FUNDAMENTALS OF CRIMINOLOGICAL AND CRIMINAL JUSTICE INQUIRY

How to think about, conduct, and evaluate research is fundamental to the study and understanding of criminology and criminal justice. Students take methods, statistics, theory, and topic-specific classes, but they struggle to integrate what they learn and to see how it fits within the broader field of criminology and criminal justice research.

This book directly tackles this problem by helping students to develop a "researcher sensibility," and demonstrates how the "nuts and bolts" of criminal justice research – including research design, theory, data, and analysis – are and can be combined.

Relying on numerous real-world examples and illustrations, this book reveals how anyone can "think like a researcher." It reveals, too, why that ability is critical for being a savvy producer or consumer of criminological and criminal justice research.

Dr. Daniel P. Mears is the Mark C. Stafford Professor of Criminology at Florida State University and a Fellow of the American Society of Criminology. He has published over 120 articles, fifteen chapters, and several books, including the award-winning *American Criminal Justice Policy* and, most recently, *Out-of-Control Criminal Justice*. His frequently cited research and funded projects have been covered in major media outlets and examine a diverse range of crime and justice topics and policies. He served as a Senior Research Associate at the Urban Institute, a Peace Corps volunteer, and a program manager and counselor working with delinquent adolescents.

Dr. Joshua C. Cochran is Assistant Professor of Criminology at the University of Cincinnati. His award-winning research appears in leading criminology and policy journals and in *Prisoner Reentry in the Era of Mass Incarceration*. He is a recipient of the American Society of Criminology's Division on Corrections and Sentencing Dissertation Award and its Distinguished New Scholar Award. He is also the recipient of the New Scholar Award from the Academy of Criminal Justice Sciences. Dr. Cochran teaches undergraduate and graduate courses on punishment, criminal justice, theory, and policy.

FUNDAMENTALS OF

Criminological and Criminal Justice Inquiry

The Science and Art of Conducting, Evaluating, and Using Research

Daniel P. Mears

Florida State University

Joshua C. Cochran

University of Cincinnati

CAMBRIDGE
UNIVERSITY PRESS

CAMBRIDGE
UNIVERSITY PRESS

University Printing House, Cambridge CB2 8BS, United Kingdom

One Liberty Plaza, 20th Floor, New York, NY 10006, USA

477 Williamstown Road, Port Melbourne, VIC 3207, Australia

314–321, 3rd Floor, Plot 3, Splendor Forum, Jasola District Centre, New Delhi – 110025, India

79 Anson Road, #06–04/06, Singapore 079906

Cambridge University Press is part of the University of Cambridge.

It furthers the University's mission by disseminating knowledge in the pursuit of education, learning, and research at the highest international levels of excellence.

www.cambridge.org
Information on this title: www.cambridge.org/9781107193703
DOI: 10.1017/9781108149815

First published 2019

Printed in the United Kingdom by TJ International Ltd. Padstow Cornwall 2019

A catalogue record for this publication is available from the British Library.

ISBN 978-1-107-19370-3 Hardback
ISBN 978-1-316-64513-0 Paperback

Brief Contents

Contents

Figures

Tables

Preface

Research can seem like an impenetrable and inaccessible undertaking, even for those who do it for a living. What exactly counts as "research"? How exactly does research get produced? How can we distinguish good studies from bad ones? What is an appropriate use of findings?

We wrote this book to provide a guide that might help readers to answer such questions and to develop what we term a "researcher sensibility." Developing fluency in criminological and criminal justice research should not be hard. It can be, though. Why? Research typically gets taught in a piecemeal fashion. Take a course on theory, a course or two on data, courses on statistical techniques or other methods, and a few on policing, the courts, and corrections – and somehow one is supposed to be off to the races. But the end result is not research fluency; it is confusion. The problem for many students or others who try to pick up research on the fly is that no good one-stop-shop source exists to obtain that fluency.

That creates a big problem. Why? Advances in science and policy depend on understanding research. How, then, can students, criminal justice policymakers and practitioners, and members of the public acquire a researcher sensibility?

We believe that it can come from thinking about research in, well, more of the way in which researchers think about it. Existing books on criminology and criminal justice do not, in our view, do that well. They help. Theory books shed light on theory, data books shed light on data, and methods books shed light on methods. Typical introduction-to-research-methods books help, too, by shedding light on core concepts in research. Many books that tackle substantive topics (e.g., criminal behavior, policing, courts, corrections) help as well by exposing students to research. But none of them shows how to integrate different parts of the research process.

Taking our cue from two classics of how to think about research – C. Wright Mill's *The Sociological Imagination* and Howard Becker's *Tricks of the Grade* – we created this book to address that gap. We wanted to highlight how science and art go into thinking about criminological and criminal justice research and, more broadly, to help readers to develop a researcher sensibility. Obtaining this sensibility is possible! And it opens the door to seeing so many more possibilities for creating knowledge and generating better crime and justice policy.

STRUCTURE OF THE BOOK

In the first part of the book, we describe what motivated us to write it, the field of criminology and criminal justice, and the nature of science. In addition, we provide an overview of the central theme of the book – that a researcher sensibility can be easily acquired and that it is essential for conducting, evaluating, and using research. It then turns to a discussion of theory, data, and analysis, the essential ingredients of research studies. Building on that account, the book identifies different types of research. We discuss science-focused versus policy-focused research, varieties of causal relationships that research can examine, and the vast array of criminological and criminal justice areas and topics that can be investigated. In the final part of the book, we conclude with a focus on how readers can appraise research. We identify specific strategies that we and many others have found useful in developing a researcher sensibility. The chapters, described below, all build to that one central goal.

Chapter 1 (Introduction). In Chapter 1, we discuss the varied motivations for the book. A central starting point is the concern that too many students – as well as criminal justice policymakers and practitioners and members of the public – do not understand how to think about research. They therefore do not know how to evaluate or use it. We argue that anyone can develop a researcher sensibility and, with it, learn to see the science and the art that go into criminological and criminal justice research.

Chapter 2 (Science and Criminological and Criminal Justice Research). Chapter 2 steps back and zeroes in on what science is and what the field of criminology and criminal justice encompasses. The chapter highlights how an understanding of science lays the foundation for understanding all types of research and "evidence-based" policy.

Chapter 3 (The Science and Art of Conducting, Evaluating, and Using Research: Initial Observations). In this chapter, we describe the science and the art of research. We demonstrate the need for a researcher sensibility and emphasize that no cookie-cutter approach works in conducting, evaluating, or using research. The chapter underscores the importance of recognizing the different goals that guide research and how these goals can and should affect research designs and studies. The goals include empirical description, understanding social meanings and the causes of crime and criminal justice phenomena, testing causal relationships, and answering different types of criminal justice policy questions.

Chapter 4 (The Role of Theory in Research). Theory constitutes a cornerstone of research. We show how theory, even if not articulated, guides all research and why it can assist us in discerning and explaining patterns and trends. We show, too, how theory dictates the types of data and analyses that go into credible research.

Chapter 5 (The Role of Data in Research). Data can be considered the second pillar of research. It grounds the scientific enterprise – indeed, without data, there is no science. In this chapter, we describe types of data, what data can best answer research questions, and consequences that flow from the limitations that attend to almost any data source. To think about data is to think like a researcher; as we argue, doing so does not require special training.

Chapter 6 (The Role of Analysis in Research). Analysis can be viewed as the third and final pillar of research. Chapter 6 showcases a range of analytic techniques and methods that can be used to discern patterns in data and to show cause-and-effect. More importantly, it identifies how theory and data together dictate the types of analyses that are appropriate. It identifies, too, how awareness of different types of analyses can lead to more creativity in thinking about and evaluating research. To think about analysis is also to think like a researcher!

Chapter 7 (Basic (Science-Focused) vs. Applied (Policy-Focused) Research). We discuss how these two types of research – studies that seek to advance science and those that seek to advance policy – have always been central to the field of criminology and criminal justice. Awareness of them can open the door to considering questions and ideas that otherwise would go unnoticed. The chapter includes a discussion of needs, theory, implementation (or process), outcome and impact, and cost-efficiency evaluations. Policy research requires use of such evaluations. Yet, these evaluations can provide unique opportunities for simultaneously advancing science.

Chapter 8 (Identifying Causal Effects). Causality stands at center stage in many criminological and criminal justice studies. But what is a causal effect? What kinds exist? This chapter presents different types of causal effects and identifies their importance in developing more accurate explanations and in improving policy.

Chapter 9 (Criminological and Criminal Justice Research Areas and Topics). The field of criminology and criminal justice covers so much terrain that it can be difficult to appreciate its scope. We present a "research matrix" to convey this scope. It provides a platform for thinking about criminological and criminal justice research possibilities. For example, considering the goals of research, different units of analysis, and types of data and analyses opens the door to imagining more research ideas than otherwise would be possible. We argue that this ability to imagine possibilities goes hand-in-hand with developing a researcher sensibility.

Chapter 10 (Criteria for Conducting, Evaluating, and Using Research). Research does not magically produce results that stand on their own. The credibility and relevance of findings instead depend on different criteria. A lack of awareness of these criteria can lead to misunderstanding and misuse of research. We therefore describe criteria that can be used to judge the credibility of studies and their relevance for science and policy.

Chapter 11 (The Science and Art of Conducting, Evaluating, and Using Research: Practical Steps). Chapter 11 wraps up the book by reinforcing the core theme – that a researcher sensibility is necessary to conduct, evaluate, and use research appropriately and effectively – and by identifying nuts-and-bolts guidance for developing this sensibility.

ACKNOWLEDGEMENTS

This book would not have happened without Robert Dreesen, Senior Editor at Cambridge University Press. We owe him a debt of gratitude. He believed in the idea before it was fully articulated and then supported it and us wholeheartedly. Thank you as well to Lisa Pinto, the Development Team Lead at the Press, and several reviewers for guidance in adding final polishes. We thank Sonja Siennick and Brandon Welsh for early conversations about possible topics to include in the book and ways to demonstrate what a researcher "sensibility" means. Frank Cullen may not know it, but he has influenced this book through many conversations with both authors and by sharing many important works in criminology and criminal justice. Dan owes a special debt of gratitude to Bill Kelly and Mark Stafford. They were and remain exemplary role models for "thinking like a researcher," and a number of the insights described in the book emanated from conversations with them. Thank you for that and for your friendship. Although they may not realize it, colleagues at the Urban Institute, Florida State University, and the University of Cincinnati have greatly influenced the content of this book as well. A "researcher sensibility" is alive and well among them. The world is a better place for it.

Thank you most especially to Emily, Eli, and Ashley. They all have an ear for "bunk." With research, as in life, that is no small part of what one needs when filtering the good, the bad, and the irrelevant!

A FINAL PERSONAL NOTE TO THE READER

We wrote this book to be useful to anyone – researchers, criminal justice policymakers and practitioners, and members of the public. But it is students who likely will find it to be the most useful. Indeed, in writing this book, we thought constantly about the undergraduate and graduate students who we have taught and with whom we work.

Their frustration at seeing how to connect different classes is palpable. One day they take a class on theory. Another day they take one on data, sampling, survey design, or the like. On yet another day they take a statistics class or two, or perhaps classes on qualitative methods or policy evaluation. In the meantime, they take classes on criminology and criminal justice that summarize and discuss large amounts of research. To many of them, it is akin to learning a language by taking a class on vocabulary, another on grammar, still another on culture, and then trying to read, speak, or write in that language. That approach does not work very well in learning any language. And it does not work well in learning to think like a researcher.

This book is meant for you and for anyone else who has struggled to make sense of crime and justice research. It is meant to help you to become "fluent" in research and to see the connections that run through all parts of the research process. It is meant ultimately to advance your own interests in criminology and criminal justice.

Research can be learned by doing. But we believe it also can be learned through a book like this one. It shows how theory, data, and analysis are connected. It shows the science and the art that go into the research process. More importantly, it shows how it is *your* ability to imagine research possibilities that creates the foundation for seeing these connections and developing the ability to conduct, evaluate, and use research.

Part I

Criminological and Criminal Justice Research

1 Introduction

Research stands at the center of the criminological and criminal justice enterprise. For scholars, it permeates their lives. They conduct research and teach students how to examine the world with it. They communicate research findings. Even so, scholars are not the sole users or purveyors of research. Research features prominently in the lives of policymakers, administrators, and practitioners and in the decisions they make. The public at large also uses research. They read about it or make assumptions about the relevance of findings and "facts" that they pick up through friends and media outlets.

In an era in which lawmakers and government officials have called for greater accountability and "evidence-based" policy, research could not be more relevant.[1] Indeed, it is critical. Vast amounts of information – good and bad – are now readily available to nearly everyone at the click of a button. The ability to evaluate research therefore has assumed even greater importance than in the past. For criminology and criminal justice there is the added consideration: At the turn of the twenty-first century, a new era of crime and justice approaches emerged that greatly expanded law enforcement, court, jail, prison, probation, and parole capacity. This shift placed a tremendous burden on taxpayers that continues to the present.[2] It also raised many critical questions. What drove the changes? Were they beneficial? Harmful? What lessons can be learned for guiding crime and justice policy today? What opportunities exist to advance the understanding of crime and criminal justice?

Enter research. Good, credible studies can provide a critical platform on which to improve knowledge *and* policy. Much depends, though, on understanding just what is meant by "research." Much depends, too, on understanding how studies are conducted, how to interpret and evaluate

---

[1] Mears (2010).   [2] Mears and Cochran (2015).

findings, and how to use them effectively and appropriately. We argue that the ability to do so requires a "researcher sensibility." This sensibility is essential for conducting research that can be trusted. It is critical as well for evaluating – that is, reading, interpreting, and judging – study results. And it is critical for using research to advance science and policy. This sensibility entails appreciating many things, but not least it involves understanding the science and art of conducting, evaluating, and using research. It has been said that "the greatest challenge of science, its art, lies in asking an important question and framing it in a way that allows it to be broken into manageable pieces."[3] Learning how to do so is an art. Science constitutes a core ingredient of research, but art comes into play as well. Fortunately, the science and art of research can be learned by everyone, not just those of us who do it for a living. That matters greatly for scientific progress and for improving policy and practice!

THE GOAL OF THIS BOOK

This book seeks to introduce students – as well as policymakers, practitioners, the public, and other researchers and scholars – to what it means to conduct criminological and criminal justice research, including how to conduct, evaluate, and use study results. It seeks to guide readers in developing what we term a "researcher sensibility" and the science and art, and many different considerations, that go into criminological and criminal justice inquiry. The practice of research can seem mysterious, or sometimes it may seem deceptively straightforward. Recidivism provides a convenient illustration. Advocates for a particular corrections program may tout it as being "effective." They point to the "low" recidivism of its participants. Perhaps only 10 percent of all participants go on to be rearrested for a new crime. Given such a low probability of recidivism, it seems that the program must be effective. In reality, though, the same percentage of individuals may have recidivated *without* the intervention. To determine if the program produced a beneficial effect requires a study with a valid comparison group.

Awareness of such possibilities and complexities, which comes with a researcher sensibility, should be part of a researcher's tool kit. It frequently is not, though. This problem does not necessarily stem from a lack of familiarity with particular theories or methodologies. Rather, it stems from a lack of familiarity with how to put together different research ingredients. More generally, it stems from a lack of familiarity with how to imagine the

---

[3] Barry (2005:60).

range of possibilities for conceptualizing and answering theoretical or policy-focused questions.

Many factors contribute to this situation. One consists of cognitive blinders that impede imagination. Consider surgeons. They understandably tend to frame medical problems from a surgical perspective. However, that can lead them to mistakenly assume that surgery constitutes the most effective treatment for a given condition, when in fact some other approach, such as radiation, medication, or physical therapy, might be better.[4] Researchers act no differently. If trained in a particular theoretical approach or methodology, they will be more likely to use these rather than some others that may be more helpful.

Academic training typically pushes individuals to specialize. What does that entail? It means that a graduate student may study a particular topic, and, in so doing, use a particular theory, data, and methodology favored by their advisor. Upon receiving a doctoral degree, the student – now an assistant professor seeking tenure and promotion – pursues this topic intensively, using the same theories, data, and methods. If he or she strays too far from the topic or these approaches, several risks arise. The newly minted PhD may alienate his or her advisor or generate fewer publications because of the time it takes to learn new theories, data, and methods. They also risk appearing to be generalists. All of these possibilities mean that they may not receive tenure or be promoted. Researchers who go into non-academic settings can face similar pressures. Confronted with a need to complete a large number of studies in short amounts of time, they may seek recourse to the conceptual and methodological tools that they acquired during graduate school. Only slowly, if at all, do they acquire new ones.

We argue that a researcher sensibility is needed for conducting better research. But it also is needed to evaluate and use research effectively and appropriately. Really? Such a sensibility may be necessary for creating credible studies, but is it really necessary for evaluating and using research? Absolutely!

Consider violence and television watching. News outlets might report that a study has found that watching violent television is associated with more violence. That seems like a common-sense finding that we can trust. Of course watching violence causes people to commit violence. But then another study finds no association between watching violent television and committing violence. We now ask ourselves, which study do we believe? While we are at it, we might start to question the television-causes-violence logic: Why exactly would watching violent shows make someone more

---

[4] Gawande (2007, 2009); Groopman (2007); Mears and Bacon (2009); Sanders (2009); Groopman and Hartzband (2011).

violent? Mere exposure to ideas does not typically suffice to change human behavior. It takes more. There is also the question of how much we can trust an identified association. If the association is spurious (i.e., not real or causal), then, by extension, there is no association to explain. For example, what about the possibility that violent people may be more likely to watch violent television shows? This possibility would result in an association between watching violent shows and engaging in violence, but the association would not be causal.

It turns out that evaluating research – that is, reading or hearing about first-hand or second-hand accounts of one or more studies and judging their merits – can be a tricky business. We can easily misinterpret the validity of study findings. We also can assume that a single straightforward theoretical logic exists to explain how A leads to B even though, upon closer inspection, we may find that many possible explanations can be identified.

The risk of misunderstanding research creates a related problem – study results may be misused. For example, if we accept a study's findings about a television–violence association, we may jump too quickly into developing theories to explain this association. *We should probably place greater priority on establishing whether a causal association exists in the first place.* What if none exists but we proceed, based on the one study, to be for or against a particular policy because of what the one study found? That would place us on poor footing. If we better understood the ins and outs of the study, we might find ourselves holding a quite different view of the policy. The ease with which studies may be misinterpreted or misused raises a profound challenge for policymakers and criminal justice administrators and practitioners. What studies should they trust? Which ones should guide their decisions? More generally, what kinds of facts should be relevant for making decisions about policy or practice?

Research can be a complicated undertaking, so proceeding carefully is warranted. Whether one seeks to advance knowledge on crime, victimization, punishment, or some other phenomenon, or whether one seeks to improve policy, many considerations come into play. But all too frequently, many people do not understand the nuts and bolts of research. They accept "facts" that accord with their personal predilections or they accept or reject them because they do not understand what went into producing the facts. This problem, as we have emphasized, affects researchers and others alike. Many students work through a Master's degree or doctoral degree program and never really learn how to conduct research. They read about bits and pieces of what goes into it. They even may help undertake a study or two. But by and large, they hold a highly circumscribed view of research. That leads them to think too narrowly about the kinds of studies that they might undertake or how to put other research into context.

The problem might be said to lie with the training offered in criminology and criminal justice programs. Actually, the problem – training versus knowing how to "do" research – pervades many scholarly disciplines. Law students struggle, for example, with it. They take three years of classes, many of which constitute core requirements, and have two summers during which they might intern. They barely get their feet wet in that time and obtain only a small taste of what the law entails.[5] Much the same holds true for criminology and criminal justice students. They take a research methods overview course, several statistics courses, perhaps a course on qualitative methods, sampling, or causal analysis, a course or two on theory, and at the same time they take courses on particular substantive topics. By the end of their third year, they complete course work and a thesis for their Master's degree. In their fourth year, they prepare for and take comprehensive exams and, at the same time, begin developing a dissertation. They know a bit about research, but have never really undertaken their own studies. Students at this point might be likened to chefs whose primary training has consisted of reading about various cooking and baking techniques and practicing specific skills (e.g., selecting the best produce, chopping vegetables). Perhaps they have prepared a small number of meals. What they have *not* done is actually cooked on a regular basis, created dishes that span a range of cuisines, successfully hosted large dinner events, or done so under pressure.

This lack of experience in doing research can be highly damaging. It can lead students to develop a myopic view of research possibilities and of their interests and strengths. They are limited in the types of research questions that they can envision and the methodologies that they can use to answer those research questions.

For those who have only passing knowledge of criminological and criminal justice research, the situation is even more problematic. To them, research may seem to belong to the realm of, well, researchers. Accordingly, facts and the very framing of questions are accepted or rejected outright because they trust the researcher's statements or because of how the findings or framing of questions accord with their personal beliefs or ideology. Undergraduate classes can do little to change that situation. Certainly, a few classes on theory and methods can provide individuals with a general sense of what research entails. However, they fall well short of preparing students for digesting study findings, requesting research, or using it effectively or appropriately.

---

[5] Turow (1977).

There are other barriers to developing a researcher sensibility. One is confusion about what distinguishes "criminology" from "criminal justice."[6] That makes sense given that scholars themselves disagree about the difference. Some view criminal justice as a sub-topic within criminology. Others view criminology as a sub-topic within criminal justice. Students frequently are confused about which term best characterizes their major or what they do professionally.

Another barrier involves policy. To some scholars, research on anything related to policy – or to programs, practices, and the everyday decision-making that is a part of crime and justice – amounts to "applied" research. Why? The focus of a given study centers on the "application" of science to inform policy in some way. That seems like an important undertaking. For some scholars, though, it amounts to second-class research.[7] The larger and more important goal for them is pure science – science for science's sake. They want researchers to focus on developing an understanding, through theory, of the "basic" or foundational causes of phenomena in society. There is, then, a seeming tension between "basic" (scientific) research and "applied" (policy-focused) research. That is so even though the two research types operate in a type of feedback loop: Important policy insights emerge from so-called "basic" research and many important scientific advances emerge from so-called "applied" research.[8]

These two barriers to developing a researcher sensibility often are intertwined. For example, to advocates of "criminology," credible and important research may be viewed as work that focuses on the causes of crime. That is "criminology." To do "criminological" work is to use theory. And theory stands as a hallmark of a true science aimed at understanding "basic," or foundational, forces in life. Consequently, "criminology" is equal to "theory" and in turn to "basic" research and, finally, "science." By implication, "criminal justice research" then must amount to an atheoretical, applied, non-scientific undertaking. Those who study criminal justice may of course disagree with this characterization. The tension around this issue pervades the field. It can be seen in part by the tendency of "criminology" programs to require a course on "theory" that primarily covers theories of crime rather than various criminal justice phenomena, such as law-making, police, courts, corrections,

---

[6] Hagan (1989); Bernard and Engel (2001); Kraska (2004, 2006); Bernard *et al.* (2005); Mears (2007, 2010); Crank and Bowman (2008); Mears and Barnes (2010); Cooper and Worrall (2012); Dooley and Rydberg (2014); Steinmetz *et al.* (2014); Thistlewaite and Wooldredge (2014); Duffee (2015).

[7] Mills (1959).   [8] Rossi (1980); Barlow and Decker (2010); Mears (2010).

and crime prevention.[9] At the same time, some programs that embrace the "criminal justice" nomenclature may not require a course on theory at all, which can make it seem that they discount the relevance of theory. It is all a bit of a muddle. And it can lead those who have ever taken "criminology" or "criminal justice" courses – or majored in or obtained a graduate degree in one or the other – confused about research.

The role of theory introduces more confusion. "Theory" can be viewed as this strange, far-removed undertaking. Some scholars may see theory as important only to advancing science. In fact, the tendency to view theory as more important than empirical research runs throughout the history of science, including the fields of math and physics.[10] In some periods, a "top-down," "theoretical" approach has been viewed as the best way to increase knowledge. In others, a "bottom-up," data-based approach, one that entails working from empirical "reality," has been viewed as best. Plato and Aristotle can be viewed as roughly representing these two polarities, respectively.[11] One can find researchers in many programs that represent them. Not surprisingly, those who study science and how it progresses find that the accumulation of knowledge progresses from many different directions, not just these two. It stems, for example, from deductively arrived-at theories, inductive reasoning, development of better measurement devices, immersion in observing a particular phenomenon, comparison of different approaches to testing an idea, and so on.[12] No matter, scholars hew to what they believe and students frequently follow suit. The end result? Students and others who take an interest in crime and justice develop a too-narrow sense of what criminology and criminal justice encompass, how studies occur in the "real world," and how to digest, request, and use research.

College and university programs are not necessarily to be faulted. An abundance of required courses can quickly drown students or require that they remain in school in perpetuity. More classes are not the answer. Involving students and others in research would be helpful, but is not always feasible. Ideally, students, policymakers, practitioners, and the public at large could magically acquire a research sensibility. That is impossible, of course. Against that backdrop, it may seem unrealistic to think that a book might help remedy the situation. In our view, though, considerable room exists for a particular type of book to at least make a dent.

What should such a book do? Before answering that question, we should describe what it should *not* do. It should not seek to replicate or extend methods, statistics, or theory books. Such books offer critically important information. Methods books, for example, cover a myriad of

---

[9] Duffee (2015); Akers *et al.* (2016).   [10] Seife (2000); Weinberg (2015).
[11] Weinberg (2015).   [12] Merton (1973); Mears and Stafford (2002).

technical topics, such as sampling, types of data, data measurement, and so on. In so doing, they primarily introduce readers to some of the "ingredients," the "nuts and bolts," that go into research, not necessarily *how* to combine them when conducting, evaluating, or using research.

Similarly, statistics books introduce readers to important information about analytic techniques. Such books clearly have their place. They do not, however, teach students to develop a researcher sensibility. Indeed, students complete courses on advanced statistics without ever using the techniques about which they learned or without understanding when the techniques should be used. They also frequently fail to learn about a range of other approaches that would enable them to answer a much broader set of research questions.

Not least, there are books about theory. They teach a critical part of the research enterprise, but typically do not provide guidance about how to create theories, integrate theory with empirical research, or appreciate the nature of scientific progress. In addition, theory frequently gets treated as a topic separate from particular substantive questions.

The best research does not come from a focus on one ingredient or another – it comes from a sensibility that enables individuals to imagine studies that would be relevant or credible in answering particular questions. All of us, whether researchers or not, can and should have this sensibility. With it, we are better able to appreciate the limits, relevance, and possibilities of studies for advancing knowledge and policy. As we seek to show in this book, this sensibility entails appreciating the science and art of research, much as a chef's sensibility goes beyond understanding the characteristics of certain ingredients or certain rules of cooking chemistry.[13]

Who might find the book helpful or interesting? We have written it with undergraduate and graduate students in mind, especially those in criminology and criminal justice programs. But we have written it, too, with an eye toward guiding students in other fields, such as sociology, psychology, political science, social work, public policy, and law, who may be interested in or who focus on crime and justice. We want it to be helpful to students who go on to have research careers. We also want it to be helpful to those who enter into policy arenas or who become administrators or work in any type of setting where research may be needed or useful. Not least, we have written the book for policymakers, criminal justice and corrections administrators and practitioners, and the public. Indeed, it is for anyone with an interest in what social scientists

---

[13] It might be said, too, that a researcher sensibility involves an ability to detect "bunk" (see Mears 2002). It is more than that, though. Discerning patently absurd or misleading research is important, but so, too, is the ability to imagine or create good research.

who study crime and criminal justice do, how they do it, and how to evaluate and use their work.

Nothing in the discussions that follow requires that readers have taken courses in criminology or criminal justice theory, methods, statistics, or various substantive topics (e.g., policing, courts, prisons). Such courses might be useful for understanding some of the material, but they are not necessary. Some readers may come to this topic with research training in other fields. This training may be helpful. At the same time, it likely will not have led to an awareness about the wide range of topics that exist in criminology and criminal justice and some of the unique research challenges and opportunities that exist. This book may be helpful to such readers in developing this awareness. We will discuss different types of analyses, including techniques typically only covered in advanced statistics courses. However, a technical foundation in statistics is emphatically not needed to understand the logic of these analyses and the kinds of questions that they can be useful in addressing.[14]

THE ARGUMENT AND STRUCTURE OF THIS BOOK

Just as being a chef entails much more than learning to dice carrots or read a recipe, the fundamentals, or "doing," of criminological and criminal justice research involves much more than learning about specific theories, methods, statistical analyses, data, and so on. *Indeed, we argue that to conduct, evaluate, and use research well requires a chef-like sensibility – a researcher sensibility – one that includes imagination and an appreciation of the science and art of the research enterprise.* To convey this idea, the book is structured in four parts.

Part I *provides the background and context for the book.* It includes Chapter 1 (this chapter), which describes the motivation for and goals of the book. It also includes Chapter 2, *which establishes the context for understanding the research enterprise.* The discussion centers on what science is and what criminology and criminal justice encompass. A focus on science matters because it provides the touchstone for appreciating the logic of research and how study findings differ from intuition and personal views.

---

[14] In so doing, the book follows in the tradition of Mills' (1959) effort in *The Sociological Imagination* to show readers how to think "sociologically." The focus here, however, is on criminology and criminal justice, a wide range of dimensions and activities that go into "doing" research, and on the salience of theory, data, methods, and both "basic" and "applied" research. This approach reflects in no small part the view that science progresses from many different avenues and serves multiple goals (Mears and Stafford 2002). The book follows, too, in the spirit of Kellstedt and Whitten's (2013) discussion of fundamentals in research in political science.

It matters not least because policymakers in recent decades increasingly have advocated "evidence-based" policy, where "evidence-based" somehow equates with "scientific." What, then, is "science"? Just as importantly, just what exactly is criminology and criminal justice as a scientific field of study? This chapter seeks to answer these and related questions. In so doing, it establishes the foundation for the subsequent chapters and the focus on developing a researcher sensibility.

Chapter 3 *describes the science and art of research and the need for a researcher sensibility in approaching research in this way*. Construction of any building begins with a blueprint. The same holds true with research studies – a blueprint, or design, is needed. Developing a credible design requires as much art as science. It requires clarity about a study's goals and research questions, relevant data, approaches for compiling and analyzing the data, and more. Developing a good research design can be likened to creating a recipe that results in a good dish. That does not mean that researchers should "cook" data. (The chef analogy only holds so far.) It means that just as creating a recipe that "works" well entails far more than listing ingredients and steps, research involves more than rote analysis of data. Science and art inform developing the goals, questions, data, and analyses for a study; they also inform appropriate evaluation and use of the results. This chapter thus identifies core elements of study designs. It describes as well the role of these designs to research and the interpretation and use of findings.

Part II of the book *focuses on "essential research ingredients," including theory, data, and analysis*. Chapter 4 *turns our attention to theory*. All research involves theory, though the theory may not be formally articulated. Scientists may not even be conscious of how it guides their work. Regardless, even research that self-avowedly focuses purely on empirical description is grounded in theory of some sort. Theory thus constitutes a critical part of the research enterprise. This chapter describes what is meant by "theory" and different ways in which it can be useful. Among other things, theory enables us to discern patterns. It can produce insights about the factors that give rise to or cause these patterns. And it can help to guide policy. Research that proceeds without theory can create more problems than not. Even so, potential harms exist. Theory can put up blinders that focus us too narrowly and lead us to miss important insights. This chapter discusses such considerations and different approaches to creating, building on, or applying theory. It then discusses types of criminological and criminal justice theories and highlights the salience of theory for guiding data collection and analysis.

Chapter 5 *centers on the role of data in research*. At the end of the day, science – and any policy built on it – depends on data. Research "findings" otherwise amount to ideology or personal beliefs. This chapter examines why data are important to the research enterprise, what data are "best" or most useful, and types of data that exist. It also discusses a range of related topics, such as measurement and what researchers do when they face nuts-and-bolts data problems. For example, in studies that rely on surveys, administrative records from the police, courts, corrections, or various agency data repositories, there may be missing information. What are the consequences of missing data and other such problems? How do researchers deal with them? This chapter addresses these types of questions and illuminates the importance of data to research, including the development and testing of theory and evaluation of policy.

Chapter 6 *introduces the role of analysis in research*. A bewildering array of research methods and analytic techniques exist to examine data. The goals generally are to provide empirical descriptions of criminological and criminal justice phenomena, identify their social meanings, test causal claims, and answer policy questions. Diverse analytic approaches exist to achieve these goals. Some of them can be quite complicated. However, our focus in this chapter is not on how to implement them (for that, many methodology and statistics textbooks exist). Rather, we discuss the logic that guides them. Why? Awareness of such approaches can open doors to thinking creatively about research questions and to evaluating studies. We also discuss the role of analysis in developing and assessing measures and in estimating causal effects. We then discuss a no less critical issue – the importance of conveying results accurately and in ways that enable readers both to understand them and to place them in context.

Part III *discusses types of criminological and criminal justice research*. Chapter 7 *zeroes in on two broad categories of criminological and criminal justice research – "basic" (science-focused) research and "applied" (policy-focused) research*. The chapter highlights that neither type of research precludes the other and that no special theories, data, or methods or analyses pertain more to one than to the other. It illuminates the range of interesting research questions that exist when one focuses on theory and on policy evaluation. Theoretically focused research leads to endless possible inquiries about the meaning and causes of various phenomena. A focus on policy leads to questions about the need for a policy as well as the theory or design, implementation, impact, and cost-efficiency of the policy. Questions focused on these different policy dimensions – what collectively are referred to as the evaluation hierarchy (need, theory, implementation, impact, and efficiency) – are important in their own right.[15] However, they also provide opportunities to contribute to scientific knowledge.

---

[15] Rossi *et al.* (2004); see also Mears (2010).

Chapter 8 *discusses causation and research that seeks to identify causal effects*. Developing and testing theories about causal relationships constitutes one of the central goals of criminological and criminal justice research. For that reason, we give it special attention as one type of research. Causation turns out to be a complicated thing to establish. Some of the analytic strategies discussed in Chapter 6 can help us to estimate causal effects. In Chapter 8, though, we step back and take more of a bird's eye view of causality. We do so to convey the complexity underlying the notion of causation, identify types of causal relationships, and highlight how awareness of them can inform theory, analysis, and policy.

Chapter 9 *describes the range of topics examined by criminological and criminal justice researchers*. In contrast to accounts that distinguish criminology from criminal justice, the book treats the two as synonymous. That approach is neither "right" nor "wrong." For our purposes, it is useful. By treating the two as synonymous, we can avoid the confusion associated with ad hoc pronouncements that place one of the two somehow "under" the other, such as the idea that "criminology" somehow belongs "under" "criminal justice" or, conversely, that "criminal justice" belongs "under" "criminology." It also avoids confusion. For example, "criminology" sometimes is equated with the study of crime, but at other times it is equated with the study of law formation and sanctioning, even though these latter topics seem more aligned with "criminal justice." Conversely, "criminal justice" studies seemingly focus on something different than that of "criminological" studies, yet they might well include research on the causes of crime.

Treating the two as different thus can result in a distorted and narrow sense of what "criminology" or "criminal justice" entails. This chapter thus seeks to map out the range of areas and topics investigated in the combined field of criminological and criminal justice research. The range – which we term the "research matrix" – can only be described as stunning. It includes the study of offending, crime rates, formal and informal social control, prisons and jails, community supervision, juvenile justice, victimization, public opinion, and much more. In each instance, research can involve one or more research goals, topics, units of analysis, types of data, and, not least, types of analytic techniques or methods. This variety creates many possibilities to generate insights, to develop, apply, and test theory, and to put research into context. Recognition of these possibilities is part of developing a researcher sensibility.

Part IV concludes the book by *focusing on the idea of developing a chef-like researcher sensibility in approaching research*. We begin with Chapter 10, which *identifies different criteria that can be used to judge research*. Interestingly, many people – students, policymakers, practitioners, citizens, and, not least, researchers – do not know what criteria to use. This situation stymies scientific progress and leads to misunderstanding and misuse of study findings. Chapter 10 therefore describes criteria that are relevant for conducting credible studies and that can be used to judge theory and research. These criteria provide guideposts for how much weight to give to particular studies and for gauging the relevance of them for science or policy.

In Chapter 11, we return to the core theme, or argument, of the book: *Credible research requires as much art as science, and conducting, evaluating, and using it well entails appreciation of that fact and a wide range of interrelated considerations.* There is no one single best way to do research any more than there exists a single best way to cook. This chapter discusses that idea. It also provides nuts-and-bolts guidance to researchers, or those seeking to become researchers; it provides guidance, too, to criminal justice administrators and practitioners and anyone with an interest in crime and justice. Research should be an accessible and useful undertaking. Our hope is that this chapter – and, indeed, the book in its entirety – helps to achieve that goal.

Figure 1.1 captures the book's core argument and reflects its organization. As shown in the top box, we seek to highlight the importance of developing a researcher sensibility. This sensibility requires an awareness of the science and art of research, how different parts of the research process are connected, and, more generally, how to think about research. It requires an awareness as well of how these considerations apply not only to conducting research, but also to evaluating and using it.

Research is not a cookie-cutter undertaking. Or, to carry the food analogy further, it is a far cry from making a smoothie. One cannot simply throw ingredients into a "research blender" and obtain accurate or useful results. Theory, data, and analysis all go hand in hand (as shown under "Research Ingredients"). Each informs the other.

But they cannot be applied willy-nilly. Much depends on the type of research that we wish to conduct, evaluate, or use (as shown under "Types of Research"). For example, is the goal to provide a more accurate scientific assessment of how X (e.g., sentencing) is related to Y (e.g., crime)? As we discuss further in the book, this type of question might be viewed as a "basic" research question. Why? It seeks not to influence policy, but instead to advance the understanding of "basic," or core, causes of phenomena. It also might be viewed, though, as an "applied" research question to the extent that it seeks to provide guidance about whether sentencing policy can be applied in ways that improve public safety.

The considerations that go into thinking about research are far-ranging. Diverse criteria exist for imagining and appraising research. Scholars typically will be interested primarily in criteria that help to ensure

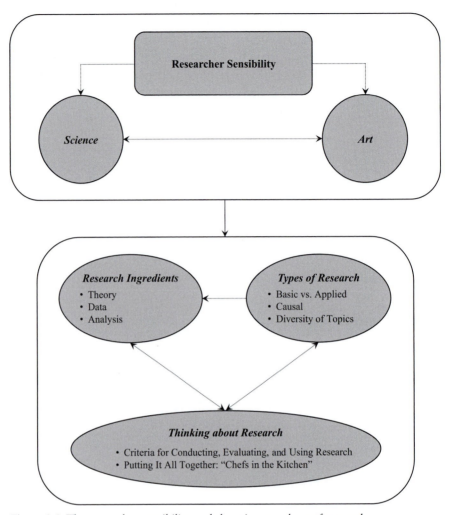

Figure 1.1 The researcher sensibility and the science and art of research

the generation of credible knowledge. However, they must consider ethical issues involved in research. Policymakers and practitioners must consider such issues as well. There is, therefore, a need to understand the criteria for conducting, evaluating, and using research appropriately (as shown under "Thinking about Research").

Writing about his view of how mathematics should be taught, Jordan Ellenberg has written: "I think we have to teach mathematics that values precise answers but also intelligent approximations, that demands the ability to deploy existing algorithms fluently but also the horse sense to work things out on the fly, that mixes rigidity with a sense of play."[16] Much the

---

[16] Ellenberg (2014:58).

same can be said about research. In fact, his recommendation encompasses much of what we mean by a "researcher sensibility." This sensibility requires a familiarity with different interrelated aspects of research, but it also requires horse sense and a willingness to think "outside the box."

When many people think about research, they may think about experiments or "statistics." Research entails much more. Our hope with this book is to contribute to readers' ability to think more broadly, creatively, and critically about research. We hope, too, that this ability – this researcher sensibility – contributes to an appreciation of how research can inform knowledge about crime and criminal justice and efforts to improve policy.

2 Science and Criminological and Criminal Justice Research

INTRODUCTION

Criminology and criminal justice is a field of study found in colleges and universities throughout the world. Sometimes it will be its own department and sometimes it is housed within others. For example, sociology programs may include criminology and criminal justice as an area of specialization. Regardless, criminology and criminal justice generally involves the scientific study of the creation, enforcement, and effects of laws, the causes and consequences of crime, and the design, operations, and impacts of the criminal justice system. It is, in short, a science that encompasses a wide range of topics.

What, though, does it mean to speak of the field as a "science"? How or when is research "scientific"? How are the social sciences – of which criminology and criminal justice is one – different from the natural sciences? Given the emphasis in recent decades on "evidence-based" policy and the attention that many criminology and criminal justice researchers give to policy, what exactly is the role of science in developing such policy? Not least, where is the "art" in conducting scientific research that we mentioned in the title and introduction of this book?

Answering such questions is of basic importance for discussing a field of study that considers itself a science. Any such discussion, though, raises additional questions. For example, what exactly is criminology and criminal justice as a distinct field or discipline? Do the two terms – "criminology" and "criminal justice" – refer to something different and, if so, how exactly? For example, it would seem that "criminology" could be viewed as encompassing "criminal justice" or that "criminal justice" could be viewed as encompassing "criminology." Why, then, use two terms when one seemingly would suffice? This chapter answers these questions. In so doing, it seeks to lay the groundwork for understanding what it means to talk about criminological and criminal justice research.

WHAT IS SCIENCE?

Science and Research

When many of us think about "research," we might equate it with "science." There is, however, a difference. Research can entail empirical assessments. Science typically entails seeking more than that. It seeks to generate knowledge about how the world works. It seeks generalizable laws or axioms. And it seeks to arrive at them through the use of empirical data, measurement, and analysis rather than the use of philosophy or mathematical logic. Science, in its emphasis on empirical assessment, is similar to research. It departs in its emphasis on seeking generalizable insights into how the world operates. Stated differently, the signature mark of science lies in the pursuit of generalizable knowledge through empirical study.

Why do scientists and the societies pursue such knowledge? The simple and yet profound answer is that they do so for knowledge's sake. Humans are curious. Evidence of that can be seen in thousands of years of efforts to investigate and understand nature, society, and, on a grander scale, the universe. At the same time, social scientists frequently focus on policies, programs, and practices that shape society. From the perspective of advancing scientific knowledge, they do so because these dimensions of social life provide unique opportunities to generate insights into how individuals, groups, organizations, and the like operate.

One example of why science appeals to many people – and why it can be relevant for understanding the world – can be seen in Figure 2.1. The scientific process involves asking questions and seeking answers through empirical analysis. In this example, the question is as follows: How high will a cord rise above the surface of the Earth's equator if we add 36 inches to it? Assume that the cord initially fits snugly around the equator and that, when we add the additional 36 inches, it rises equally above the Earth's surface.[1] We might ask a related question: How much would the cord rise if instead of the Earth we used a golf ball?

Why juxtapose the two questions? It helps to clarify how our intuition affects our understanding of the world. In the case of the Earth, we anticipate that the cord barely rises. How could it do more than rise imperceptibly given the tremendous circumference of the Earth and the fact that we only added 36 inches to the cord? By contrast, in the case of the golf ball, we assume that, given the small circumference, adding 36 inches will lead the cord to rise a great deal off the surface of the ball. In reality, however, the

---

[1] Versions of this illustration have been used in Mears and Stafford (2002:10), Mears (2010:170), and Mears (2017:47); it derives from a discussion in Malcolm (1958).

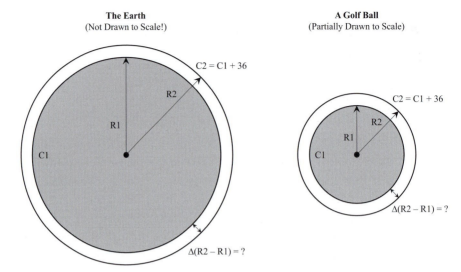

The Earth
(Not Drawn to Scale!)

A Golf Ball
(Partially Drawn to Scale)

Question: How much does a levitating cord, bound to the Earth's surface, rise if we add 36 inches to it? How much does it rise if instead we use a golf ball? That is, in each instance, what is $\Delta(R2-R1)$? Intuition says that it will be infinitesimal in the case of the Earth and a lot in the case of a golf ball. That intuition is incorrect.

Answer: The formula for radius is $C/2\pi$. So, the change in radius, $\Delta(R2-R1)$, is equal to $(C2/2\pi)-(C1/2\pi)$. This formula reduces to $\Delta(R2-R1) = (C2-C1)/2\pi$. Since π is a constant (typically approximated to be 3.14), the formula further reduces to $\Delta(R2-R1) = (C2-C1)/6.28$. Here, $C2-C1$ is equal to 36. So, the solution then is $\Delta(R2-R1) = 36/6.28$. The cord thus rises 5.73 inches. It does so if the sphere is the Earth or a golf ball.

Figure 2.1 Science vs. intuition: An illustration using the Earth and a golf ball
Note: Adapted from Mears (2017:47).

cord will rise by the *exact* same amount – roughly 6 inches – in both cases. Our intuition here leads us wildly astray.

The figure depicts the reason for our mistake. For both spheres, we want to determine the difference (Δ) between the radius of the sphere when the cord is tightly bound to it (R1) and the radius when the cord levitates above the sphere (R2). That is, we want to find Δ(R2 – R1). We can do so using a variation of the formula for circumference, $2\pi r$ (π is a constant that is approximately equal to 3.14 and "r" is the radius). This formula can be revised such that r = C / 2π, or, even simpler, r = C / 6.28. We then can compute the difference between R2 and R1 by using the following calculation: Δ(R2 – R1) = (C2 / 6.28) – (C1 / 6.28). Recall that C2 is the same as C1, except that we added 36 inches to it. That is, C2 = C1 + 36. Accordingly, the formula becomes Δ(R2 – R1) = ((C1 + 36) / 6.28) – (C1 / 6.28). Put differently, Δ(R2 – R1) = 36 / 6.28 = 5.73, or approximately 6 inches. Observe that in this formula, the difference will always be the same regardless of a sphere's initial circumference (i.e., C1).

Sometimes our intuition correctly guides us to an understanding about patterns and causal relationships. But sometimes, as in this example, it can blind us to them.[2] Science exists in part to help avoid the problems with intuition. It exists, more broadly, to satisfy our curiosity. This curiosity leads to interest in mathematical questions, as in this example, and questions about everyday life, humans, societies, animals, and the natural world.[3] We investigate, explore, and, in turn, frequently encounter mysteries that we want or need to understand.

Science helps us in that endeavor. It provides a foundation for more systematically investigating and exploring phenomena. It helps us, at the same time, to avoid the pitfalls of intuition. In the realm of criminal justice, the need for science as a corrective to intuition is sorely needed.[4] Many criminal justice policies, programs, and policies rest on what seems like "common sense," but in reality amounts to the equivalent of "quackery."[5]

What exactly counts as scientific "knowledge"? Scientists and philosophers of science have debated the issue for eons.[6] In general, scientific knowledge differs from other types in relying not only on theory, but also on empirical analysis, to depict the nature of reality and how various factors influence one another. The emphasis on empirical analysis provides the foundation on which to test ideas. Science rises or falls with this emphasis.

Consider the alternatives. As highlighted above, intuition can mislead us. Worse yet, sometimes belief systems blind us to how the world works. For example, from a philosophical vantage point, we might assume that people are inherently good or bad. We might make assumptions about the ways of the natural world, too: The Earth is square, oceans come from the tears of the Greek gods, and the flu results from having impure thoughts. Not least, and of central relevance for this book, we might make assumptions about crime and efforts to address it. For example, we might assume that individuals commit crime because they lack moral fiber and that severe punishments deter.

In every instance, people may disagree about what is "correct" or "true." The political realm provides a perfect illustration. By and large, those who hew to one political orientation (e.g., liberal) or another (e.g., conservative) tend to believe in the assumptions that inhere to these orientations.[7] Deeply religious people may tend to do the same – they proceed from the assumption that their religion somehow must be more "correct" or "true" than another.

Science resides in a different realm. It examines phenomena that lend themselves to empirical analysis. It cannot shed light on whether one

---

[2] Kahneman (2011). [3] Weinberg (2015). [4] Mears (2010).
[5] Latessa *et al.* (2014); see, generally, Farabee (2005), Mears and Cochran (2015), Cullen *et al.* (2016), and Mears (2017).
[6] Staley (2014); Weinberg (2015). [7] Miller (1973).

political ideology or religion is somehow "better" or more "true" than another. The political, religious, cultural, and other such dimensions fall outside the purview of science.[8] Certainly, social scientists can empirically study how individuals think about these areas of life. For example, they can ask individuals whether they support the death penalty, if they think that people are inherently sinful or good, and which foods are "best." But they cannot establish that one or another view is "correct." Individuals disagree, for example, about the morality of the death penalty, abortion, corporal punishment, and less weighty issues, such as whether New Hampshire maple syrup tastes better than New York maple syrup. No amount of scientific observation will ever be able to establish the truth of the matter. (If it could, the clear winner would be New Hampshire maple syrup! Full disclosure: Dan grew up in New Hampshire and so may hold a biased view on this issue.)

All that said, no cookie-cutter formula exists for determining exactly what counts as science. We can, though, identify some hallmarks of science. *First, science stands apart from philosophy in its reliance on methods, data, and data analysis.* Scientists use methods, such as observation (e.g., interviews, surveys), experiments, and statistical techniques, to identify the prevalence of certain phenomena, factors associated with them, and what may cause them.

A second way in which we can distinguish science involves replication. Scientists generally assume that no one study typically should be trusted. Rather, only through repeated study, and only when the additional studies consistently agree with one another, do we begin to trust that maybe an identified pattern exists or that some posited explanation is "true." In science, replication is critical. The more studies that accumulate and come to the same conclusion, the more that we can trust that the conclusion approximates "truth." Consider experimental studies in medicine. Reviews have shown that, though experiments constitute a "gold standard" for when we can trust studies, they can still be highly problematic.[9] Thus, only after a large number of experiments accumulate can we trust that an identified association or pattern actually exists.

Third, science tends to emphasize approximations to "truth." That can be seen in the language used by most scientists. They "test hypotheses" and they "find support" or "fail to find support" for a given hypothesis. They do not find "the" truth, they do not "confirm" "reality," and they do not "show" that some force, X, "caused" some outcome, Y. Rather, they simply come closer and closer to approximating "truth."

---

[8] Gould (2003).
[9] Ioannidis (2005a, 2005b); Mears (2010); Mears and Cochran (2015); Mears (2017); Harris (2017).

A related idea that tends to guide most scientists is the notion that science involves the ability to falsify theories or statements about reality. From this perspective, a theory amounts to simply one person's story about a given phenomenon and is not much different than a fictional account. However, if it can be falsified, and if empirical tests occur that seek to do so, then we can trust better that we are approximating an accurate account of the world.

The reliance on "falsification" as a criterion has merit, but it also has been hotly contested among scientists.[10] For example, we might develop a theory that presently cannot be tested, but that someday, with better methods or data, can be. Some scholars would view the theory as scientific. Others would say it is not. Why? Without an empirical test and thus the ability to falsify the theory, we have no way to differentiate it from fiction.

Fourth, science typically entails thinking and talking about the world in terms of probabilities. Some force, X, "likely" causes Y. Why think or talk this way? Philosophical debates attend to this issue, but a simple response is that the theories, methods, data, and analytic techniques of science entail error. That does not mean that guessing at the "truth" is better. It simply means that even with the best, most rigorous studies, error can arise.

That, indeed, tends to be a theme in the history of science: Each answer to a question opens the door to new questions. Frequently, the advance in knowledge lies in learning how to reframe a question in ways that allow for more accurately understanding the conditions under which certain phenomena or effects arise.[11]

A simple example: We can conduct an experiment in which we randomly assign felons to a drug court and others to "business as usual." Assume that the study findings indicate that the treatment group (i.e., drug court participants) had lower rates of recidivism. If the study is well done, we trust the results. But that does not mean that a better designed study would identify the same results.[12] Perhaps, unbeknown to the researchers, some non-randomness in the experiment arose, such that some lower-risk individuals ended up in the treatment pool. The study thus becomes biased toward finding a treatment effect. In addition, the identified effect may not hold in other places. Perhaps the drug court effect might only arise in areas where "business as usual" entails a reliance on highly ineffective programs. In areas that rely on ones that are effective, the drug court effect may not arise since the non-treated group likely would be receiving beneficial treatment. Such possibilities should lead us to reframe our original question. Instead of asking whether drug courts are effective, we might ask,

[10] For an overview, see Okasha's (2002) discussion of Karl Popper and "falsification."
[11] Mills (1959).   [12] Mears *et al.* (2011); Mears *et al.* (2015).

"Under what conditions can they be effective?" There may still be other possibilities to take into account. What about the possibility that drug courts cause harms? This possibility is certainly plausible and so we might find it more productive to be even more precise and to cast the question in this way: "Under what conditions are drug courts effective and under what conditions do they cause harms?"

Fifth, science relies on peer review. Why? Scientists make mistakes. Peer review provides a critical opportunity to weed out studies that do not pass muster. Perhaps the studies failed to build in any clear way on prior work, relied on unrepresentative data, used inappropriate measures, and so on. Peer review is not perfect. Indeed, some published research should not have gotten through peer review. That is another reason for viewing any given study as an approximation to reality, one that we view skeptically until a larger body of studies emerges that arrives at a similar conclusion. Even then, skepticism holds reign. Why? It is not just a lone scientist or two that can be wrong. Entire fields of study sometimes engage in "group think" that can blind scientists to theoretical explanations that should be considered.

Science thus involves the pursuit of the approximation of truth through methods and processes designed to identify empirically how the social or natural world works. It also involves skepticism. That distinguishes it from various philosophies and personal opinions, or from the results of studies that rely on flawed, or no, systematic reliance on the tools of science.

Once again, then, how does science differ from research? No correct answer exists. We can say that researchers who seek to create generalizable insights about the way the world works are contributing to science and can be called "scientists." That differs, say, from a situation where a researcher simply seeks to know about one particular event or pattern and not to generalize from it to advance knowledge about the world.

What, then, of someone who conducts research, but does so without an interest per se in advancing science? For example, researchers at a local, state, or federal agency might conduct studies that rely on scientific methods, but with a focus on improving agency operations, not increasing scientific knowledge. We likely would call such individuals "researchers," not "scientists."

That seems like a straightforward call, but it is not. Why? It misses the fact that scientific knowledge accumulates in unanticipated ways. Some of the biggest leaps in knowledge, including so-called "paradigm shifts" that change how we conceptualize phenomena, come from as simple a step as creating a better measurement device or statistical technique.[13]

---

[13] Kuhn (1962); Merton (1973); Weinberg (2015).

For example, perhaps a police department surveys its street patrol officers as part of creating an annual report on agency performance. It identifies substantial differences in the reported job satisfaction of male officers and female officers. Why? The report may not say. In that sense, it fails to advance scientific knowledge. Yet, the study may be read by researchers who then wonder why such a difference exists. They proceed to develop a theory and to test it. Other researchers – we might call them "scientists" or "scholars" – build on that work. Eventually, a theory emerges and comes to be viewed, after considerable empirical testing, as a credible, trustworthy account about the factors that influence employment satisfaction.

Was the initial department report scientific? Yes, to the extent that it relied on credible data and scientific methodologies. It was not, however, peer reviewed and did not seek to explain a phenomenon, much less to do so for knowledge's sake only. From that perspective, it was not a scientific undertaking. Even so, it contributed to scientific progress. At the end of the day, then, when scientific methods guide any research activity, we can view that activity as a scientific undertaking, one that may directly or indirectly contribute to advances in knowledge.

Scientific Progress and the Accumulation of Knowledge

The field of criminology and criminal justice is a science, or it aspires to be one. Scholars differ about what that can mean, but it includes an emphasis on methods, data, and analyses designed to provide as accurate as possible a depiction of reality. It means progress, too, in advancing knowledge. What, though, is scientific progress? Viewed somewhat differently, how does scientific knowledge accumulate?

When we consider progress in science, it can be natural to think about tremendous jumps in knowledge, like the discovery of gravity or the various discoveries that lead to Nobel prizes. Such cases stand out because they are so striking. They are unusual in that way. They also somehow seem like absolutely clear statements about advances in science. However, decisions about the importance of any given theory or finding rests with a community of scientists. It rests, in turn, with their collective – and imperfect – judgements about the importance of different studies. Pronouncements about the relative importance of any one study can be misleading for this reason.

It is, we think, more constructive to think about science as progressing along many different fronts.[14] View science perhaps as a track meet. There are different events that go into the final tally of which team "wins" or "loses." Collectively, a team may win, but even when it does not,

---

[14] Mears and Stafford (2002).

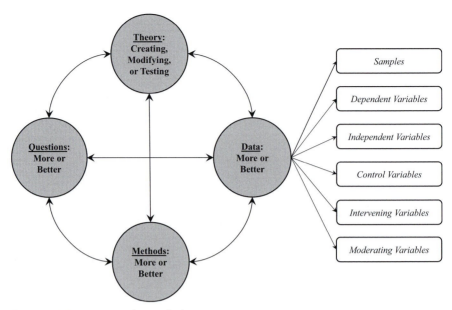

Figure 2.2 Dimensions along which science progresses

individuals may do so. Similarly, scientific progress can occur along a variety of dimensions. Growth along one dimension sometimes may outpace growth in another. In some years, there may be an especially noteworthy advance in statistical methodologies. In other years, there may be tremendous strides in developing particular theories or sources of data. And in still others, there may be a steady march toward more productive, insightful ways of framing questions, which lead to leaps in knowledge.

Figure 2.2 provides an illustration of this idea. As depicted in the figure, knowledge can progress, or accumulate, through (1) the creation of new theories, modification of existing theories, or testing of theory, (2) development of more and better data, (3) creation of more or better methods of analysis or of designing studies, or (4) asking more or better questions.

Each dimension in turn brings with it additional possibilities for the accumulation of knowledge. Consider data. The generation of new or better data can entail obtaining more representative samples for a study or better measures of dependent, independent, control, intervening, and moderating variables. *Samples* involve the selection of representative cases that we then use to identify patterns that may be typical of the larger population of people or places. *Dependent variables*, or outcomes, are those phenomena – such as variation in crime rates, support for the death penalty, or punitive criminal laws – that we wish to predict or explain. *Independent variables* are those forces that we think may explain some or all of the variation in an outcome. For example, we might test a theory that predicts that income inequality in communities (an independent variable) causes more crime (a dependent variable, or outcome). *Control variables* represent various forces, the omission of which, for some kinds of analyses, may lead us to question whether an identified relationship between two other forces (e.g., X and Y) is "real" or spurious. A spurious relationship is one that is not real, even though an observed association may seem to represent a causal effect. *Intervening variables* are those factors (or forces) that may help us to explain how one factor influences another. For example, the association between X and Z might be explained by Y, such that X → Y → Z. Finally, *moderating variables* are those factors that we think may amplify or diminish the effect of another factor on some outcome. Consider fatigue and irritability. The more fatigued we feel, the more likely we may be to grump at somebody. The effect of fatigue may be even greater, however, if we are hungry. Put differently, being hungry may amplify the probability that fatigue will cause us to be grumpy and irritable.

Similar types of nuances can arise with theory and methods, respectively. Different approaches exist to "doing" theory. Many scholars advocate the use of "formal theory" construction, for example, while others promote the use of "grounded theory" construction.[15] In addition, different approaches exist for conducting analyses. Sometimes a new theory or method can shed light on critical questions that to date have been difficult to answer. In this way, science can be a bit like detective work. Conceptual roadblocks sometimes block scientists and detectives alike from solving a problem. Then some event shakes them up and they "see" the problem in a light that enables them to answer it. "Aha" moments can happen for scientists as much as for detectives. Application of new or different theories and methods provide a critical platform from which scientists create such moments.

Perhaps the "fuzziest" way science can progress lies with asking new or better questions (shown in the left-hand side of the figure). Science can lead to lots of dead ends, but it also can lead to new ways of discerning patterns. Thomas A. Edison reportedly said that, after 10,000 seemingly unsuccessful experiments aimed at creating a storage battery, "I have not failed. I have just found 10,000 ways that won't work."[16] Identifying that certain strategies do not work amounts in fact to progress. We know what not to do and can turn our focus to other directions.

---

[15] Compare the discussions, for example, in Lewin (1952), Homans (1964), Dubin (1978), Gibbs (1985), Gottfredson and Hirschi (1990), Hage (1994), Crank and Bowman (2008), and Jaccard and Jacoby (2010).
[16] Elkhorne (1967:52).

Failure to understand various phenomena – whether those in nature or in the social world – can be frustrating. Yet, each time that scientists "fail," they come closer to gaining critical insights. Failure can lead us to revisit how we frame research questions and, in so doing, it can lead to big advances. From where do new questions, or new ways of framing questions, come? *They can emerge from almost any aspect of the research enterprise.* Consider a new theory. It might not be testable, thus casting into doubt its relevance for science. Yet, it may nonetheless spark insights among other scientists that lead to new questions or ways of examining old ones.

The importance of generating such insights is so important that we might view it as a criterion on which we evaluate theories – all else equal, a theory that generates more, and more important, avenues of inquiry may be viewed as the better theory.[17] That criterion does not necessarily hold only for theories. Methods or data sources that provide the foundation for generating more scientific research may be viewed as better than those that do not. Here, again, though, what amounts to "better" typically can only be understood in hindsight.

A final observation about progress in science concerns laboratories and universities. For many people, the very word "science" conjures up an image of a laboratory. Scientists, typically in a university or college setting, undertake experiments and do so far from the hustle and bustle of the "real world." In reality, a great deal of science does not involve laboratories or experiments or occurs only in academic settings. It can consist of a wide range of approaches to research, not just experiments. And it may occur in research institutes and research divisions of local, state, or federal agencies. It also may occur in businesses and corporations.

Not least, science may begin with purely "academic" questions about the nature of the world or it may begin with a focus on policy. Indeed, many theories in the social sciences emanate from policy research.[18] The same holds for many other sciences. For example, in medicine, efforts to address an epidemic can lead to greater understanding about the human body even as they help in developing vaccines to prevent future epidemics.[19] All such research should be considered when we contemplate the different ways in which science progresses.

---

[17] See, generally, Gibbs (1972, 1985, 1997), Mears and Stafford (2002), and Ekland-Olson and Gibbs (2018).

[18] Rossi (1980).

[19] See, for example, Barry's (2005) account of the 1917 flu pandemic; see also Mukherjee's (2010) account of progress in understanding and treating cancer.

Natural Sciences vs. Social Sciences

Science is science, whether the focus is on biology, oceans, physics, and other "hard" sciences or on criminology and criminal justice, psychology, sociology, and other "soft" sciences. They are unified by a focus on systematic observation and replication, as well as theory, data, and methods that collectively serve to help us come closer to understanding reality.

The very notion of a "hard" science stems from the fact that some topics lend themselves more readily to measurement and manipulation. In chemistry, for example, scientists can mix different chemicals or subject them to tests that allow theories to be tested.

By contrast, much of what gets studied in the "soft" sciences cannot be directly measured. For example, almost no studies measure criminal acts as they occur in "real time." Rather, scientists conduct surveys and ask individuals about whether they have committed crimes or been victimized, or they rely on court records that provide information about arrests or convictions. Even if a scientist wanted to capture a crime in "real time," there is no definitive criminal act. Rather, behaviors unfold over time and are subject to interpretation. To illustrate, there is no clear beginning or end to a criminal act. In addition, we cannot see all aspects of criminal behavior and we cannot see inside individuals' brains to determine what they intended.

The social sciences generally must rely on *indirect* measures of various aspects of the world. When scientists study why individuals commit crime, they necessarily must rely on imperfect information about offending and the various causes thought to contribute to the offending. Similarly, when they study why some areas have higher crime rates than others, they invariably rely on indirect measures of such phenomena as community "cohesion" or "inequality." The same holds true for studying various aspects of the criminal justice and correctional systems. In all instances, scientists rely on "soft" information – that is, indirect measures – to identify associations and patterns.

Social scientists also rely on "soft" methods, which we might define as any approach other than an experiment. In the social sciences, experiments can happen. However, they generally constitute the exception rather than the rule. That reflects the phenomena under study. For example, a researcher might want to shed light on variation in the extent to which different courts issue incarcerative sanctions. An experimental study, one in which we randomly allocate some courts to have one characteristic and others to have a different one – perhaps to see how the characteristic affects sentencing decisions – simply is not possible. Rather than give up the ghost, though, social scientists have developed a variety of methodological approaches to investigating court decision-making.

Does the reliance on indirect measures and a range of non-experimental methodologies make the "soft" sciences less "scientific" than the "hard" sciences? We know of no clear way to answer that question. Consider medicine. We might view it as a "hard" science. Yet, many aspects of medicine, including illness and treatments, cannot be studied through experiments. Consider that physicians make decisions every day that reflect their knowledge, skill, resources, and the time available to render an assessment. A wide range of individual, organizational, and societal factors can influence their decision-making. No experimental design can neatly disentangle all of those factors or how they may interact to influence medical decisions.[20]

One of the central factors that makes the study of crime and criminal justice – and most phenomena in the social sciences – so difficult is human volition. This difficulty can make research in the "hard" sciences look easy. As Neal deGrasse Tyson, a physicist, has commented, "In science, when human behavior enters the equation, things go nonlinear. That's why Physics is easy and Sociology is hard."[21]

Studying crime and criminal justice can also be difficult because of the myriad of factors that, as with medical practice, influence the actions of individuals, organizations, governments, and communities. Consider judicial decision-making in parole hearings. The decisions about whether to parole individuals may be influenced by state law, parole hearing caseloads, the political or philosophical leanings of particular parole boards, and so on. In fact, one study found yet another factor that may influence parole decisions – hunger. Shai Danziger and colleagues studied judicial rulings. They found that the favorable rulings declined as judges became hungry and then, after food breaks, favorable rulings became more likely![22] Many factors influence crime and criminal justice phenomena. In addition, these factors may interact with one another. There can be thresholds, too, such that a given factor may not, say, influence an outcome greatly until it reaches a certain level.[23]

Criminology and criminal justice thus can be seen as a "soft" science. At bottom, though, it shares with the natural sciences the goal of seeking to create knowledge and to do so using the best theory, data, and methods possible.

Science and "Evidence-Based" Policy

In recent decades, policymakers and government officials have called for "evidence-based" policy. There exists, however, little consensus about what "evidence-based" actually means.[24]

---

[20] See, generally, Mears and Bacon (2009).   [21] Tyson (2016).
[22] Danziger *et al.* (2011).
[23] Agnew (2005); Mears and Cochran (2013); Mears *et al.* (2013a).   [24] Mears (2010).

One assumption that runs through many accounts views "evidence-based" policy as that which rests on scientific "evidence," where such evidence refers to results from experimental-design studies. Such a view is striking. Why? To the extent that evidence-based policy refers only to experimental evidence, there is little chance of placing the bulk of crime and justice policy on an "evidence-based" foundation. We simply cannot do experiments that cover the vast expanse of criminal justice and corrections. For example, scientists cannot ethically assign inmates randomly to super-max prisons or to the death penalty. And they literally cannot randomly assign poverty and inequality to some communities and not others.

Can experiments be undertaken to investigate the effectiveness of this or that program, such as a drug court? Absolutely. But no local, state, or federal agency – or any organization – can experimentally evaluate all programs. Even if one could, it still would not be possible to conduct experiments on the entire criminal justice system, various combinations of state laws, elimination of the juvenile justice system, and so on.[25]

Policy nonetheless can rest on scientific evidence, depending on how one defines "evidence." Science can include many types of studies. It can consist of the results from experiments. But it can also consist of the results that come from other approaches to studying crime and criminal justice. There are, for example, numerous "quasi-experimental" research designs, which we will discuss further in the book, that can provide credible estimates of how some factors influence others or the effectiveness of various policies, programs, or practices. When policy builds on such research designs, it might be said to be "evidence-based."

A more general view sees evidence-based policy as efforts that rely on the results of scientific methods and that seek to answer a range of policy-relevant questions. In Chapter 7, we discuss the evaluation hierarchy. Briefly, it refers to empirical research that seeks to answer five policy questions: What is the need for a policy? What is the theoretical foundation of the policy, and how credible is that foundation? How well is the policy implemented and what factors influence its implementation? What is its impact on intended and unintended outcomes? And how cost-efficient is the policy?[26] The notion of a hierarchy stems from the fact that policy efforts ideally proceed by answering each question sequentially. For example, it makes little sense to implement a policy that society does not need. Accordingly, before implementing a policy, we would first want to establish whether we need it.

Viewed in this light, "evidence-based" policy consists of efforts that draw on credible, scientific research that examines these questions.

[25] See, however, Mears (2017).   [26] See Rossi *et al.* (2004) and Mears (2010).

For example, an evidence-based policy is one for which a clearly established need, based on empirical research, exists. It is one that has a clear theoretical, or causal, logic that has been empirically supported. It is one that has been shown through empirical assessment to be consistently and well-implemented. It is one that research shows to create a clear and substantial impact. And, not least, it is one that can be shown empirically to result in improvements that result in more benefits than costs to society.

What counts as "credible" research? It can be defined as studies that (1) rely on theories, methods, data, measures, and analytic approaches used by scientists and (2) the scientific community views as valid in providing information about the prevalence and causes of various phenomena. If that sounds a little "squishy," it should. No social scientific theory or set of data, measures, or analyses in any absolute way provides the "truth." They also do not provide the only or best way to understand some phenomena, including not least crime and criminal justice. The defining characteristic of credible research is simply that it uses the best available scientific methods to describe and understand the world around us.

In short, science has much to contribute to efforts to place policy on an "evidence-based" foundation, especially if "evidence" means the results of using scientific methods to examine the five categories of questions that comprise the evaluation hierarchy. Even then, there likely will remain considerable confusion about what counts as "evidence-based." For example, even after ten or twenty experimental evaluations, there may not be sufficient basis to claim with confidence that a particular law or program can reduce crime. In addition, even if such confidence were warranted, that would not mean that the law or program would be well-implemented or effective in a particular community or state.

The Art of Conducting Scientific Research

Media accounts sometimes portray scientists as hyper-rational individuals. There may be truth in that view, but only a bit. Scientists generally do go about their lives systematically observing and making sense of the world. Yet, the precise focus of their inquiries and how they go about them can be influenced by all manner of forces. One researcher, for example, may spend his or her entire career studying law enforcement officer decision-making. Why? Perhaps that topic happened to be a primary focus of the program in which he or she studied. Perhaps his or her advisor had a large-scale study and roped the researcher into it. Perhaps the researcher had intended to pursue some other phenomenon, but then, seemingly by chance, tripped into a research collaboration on law enforcement that sparked a lifelong interest in the topic. Perhaps a unique funding opportunity arose that he or she pursued simply to help "pay the bills."

Observe here that the researcher's emphasis in no clear way emanates from a systematic stocktaking of the state of criminological and criminal justice research and the gaps that most warrant addressing. Rather, the emphasis derives from other considerations. Other types of seeming randomness might drive a research agenda. Consider Robert Merton, whose 1938 article, "Social Structure and Anomie," is among the most cited in criminology.[27] An oral history that Francis Cullen and Steven Messner conducted with him highlighted how the cultural conditions in the time in which he lived – including the near-universal emphasis in the early part of the twentieth century on "limitless possibilities" for social mobility – shaped his theorizing about social organization.[28] In short, the era and neighborhoods in which he grew up influenced the theories he developed. More mundane factors, though, can shape research and in no way conform with a cookie-cutter approach to research. For example, a student might learn about a particular methodology during graduate school, become expert in its use, and then continuously investigate questions that can be answered with that methodology. Such an approach seems far from "scientific." Yet, it might well result in the development of theories and empirical analyses that greatly advance criminological and criminal justice knowledge.

We make these points to highlight that scientific advancements occur in any number of ways. There will be strong viewpoints about how any given study or research project should be undertaken, but there is no single formulaic approach to scientific progress. That in turn suggests the need to pursue research with a bit of an "explorer's" mindset, one that allows for seizing on opportunities as they arise, exploring paths that may seem like dead ends, and imagining different ways to overcome them. The "art" in scientific research lies in adopting such a mindset. It lies as well in being adaptable, curious, thinking creatively about the types of studies that may be possible, and following one's interests. It lies, too, in knowing what questions to ask that may most advance science or policy. We discuss the science and art of criminological and criminal justice research throughout this book. First, however, there is a need to discuss what exactly "criminological and criminal justice" research entails.

WHAT IS CRIMINOLOGICAL AND CRIMINAL JUSTICE RESEARCH?

Preliminary Observations

It seems a bit clunky and unnecessary to have to refer repeatedly to "criminology and criminal justice," no? Consider the field of medicine. Most universities and colleges do not have a field of study entitled "Medicine

[27] Merton (1938); Cullen and Messner (2007:8).   [28] Cullen and Messner (2007:14).

and Health Care." Instead, there typically are departments, schools, or colleges of medicine.

The issue here centers on theory versus practice. If we are interested purely in the causes of crime or illness, perhaps "criminology" and "medicine," respectively, may seem like the way to go. Conversely, if we are interested purely in the laws, organizations, systems, and the like devoted to addressing crime and illness, respectively, then perhaps "criminal justice" and "health care," respectively, would be the better terminological options.

What, though, if we come to the table armed with a bias in one direction or the other? Perhaps we think that health-care systems ultimately require illness to even exist. Consequently, the terminology that we should always use is college of "medicine," where "medicine" encompasses both the causes of illness and our responses to it. Someone else, though, might think that the focus on responses belongs to another field of study. In addition, he or she might think that a study of responses seems too centered on policy or practice and consequently too removed from a focus on advancing science. This person might also view the study of medical practice as atheoretical. What really matters, for this individual, is understanding illness and developing and testing theories about its causes. In this case, he or she would likely argue that "medicine" should refer only to the study of illness and its causes.

Here, we have varying meanings associated with the same term ("medicine"). And we can see a clear tension in what scholars might view as the more important domain of study. The logic is, admittedly, a bit odd. A focus on health-care laws, practices, and systems can be no less theoretical an undertaking than a study of how certain diseases arise among certain individuals or groups or in certain areas. And this focus can be no less important in advancing knowledge. The main difference lies in the outcomes under scrutiny.

This same set of problems exists with the terms "criminology" and "criminal justice." Scholars, policymakers, criminal justice administrators and practitioners, and the public all use these terms inconsistently. Some view "criminology" as the study of crime causation only, while others view it as encompassing both crime causation and the laws, systems, and responses that society uses to reduce and respond to crime.[29] By contrast, some view "criminal justice" as focused only on the latter, and others view it as encompassing both the study of crime causation and policy responses to it.

---

[29] See, generally, discussions in Kraska (2006) and Duffee (2015).

To add to the confusion, some scholarship assumes that "theoretical" research must be "criminological" and that it has little relevance for policy or practice. Other scholarship assumes that "policy" research cannot be or typically is not grounded in theory and does not contribute to the development of it. There is little logical basis for holding such views, but they exist nonetheless.[30]

More confusion: In contemporary times, there are "criminology" programs, "criminal justice" programs, and "criminology and criminal justice" programs. They all cover much the same terrain. Perhaps some programs lean more toward studying the causes of crime and others toward the study of criminal justice, but that is to be expected. Not all programs are sufficiently large enough to cover a wide range of topics and the culture in some may foster an interest in or commitment to topics.

Even more confusion: What are the varying topics that get covered? As we discuss in Chapter 9, the range of topics is vast. For example, criminological and criminal justice researchers study: variation in crime among individuals and across areas (e.g., neighborhoods, cities, states, and countries); the creation, application, and effects of formal social control (e.g., enactment of laws, sentencing decisions, community policing); the nature and effects of informal social control (e.g., how perceptions about friends', family members', or others' views of oneself may affect behavior); the nature, implementation, and effects of various sanctions (e.g., probation, jail, prison); how environmental and physical spaces influence deviance and criminal activity; the nature and effects of laws, crime prevention programs, and juvenile and criminal justice systems as a whole; the causes and consequences of victimization; public views about crime and justice and what explains variation in these views; and more.

In addition, these researchers draw on a diverse range of disciplines. They create theories, but they also draw on theories and methodologies from other disciplines, such as biology, economics, law, psychology, public administration and policy, sociology, social work, and more.

In short, it would seem that one could use "criminology" or "criminal justice" as a shorthand for "criminology and criminal justice" or "criminal justice and criminology." So, why not use "criminology" or "criminal justice" throughout the book? The reason is that we want to avoid misunderstanding. If, for example, we use only the term "criminology," the risk arises that some readers may assume that the focus centers only on the causes of crime. That is not how we use the term, but some readers might do so. Similarly, if we use

---

[30] Mears (2010); Cooper and Worrall (2012); see, generally, Duffee (2015); see also Rossi (1980).

"criminal justice" throughout, some readers might assume that the focus centers on criminal justice, not on theories about crime.

This dilemma can be found in many fields, including medicine and health care, as discussed above, and in economics, psychology, law, and so on. Specifically, some scholars may focus only on developing theories or examining the causes of various phenomena. Their goal is to understand the nature of the universe. Such an approach, as we discuss in Chapter 7, entails a focus on the "basic" causes of things. Here, "basic" does not mean simple; rather, it means the root causes of, in this case, crime and justice. By contrast, "applied" researchers may focus more on how to improve the world by developing or applying knowledge that may aid in efforts to reduce crime. We view both endeavors as equally important. Each entails the need for theory and empirical analysis. Even so, the divides exist and can influence the perceptions that some have about the relative importance of certain kinds of research.[31]

To say that this situation can be confusing is an understatement. Consider another example from America. Some members of the American Society of Criminology (ASC) may feel that its lead journal, *Criminology*, and the ASC should focus primarily on "theory." Yet, the ASC also publishes a journal called *Criminology and Public Policy*. In addition, *Criminology* annually features presidential addresses that emphasize the importance of theoretically *and* policy-focused research.[32] Conversely, the Academy of Criminal Justice Sciences (ACJS), which some scholars may view as focused more on "applied" policy and practice topics, features publications, *Justice Quarterly* in particular, that publish theoretically focused papers on crime causation. Similar confusion can be seen in criminology and criminal justice associations internationally.

One simple solution, then, is to use both terms. Doing so may be clunky, but it can avoid misunderstanding. Even so, it still creates the impression that one term, "criminology," differs from the other, "criminal justice." That is unfortunate, but largely unavoidable. A second solution is to understand the historical context that has given rise to this situation. It is to this context that we now turn.

Some Historical Context

Cesare Lombroso (1835–1909) has been referred to in patriarchal terms as the "father of criminology."[33] He earned a medical degree in 1858 from the University of Pavia.[34] Pilloried in recent times for his seemingly simplistic

---

[31] Wolfgang (1963); Petersilia (1991).   [32] Mears (2010:3).
[33] Wolfgang (1961:361); see, generally, Devroye (2010).   [34] Wolfgang (1961:362).

arguments about the biological bases of criminal behavior, Lombroso in his era was a prominent and prolific scholar who, reflecting the emerging development of science and its emphasis on observation and measurement, wrote many articles and books about crime. As Marvin Wolfgang has highlighted, Lombroso was far from alone in his views or approach. Wolfgang noted, for example, that "Havelock Ellis, in *The Criminal*, gives a brief history of the precursors of Lombroso, and in the second chapter, no less than twenty-two scholars in Europe who had anticipated Lombroso in pointing out the relationship between the criminal's physical and mental characteristics and his behavior."[35] Ellis wrote his book in 1890; the influence that Charles Darwin and evolutionary theories had on Lombroso and these scholars is clear. Darwin's book, it may be recalled, was published in 1859 and was striking for advancing arguments about natural selection. Entitled *On the Origin of Species by Means of Natural Selection, or the Preservation of Favoured Races in the Struggle for Life*, it contributed to Lombroso's work and that of many others.[36]

Long before Lombroso, there were other famous scholars of crime and justice. For example, in 1764, Cesare Beccaria published *An Essay on Crimes and Punishment*.[37] His work and that of many other scholars drew attention to the importance of inherited, psychological, and social conditions for understanding and addressing crime in a rational manner, one that might, for example, deter offending. In subsequent decades, scholars embraced positivism, or the notion that behavior and the world at large can be understood through logic, mathematics, and measurement. From this perspective, philosophy takes a back seat to a scientific, empirically based approach to understanding the world. Indeed, in contemporary times, we generally think of criminology and criminal justice as a scientific, not a philosophical, undertaking.[38]

Lombroso represented this shift in thinking. He adopted a "scientific" approach to understanding crime and thus has come to be viewed as a founder of "criminology." Even in the 1800s, though, an interesting tension arose. Lombroso focused primarily on trying to understand who offends and who does not. During this time, philosophical and legal treatises advanced by Beccaria laid the foundation for continued scholarship aimed at understanding how to structure laws and policies. They did not necessarily entail "science." Rather, they entailed assumptions about the appropriate moral response to crime and about what somehow must be effective in reducing or "curing" it. Then, during the 1800s, police departments emerged – the first was implemented by Boston in 1833 – as a formal,

---

[35] Wolfgang (1961:366), citing Ellis (1913).   [36] Darwin (1859).   [37] Beccaria (1986).
[38] Rafter (2009); Bosworth and Hoyle (2011).

institutionalized way to respond to and address crime.[39] Corrections experts concomitantly devised approaches that sought to be scientific. In the mid 1800s, for example, Alexander Machonochie, a British naval officer, developed a carrots-and-sticks "marks" system while running a penal colony on Norfolk Island.[40] He sought to use science to guide reforms; his efforts informed correctional practices in his home country and abroad. In short, scientific attention turned not only to the study of criminal behaviour, but also to how best to prevent and reduce it through scientific understanding.

These topics came under study from many different fields. As Nicole Rafter has written, during the 1800s, medical doctors and scientists from diverse fields studied "moral insanity," created "criminal statistics," developed theories of criminal behavior, linked poverty to crime, and so on. There was not, however, as yet a field of criminology.[41]

That all changed by the end of the 1800s.[42] The term "criminology" increasingly came into use. Raffaele Garofalo, for example, a student of Lombroso, published the first of several editions of his book, *Criminology*, in 1885.[43] And then, during the 1900s, it became a field of study. In 1909, for example, scholars and practitioners from around the United States convened at Northwestern University's School of Law for the inaugural Conference on Criminal Law and Criminology.[44] Members of the conference voted to create the American Institute of Criminal Law and Criminology.[45] The founders envisioned an interdisciplinary effort to understand crime and how to address it. Within a decade, contentious debates about the proper theoretical and substantive focus, along with limited funding, led to the Institute's demise.[46]

This outcome reflected something of an identity crisis for the "field." Was it focused on the study of crime? Or criminal justice? Was it a particular theoretical orientation, such as biological or environmental causes of crime? Or was it "simply" the application of different perspectives – from different scientific fields – to topics related to crime and justice?

There is today no "correct" definition of criminology or "criminal justice." Indeed, as we discuss below, there is debate about the field's proper focus of study and the terminology of "criminology" versus "criminal justice." Even so, a characterization of the field that is still commonly used emerged in the early 1930s. Specifically, in 1934, Edwin Sutherland published the widely used *Principles of Criminology*, which subsequently was

---

[39] Harring (1983); Walker and Katz (2017).   [40] Morris (2002).
[41] Rafter (2011); see also Laub (1983).   [42] Devroye (2010).
[43] Garofalo (1885); see the discussion of this work in Allen (1954).   [44] Devroye (2010:7).
[45] Devroye (2010:7).   [46] Devroye (2017:30).

updated through a series of new editions. It defined criminology as a field that was focused on law-making, law-breaking, and responses to crime.[47]

That broad description likely accords with what many criminology and criminal justice scholars think.[48] No definitions are, however, "right" or "wrong." They simply are more or less useful. This definition, in our view, seems *most* useful – it draws our attention to many dimensions related to crime. For example, there is no crime without a law to define it as such. Why, then, are some behaviors deemed, by law, to be criminal? What explains differential enforcement of the law? Or its effects? Why do some individuals commit crime and others do not? Why do some individuals persist in offending, others escalate their offending, and still others desist? What explains why the public supports some approaches to crime more than others or why support for some sanctions, such as the death penalty, varies over time? This broad definition of criminology – and, we would submit, of "criminal justice" as part of the same field – works to draw our attention to these and many other related questions of interest in and of their own right and because they may help guide policy.

Sutherland provided such clarity and parsimony. So, the question arises again – why the terminological confusion? A little more history is in order.

An obvious starting point for thinking about the history of the field of criminology and criminal justice might begin with scholarly organizations. As described by the ASC[49] and the ACJS,[50] criminology first emerged as a distinct field of study in the 1940s.[51] The groundwork for this new field of study was laid earlier, however. In 1928, August Vollmer, the Police Chief of Berkeley, California, and Alexander Kidd, a law professor, submitted a proposal to create a school of criminology at the University of California at Berkeley.[52] Subsequently, in 1933, the university created an undergraduate major in criminology. Notably, the Federal Bureau of Investigation (FBI) – which acts as America's national law enforcement agency – arose in nascent form in 1908 and later was named the FBI in 1935, just two years after the emergence of this new major at a prominent university.[53]

Other historical accounts of criminology and criminal justice make clear that this field had its roots in developments internationally. Indeed, it would be a mistake to view its development as a distinctly American phenomenon. To the contrary, parallel efforts to organize a coherent field of

---

[47] Sutherland (1934).   [48] See, for example, Akers *et al.* (2016).

[49] The ASC's historical account is available online at www.asc41.com/History.html.

[50] The ACJS's historical account is available online at www.acjs.org/page/Historian.

[51] The ASC's account was first published as an article by Morris (1975); see also Clear (2001).

[52] Morris (1975).   [53] Weiner (2012).

study surfaced in England – as reflected in historical accounts of the development of the British Society of Criminology[54] – and, indeed, worldwide.[55] These efforts, like those in America, involved tensions around what precisely should be the focal point of study.

The tensions can be seen in Vollmer's efforts. He and his colleagues sought to develop an organization devoted to "criminology." They called it the National Association of College Police Officials, which was formed in 1941. World War II intervened and slowed progress toward this goal. After the war, in 1946, the founders of this association met and renamed the organization the "Society for the Advancement of Criminology." The focus of the Society, which had forty members, was to be on:

> The study of the causes, treatment, and prevention of crime, including, but not restricted to: (1) Scientific crime detection, investigation and identification; (2) Crime prevention, public safety and security; (3) Law enforcement administration; (4) Administration of criminal justice; (5) Traffic administration; (6) Probation; (7) Juvenile delinquency control; and (8) Related aspects of penology.[56]

Soon after, in 1950, the University of California at Berkeley created the first "School of Criminology." (The creation of a program of criminological study in 1933 had not resulted in creation of an organizational unit devoted to criminology.[57]) Eventually, departments, schools, and colleges of criminology emerged. For the next two decades criminology, as a field of study, proliferated nationally. Along the way, in 1958, the Society for the Advancement of Criminology formally changed its name to the American Society of Criminology.[58]

Despite the rapid growth of criminology throughout the 1950s and 1960s, a tension existed regarding whether the field should focus on basic or applied work. Some members of the Society, especially the early founders, wanted the focus to center on how to apply research to inform policy and practice. This focus understandably reflected their policing backgrounds. However, as Albert Morris has recounted, even as early as 1946, there "emerged a consensus that the problems of crime control were both too broad and too complex to be examined solely in terms of police tasks."[59]

---

[54] The BSC's historical account is available online at www.britsoccrim.org/history/.

[55] Jones (1986); Becker and Wetzell (2006); Jones and Johnstone (2015); Pifferi (2016); see, generally, Tonry (2011), Cullen and Wilcox (2012), Farrington and Welsh (2012), Petersilia and Reitz (2012), Reisig and Kane (2014), Wooldredge and Smith (2016), and Liebling *et al.* (2017).

[56] Morris (1975:128).   [57] Morris (1975).   [58] Morris (1975:134).

[59] Morris (1975:149).

"This consensus," Morris observed, "became reflected in the acceptance into membership of those whose primary interests lay outside of the police field, particularly in corrections – a movement that led ultimately to the interdisciplinary Society of today."[60] The interdisciplinary emphasis was, it will be recalled, present throughout the history of what has come to be "criminology" or "criminal justice."

As a result of this shift, the membership of the Society began to include not only those committed to an applied focus, but also those who wanted to study crime and justice for the sake of advancing knowledge. During the 1950s and 1960s, sociologists in particular increasingly shaped the direction of the Society. Simultaneously, debates began to surface about what exactly fell within the purview of "criminology." For example, in a 1963 editorial in *Criminologica*, Charles Newman asked:

> Can criminology become the meeting ground for adjunct professions concerned with the scientific study of crime and criminal behavior? Can it allow the mantle of "criminologist" to be bestowed upon those persons who seek affinity even though their major professional identity may lie in the adjunct areas of law, medicine, social work, psychology, psychiatry, and enforcement?[61]

No clear answer emerged in America or elsewhere. Some scholars argued that only a professional criminological organization and training in the scientific field of criminology could allow an individual to claim to be a "criminologist."[62] Others expressed concern about efforts to certify an individual as a professional "criminologist." The field of social work, for example, sought at one point "to eliminate from the correctional field those who do not have social work degrees."[63] William Dienstein, the Society's President, responded in a 1959 letter by observing:

> My opinion is that if we keep on over-specializing we are going to have a society of cultural ignoramuses; specialists who know how to do it but little or nothing about why and consequences; who know much about a minute aspect of some field as determined by some group and are ignorant of the purposes and functions of their specialty in relation to the purposes and functions of the whole society.[64]

An extension of Dienstein's view is that the scientific study of crime and justice does not require an applied focus. It thus does not require that individuals be certified to "practice" criminology in the way in which individuals are certified to become social workers. Accordingly, programs

---

[60] *Ibid.* [61] As recounted in Morris (1975:151); see also Wolfgang (1961).
[62] Wolfgang (1961). [63] Morris (1975:155). [64] As recounted in Morris (1975:156).

do not need to engage in training individuals for work as professional police or corrections officers.

Here, then, we can see the tension: Some programs, depending on the interest of faculty, may want to emphasize policy and practice. They therefore might be interested in preparing individuals for the professional world of policing or corrections. Others might eschew that focus. They instead emphasize "basic" science, that is, the study of the basic causes of law-making, crime, and criminal justice. Both endeavors can be viewed as falling under the umbrella of "criminology" or "criminal justice," yet we can see how the two groups might look askance at each other. The first might view pure academic studies – knowledge for knowledge's sake – as a waste of time, while the latter might view efforts to train professionals as a task suited to, well, training programs, not to programs engaged in the scientific study of law, crime, and justice.

This divide can be seen further in the splitting off of many members of the ASC to create the International Association of Police Professionals (IAPP) in 1963.[65] Part of the concern stemmed from a feeling among those with a more applied bent that sociologists had turned the field into too theoretical an undertaking. Shortly thereafter, in 1965, an impetus for a more applied direction emerged – President Johnson created a commission to study crime and criminal justice that culminated with a report, published in 1967 and entitled, *The Challenge of Crime in a Free Society*.[66] The report laid the foundation for the Omnibus Crime Control and Safe Streets Act of 1968, which in turn contributed to the establishment of criminal justice programs nationally. As William Oliver has written:

> The bill created the Law Enforcement Assistance Administration (LEAA) within the Department of Justice, which became the criminal justice grant funding organization for the national government. These grants were then passed on to State Planning Agencies (SPA), which were created in each of the 50 states. One of the grant programs created was the Law Enforcement Education Program (LEEP) which provided loans and grants to police officers and those wanting to enter law enforcement. The LEEP funds were also designated to create criminal justice programs in higher education.[67]

In short order, bachelor degree programs increased. At the time the Commission's report appeared, in 1967, only thirty-nine existed. Ten years later,

---

[65] Oliver (2014:16).

[66] President's Commission on Law Enforcement and Administration of Justice (1967). See volume 17, issue 2, of *Criminology and Public Policy* for a fifty-year retrospective account of the President's Commission and *The Challenge of Crime in a Free Society*.

[67] Oliver (2014:19).

in 1977, there were 376.[68] The funding thus helped to "establish criminal justice as an academic discipline in colleges and universities."[69] It also helped to create an applied, or policy-focused, emphasis in the resulting programs.

The IAPP became concerned that, as *The Challenge of Crime in a Free Society* had emphasized, criminal justice should be understood as a system, one with independent yet interrelated parts, including law enforcement, courts, and corrections.[70] "In light of this fact, the group felt that the IAPP should focus more broadly; it should incorporate the study of courts, corrections, and juvenile justice, into its study of the police. That, however, would necessitate a name change to the organization."[71] In 1970, at a conference in Seattle, Washington, the IAPP changed its name to the Academy of Criminal Justice Sciences.[72]

This new association, like the ASC, transformed over time. For example, although it emphasized police training, the emphasis began to include "the study of the criminal justice system through a more liberal arts approach."[73] And its growth did not occur independent of the ASC. For example, an LEAA grant led to the creation of a Joint Commission on Criminology and Criminal Justice Education and Standards that included members from the ACJS and the ASC as well as from other professional associations representing other fields, such as sociology, psychology, and public administration.

As with the ASC, the ACJS gradually assumed a more interdisciplinary focus. Also, the range of topics it covered increasingly broadened. Perhaps not surprisingly, then, discussions about merging the two organizations surfaced. Some felt that the causes for the "divorce" in 1963 no longer existed, that more similarities than not now existed, and that "by merging the two organizations together they would grow stronger."[74] Others felt that the two organizations still had divergent emphases. A committee formed in 1976 to examine the pros and cons of merger; in 1978, the ACJS membership voted against unification of the ASC and the ACJS.

During the 1980s and 1990s, the two organizations continued along parallel paths. They each grew in membership and complexity (e.g., more committees and specialized sections and divisions devoted to specific areas emerged). They also became more interdisciplinary in their focus. Simultaneously, criminology and criminal justice programs increasingly gained greater prominence in colleges and universities. In earlier decades, these programs tended to be housed within other departments, schools, and

---

[68] Oliver (2014:19–20), citing Walker (1998).
[69] Walker (1998:205), as quoted by Oliver (2014:20).   [70] Oliver (2014:20).   [71] *Ibid.*
[72] *Ibid.*   [73] *Ibid.*   [74] *Ibid.*

academic units, such as sociology or political science. They also sometimes were viewed as less than fully academic. "The discipline was," as Craig Hemmens, the 2012–2013 ACJS President, emphasized, "frequently derided as a 'cop shop' that did little more than provide training for future police officers."[75] That changed. In the 1980s and 1990s, "undergraduate and graduate criminal justice enrollments soared, and the discipline began to create its own identity, separating from sociology and political science."[76]

Reflecting on this shift, Hemmens, an active member of the ACJS *and* the ASC, wondered what if any difference existed between criminology and criminal justice and if there was any reasonable basis for continuing to have two parallel organizations. After considering the issue, he ultimately saw little difference between the two and argued that they should be merged. He highlighted, for example, the following similarities: Both organizations have conferences that feature papers with similar topics, theories, methods, and emphases; they each seek to influence policy; and they each emphasize curriculum and professional development.[77] The courses offered in various programs – regardless of program name – overlapped as well. As he noted, "I have worked in a Department of Criminal Justice, a Department of Criminology and Criminal Justice, and a Department of Criminal Justice and Criminology. Each department has offered similar courses and had faculty engaged in similar research areas."[78]

Hemmens encountered substantial resistance to his proposal. Why? Members of the ACJS seemingly felt that the ASC was "too big, too impersonal, and not as inclusive in its treatment of academics from different types of institutions," whereas the ACJS was viewed as "more welcoming to academics regardless of their institutional affiliation and to practitioners."[79] Whether such perceptions were well-founded or baseless, or premised on a different era when the two organizations may have differed more, is open to debate. Regardless, it remains a somewhat odd situation for the field and the two organizations. For example, many members of the ASC are members of the ACJS; conversely, members of the ACJS frequently are members of the ASC.[80] The presidents of the ASC frequently have been presidents of the ACJS, and, vice versa, presidents of the ACJS have been presidents of the ASC. Not least, efforts have continued to create bridges between the two organizations through the creation of such collaborations as the Crime and Justice Research Alliance (CJRA), which serves to make

[75] Hemmens (2015:21).   [76] *Ibid.*   [77] Hemmens (2015:22).
[78] Hemmens (2015:23).   [79] Hemmens (2015:22).   [80] Sorensen *et al.* (2006).

scientific experts and research available to the policymaking and practitioner community.[81]

Criminological and Criminal Justice Research

What is clear is from the above discussion is that the tension – between "basic" vs. "applied" research and "criminology" vs. "criminal justice" – has persisted throughout the decades, not only in the United States, but also in many other countries. From the late 1880s to the present, there have been repeated shifts in the emphasis that "the" field should address. Debates about these shifts frequently involve claims about the relevance of particular theoretical perspectives (e.g., biological or sociological), substantive foci (e.g., crime, law, police, courts, prisons), or the goal of advancing science versus the goal of advancing policy.

The ongoing tension persists to the present. It can be seen, for example, not only between the ASC and the ACJS, but also *within* the two respective organizations.[82] It can be seen, too, in the conflicts that have arisen in the development of similar international associations. In the end, we believe that a few conclusions can be made when one looks back on these developments.

First, the field of "criminology," "criminal justice," "criminology and criminal justice," or "criminal justice and criminology" exists. Programs whose names use these terms have proliferated since the 1970s. Whatever one wants to call it, this field seems here to stay.

Second, regardless of terminology, this field has, since the 1800s, emphasized a *scientific* approach to understanding individual-level offending and variation in crime rates as well as the operations and effects of the criminal justice and correctional systems. That is, it has emphasized science as a goal and it has emphasized a broad-based view of its scope or purview.

Third, this field continues to prioritize theory *and* policy.[83] Earlier in the chapter, we discussed the nature of science. That discussion highlighted the importance of theory, data, and methods to illuminating how the world works. It also highlighted that science does not have to be divorced from policy and that, conversely, policy studies can provide innumerable opportunities to develop and test theory. The two go hand in hand. That may be

---

[81] Applegate (2016).

[82] See, generally, Hagan (1989), Bernard and Engel (2001), Clear (2001), Kraska (2004, 2006), Bernard *et al.* (2005), Crank and Bowman (2008), Cooper and Worrall (2012), Dooley and Rydberg (2014), Steinmetz *et al.* (2014), Duffee (2015), Hemmens (2015), Mears and Cochran (2015), Snipes and Maguire (2015).

[83] See, e.g., Petersilia (1991) and Clear (2001); see, generally, Mears (2010).

one reason why, even among those who hew to one emphasis or another, the field of criminology and criminal justice has continuously prioritized theory and policy.

There has been and likely will continue to be debate about the relative importance of "theory-focused" or "policy-focused" research. For that reason alone, care should be taken in using "criminology" and "criminal justice" as terms. They can be viewed as synonymous. Yet, some scholars argue that the terms convey different meanings. There remains, then, a need for appreciating this situation and how it can lead to misunderstanding.

Fourth, the field continues to evolve and broaden. For example, victimization and public opinion historically received relatively little attention. They now feature prominently in criminological and criminal justice research. Similarly, biological perspectives initially grounded research in criminology and criminal justice. Then these perspectives receded into the background only, in recent years, to resurface. Not all scholars embrace these changes. However, the growth of the field clearly lies in the direction of expanded domains of theory and inquiry.[84]

Fifth, the field increasingly is interdisciplinary, which reflects in many ways the make-up of those who helped to create it in the late 1800s and early 1900s. In fact, it always has been interdisciplinary, but there have been periods when one discipline or another held more sway. There exists today a diverse range of disciplines that inform criminological and criminal justice research. Biosocial researchers have become more prominent in the field, but alongside them are researchers from psychology, social work, political science, economics, and more who play a role in advancing the study of crime, law, and justice.[85]

Sixth, this field – what we here will term "criminology and criminal justice" – not only is here to stay, it also is, in our view, needed. No other field of study puts crime and criminal justice at the center of its focus. The theories required to explain various crime and justice phenomena – including law-making, law-breaking, and responses to it – come from diverse academic disciplines. None of these disciplines, however, prioritizes crime and justice. By contrast, the field of criminology and criminal justice does so. In so doing, it helps to ensure that greater scientific progress in understanding the diverse array of topics that fall within its purview occurs.

---

[84] We disagree with Marvin Wolfgang's (1963:161) description of criminology as the study of crime. In our view, it encompasses as well the scientific study of law-making and responses to crime, which is precisely the definition advocated by Sutherland (1934) and many crime and justice researchers (see, e.g., Clear (2001); Cullen (2005); Sherman (2003b); Maguire *et al.* (2012); Hemmens 2015; Akers *et al.* 2016).

[85] Morris (1975); Clear (2001); Mears (2010); Mears and Cochran (2015).

In addition, no other field provides systematic education and training to students and practitioners in crime and criminal justice.[86]

Is this establishment of criminology and criminal justice as an independent field truly ideal? That is hard to say. Virtually all academic disciplines can suffer from insularity. When cut off from other disciplines, they tend to adopt an unduly narrow view of the world. They can miss out on opportunities to gain insights by viewing the world through other academic disciplines. Time will tell. However, in our view, the interdisciplinary nature of criminology and criminal justice likely will protect it from becoming too insular.

CONCLUSION

Science distinguishes itself from other fields by its effort to identify reality through empirical measurement and analysis. It develops theory and tests it with research designs that themselves entail data, measures, and various analytic methods. The end goal? For many scientists it is, quite simply, knowledge for knowledge's sake. They want to contribute to developing greater understanding of the world. At the same time, many scientists seek to create knowledge that can help inform the development of policies, programs, and practices that can improve the world.

That is true in many sciences, and no less true with criminology and criminal justice. Scholars in this field seek to understand law, crime, criminal justice, and a diverse array of related areas simply because they want to contribute to knowledge about such matters. Yet, many of them also seek to inform policy. They want to help policymakers and practitioners, and the public at large, devise efforts that can reduce crime, assist victims, and improve justice, and do so cost-efficiently.

Fortunately, these goals do not have to be at odds with one another. To the contrary, many scientific advances come from examining policy and practice, and many policies and practices can be informed by efforts that seek primarily to advance science.

Much of the art of conducting research entails the ability to discern possibilities for advancing knowledge and policy. That can come in part from a willingness to embrace different types of research. In some ways, the field of criminology and criminal justice reflects a history of researchers who have recognized, whether consciously or not, that possibility.

Since its beginnings in the 1800s, many scholars have started with a science-focused bent and others have started with a policy-focused bent.

---

[86] Wolfgang (1963).

As the field has grown, these dual emphases have persisted. Sometimes one seemingly "wins" out over the other. When that happens, divides have occurred. In the early 1960s in America, for example, conflict over the primary mission of the field led to a split and, ultimately, the creation of a new association, the ACJS, devoted to the study of crime and justice. Yet, in subsequent decades, the ACJS and the ASC, which was founded several decades before the ACJS, grew in a parallel manner, to the point where they both now largely resemble each other. They each emphasize theory *and* policy. They also each embrace interdisciplinary research and the study of an incredibly diverse range of topics.

In the end, the field of criminology and criminal justice stands on its own as an independent and important area of inquiry. No other scientific field or discipline exclusively or systematically examines crime and justice. Because of its interdisciplinary focus and dual emphasis on theory and policy, this field in its own way requires artfulness on the part of researchers. For example, those who conduct, consume, or use criminological and criminal justice research typically must be able to see topics from diverse angles.

We suspect this situation will always characterize the field. As long as the focus centers on advancing science or using science to inform policy, criminology and criminal justice researchers will be challenged to devise new theories, data sources, methods, and domains of inquiry. That has been true over the course of the development of criminological and criminal justice research, and it shows every sign of continuing in that direction.

3 The Science and Art of Conducting, Evaluating, and Using Research

Initial Observations

INTRODUCTION

Research requires as much art as science. It goes beyond "data," "analysis," or "results." It involves framing questions with reference to a study's goals, prior research, available data, and methods for analyzing the data. It demands consideration of what can feasibly be accomplished with available time and resources. And, most of all, it entails being able to see possibilities.

What, then, is research? What, in fact, are the goals of research? How do they influence research? On a more down-to-earth level, what activities comprise the research process? When many people think about research, they equate it with experiments. In reality, though, research entails much more than experiments. How? And what relevance do answers to questions about goals and process have for conducting and evaluating criminological and criminal justice research or for using it effectively and appropriately?

This chapter addresses these questions. In so doing, it seeks to build on the previous chapter in establishing the groundwork for our argument that a chef-like researcher sensibility is needed for conducting, evaluating, and appropriately using credible research. Developing this sensibility requires a knowledge of different aspects of the research process. That includes, as we discuss below, development of research designs, clear identification of research goals, and a range of activities such that, when done well, can advance knowledge or policy. Subsequent chapters extend and illuminate this idea. Then, in Chapter 11, we identify pragmatic steps that can be taken to develop a researcher sensibility.

WHAT IS RESEARCH DESIGN?

Research design can be viewed as the blueprint and work plan for a study. Just as with building a house, a blueprint is needed for guiding the selection of materials and how to combine them. A work plan is needed for thinking through the precise sequence of steps to be followed and how each step will be completed. For a house, one must think about a multitude of considerations: budget, lot size, permits, available materials, who builds what part of the house in what order, planning on the unpredictable, putting finishing touches on a house, allowing time to address various "warts and blemishes," and so on.

For research, a blueprint and work plan also are needed. We can think of "research design" as the task both of designing a blueprint for a study and of creating a work plan to execute the blueprint. The two go hand in hand. For example, we might design an experiment. Then we realize, in developing a work plan, that we have insufficient funds or staffing to conduct it. That leads us in turn to consider alternative "blueprints" – that is, studies that may be less costly to undertake, but that still enable us to answer our research questions.

How do science and art come into play? There are many ways they do, but consider first the building example and, specifically, a situation where an architect wants to help clients identify the best design for a new home or building. The clients may not fully know what they want. Even so, they may have a strong sense of what they do *not* want. In addition, they undoubtedly will impose financial limits on what can be built. The environmental terrain may impose further limits, or perhaps, depending on the architect's inventiveness, create unique opportunities for designing the home or building. The architect has to work with the clients to help them gain clarity about what they really want in a home, what compromises they can tolerate, and what their budget will allow. He or she has to balance all of these considerations and more in arriving at a plan that will be viable and leave all parties happy.

A similar task confronts anyone seeking to do research. Developing a successful research design requires that a scientist work through a series of important questions. They include, but are not limited to, the following: What exactly is the goal of the study? What theory does it advance or critical research gap does it address? What funds or resources are needed to undertake it? What data exist or can be created? How "good" or complete are the data? What kind of analyses would be best? Is there special software or training required to undertake them? What checks should be pursued to ensure that the results can be trusted? What caveats or limitations should be emphasized in describing the results?

Just as there exists no magic formula for architects to follow in designing homes or buildings, there exists – as this constellation of questions illuminates – none for creating the most useful and scientifically credible research studies. There is instead the science and art of doing so. The science lies in understanding the different activities – such as sampling, theorizing, analysis – that go into research. The art lies in knowing how to bring different aspects of research together to address important gaps in knowledge or to answer questions that might best inform policy. And it lies in seeing how to devise credible, scientific studies with available resources.

That view runs counter to what many people may think when they contemplate "research." They see research as a technical undertaking. Mix a little data and statistical analysis, or do an experiment, and out pop "results."

In reality, data and analysis constitute but one part of a more general process for generating "good," that is, credible, science. Research that addresses important questions in fact frequently does not begin with data or analysis. *It begins with identifying a question, learning about its various contours, and embarking on a creative process of identifying how best to answer it.* Some individuals might discover a data set and wonder what they can do with it. The creative process here begins in more of a bottom-up rather than a top-down manner in such instances. Ultimately, though, the researcher must identify study questions, how to answer them, and the various implications or contributions of the new answers.

Precisely because it requires consideration of the "big picture" *and* "nuts-and-bolts" issues, research can seem daunting in its potential complexity. In this way, consider a different analogy – we might view research design as akin to speaking a foreign language. To speak fluently, we must *integrate* knowledge of grammar, vocabulary, and cultural context. Similarly, to "speak" research requires an ability to integrate information about multiple aspects of the research process. Other analogies convey this idea as well. For example, research might be viewed as an undertaking akin to creating a musical score or novel: Composers and authors must think about how to bring notes or words together to convey a particular feeling or idea. Or, to use the analogy with which we began the book, chefs must know how to combine different ingredients in just such a way as to create great food that fits a particular occasion. In so doing, they must adjust to a variety of constraints, including the availability of certain foods, staff skill levels, customer volume, and time. If they do not, the food and dining experience will suffer.

Research entails a similar balancing act. To develop and implement research design well requires navigating a host of considerations and constraints. And to appraise it accurately and use it appropriately requires appreciation of that fact. To convey this idea further, we discuss essential parts of the research process and the science and art involved.

RESEARCH GOALS

Conducting credible and useful research can be likened to making smart financial investments. For many of us, the phrase "financial investment" calls to mind the idea of selecting stocks in the hopes of securing a large return. However, financial investment, as with research, only makes sense with respect to particular goals. For example, stock investing would not be wise for a person who has trouble paying for rent and food. Similarly, someone saving to purchase a new car also should not likely invest his or her car fund in stocks. In each case, the market can go down substantially in the short term and leave the individual with no ability to pay their bills or purchase a vehicle. If, however, those goals are covered and if the individual has additional funds and time to wait on the market, then investing in stocks as part of a retirement plan could be a sensible move. Even so, stock investing carries risks. And not everyone has the same tolerance for risk or the same retirement goals. Some individuals want to live out in the country and fish, hike, or read all day long; others may want to travel the world; and still others may need to continue working during "retirement" to help pay the bills and take care of dependents. Risk tolerance, retirement timelines, family context, and other considerations all influence what would constitute a wise investment strategy.

Much the same observation holds for research design. Studies that contribute to knowledge or science-based policy entail not just adherence to canons of credible scientific research. They also entail consideration of specific study goals, questions that should be asked to achieve these goals, and designs that are scientifically defensible and can feasibly be adopted.

This entire process – articulating research goals, questions, and designs – can be much harder than it seems. For example, in devising a study, we may discover that we lack adequate funding for the design that we want to pursue. The data may not exist or may not be possible to obtain. The amount of time required to undertake the study could exceed that which we can reasonably allocate. Ethical considerations may eliminate certain methodologies. And so on.

Such constraints make designing a credible criminological or criminal justice study a bit like solving a puzzle. Resource and ethical constraints contribute to this puzzle, but so does the state of prior theory and research. Solving the puzzle requires careful consideration of whether a given study can be done and is likely to yield credible scientific information.

A starting point for any study begins with goals. There generally are four that motivate research. As shown in Figure 3.1, they include: (1) describing the social world; (2) understanding the social meaning of social phenomena; (3) identifying and testing causal relationships; and (4) answering criminal justice policy questions. We discuss each one below. Before doing so, however, several observations warrant emphasis.

First, in each instance, the goals dictate the types of questions that are asked. The questions then determine the types of research designs that are

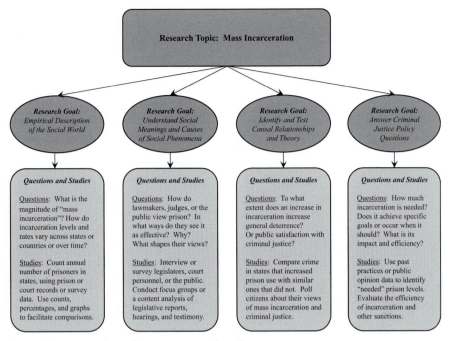

Figure 3.1 Research goals, questions, and studies

appropriate. For example, if we want to identify whether a given factor, such as incarceration, reduces recidivism, we need a research design that allows for generating a credible estimate of impact. In this instance, then, we do not want to rely on interviews with a few select individuals off the street about the effects of prison on recidivism. We would want a more representative sample.

As shown in the figure, the starting point for almost any study begins with a general research interest or topic, such as mass incarceration. Sometimes, as with policy studies, the interest may be dictated by law. For example, a statute might require evaluation of whether a civil commitment law for sex offenders is being implemented appropriately. Other times, the reason for the interest stems from a social scientist's curiosity or from his or her assessment of where important gaps exist in theory and research. The interest could lie with empirical relationships that the scientist thinks may exist. Why, for example, do some states use the death penalty more than others?[1] Alternatively, the interest could lie at a high level of generality, such as an interest in understanding the nature and causes of order in prisons.[2]

Second, not all research progresses in a top-down way (i.e., goals → questions → research design). Indeed, as with any creative activity, research

---

[1] Paternoster *et al.* (2007).
[2] Sparks *et al.* (1996); Bottoms (1999); Griffin and Hepburn (2013).

evolves through a myriad of pathways.[3] Studies might begin, as noted earlier, with exploring the possibilities that an existing data set provides.[4] Or they might begin with random observations that one hears on the subway or while taking a walk. These observations can spark an insight or a line of inquiry that seems intriguing or worth investigating. Studies might begin, not least, with concerns about a social problem, such as homelessness and its possible contribution to crime. The end result in these and other instances is the same – any given research study addresses specific questions and does so with the hope of achieving a more general goal.

Third, although we are presenting these goals as distinct from one another, they can and frequently do implicate one another. To illustrate, a study of the impact of incarceration on recidivism might seek at the same time to uncover the mechanisms through which any reduction in offending – referred to as "desistance" – occurs.[5] In so doing, the study might draw on theories of crime to identify different causal pathways and then test which ones are empirically supported.[6] The study thus seeks to contribute to policy discussions *and* to test causal claims implied by different theories. Similarly, studies that seek to describe crime and justice phenomena require the identification of socially meaningful views of them. Consider that if we want to estimate the total amount of criminal punishment in a society, creating rates of incarceration will not suffice. We need to include other punishments. Which ones? The only way to know is to draw on extant accounts about the actions that a given culture views as punishment for violating criminal law. If those do not exist, then we need to conduct our own study that identifies examples of culturally meaningful punishments.

Empirical Description of the Social World

We turn now to the first of the four goals that typically guide research. A central goal of social scientific research is to describe the social world. For criminology and criminal justice researchers, that entails efforts to describe a diverse range of crime and justice phenomena (see Chapter 9). This idea seems simple. In reality, it is anything but that.

Consider that no objective basis exists for classifying behavior as meaningful without reference to a cultural frame of reference. That is, the meaning of action comes from culture. In some communities or countries, a

---

[3] Mears and Stafford (2002).   [4] Gibbs (1972).

[5] Maruna (2001, 2011); Laub and Sampson (2003); LeBel *et al.* (2008); Kurlychek *et al.* (2012); Paternoster *et al.* (2016).

[6] Mears *et al.* (2013b).

middle finger raised in the air may be viewed as a sign of disrespect, while in others it has no clear meaning. Yes, but what about murder? It must be an objective act about which surely no disagreement could exist about its meaning, right? Actually, no. Any careful observer of the criminal justice system will see that many contextual considerations influence how we interpret an individual's behavior. The courts, for example, expend considerable effort in determining if a given individual acted with criminal intent, what in criminal law is referred to as *mens rea*.[7] Without it, no "crime" – in the legal sense – exists.

The identification of culturally meaningful descriptions of social phenomena is a distinct goal of many research studies, one that we discuss in the following section. Here, we want to distinguish it from the goal of creating empirical descriptions of phenomena. The two go hand in hand. For example, any descriptive empirical account reflects an understanding about how to classify behavior based on culturally meaningful views or interpretations of such behavior. Once such behavior has been identified, the task of an empirical description lies in quantifying dimensions of the behavior. Even so, studies frequently measure phenomena without clearly identifying their social or cultural meaning. Census data are illustrative, as are court processing and prison system data.

Empirical description of behavior or actions – including those of organizations and systems – encompasses many possibilities. We might study the prevalence of all crime or particular types of crimes, victimization, get-tough legislation among states or countries, public support for the death penalty, prison officer use of excessive force, wrongful convictions, rates of prison sentences in rural versus urban counties, criminal justice system expenditures among states, and much more.

Prevalence estimates constitute one type of empirical description. Other types exist as well. To illustrate, we might compare crime rates in different cities, counties, states, or countries, or the relative prevalence of arrests of males versus females. In so doing, we are not necessarily seeking to show that some factor (e.g., urbanization) contributes to another (e.g., crime rates). Rather, we seek to convey the potential variability in the prevalence of a phenomenon across a range of potential dimensions. To illustrate, government reports frequently provide descriptions of how age, sex, and race may act as divides along which variation in many behaviors or actions, such as crime or arrests, occur. Such descriptive accounts may be interesting in their own right or be useful as groundwork for identifying causal relationships or guiding policy.

---

[7] Deigh and Dolinko (2011).

Empirical description may, again, seem simple, but it is not. Why? The usefulness of description relies heavily on pre-established understanding about how to interpret behavior or actions. Thus, from a scientific perspective, researchers must proceed with a clear awareness of culturally or socially meaningful categories of behavior. They also must proceed with knowledge about how best to measure such behavior in ways that accurately tap into a concept or construct.[8] Consider crime. If we seek to measure it, calls to the police and arrest data – such as those collected through the Uniform Crime Report (UCR) program – will only be partially useful. Why? They reflect not only offending, but also citizen willingness to call the police. Better would be self-report data collected from citizens about their offending and victimization experiences. Even then, questions must be addressed. For example, among the many ways we might ask individuals about crime, which will provide the most accurate accounts? Among those accounts, which should be used as our estimate of "crime"? Should we use an "any crime" measure, a count measure (i.e., the number of times an individual committed crime), or a severity measure (i.e., some indicator of how severe the various crimes were that an individual committed)?[9] Such questions arise for many phenomena, such as self-reported versus officially recorded counts of inmate misconduct.[10]

Part of the art of developing scientifically credible empirical descriptions lies in awareness of these diverse possibilities and how to select from among them. Part of the science lies in being careful not to accept, willy-nilly, existing empirical accounts as somehow self-evident in their meaning. Empirical descriptions, like any fact, require frames of reference from within which to interpret them.[11] Producing accurate empirical descriptions requires an ability to appreciate a diverse range of methods for measuring phenomena *and* an ability to appreciate the diverse range of conceptual frameworks for interpreting them.

This awareness is directly relevant to being able to conceptualize different types of research questions and studies. In the above example, our focus centered on the causes of crime. We might, though, be interested in understanding variation in *reported* crime. Consider a situation in which two cities have comparable levels of reported crime, but where one has a great deal more unreported crime. We might establish this divergence by comparing UCR estimates to those from the National Crime Victimization Survey (NCVS). (The NCVS data provide estimates of victimization, but tell us little about offenders, their frequency of offending, or crime rates among states or most cities.[12]) The two cities look like they have the same amount

---

[8] Gibbs (1972, 1997).   [9] Sweeten (2012).   [10] Steiner and Wooldredge (2014).
[11] Parsons (1968).   [12] Lynch and Addington (2007).

of crime, but in reality one has far more than the other. Use of different data sources can help us determine the extent to which crime may go unreported and sets the stage for studies that can unpack why discrepancies between actual crime and reported crime arise. The topic is interesting in its own right and is certainly relevant for policy. Consider, for example, that in the United States, roughly half of all violent crime is not reported to the police.[13] Consider, too, that under-reporting can vary across racial, ethnic, gender, age, and other groups or by area. And it can result from diverse causes, such as differences among groups in their trust of the police.[14]

Identifying Socially Meaningful Descriptions and Possible Causes of Social Phenomena

Measuring and counting phenomena that interest criminology and criminal justice researchers requires an understanding of how to describe and discern such phenomena. When such understanding already exists, then empirical descriptive accounts can readily proceed. However, when it does not, research is needed for creating this understanding.

Consider a community in which attending church is expected of everyone. In such a community, not attending church amounts to defiance against the community's way of life and even its laws. If we want to count crime in such a community, we would need first to understand how citizens view church attendance. We otherwise would fail to include non-attendance as a type of crime or, at the least, as a type of antisocial behavior.

A prominent goal of social scientific research thus consists of identifying cultural and social frames of reference for how to interpret certain behaviors or actions in particular societies. Such research seeks to determine how individuals, groups, organizations, or communities discuss, describe, or think about ways of acting. In all instances, the focus lies with the "social world" or "social phenomena," not with the natural world. The latter focus of course is the purview of biology, chemistry, physics, and so on. For criminology and criminal justice researchers, the emphasis centers on how crime and criminal justice are viewed from a cultural perspective.

This emphasis sometimes is referred to as "interpretive" research because researchers seek to identify how to interpret behaviors or actions. Many debates exist about its importance.[15] Much of the debate stems from efforts to view one type of research (e.g., tests of generalizable causal relationships predicted by theory) as more important than another (e.g.,

---

[13] Langton *et al.* (2012:1).   [14] Langton *et al.* (2012).
[15] Compare, for example, discussions in Gibbs (1972, 1997), Kraska (2004, 2006), and Crank and Bowman (2008).

identification of culturally meaningful phenomena). Our view is that they are just that – types of research that are part and parcel of the more general goal of generating scientific knowledge.

An illustration can convey the point: We seek to conduct an empirical examination of the effects of police experiences on officer decision-making. However, what if no theory exists to inform this examination? Indeed, what if we do not know what experiences may be relevant? In that case, we first must identify such experiences. We need a study that aids us in that endeavor. Without it, we might grab on to whatever measures in a given data set strike us as relevant. Prior criminal experiences, victimization, divorce, financial strain, and so on, might all seem important to examine in a study of decision-making among officers. We likely would miss the mark, though. It would be far more productive to begin with observing or interviewing officers to learn about how they view their work and how they characterize, or interpret, what occurs on the job. In so doing, we might learn about categories of officer experiences that exist and that we never would have considered. Documenting such categories would be important in its own right. It also would create the foundation for a study that collects data on these experiences and seeks to identify their causes or effects. Here, we can see both types of research – interpretive and causal – at play and how each is necessary to measure socially meaningful phenomena and demonstrate cause-and-effect.[16]

Does a focus on cultural or social meaning imply that somehow all behavior or actions are "relative"? Yes and no. Interpretation of behavior or social actions does require a conceptual frame of reference. At the same time, within that frame of reference, actions do have what might be viewed as "objective" meaning. If, for example, sticking one's middle finger up signals, in a given culture, disrespect, then when an individual sticks his or her middle finger up at someone, we can conclude that disrespect was intended and would be interpreted as such by others. It was objectively an act of disrespect. What if the individual did not mean to show disrespect? In that culture, it still would objectively be viewed as such.

A scientific study of crime and justice thus requires studies that can identify culturally or socially meaningful behaviors or actions. In turn, that means that studies must be devised to achieve this goal. They typically entail different approaches than might be used to establish the prevalence of a phenomenon. For example, researchers observe individuals, groups, organizations, or the like, conduct interviews, dig through archival records to determine how various behaviors or actions are characterized, and so on.

---

[16] See, for example, Skolnick's (1966) classic study of policing.

The groundwork for testing causal claims consists of identifying culturally or socially meaningful actions. It also consists of identifying possible causal relations between these actions and other forces. That is, it entails developing a theory. For example, we might be interested in studying domestic violence. To study it requires first identifying what domestic violence is and how we can determine that it has occurred. A related step entails identifying its causes. Absent a theory or body of research to guide us, we need a study approach – such as interviewing individuals whose partners have been arrested for abuse – that can help us to identify possible causes. We then can devise a theory from what we learn, and test it empirically.

Once again, science and art come into play. Identifying the cultural meaning of certain actions, for example, can entail many pitfalls. Perhaps we interview individuals whose views fall far outside the statistical "norm" for a given group. Relying on them to convey how we should interpret certain actions would be risky. How, though, do we know whose views somehow best represent societal views? We don't. Instead, researchers must be aware of the diverse views that may exist and the need to triangulate – that is, use multiple data sources – to determine if agreement exists across them. They must be aware as well of when and how to employ particular methodologies for gaining insight into possible causal relationships.

Identifying and Testing Causal Relationships and Theory

Science ultimately seeks to arrive at an understanding of causal relationships through the use of theory and empirical tests. Tremendous debate exists about defining and demonstrating causation.[17] Regardless of such debate, however, the goal remains central to the scientific enterprise.

For criminology and criminal justice, the focus centers on how biological, organizational, cultural, social, and other factors may cause crime and justice outcomes. A few examples: To what extent does strain cause offending? Does any such effect arise through increased anger and frustration? What is the contribution of strain to crime, relative to many other potential causes, such as genetic differences among individuals or differences in the family or community conditions where they reside? How do racist views influence jury deliberations? What factors cause some states or countries to criminalize some behaviors but not others, and why have they done so only at particular times? Why, for example, did the United States, in

[17] Blalock (1964, 1994); Gibbs (1982); Mears and Stafford (2002); Sampson *et al.* (2013); Stafford and Mears (2015).

the 1990s, toughen its response to sex crimes even though such crime appeared to have been on the decline?[18]

From a policy perspective, an equally wide range of causal questions exists. Broadly, the focus in each instance is on whether a given policy, program, or practice improved some outcome. Did it, for example, create less crime, fewer errors in police or court decision-making, greater public satisfaction with the criminal justice system, and so on?

In developing and testing causal accounts, several considerations arise. First, the causes of any criminology or criminal justice outcome of interest almost invariably will be specific to the outcome. For example, the causes of higher crime rates in some areas can be anticipated to differ from the causes of differences among liberals and conservatives in their support for particular types of policies. Research on particular outcomes thus must be directed toward outcome-specific causes. Second, the possibility exists that some causes may influence multiple outcomes; research thus can and frequently is aimed at identifying causes that may have effects that extend beyond one outcome. Third, theory, data, and methodology all go into identifying causal relationships; they are not goals in and of themselves. Rather, they serve as tools for identifying causal relationships.

In a world where endless resources exist for research and where no ethical concerns about experiments existed, research would be easier, but still challenging. Social scientists, however, live in a world where resources are limited, ethical constraints exist, and experiments frequently are not feasible. They cannot, for example, conduct an experiment – a central way in which science typically seeks to identify causation – that involves randomly assigning some convicted felons to receive one-year prison sentences and others to a year of physical torture to determine which may have the greatest deterrent effect. Similarly, we cannot randomly assign some states to have less poverty and others to have more to understand the effects of poverty on crime.

A challenge that confronts all scientists consists of identifying ways to identify underlying patterns – possible causal relationships – that may exist. In accounts of scientific advances, it frequently seems in fact that advances arise in a haphazard, unpredictable manner.[19] Scientific advances sometimes come from a stroke of luck. Even so, the accounts identify that individuals or groups of researchers can increase their chances of scientific insights through different strategies. These can include working hard, immersing one's self in relevant literature and keeping abreast of advances in theory and empirical studies, tackling a topic in a systematic manner,

---

[18] Mancini and Mears (2016).
[19] Kuhn (1962); Merton (1973); Mukherjee (2010); Weinberg (2015).

adopting different perspectives, being willing to capitalize on new opportunities, knowing how to leverage limited resources to the greatest advantage, and so on.[20] There is no way to adopt these strategies in a "cookbook"
manner. Rather, one must develop a sensibility about how to approach the
study of causal effects in a way that maximizes the likelihood of achieving
credible estimates. That sensibility inescapably requires more than science –
it requires art, or what might be viewed as creativity in weighing and
balancing diverse considerations and possibilities. It includes knowing, not
least, what works best for you.

We should emphasize that the different goals of research can interact
with one another. As noted above, description is itself a theoretical act.
Theory can help us to describe phenomena more accurately. At the same
time, efforts to describe phenomena can help us to develop theory. This
dynamic arises in the natural sciences as well. Consider the extensive public
and scholarly debate about whether Pluto is a planet or something else.
Pluto is of course Pluto regardless of what we call it. What characterization,
though, should we use? To accurately call it a planet requires a definition
and theory about what makes something a planet. But scientists, it appears,
do not agree on the proper definition or theory of a planet. That in turn has
contributed to the debate about how best to classify Pluto![21]

Criminal Justice Policy-Focused Questions

Another goal of research is to answer policy-focused questions to inform
policy discussions and to put criminal justice decision-making on a science-
based foundation.[22] Studies that focus on policy are referred to as "evaluation research." As discussed in Chapter 2 and as will be discussed in more
detail in Chapter 7, the evaluation hierarchy leads us to think about five
types of questions: (1) Is a policy needed? (2) What is the causal logic that
guides the policy? (3) How well implemented is the policy, and what factors
influence implementation? (4) What is the policy's impact? (5) And to what
extent is the policy cost-efficient?[23]

Which questions warrant attention depends entirely on the needs or
interests of criminal justice policymakers, administrators, and practitioners.
Determining those needs or interests, as with other research activities,
entails, once again, as much art as science. For example, if asked to evaluate
the effectiveness of a new community policing program in reducing crime,
should the researcher proceed? Perhaps. Some considerations might lead us
to consider holding off, though. To illustrate, what if the program recently

---

[20] See, for example, Berger (1990); see also Merton (1973) and Weinberg (2015).
[21] Tyson (2014).   [22] Mears (2010).   [23] See Rossi *et al.* (2004) and Mears (2010).

started and had encountered hurdles? New training was supposed to occur, but the curriculum was not yet ready. Administrative staff turnover delayed hiring additional officers. A group of neighborhood residents raised concerns that the program was proceeding without their input. These and other factors likely would need to be addressed before the program would have a fighting chance of appreciably reducing crime.[24] If we proceed with an impact evaluation, we likely will conclude that community policing does not work. That, however, would be misleading. The policy, as designed, was never effectively implemented in the first place.

How should we proceed? One option is to ignore our concerns. Alternatively, we can embrace them and refuse to do the study. Or we can see if a middle ground may exist, one where we provide a tentative assessment of impact, but focus more on how the program's implementation could be improved. Science and art can guide us in determining how best to proceed. In such situations, "the 'art' lies in helping the evaluation sponsors determine what they really need to know and what can be done with the resources that they have at their disposal. The 'science' lies in applying the best methodological approaches one can to answer a given question given the available data, resources, and funding to support an evaluation."[25]

THE RESEARCH PROCESS

Many books, chapters, articles, reports, and more offer useful guidance on parts of the research process.[26] They tend to focus more on what might be viewed as the "grammar" and "vocabulary" of research. That can be helpful, much as learning grammar and vocabulary can be instrumental in learning a foreign language. But it does not capture the way in which research or speaking a different language occurs in the "real world."

We see the results of this problem arise with many doctoral students. They take classes for several years. They read about different topics and learn about measurement, introductory statistics, some advanced statistics, and the like. They take comprehensive exams. Then they begin work on a dissertation. At that point, many of them stumble, surprised that they really cannot do research. A similar problem arises with language acquisition. Taking classes for several years will not take many of us very far in learning to converse fluently in a new language, though we may well pass tests on grammar and vocabulary. To learn to converse in a new language,

---

[24] Maguire and Katz (2002).   [25] Mears (2010:48).

[26] For accounts that center specifically on crime and criminal justice, see, for example, Lasley (1998), Davies *et al.* (2011), Maxfield and Babbie (2015), Bachman and Schutt (2018), or Dantzker *et al.* (2018).

immersion is ideal: listening to music, reading cartoons, newspapers, and books, using software programs, talking to anyone who will listen, and yes, taking classes.

Much the same can be said of research. To learn it well requires involvement in many different types of research studies, ones that ideally force us to take charge of organizing and executing research designs. Exposure to a diversity of topics and experience with different aspects of research contributes to the development of a researcher sensibility. Designing a survey, for example, requires markedly different considerations from identifying an appropriate statistical methodology. Both differ from the skills required to conceptualize a research study's goals and questions or to manage a large project with many staff.

With this book, we cannot substitute for immersion in different research projects. Nor can reading a book substitute for immersion in different *types* of research projects. Our hope, however, is that it can provide a "bird's eye" view of how research can unfold and insights about considerations that go into such research. Necessarily, this approach means that we cannot provide in-depth accounts of certain topics. That is fine – many introductory and in-depth books on research methods, theory, and statistics do just that. Existence of such works frees us to focus less on the trees and more on the forest. It enables us to try to convey what a researcher sensibility entails and how science and art go into all aspects of research.

Thinking Like a Chef, Architect, Composer, or . . . a Researcher

Given the discussion to this point, it perhaps will not be surprising that our account of the research process begins with the notion that research is a craft. It requires an ability to be creative and to draw on technical skills to generate useful and scientifically credible knowledge. The two go together. Creativity can lead researchers to see opportunities that otherwise would go missed and to identify ways to adapt research methods to capitalize on these opportunities. At the same time, methodological awareness opens the door to seeing opportunities to undertake research.

A similar idea surfaces when we think about many professional pursuits. For example, a good chef thinks creatively about how to combine various ingredients for a particular occasion, and thinks at length about what his or her customers want. A good architect must do the same. What exactly does a client want from a new building? How might different architectural designs meet the client's needs and preferences? What materials and resources could be brought together to execute a design and do so within a set budget? A creative mindset and familiarity with diverse materials, code requirements, and other technical considerations are needed to answer such questions. Similarly, a composer must find a way to combine notes in sequences that somehow, when played by certain combinations of instruments, convey a particular message that resonates for audiences. Knowledge of other music, scales, different ways of arranging notes, characteristics of specific instruments, and so on can help, as can inspiration. But both together create the platform for a composer to realize his or her vision.

The point bears emphasis: The craft of good research – research that uses scientific methods to generate credible insights that advance our knowledge about crime, criminal justice, or policy – stems from an ability to simultaneously contemplate diverse research designs, draw on different methods, and adapt them to particular goals and resource constraints. As with chefs, architects, composers, or any other craft, it requires more than a formulaic approach.

One might conclude, then, that only experts can conduct or evaluate research well. We disagree. Research "experts" do not have an exclusive claim to research. Consider that even the best researchers have little familiarity with certain theories, topics, data sources, and methods. No one can know everything. Top researchers compensate by thinking creatively. They leverage the technical skills that they have or that they learn about from colleagues. And they continuously hone their creative and technical skills. It is that continuous pursuit – one focused on acquiring not just the technical skills, but also the ability to think creatively – that anyone, regardless of their level of experience, can use to conduct, evaluate, or use research well.

Framing the Question

The challenge in science – "its art," as John Barry has written – consists of identifying important questions that can be answered and, if answered, will advance knowledge or policy.[27] Framing research questions sounds easy. But framing questions in ways that can be answered and that also speak to our research goals is another undertaking altogether.

The ability to frame a research question cannot be reduced to a cookie-cutter approach. Why? Science progresses in different ways. Sometimes better measurement leads to tremendous advances, or "paradigm shifts," in how we understand the world. Sometimes a new theory or application of a novel method to a new field of study achieves the same outcomes. And sometimes these advances result from dogged pursuit of a particular line of inquiry.[28]

---

[27] Barry (2005:60).
[28] Kuhn (1962); Merton (1973); Mears and Stafford (2002); Mukherjee (2010); Weinberg (2015).

This consideration alone makes framing a study question as much an art as a science. Another involves pragmatic constraints. One of the biggest such constraints involves resources. Without them, studies cannot occur. Time is another. Few people or organizations have the time or inclination to undertake studies that unfold over decades. For policymakers, the need for "real-time" information in particular demands that studies provide results in weeks, months, or a few years, not decades.

Consider a typical request that a legislative committee might make to a research agency: Conduct a study that shows that private prisons "work." What exactly does the committee mean by "work"? Without an answer, the agency might well undertake any number of studies – an evaluation of how well private prisons in general are operated, whether they offer better services and treatment than do public prisons, whether they improve inmate transitions into society (e.g., less recidivism, homelessness, and unemployment) more so than their publicly run counterparts, whether they are safer, and whether they save taxpayers money. The agency interprets the request to mean that the legislature wants to know if the private prison offered required services. Why? The agency researchers may believe that this question is really what the legislature wanted answered. The agency researchers may be influenced at the same time by their view that any other study would require a much longer time frame than the legislature wanted. A year later, when presenting the results, they learn that what the legislature *actually* wanted was a cost-efficiency evaluation.

What if, in fact, the legislature wanted a study of the impacts *and* cost-efficiency of private prisons? That would be ideal, but the agency researchers might be correct in believing that they could not conduct such a study in one year.

Here, then, we have a request that at first blush seems simple, but upon closer inspection entails challenges that may be difficult to satisfactorily resolve, especially when the legislature wants an answer within a short time span. Observe that it is no simple matter to show that the state spent fewer funds on a private prison than it would have for a public prison. An appropriate cost comparison requires, among other things, (1) identification of a similar publicly run prison, (2) assessment of whether the private prison offered the same amount and quality of services and treatment, (3) evaluation of the private prison's impact on recidivism, homelessness, unemployment, and other re-entry outcomes relative to outcomes among inmates released from a public prison that serves similar inmates, and (4) monetization of all costs and benefits.[29]

[29] Gaes *et al.* (2004); Mears (2010); Lindsey *et al.* (2016).

The only way in which an agency can ensure that it conducts a study that speaks to the legislative committee's goal is, first, to understand what those goals are, second, to appreciate the complexities and costs of different studies, and, third, to work with the committee to identify a study that could be feasibly completed in a year with available resources. Through communication with the committee, the agency might identify several possible studies that address relevant and answerable questions. For example, to what extent have private prison vendors complied with requirements set forth in state-issued contracts? What has contributed to non-compliance and what can be done to remedy any shortfalls? These questions might be answered through a number of research strategies and could be used by the legislature as it deliberates about whether to continue or terminate funding. That said, answers to these questions would not shed any light into whether private prisons produce comparable or better returns to what arises with private prisons. Whether that matters to the legislative committee could only be determined by them. The art, then, for the agency lies in helping the legislature understand the range of possible questions that can be answered and, at the same time, the limitations that attend to resulting studies.

Even then, the context for framing the study would still need to be established. Is the legislature, for example, making a decision about whether to terminate or extend a contract? Is it seeking to make a decision based on credible empirical evidence of cost-efficiency? Does it seek to hold a private prison contractor accountable as part of a broader effort to demonstrate government accountability, but with no clear intention of terminating a contract? To frame the research question, the agency would want to identify the broader goal sought by the legislature. That then would set the context for why a given research question makes sense and, in turn, why the agency pursued a particular research strategy.

In this illustration, we can see that researchers would not likely create useful information if they did not work closely with the legislative committee. They might undertake a credible study in the sense of relying on scientific methods. The information, though, would probably not advance the legislature's deliberations because it emanated from a poor understanding of what the legislature truly wanted.

Part of the art of framing questions comes from placing a study in context. Why, for example, will science benefit from publishing results of a given study? Poor framing of a study frequently dooms it from the outset, precisely because its contribution may not be clear. Consider the experience of Dr. Robert Warren. In recounting his time as an editor of a top-tier journal, he noted that many papers submitted to the journal lacked a "soul," that is, a "compelling and well-articulated reason to exist."[30] The papers never made it clear why they were important.

Why does that happen? There are many reasons. One is that framing studies can be difficult. Another is that researchers can become so enmeshed in a topic, theory, data, or method that they lose sight of why exactly the focus of their study matters. It also may result from tunnel vision. Scientists frequently must and do specialize. That can create a sense that somehow only specialists can understand their work. They thus write only for that audience and see no need to frame the study in a broader context.

Whatever the cause, the problem can be solved only by good writing and a clear discussion about the reasons for a study and the ways in which it advances understanding. Researchers too often shorten the framing of the question. They forget to couch an empirical analysis in relation to prior research or to its potential implications for scholarship. Instead, they give in to the temptation to allow solid data and analysis to "speak for themselves." They rarely do. In science, as in architecture, form and function go hand in hand. Good studies are ones where the authors address the "So what?" question *and* rely on credible research designs.[31]

How do researchers arrive at a clear and defensible justification for a study? The first and simplest one lies with describing the justification for the study! It seems like an obvious step, but many researchers skip it.

A second strategy is to frame a study in a "nested" manner. Figure 3.2 provides an illustration of this strategy. It shows how a study of racial and ethnic sentencing disparities might be placed within two broader contexts, each of which helps to situate the study for a reader and helps them to understand its contribution. The first and most general context, or goal, of the study, is to contribute to theory and research aimed at understanding *inequality in society*. Then, within that broader context, a second exists – the study seeks more specifically to contribute to theory and research aimed at understanding the *causes of inequality*. Finally, within that context, the study seeks in particular to contribute to scholarship on the *causes of racial and ethnic disparities in criminal punishments*.

The empirical study might focus only on sentencing decisions. However, its broader relevance lies in its potential to shed light not only on such decisions, but also on inequality in general and, specifically, the causes of inequality. Could a researcher begin with the first, most general research goal? Absolutely. But he or she then would need to work "down" to an empirical study that could address that goal.[32] Conversely, he or she could

---

[30] Warren (2016:4).   [31] *Ibid.*
[32] Mills (1959) and Becker (1998) have offered wonderful examples of this process.

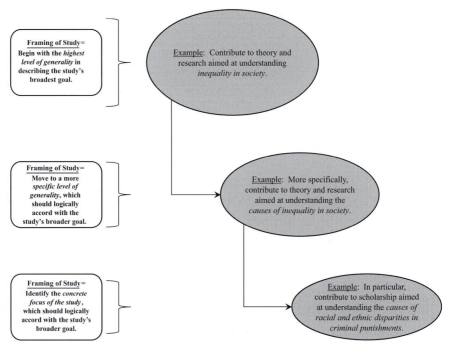

Figure 3.2 The art and science of framing and contextualizing a research study

begin with the more concrete focus on racial and ethnic disparities in sentencing. In that case, the next step would be to work "up" to the more general contexts, or research goals, that help to frame the importance of the study and why a particular research design was employed.

Some additional context still would be needed. What, for example, does prior theory and research say about the causes of racial and ethnic disparities? Does the study seek to resolve a debate about one of the putative causes? To show how one or more of the causes may be greater for some groups (e.g., females or the economically disadvantaged) than for others? To evaluate which causes may explain more of the variation in sentencing disparities? Or to identify a cause that others have not identified, but that a particular theory suggests may be relevant?

Regardless of the question, the implication is straightforward: The researcher needs to provide additional context for situating the relevance of the study. If the study sought to compare the relative influence of several causes of disparities, it would want to highlight that fact at the outset of a paper. It would want to highlight the specific research gap that is being addressed. It may be, for example, that few credible studies exist that have shown which causes most contribute to racial and ethnic disparities in sentencing.

Identifying the different contexts or goals of a study takes effort. It requires familiarity with prior studies and what they have found. It requires identification of research gaps and which ones, if filled, would be most likely to constitute a significant contribution to knowledge. It requires not least awareness of relevant theories and how a study could be used to test them. Many theories, for example, are like the US Constitution – they are stated at a high level of generality and therefore require interpretation. The Supreme Court renders decisions that seek to identify how aspects of the Constitution apply to particular cases or, conversely, to the implications of a decision from a particular case for how the Constitution might be viewed as applying to a range of other cases. Likewise, researchers must think about how a general theory may apply to particular instances of crime or criminal justice, or, conversely, how an empirical study may have implications for a general theory.

Theorizing, Hypothesizing, and Mapping Out Causal Pathways

Many studies focus on identifying whether two factors – for example, X and Y – are associated and, if they are, whether the association is causal. The outcome is the factor caused by another. Here, for example, we would say that X causes the outcome Y. The outcomes that we might wish to explain are as varied as the field of criminology and criminal justice. Similarly, the causes of any given outcome may vary. In some instances, there might just be one factor. Social outcomes, however, such as crime and various aspects of the criminal justice system, typically result from many causes.

A related line of research seeks to explain the causal mechanisms that explain a given causal association. For example, a study might seek to identify if a causal association between X and Y arises through X's effect on A and then A's effect on Y.

Identifying possible causal relationships (e.g., X $\rightarrow$ Y) or causal pathways (e.g., X $\rightarrow$ A $\rightarrow$ Y) can be done in many ways. We might rely on a formally articulated theory.[33] Alternatively, we might proceed in an "atheoretical" manner. No particular theory may guide the study in this instance. Even so, characterizing such research as "atheoretical" is a misnomer. Why? The study may be guided indirectly by theory. In addition, there may be little theory on which to draw. The investigator then must rely on different strategies – typically, qualitative data collection approaches – to generate a theory about how different social forces may be causally related.[34]

---

[33] See, for example, Gibbs (1972).
[34] See, for example, Corbin and Strauss (1990), Feagin *et al.* (1991), and Charmaz (2014).

Scientific criminological and criminal justice research proceeds along both of these fronts: That is, it seeks to answer questions through development of theory or through empirical research. There rarely is a final, conclusive theoretical account of a given outcome. Science generally cannot provide such accounts. In the social sciences, that axiom holds even more. Knowledge can, though, accumulate. We develop theories that build on other established theories, we test parts or all of theories and modify those parts that do not enjoy empirical support. Quite frequently, we run into dead ends that require us to go back to the proverbial drawing board to begin anew. Against such a backdrop, no one study typically constitutes a single turning point. Rather, a body of studies grows that helps scientists to identify more accurate ways to measure outcomes, assess which causal forces influence the outcomes and in what ways, and how to conceptualize the outcomes in different ways.[35]

Even "descriptive" accounts – such as one that seeks simply to provide summary statistical portraits of a given phenomenon – typically flow from a theoretical framework, though it may be an unarticulated one. Consider, for example, government reports that depict the age, sex, and racial and ethnic background of all prisoners.[36] Although such reports may be required by law, they typically build on a presumption that variation in some outcome may be related to and possibly caused by another factor. To illustrate, a report might present information on rates of incarceration nationally. It then may show that the rate among minorities is higher than that for whites. The fact that government reports seek to provide this information implies that we suspect minority status somehow "matters" in determining criminal justice outcomes. And that descriptive finding implies that indeed there is something about minorities, the contexts in which they reside, or how they are treated by the criminal justice system that causes them to be more likely to be incarcerated.[37] These three possibilities can be viewed broadly as theories that could help explain how the higher minority incarceration rate could occur. Each theory in turn opens the door to a wide range of more specific theoretical possibilities. For example, there are many potential ecological factors, such as poverty, employment opportunities, cultural and political capital, and so on that could affect minorities, the areas where they live, or how the criminal justice system treats them. Although government agencies do not typically provide theories that explain patterns in their descriptive reports, this does not mean that the reports are "atheoretical."

---

[35] Merton (1973).   [36] See, for example, Carson (2016).   [37] Mears *et al.* (2016b).

The relevance here is that the research process always begins with a research question and usually entails the development or application of theory. The word "theory" may not necessarily appear in every study. Most social scientific studies of crime and criminal justice, however, involve some reference to causal accounts that place the studies in context and that situate the relevance of any observed findings.

In the traditional view of science, of course, researchers derive hypotheses, then empirically test them. If the hypothesis is supported, they conclude that evidence exists to support the theory. If it is rejected, then they conclude that there is no evidence from the particular study to support the theory. As emphasized above, however, not all research always involves application of a particular theory or, by extension, hypothesis testing.

Regardless of the specific approach taken, the research process typically involves an effort to theorize, hypothesize, or map out the causal pathways thought to exist between different factors. That can involve straightforward application or testing of particular theories. More often than not, however, this effort requires creativity and an ability to consider all parts of the research process.

Sampling People, Places, Organizations

The research process invariably requires sampling people, places, organizations, or some "unit of analysis." That is true of empirical studies. It also is true of efforts aimed at developing theory.

What is the "unit of analysis"? It is the unit for which some causal relationship makes sense. For example, if a theory states that an individual's level of self-control affects their propensity to offend, the unit of analysis is "individuals."[38] Why? The explanation only makes sense for individuals. Consider this claim: Communities, cities, or countries with low self-control engage in more crime. This makes no sense. Communities, cities, and countries do not possess "self-control." (We discuss units of analysis at more length in Chapter 6.)

Recognition of the notion of a "unit of analysis" can help guide development of theories of crime and criminal justice. To illustrate, a theory might argue that dysfunctional family dynamics cause more offending in these families. The focus on families requires that we think clearly about family structure and what occurs in families rather than on individual or community characteristics. In so doing, we develop a theory that centers on and only makes sense in the context of thinking about "families."

---

[38] Gottfredson and Hirschi (1990); Hay and Meldrum (2016).

Recognition of "units of analysis" also can alert us to the fact that any one study likely is generalizable, if at all, only to that one unit of analysis. For example, a study might examine whether, in Ohio, neighborhoods with more non-profit organizations have lower crime rates. Whatever the finding, we know that it likely extends only to neighborhoods (the study's unit of analysis), not to counties, cities, states, or countries (which were not the study's unit of analysis). In addition, we know that it may extend only to neighborhoods in Ohio.

Not least, recognition of the concept of "units of analysis" highlights that when we are thinking about conducting, evaluating, or using the results from a study, we need to think carefully about the appropriate unit of analysis. Sometimes, as with a study of self-control, it might be clear what the unit should be. Frequently, though, the appropriate unit only becomes evident after clarifying a study's goals, questions, and the causal associations that we think exist. Consider, a study of sentencing. A theory might posit that in areas where court actors perceive there to be a greater criminal threat, tougher, more punitive punishments will be used. Should the study use courts as the unit of analysis? That would seem logical. What, though, about the notion that community characteristics, such as the amount of crime or social disadvantage, may influence court actors? Consideration of that question may lead us to include community information in our study. In so doing, we might end up with a study that includes two units of analysis.[39] Also, what about the notion that court actors might target their punitive tendencies toward groups that they assume are more criminal? Consideration of that question may lead us to include information about individual defendants. In this instance, we arrive at a study that includes three units, or levels, of analysis: communities, courts, and defendants.[40]

Part of the science and art of the research process entails thinking clearly about units of analysis. Doing so is critical for collecting and analyzing data. It also is critical for identifying the theoretical basis for understanding how different factors may influence one another.

Collecting Data

The hallmark of research is data, but not just any data. Scientific studies seek to obtain data that accurately measure the constructs, or forces, that we think may influence crime and criminal justice outcomes. These studies ideally draw on extant theories and scholarship to identify the data that best

---

[39] Johnson (2010).
[40] See, for example, Wang and Mears (2010a, 2010b, 2015) and Wang *et al.* (2013).

help to describe and explain outcomes. In many instances, the information that we want cannot be obtained. For example, there is no way of directly measuring someone's self-control or their support for the death penalty. Accordingly, we have to rely on imperfect sources of information. That can include reliance on self-report surveys, observation, or reliance on administrative records from schools, courts, prisons, and the like. Our goal is to obtain the most relevant data and to do so with the limited time and resources available to us.

Scientific studies also typically seek data that are representative. Random samples can provide one basis for obtaining results that we think represent a broader universe of individuals, courts, police agencies, and so on. Clarity about how to sample requires that we identify clearly our unit of analysis and the distribution in space and time of that unit. For example, if we want to understand police department culture, then we need to know something about the distribution of police departments nationally and within states, and we need to know how many individuals work within each department. We then can devise a sampling strategy that will allow us to answer our questions. How, though, does time enter into the equation? Perhaps officer culture is known to change greatly just before or after a presidential election. If so, and if that change is not our focus, we might want to conduct our survey well before or well after an election.

One sometimes hears the expression, "The data speak for themselves." As noted earlier, from a researcher's perspective, that rarely, if ever, is the case. Data only make sense within a larger context. That includes consideration of sampling representativeness, how well the measures capture particular constructs, the distribution of the measures across the units of analysis, the generalizability of the results to other places, and similar issues.

Here, again, although data collection constitutes a distinct aspect of the research process, it is inextricably intertwined with other parts of this process. To sample well includes awareness of the broader goal of a study, the study's questions, and the theory that guides the study. The science and art of research involve the ability to discern the intertwined nature of different aspects of the research process and how decisions in one part can have ripple effects to others.

What, though, of research that does not involve random samples? That occurs frequently. Studies without random samples need be no less scientific than those that do.[41] For example, scholars might interview a small number of prison officials or examine archival records, including newspaper accounts, about informal punishment policies at two different prisons.

---

[41] Corbin and Strauss (1990); Feagin *et al.* (1991); Charmaz (2014); see also Crank and Bowman (2008).

The considerations for sampling may differ when we cannot obtain random samples. But the logic is similar in both instances – we ultimately seek samples that will help us to obtain insights about how the social world operates.[42] Even the most representative samples, for example, are only representative at a particular point in time; in that sense, all studies are historically contingent and non-representative.[43] A study of prison effectiveness might show that in one decade incarceration increased recidivism, while decreasing it in another.[44] Many reasons might explain such a difference. Perhaps in the earlier decade, prisons antagonized inmates and offered no rehabilitative programming, while in the later decade they provided consistent supervision and evidence-based correctional interventions. The point is that all studies entail sampling considerations that should be governed by our research goals and questions, and they all confront constraints that limit their potential validity and generalizability.

Analysis

All analysis flows directly from what the data permit. In some studies, for example, there may be a great deal of missing data. If too much information is missing, we may need to refrain from analysis or introduce analyses that adjust for the missingness. If the outcomes are continuous, we should use certain types of statistical analyses; if they are binary (e.g., committed a crime or not, arrested or not), we should use others. Outcomes can vary greatly in their distribution. They may be continuous or binary, they may involve counts or ordered sets of categories (e.g., low, medium, high), or they may consist of non-ordered sets of categories (e.g., placement in different types of rehabilitative treatment). The nature of these distributions dictates the types of statistical analyses that researchers use.

The same holds for qualitative data – that is, the types of phenomena that we wish to explain and the information used in the explanation collectively determine the mode of analysis. That said, the analytic techniques for examining qualitative data, such as a case study based on interviewing one person, court, prison, or community, vary from those used in most quantitative analyses. That is true as well for analysis of historical comparative sources of data.[45]

In all instances, scientific analysis proceeds differently than most other approaches in that it seeks both to examine the data systematically and to counter-argue hypothesized effects. Systematic analysis entails attempts to

[42] Corbin and Strauss (1990).   [43] Feagin *et al.* (1991).
[44] See, generally, Mears *et al.* (2015).
[45] See, for example, Gould (1987) and Barker (2009).

repeatedly examine data in diverse ways to ensure that a set of findings holds up consistently. If they do not, then questions arise about whether identified patterns or causal relations actually exist. The effort to counter-argue points is critical to the scientific enterprise as well. Scientists seek to determine if certain patterns or causal relationships exist, not to advance a particular view of the world. To that end, they employ a range of analyses to determine if the results perhaps are counter to what they hypothesize.

This reliance on systematic analysis and efforts to counter one's expect-ations make science a slower undertaking than what might arise through cursory analysis of data. It is, however, precisely what makes scientific insights "scientific." Conclusions flow from careful consideration of research goals and questions, causal pathways, sampling, data, analyses that seek to show how the world actually operates as opposed to how we assume it does, and systematic description of the processes followed to arrive at a given set of findings. The latter allow others to evaluate the credibility of a set of findings and to undertake replications or extensions of a study.

Presenting Findings in an Accurate and Useful Manner

Outside the scientific arena, it may be acceptable to "cherry pick" findings – that is, to emphasize those results that may accord with what we think must be true. This approach can be found not only in political arenas, but also in the "applied" world of criminal justice. Administrators, practitioners, and anyone who works in the criminal justice system may hold strong views about the prevalence and causes of such phenomena as crime, police officer abuse of citizens, and racial disparities in sentencing, as well as a myriad of other issues, such as the effectiveness of the death penalty or solitary confinement.

Within the scientific arena, however, the avowed goal is to present findings as objectively as possible. That means presenting results accurately and identifying clearly the uncertainty that attends them. It also means describing a study's limitations, such as the populations or areas to which a study may or may not generalize.

Researchers are, it will not be shocking to learn, human. They can hold biases that color how they frame studies, the questions they ask, the data that they think are relevant, the analyses that they view as more trust-worthy, and the findings that seem most important. They do not magically arrive at objective research or presentation of results. Fortunately, at least three factors reduce this problem, though they do not eliminate it. First, researchers by training aspire to objectivity, to the extent that such is possible. Second, researchers rely on procedures – including theory, the situating of studies in the context of prior research, careful justification for use of particular sources of data, and selection and use of analytic methods that scientists have found to be useful in analyzing certain types of data. Third, they work within an institutional context that provides checks and balances. That context consists of the broader scientific community and reliance on peer review to assess the integrity of a study. Research that other scientists view as passing muster gets published in peer-review journals. These three factors collectively create a greater likelihood, but do not guarantee, that research will be accurate or accurately presented.

Communicating to the broader scientific community constitutes a critical part of the research process. As with any craft, learning to communicate effectively can take time and entails both technical training and a bit of "art." Those who are trained in research and then go on to conduct studies ideally merge both. They find a way to convey scientific studies effectively to diverse audiences. The typical problem, however – one that movies and television shows frequently parody – is that researchers seem to talk in a language that only other researchers can understand. In the policy arena, this problem can become a significant barrier to research exerting an influence on decisions about laws, policies, programs, practices, and the like.[46] The findings from studies may be relevant for policymakers and criminal justice administrators and practitioners. Yet, if the scientific community cannot communicate the findings in an accessible manner, there will be little chance that the research informs policy discussions. As Joan Petersilia observed several decades ago, that situation has changed over time. Students increasingly are being trained not only to undertake a wide range of "basic" and "applied" research, but also to communicate the results to diverse audiences.[47] Here, again, technical proficiency in research only takes one so far. The art of conveying material to diverse groups takes practice and requires an ability to tailor information in ways that appeal and are accessible to these groups.

EXPERIMENTS ARE AN IMPORTANT TYPE OF RESEARCH DESIGN, BUT FAR FROM THE ONLY KIND

We purposely did not center a discussion about the research process with a focus on experiments. Why? Experiments clearly are central to science. They occur most frequently in the natural sciences, such as chemistry and physics, and in medicine. They occur in the social sciences as well, but not

[46] Petersilia (1991).
[47] Petersilia (1991); see, generally, Cullen (2005), Mears (2010), and Blomberg *et al.* (2016).

nearly as frequently.[48] And many times experiments simply cannot be done. For example, despite a plethora of death penalty studies, none yet exist or likely will in which some states are randomly assigned to implement capital punishment and others are not.[49]

Experiments constitute an important way in which science advances. But they are only one of many approaches used by researchers to study the causal effect of an intervention, such as particular policies or programs, on various outcomes, such as crime or sentencing decisions. We discuss in Chapter 6 a wide range of quasi-experimental designs that under certain conditions can approximate the findings that we might obtain from experiments.[50] In addition, scientific studies do not focus exclusively on causal effects. They include, as we discussed earlier, efforts to describe the social world, to identify the social meanings of diverse social phenomena, and, not least, to answer policy-focused questions.

CONCLUSION

We have sought to identify the central role of study designs, goals, and particular research activities in scientific accounts of crime and criminal justice. The science and art of research lies in seeing how these different dimensions intersect. To develop an appropriate, useful, viable study design relies on clarity about one's research goals. At the same time, these goals dictate the types of studies that should be conducted. Similarly, although research goals dictate the questions that we ask, our final study design may be governed by data that already exist. Perhaps, for example, funding does not permit collection of new data. In that case, we may have to work "backwards" and reframe our research questions to make them amenable to empirical study. All of these aspects and more – including the samples that we use, the types of analyses that we present, and how we discuss the results – go into research.

It should be evident that no cookie-cutter approach to research can work. Judgement calls must be made at the start of a study, during it, and even at the end when describing results. For researchers, the ability to make these calls stems from development of what we have termed a researcher sensibility. With such a sensibility, one can adjust studies in ways that are more likely to produce credible results; without it, studies are likely to be framed in ways that do not align with research goals. In such cases, we might use a data set just because it happens to be available. We might use a methodology because it somehow seems

---

[48] See, however, Welsh *et al.* (2013).   [49] Nagin and Pepper (2012).
[50] See also Sullivan's (2013) discussion of simulation studies.

"advanced." Or we might describe data endlessly, with no clear link to a broader research goal. Such studies achieve little.

We hope it is clear that this researcher sensibility not only is critical for conducting research, but also for evaluating and using it. Without it, we are left accepting the claims that researchers make about the importance or credibility of their studies. Consider a study that relies on a non-random set of interviews with prison inmates and finds supermax housing to be harmful to inmate mental health. A policymaker (or his or her staff) reads the study and concludes therefore that such housing should be abolished. Although many arguments can be leveled against supermax housing, reliance on this study's results to justify abolishing the housing would be folly. For example, the study would not have provided a valid estimate of the housing's effect on inmate mental health. It also would not have provided any estimate of the benefits or harms of the housing on other critical outcomes, such as prison system safety and order.[51]

In this illustration, the study may have merit. Perhaps it sheds light on different ways in which supermax housing may affect inmate mental health. However, the ability to recognize the appropriate uses and limitations of the study requires that we not accept research findings at face value. It also requires an ability to understand the study's goals, the precise questions it was designed to answer, and the ways in which these goals and questions – as well as the sampling, data, and analyses – shape how we should evaluate and use the findings.

There is, we think, no short cut. To undertake credible science requires a researcher sensibility. And to evaluate and use it appropriately requires one as well.

---

[51] Mears and Watson (2006); see, generally, Frost and Monteiro (2016) and Mears (2016a).

Part II

Essential Research Ingredients: Theory, Data, and Analysis

4 The Role of Theory in Research

INTRODUCTION

The essential "ingredients" of research include theory, data, and analysis. They interact and inform one another and in that sense they cannot readily be separated from one another. Theory can dictate the data and methods that we use. By the same token, data can dictate the theories from which we draw (or the theories we develop). And our knowledge of analytic techniques can shape the questions and theories that we develop and, accordingly, the data we use. Even so, each ingredient can be viewed as serving a distinct role in the science and art of research.

Here, we focus on the role of theory. In Chapters 5 and 6, we focus on data and analysis, respectively. Theory is critical to the research enterprise. It guides the questions that get asked. And it enables us both to discover patterns that we otherwise might miss and to understand what gives rise to them. The goal of this chapter, then, is to describe what is meant by "theory," identify ways in which theory can be helpful and sometimes harmful for advancing science and policy, highlight ways to "do" theoretical research, discuss types of criminological and criminal justice theories, and illuminate the salience of theory for data and analysis.

Stated differently, the chapter seeks to answer a series of questions. What is theory? In what ways is it useful? In what ways might theory interfere with advancing scientific understanding and policy? How does one go about "doing" – creating, applying, or evaluating – theory? What types of criminological and criminal justice theories exist? And what relevance does theory have for data and analysis? In answering these questions, we hope to convey the role of theory, and of a researcher sensibility, in studies of crime and criminal justice.

WHAT IS THEORY?

Theory as a Guide

Theory guides research, much as it guides our everyday decisions. We may not consciously articulate the theories that inform our decisions, but they nonetheless exist. Advances in cognitive psychology have found that all of us appear to be "wired" to search for patterns. We rely on cognitive "short cuts," or heuristics, to make sense of disparate sources of data that we absorb from our environments.[1] These heuristics aid us in interpreting the data that our senses provide. They amount, in short, to theories that enable us to organize information and discern patterns and relationships. We may make mistakes – we assume, for example, something about a particular event, person, situation, or the like, that turns out to be incorrect. Regardless, the heuristics enable us to navigate the social and physical world; without them, we would be lost.

Social science theories operate in much the same manner. They enable us to identify patterns that we otherwise might miss. Figure 4.1 conveys this idea. In panel A, there is a "smiley" face, but the mish-mash of lines obscures its presence. In panel B, the bolded contours of the face make it jump out at us. Theory operates in a similar manner. It draws our attention to patterns that may exist. We then use data and analyses to confirm the presence of the patterns.

Theories can do more than that, though. They not only can help us to discern patterns, they can aid in identifying the causes and the consequences of them. Put differently, theories amount to written statements that describe phenomena, what produces them, and what effects they have. As with individual decision-making that we all make, theories may reflect an accurate *or* an inaccurate understanding of the world. What is the difference? Researchers state their theories in writing. They also articulate the causal reasoning, or logic. They then test parts or all of a given theory empirically.

This emphasis in science on empirical tests constitutes an especially important difference from how most of us proceed in our day-to-day theorizing and decision-making. Most of us do not formally articulate the reasons for how we view the world and the explicit logic behind any given decision. And we typically do not test these reasons empirically, much less with established research methodologies!

Theory Defined

What, then, is a theory? How do we know a theory when we see one? For example, does it suffice for a scholar simply to call an explanation that they

[1] Kahneman (2011).

A. Pattern Exists–But Cannot Be Seen   B. Pattern Exists–Theory Helps Us to See It

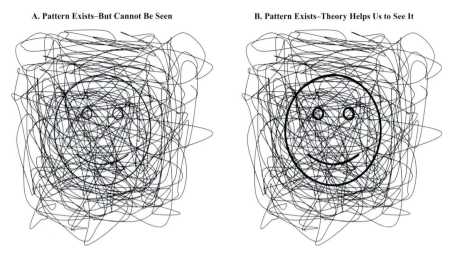

Figure 4.1 Theory helps us to discern patterns

develop about some phenomenon a theory? Or must certain criteria be met for an explanation to be called a "theory"?

At the most general level, a theory consists of a set of statements that explain how one or more forces contribute to another. A more precise definition comes from Robert Merton, who wrote at length about the history and nature of social scientific theory: "Theory refers to logically interconnected sets of propositions from which empirical uniformities can be derived."[2] A similar definition can be found in many accounts of social science theory.[3] Scott Decker, for example, has described theory as "a set of logically interrelated propositions" and has noted that we can view the "propositions as the 'mortar' that holds the bricks of theory together, with the bricks being the variables."[4] This type of definition is useful, and it is one that arguably guides most criminological and criminal justice researchers.[5]

Even so, one might add to this type of definition the requirement that a theory not only identify propositions and how they are related, but also, as Jack Gibbs has advocated, state explicitly the assumptions that underlie it, rules for deriving testable hypotheses, and procedures for measuring the constructs used by the theory.[6] "Constructs" are phenomena that cannot be

---

[2] Merton (1968:39); see also Merton (1973).

[3] See, for example, Blalock (1964), Cole (1975), Dubin (1978), Marini and Singer (1988), Hage (1994), Elliott (1999), Mears and Stafford (2002), Reynolds (2006), Jaccard and Jacoby (2010), Swanson and Chermack (2013), and Swedberg (2014).

[4] Decker (2015:382).

[5] See, generally, Lilly *et al.* (2015), Snipes and Maguire (2015), and Akers *et al.* (2016).

[6] Gibbs (1972, 1985, 1997); many other scholars have advocated such a definition (see, e.g., Homans (1964); Berger and Zelditch (1993)).

directly measured. Most social scientific research, including criminological and criminal justice studies, faces this problem. Scientists thus rely on empirical data that indirectly measure a construct. There is, for example, no direct measure of intelligence. For that reason, we have to rely on indirect measures, such as responses individuals give to a variety of survey questions.

Without clarity about proper measurement of a theory's core constructs, researchers flounder in seeking to identify the most accurate way to measure these constructs. Similarly, without clear procedures for how to derive hypotheses, researchers must guess at how best to test a theory. For example, one of the most famous theories of offending, differential association, provides no clear rules for deriving hypotheses.[7] That leads to a situation in which researchers guess at the hypotheses that provide a test of the theory. Without guidance about measurement of the theory's constructs, they have to guess at the best measures to use as well.[8]

Here is another way to consider the matter. Imagine a board game that comes with enough graphics and pieces that we have a general sense of what the game entails. There may even be an instruction manual that says something to the effect of, "Whoever accrues the most money wins." What, though, if no other instructions come with the game? How do turns progress? What counts as a "turn"? In this situation, we could make up rules, but we would end up in a situation where everyone plays the game differently.

That situation characterizes the problem that attends many theories. They lack clear instructions for how we should derive hypotheses or what hypotheses count as valid tests. They lack, too, clear instructions about measurement of key constructs. As with the imaginary board game, the end result can be marked inconsistency. In this case, the inconsistency lies not with how we play a game, but how researchers empirically test a theory or judge its quality.

Still other views – beyond those that emphasize statements, propositions, and rules – exist about what counts as theory. For example, some scholars view theory as generalizations, laws, or axioms about how two or more factors are related to one another, or as statements about the conditions under which relationships among these factors arise.[9] Others see theory as a conceptual framework for describing a phenomenon and what causes it.[10]

[7] Sutherland (1934).   [8] See, for example, Mears *et al.* (1998).
[9] Reynolds (2006); Williams and McShane (2014).
[10] Crank and Bowman (2008); see also Parsons (1977).

Theory in Practice

Unfortunately, no consensus exists about which definition of theory is best.[11] Valid criticisms can be made of almost all definitions. Conceptual frameworks are illustrative. They can seem useful, yet are difficult to test. "Conflict theory" constitutes a case in point. Many textbooks discuss conflict theory as if it is just that, a single theory. The underlying idea consists of the notion that groups compete for power; this competition leads each group to devise means by which to control one another. But there is no single "conflict theory." Rather, many specific theoretical accounts exist that differ markedly from one another, and yet may be categorized together simply because they emphasize political, economic, or other dimensions of power. Beyond that common overlap, however, there is little uniformity in the core logic and arguments of each theory. There is, then, no "conflict theory" per se, and many of the theories so classified do not appear to be similar. This situation engenders a wealth of empirical tests that do not in any coherent way test "conflict theory."[12]

Another illustration – "middle-range" theories, which Merton advocated, consist of "theories that lie between the minor but necessary working hypotheses that evolve in abundance during day-to-day research and the all-inclusive systematic efforts to develop a unified theory that will explain all the observed uniformities of social behavior, social organization, and change."[13] That is well and fine. Yet, it in fact is unclear what middle-range theories are or how they can be incorporated into other theories.[14] To Merton, most theoretical ideas or working hypotheses are middle-range theories. They are the stuff of everyday research. How, though, do such theories differ from "low-range" or "high-range" theories? One of the most prominent theories of offending, self-control theory, posits that individuals with low self-control are more likely to commit crime.[15] From some perspectives, that amounts to a hypothesis, not a theory.[16] Even so, many scholars would view the hypothesis as a theory because authors of self-control theory, Michael Gottfredson and Travis Hirschi, provided extensive reasons for the expected relationship between self-control and criminal behavior. In addition, self-control theory was presented as a "general theory of crime." It therefore is difficult to see how it could be viewed as a "middle-range" theory even though Merton's classification would categorize it as such.

---

[11] Mears and Stafford (2002).
[12] Mills (1959); Merton (1968); Freese (1972); Gibbs (1972); Blalock (1989); Mears and Stafford (2002).
[13] Merton (1968:39).   [14] Mears and Stafford (2002).
[15] Gottfredson and Hirschi (1990); Hay and Meldrum (2016).
[16] See, for example, Freese (1972), Gibbs (1972), Blalock (1994), and Hage (1994).

We can view the debate about what is theory and how to use it from an optimistic or pessimistic perspective. From an optimistic perspective, the diverse definitions all emphasize the importance of describing relationships in writing so that others can test them. They encourage us to develop clear and coherent arguments and predictions and ways to test them. That differentiates them from the sundry ideas that are never verbalized, but may guide many of us in our day-to-day lives. And it paves the way for the notion that empirical tests of theories are important for adjudicating what may be an accurate view of the world. We should not, for example, simply accept a theory at face value; we should test it empirically. Viewed in this light, we can rely on any of a range of definitions and probably not go too far wrong.

From a pessimistic perspective, the situation results in a great deal of writing, data collection, and research that does not accumulate into a coherent body of knowledge.[17] Hypotheses get tested, for example, that have no bearing on the validity of a theory. Perhaps the clearest example of this problem lies in the tendency for many studies to identify an empirical association between two measures and to do so with no clear connection to a theory. The problem? No clear basis exists for interpreting the association or its relevance for a larger body of knowledge.

In the end, there are some grounds for adhering to either view. Considerable theorizing occurs that entails needless imprecision and confusion that inhibits scientific progress. At the same time, the diverse efforts point in the same direction: They seek to develop accounts of the social world that ideally can be tested empirically and shed light on the existence of various phenomena, what contributes to them, and how they influence other phenomena.

HOW IS THEORY USEFUL?

Theory is nothing more or less than a tool. It serves not as an end in and of itself. Rather, it provides a means by which we can obtain a greater understanding of a diverse array of social phenomena, not least crime and criminal justice. Like any tool, theory can be used to different ends. Here, we discuss several ways in which theory can be useful.

Theory Can Help in Describing and Understanding Social Phenomena

In some debates about theory, scholars sometimes place one goal, such as description, above another, such as prediction. These debates miss the fact

[17] Mears and Stafford (2002).

that each goal implicates the other. To predict a phenomenon, we must be able to describe it. For example, tallying fielding errors at a baseball game requires that we first understand what counts as an error and, as importantly, the very meaning of an error within the context of the game. At the same time, a description of a phenomenon can be wrong. Thus, efforts to describe phenomena require empirical evaluation. It may be that we rely on someone who knows nothing about baseball for insight about the game. We are told that any hit over the outer wall or fence is an error – it must certainly be unintended and problematic since we now have no ball! If we interviewed more people, however, and targeted particular individuals who know more about the game, we would quickly learn that hits out of the park are not errors, but instead "homeruns" (and they are good!).

The same logic holds for criminological and criminal justice research. For example, we might develop a theory about when and why people support severe punishments for offenders. To develop and test this theory, we first would need an understanding of what counts as punishment in a given society and which punishments citizens view as more severe. In developing this understanding, we simultaneously may learn about when and why punishment is used. Our descriptive effort thus involves the creation of a theoretical model of punishment, one that may generate predictions about variation in punishment among individuals or places.

In short, as emphasized in Chapter 3, one prominent line of inquiry for social scientists consists of developing or using existing theory to describe various social phenomena in a socially meaningful way that citizens or particular groups would recognize as culturally intelligible. For example, in some schools, there may be a greater tolerance for minor infractions, such as hallway pranks that one youth might play on another; indeed, the infractions may be interpreted as normal adolescent behavior. By contrast, in other schools, such acts may be viewed as delinquent, abnormal, and warranting referral to the police.[18] A predictive theory of delinquency that failed to draw on these descriptive insights would miss that youth in both schools engaged in identical behaviors and that labeling processes, not absolute differences in offending, determined whether these behaviors were classified as "delinquent."[19]

A classic example of how theory can aid in description can be seen in Merton's famous deviance typology. With knowledge of this typology, one can see that certain behaviors constitute distinct types of deviance. Without it, these behaviors might be viewed as seemingly innocuous or random events with little evident pattern to them. Merton distinguished four types

[18] Mears *et al.* (2016c); Ripley (2016).   [19] Singer (1996); Mears *et al.* (2016c).

of deviance, and did so by cross-classifying acceptance (+) or rejection (–) of societal goals and acceptance (+) or rejection (–) of societally approved means to these goals, respectively.[20] His premise for this classification stemmed from the observation that goals guide human behavior and that diverse means to achieve those goals exist. It also stemmed from the observation that society endorses some goals, and some means to those goals, but not others. Not least, it stemmed from the observation that some individuals or groups may have differential interest in or ability to achieve certain goals or to use legitimate (societally approved) means to pursue them.

The four resulting types of deviance were: conformity (+, +), innovation (+, –), ritualism (–, +), and retreatism (–, –). Deviant conformists are those individuals who adapt to societal pressures by accepting societal goals and the means to them. Of course, conformity can be viewed as an appropriate, non-deviant response to societal pressures. But individuals or groups may go too far and pursue conformity at all times. At least three other deviant adaptations exist. For example, individuals may accept societal goals, but reject the means to them (deviant innovation), they may reject societal goals, but accept the means to them (deviant ritualism), or they may reject societal goals and means to the goals (deviant retreatism). A fifth deviant type consists of individuals who reject societal goals and means and instead seek to substitute new goals and means for them (deviant rebellion).

This theory helps us to classify individuals in ways in which we otherwise would not be able to do. It illuminates a potential pattern from a wealth of information. It at the same time provides some insight into possible causes. For example, individuals who have access to legitimate means may be far more likely to engage in deviant conformity and less in deviant innovation, ritualism, retreatism, or rebellion. Even so, simply because the typology makes intuitive sense does not mean that the theory accurately predicts who engages in deviance. Empirical research, as well as additional theorizing, is needed for that endeavor.

Another, more light-hearted but no less relevant example involves the description of winking. Clifford Geertz, an anthropologist, used winking to convey what he meant by the "thick description" that ethnographers undertake. For our purposes, we can think of thick description as theory that helps us to describe social behavior in culturally meaningful or intelligible terms.[21]

> The point is that between ... the "thin description" of what the
> rehearser ... is doing ("rapidly contracting his right eyelids") and the
> "thick description" of what he is doing ("practicing a burlesque of a friend

---

[20] Merton (1968:194).   [21] Geertz (1973); see, generally, Weber (1978:3–24).

faking a wink to deceive an innocent into thinking a conspiracy is in motion") lies the object of ethnography: a stratified hierarchy of meaningful structures in terms of which twitches, winks, fake-winks, parodies, rehearsals of parodies are produced, perceived, and interpreted, and without which they would not ... in fact exist, no matter what anyone did or didn't do with his eyelids.[22]

As Geertz's account highlights, physical actions in and of themselves do not magically mean something in isolation. Their meaning stems from society and culture. Scientific efforts to predict social phenomena thus require theories that enable us to define phenomena in societally or culturally intelligible ways. Theorists then can build on such work to develop accounts of the causes and effects of these phenomena.

This observation leads to a critical point: Any effort to describe a socially meaningful behavior or action requires some understanding of society and culture.[23] In the above illustration, one needs to be familiar with the very notion of using physical cues to connote intention and, more specifically, the idea that winking, when done in a certain way, signifies an intention to deceive or engage in a conspiracy of sorts. Without this information, a scientist would not even know that there was a phenomenon – let us call it "conspiracy winking" – to explain. Even something as serious as a death is not intrinsically a "meaningful" occurrence. There are accidental deaths, suicides, and murders, for example. Each involves death, but their social or cultural meanings among various groups or communities may vary enormously, as may their causes and effects. Without understanding these meanings, we might create a general theory of death. But we likely would have a theory that was so general as to be meaningless. For example, the theory might argue that people die when their hearts stop beating. It thus would miss out on the social meaning of deaths that arise through different circumstances and how the causes of different types of deaths vary.

In short, description can be viewed as a form of theoretical activity. We can use it, and the process of arriving at description (e.g., interviews, observation, or ethnographies), to help make sense of behavior. Such activity sometimes has been termed "verstehen" theorizing, from the German word for "understand." Max Weber, who helped to found sociology, employed this terminology.[24] "Verstehen" theorizing – what some scholars call "interpretative" theorizing – can be viewed as an effort to describe social behaviors and actions in socially and culturally intelligible ways.[25]

---

[22] Geertz (1973:7).   [23] See, generally, Weber (1978).   [24] Weber (1978).
[25] See, generally, Parsons (1968), Gibbs (1972), Dubin (1978), Hage (1994), Mears and Stafford (2002), and Reynolds (2006).

It helps us to understand and discern when a twitch is a twitch and when it is a wink.

Description can provide us with a clear causal account of behavior. As in the above example, it may tell us that there are multiple forms of winking, including one in which individuals mean to jokingly convey conspiratorial activity. In turn, we can use descriptive theoretical accounts to guide data collection efforts and analysis. However, these accounts do not necessarily tell us why some individuals engage in a particular activity (e.g., conspiracy winking, crime) and others do not, or why some groups engage in higher rates of the activity (e.g., conspiracy winking rates, crime rates). For that, we need theory that can identify and explain causal relationships.[26]

Theory Can Help in Providing Causal Explanations

A basic goal of science is to solve mysteries and, in particular, to explain what gives rise to various phenomena. Theory aids in that endeavor. It helps us to identify causes and how they influence phenomena. For criminological and criminal justice research, theory is used to explain an incredibly wide range of social behaviors among individuals, organizations, cities, states, systems, and so on. As we discuss in Chapter 9, these behaviors, or phenomena, include crime, the exercise of formal and informal social control (e.g., law-making, policing, and sentencing), what happens inside prisons and jails, community supervision (e.g., probation and parole), juvenile justice, victimization, media studies, public opinion about diverse issues, and more. In every instance, researchers typically seek recourse to one or more theories. The theories in turn identify factors that may cause a particular phenomenon.

This view of theory – one that emphasizes a focus on how two or more phenomena may be causally related to one another – is the one that dominates the bulk of criminological and criminal justice research.[27] It sounds simple. Indeed, as depicted in Figure 4.2, it can be. At bottom, the effort can be likened to solving a puzzle. We zero in on some phenomenon and examine it from diverse angles until we have a "lightbulb" moment where we can identify a plausible explanation. For example, if we want to know what causes crime, we can brainstorm about a range of possible factors that might be relevant. Part of our brainstorming almost assuredly will entail thinking about the mechanisms through which a given factor may cause the outcome. Strain, for example, might cause crime and do so by

---

[26] The tension between "verstehen" analysis and causal analysis is captured in an exchange between Turco and Zuckerman (2017) and Watts (2017).
[27] Akers *et al.* (2016:1); see also Mears and Stafford (2002) and Reynolds (2006).

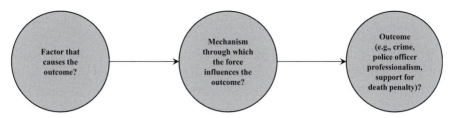

Figure 4.2 Theory as a guide for identifying causal relationships and mechanisms

lowering our self-control or increasing our need for resources, both of which might contribute to crime. Each causal pathway seems plausible. Each therefore could serve as a starting point for thinking more carefully about the causal force and the pathways through which it might affect some outcome, such as crime, police officer professionalism, public support for the death penalty, and so on.

The development of a causal account can quickly become complicated. We describe how in more detail below, but much depends on the state of prior theory and research. For example, if many theories about the phenomenon already exist, we can draw on them for insight. If none exists, we must work out the causal possibilities ourselves. Much also depends on one's approach to theory. To illustrate, formal theoretical approaches demand a level of rigor that can be sufficiently daunting as to deter many scholars from relying on them to explain some type of behavior. Informal approaches can be easier to use. However, they run the risk of creating problems in articulating a clear and consistent explanation for the phenomenon that we wish to understand. There are additional considerations. For example, do we seek to determine if one particular social force may be causal? Or do we seek to show that a causal force identified by a prior theory may not be the only relevant one? Perhaps instead we seek to explicate a sequence of causal forces between two others. Or perhaps we speculate that several causal forces interact. Still another possibility among many is that a causal force exerts a nonlinear (or what might be termed a "curvilinear") effect on an outcome. Perhaps, for example, a "dose" effect exists, such that more of a causal force does little until a threshold is reached, after which a large influence on the outcome occurs.

A theory ultimately must be tested empirically or it remains at the level of what might be called a plausible "story." It may provide an account that seems intuitive. And there may even be pieces of the theoretical argument that rest indirectly on empirical research. Consider an architect's blueprint for a house. It may contain elements that rest on sound science. Perhaps, for example, it calls for the use of types of concrete, wood, roofing materials, and the like, that have been shown to have particular suitability for some

types of buildings. The overall design, however, may bring these elements –
and perhaps elements of questionable construction-worthiness – together in
ways that will result in structural instability. That parts of the design look
credible does not mean that the overarching design should be trusted.

Much the same can be said of theories. Although parts of them may
have a certain logical appeal and rest on credible research, the totality may
not result in predictions that hold up under empirical scrutiny. The theory
may not actually take us very far in accurately explaining or predicting
causal relationships. That is why scientific research of criminological and
criminal justice theory emphasizes empirical tests.[28]

Theory Can Help in Guiding Policy

Another important use of theory is to guide policy. For example, in
the corrections system, theory can be used to develop or identify the
theoretical rationale for how a proposed or existing policy, law, program,
practice, or rule may contribute to an intended outcome.[29] All too frequently, however, policymakers and administrators rely on what Edward
Latessa and his colleagues have referred to as "correctional quackery."[30]
This approach involves a reliance on gut instincts or intuition, anecdotal
accounts, or highly publicized and sensationalized accounts of new programs. We should not be too quick to blame policymakers or administrators for adopting this approach. Many of us rely on our gut instincts to
guide our decisions.

Regardless, the approach suffers from a basic problem – the theoretical
logic for the policies may be inconsistent or lacking. Then, to add insult to
injury, it may turn out that little to no credible empirical research has been
undertaken to support the theoretical foundation of the policy. Consider
drug courts. Figure 4.3 presents a simplified description of the theoretical
(or causal) logic that guides them. The logic assumes that timely sentencing,
close supervision of offenders, and frequent check-ins with the court
collectively exert a specific deterrent effect that reduces recidivism. It also
assumes that drug treatment will reduce drug abuse and addiction and that,
in turn, individuals will be less motivated to offend. Not least, it assumes
that rehabilitative services, such as counseling or life skills training, may
enable individuals to obtain work and manage strain better, thus reducing
the likelihood of criminal behavior. The theoretical logic gives us a better
ability to determine why a given drug court may be effective and what might
be done to increase its effectiveness. The logic identifies that when close

[28] Watts (2014, 2017); cf. Turco and Zuckerman (2017).
[29] Mears (2007, 2010, 2016b, 2017); Welsh *et al.* (2018).   [30] Latessa *et al.* (2014).

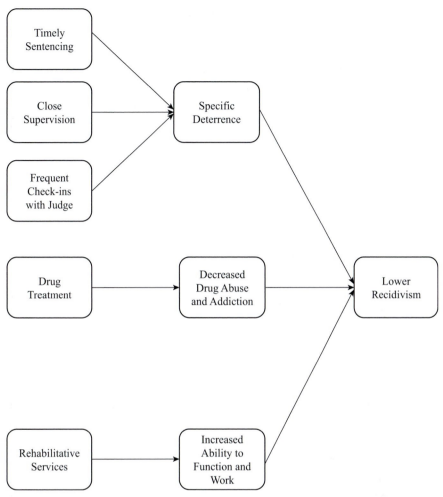

Figure 4.3 Drug court theoretical (causal) logic
Note: Adapted from Mears (2010:102).

supervision or drug treatment occur infrequently, we can anticipate minimal reductions in recidivism. Unfortunately, many drug courts have been created with little attention to documenting their specific theoretical logic (drug courts in fact vary greatly in their design) or the extent to which implementation of the courts adheres to the logic.[31]

An illustration of this problem can be seen in calls for longer prison sentences. One can justify tougher sentencing in many ways. A prominent justification, however, consists of the argument that serving a longer amount of time in prison has a specific deterrent effect. Little empirical research supports that claim.

[31] Butts and Roman (2004); National Institute of Justice (2006); Mears (2010).

This lack of support likely stems from the existence of a variety of theoretical pathways through which imprisonment influences individuals.[32] Let us assume that specific deterrence, via longer prison stays, lowers the probability of offending. The possibility exists that this effect may be offset by countervailing causal effects. For example, some theoretical perspectives point to the possibility that longer stays have a criminogenic effect. To illustrate, social bond theory can be viewed as predicting that an individual's ties to conventional society, including conventional values and beliefs, may weaken throughout the course of incarceration. Similarly, strain theory can be viewed as predicting that longer stays would weaken an individual's ability to reunify with family or friends or to secure housing or employment. The net effect of these different causal processes may be that prison terms increase rather than decrease recidivism.[33]

Long ago, Kurt Lewin observed that "there is nothing more practical than a good theory."[34] Indeed, a central benefit of theory is that it can help us to identify a policy's causal logic and how it might achieve intended outcomes or, conversely, how it might undermine them. It also can help us to identify the conditions that need to be met for a policy to be effective.[35] The theory, it should be emphasized, need not come directly from university or research institute scholars. It can come from those who develop policies and programs.

What most matters is the effort to think clearly about all the ways in which a policy might or might not achieve its intended goals. Consider many gang initiatives – they frequently fail to achieve their goals because they do not address key dynamics involved in gang-related criminal activity. To illustrate, theoretical accounts emphasize the possibility that gangs contribute to crime through group processes. Failure to interrupt or channel these processes may do little, then, to reduce crime. Prosecution of high-profile gang leaders might influence these processes; more likely, though, is the possibility that they engender stronger solidarity among other gang members and that a new leader steps up. Conversely, efforts to go beyond selective prosecution may prove more helpful. For example, the police and prosecutors might enlist the support of gang members and community residents to activate group processes in ways that reduce crime.[36] Another illustration involves supermax housing. One need not have studied supermax housing extensively to arrive at the insight that it may deter some

---

[32] See, generally, Mears *et al.* (2011), Mears *et al.* (2015), Mears and Cochran (2015), and Mears *et al.* (2016a).
[33] Nagin *et al.* (2009); Cullen *et al.* (2011b); Mears *et al.* (2016a).   [34] Lewin (1952:169).
[35] Decker (2015:382).   [36] Decker (2015).

inmates, but not deter others. Which inmates might be deterred by a stay in supermax housing? Why? How many days in isolation can be expected to produce a reduction in misconduct? Why?

These are the types of questions that, if answered, can aid in determining whether a credible theoretical basis exists for a policy to be effective.[37] If answers to these theoretical questions do not exist, this should raise questions about warrant for the policy. In fact, a broad array of similar questions exist that can help in formulating the theoretical foundation for a policy. For example, what causal mechanisms most contribute to an intended outcome, such as reduced crime? If we can identify a factor or two that exert the greatest influence, a policy might be modified to emphasize them. Another example: What factors may interact to contribute to an intended goal, such as reduced minority disparities in arrests? Consider a program that seeks to educate police officers to be more aware of cultural differences in certain communities. This program might be more effective in improving police–citizen relations when the organizational culture of a police department actively supports these educational efforts.[38] To the extent that such an interaction exists, an officer training program would be more effective if coupled with a simultaneous focus on improving a law enforcement agency's organizational culture.

If we pursue such questions with an eye toward only finding support for a given policy, little will be gained. However, if pursued in an objective manner, we may be more likely to arrive at an accurate assessment of whether a policy is likely to be effective and the conditions necessary for benefits to arise. For policymakers, this effort can lead to more effective policies; for scholars, it can lead to greater insight into crime and criminal justice.[39]

The Problem of Proceeding without Theory

Consider a spur-of-the-moment vacation. We get in the car and just start driving. Or we ask the train or bus ticket-master to select some destination for us. No return date has been set. No agenda or plan exists. We may not even have the time for a vacation, or we may have responsibilities that, if left unattended, cause hardship for others. Spontaneity sometimes can be the better path in life, but in this instance we can anticipate that the vacation will be a failure.

---

[37] Decker (2015:383); see also Mears (2016a).
[38] See, generally, Engel and Smith (2009), Mears and Bacon (2009), Reisig (2010), Rojek *et al.* (2012), Sampson (2013), and Lum and Nagin (2017).
[39] Rossi (1980).

Similarly, undertaking research or creating policy without theory is unlikely to achieve much and may simply leave us expending a great deal of time and resources to little end. Intuition can lead to all manner of insights. When it does, mainstream media accounts or books on the history of science regale us with how the intuition arose and its influence. What these accounts typically leave out are all the times that intuition went astray or simply was wrong.

These accounts also tend to emphasize simple associations. Why? Such associations are much easier to discuss. It is, for example, easy enough to say that more of X (e.g., drug laws, community policing, prison sentences, supervision of probationers and parolees) is associated with more (or less) of Y (e.g., drug dealing, crime, police misconduct, racial and ethnic disparities in law enforcement or sentencing). Associations are not, however, theories. They typically constitute, at most, a starting point. Consider a detective show about a murder – there may be many possible suspects, all of whom might plausibly have committed the crime. Associations are like that – there may be many possible explanations for them.

The risk lies in the fact that we – scholars, policymakers, or the public – may unconsciously select the explanation that we think most makes sense. And we stop. Our search for an explanation led to one that seemed plausible. Then, over time, every time we see or read about the association, we view it as confirmation of our explanation. Researchers, like everyone else, are vulnerable to "confirmation bias," a process by which one emphasizes information that supports our view and downplays or ignores that which does not.[40]

Theory provides an important check against this problem. It can prevent us from adopting or embracing an intuition that may be incorrect or lead us to miss out on other explanations that may be more plausible. When coupled with credible empirical analyses, theory can serve as an even more powerful check against that problem.

Another risk of proceeding without theory is that we have no idea what we are "seeing." Recall the "winking" example above. If we do not know how to interpret certain behaviors, we cannot develop theories that identify causal relationships for these behaviors or their effects. In turn, we cannot test the theories. Consider studies of the "code of the street." This code, described by Elijah Anderson, dictates how certain actions are interpreted. For example, in some neighborhoods, what otherwise might be viewed by an outsider as a non-event might be construed as a failure to afford an individual the respect that he or she expects.[41] Without knowledge of the code of the street, we cannot identify occurrences of disrespect or whether,

---

[40] Kahneman (2011).   [41] Anderson (1999).

as Anderson's theory anticipates, it contributes to violence. With knowledge of it, one can undertake studies that examine various manifestations of the street code and its potential influence not only on violence in society, but also inside prisons or on ways in which the police and courts sanction individuals.[42]

A third risk is that we accumulate an endless array of "facts" – empirical descriptions – with no way to make sense of them or to discern patterns. Of course, such descriptions can and frequently do provide fodder for developing important scientific advances. Science progresses in many ways. One of them consists of simple exploration – chart new territory by collecting lots of information, even when one is not sure why or what to do with it. The risk nonetheless bears emphasis. Why? The last two decades have been witness to tremendous advances in computers and, in turn, the collection of data and increases in analytic capacity. Researchers now can churn out empirical analyses – "facts" concerning the distribution of some phenomenon, such as arrests, or the association between a given phenomenon and another – at a much faster rate than in the past. Availability of more data creates many opportunities to advance our understanding of crime and criminal justice. It also creates many opportunities to create a mountain of facts with far too little theory to help us make sense of it all. (A similar problem was identified as contributing to problems in detecting the 9/11 attacks.[43])

Yet another risk of proceeding without theory – or without seeking to develop theoretical accounts – is that we fail to consider the precise way in which a potential causal force contributes to some phenomenon. Functional form refers to the precise way in which a causal force, X, is associated with a phenomenon, Y. The functional form might be linear. For example, each unit increase in X always leads to the same increase in Y. But it instead might be curvilinear. For example, each additional unit of X may provide less of an increase in Y, a situation of diminishing returns. Theoretical approaches to research entail consideration of these and other possible causal relationships (we discuss more possibilities in Chapter 8). In so doing, they can shed considerable light on the causes of the phenomena that we wish to explain. And they can provide a platform for developing more effective crime and criminal justice policy.[44]

The Problem of Proceeding with Theory

Like any tool, theory can be misused. When that happens, it can interfere with scientific progress and developing credible evidence about policy.

---

[42] Mears *et al.* (2013c); Mears *et al.* (2017c).   [43] Silver (2012); Mears (2017).
[44] Mears (2017).

Consider a situation in which a researcher becomes enamored of a theory. That can be beneficial. For example, the researcher may come to know the intricacies of the theory and how it might be applied to many phenomena. Persistent pursuit of a particular social scientific question or theory may pay dividends. Thomas Edison's many thousands of attempts to create a storage battery illustrate this idea.[45]

But the strategy may backfire, too. Sometimes we purchase a bad product, a "lemon." Think here of a used car that constantly breaks down and requires ongoing expensive repairs. What we likely should do is get rid of it. Instead, many of us continue to invest time and money in the "lemon," hoping that maybe we have turned a corner and that the "lemon" will work without further investment. Much the same can happen with theories. We invest tremendous amounts of time and energy in them despite many failures and signals that tell us to move on to other avenues of inquiry that may create greater insight.

A commitment to one theory or to one approach to theorizing has another downside – it can put up blinders. That problem attends many aspects of life. We get locked into viewing a problem, situation, issue, or the like in only one way. In so doing, we fail to adopt other perspectives. That can be especially problematic if these other perspectives illuminate better the phenomenon that we wish to understand or change. It is best, then, to remember that a theory is precisely that – a possibly valid explanation among many for why some phenomenon occurs. We should invest in theoretically informed research, not the theories themselves.

HOW TO "DO" THEORETICAL RESEARCH?

It may seem strange to think that many researchers do not have training in how to undertake theoretical research, but that is the case. Many university and college programs offer courses about theories of crime or criminal justice. These courses, however, typically focus on specific theories, not on how to create or augment theories. This situation is unfortunate because, as Howard Becker has argued, a "theoretically informed way of working" provides a critical platform on which to advance scientific understanding.[46] As he also has argued, there is no one way to undertake theoretical work – rather, many "tricks of the trade" exist.[47]

One can view these "tricks" as various strategies that researchers can use to develop theories about the world around us and, of special relevance for us, crime and criminal justice. No formulaic approach exists for

---

[45] Elkhorne (1967:52).   [46] Becker (1998:3).

[47] Becker (1998); the phrase is, in fact, the title of his book. See also Swedberg (2014).

tackling research in a "theoretically informed" manner. If there were, it almost assuredly would be widely used. What that means is that all of us – active researchers or consumers or users of research – must rely on a sensibility, an awareness of the different ways in which theory can be developed. The sensibility entails more than an awareness of different strategies. It entails an ability to consider all parts of the research process and the importance of "thinking theoretically" to advance scientific understanding.

Given that little consensus exists about the "right" way to "do" theory, how then can one proceed? Scholars have identified many strategies for how to create or build on theory. We discuss several of them, but emphasize that what ultimately may be best is to attempt to use a variety of them and then devolve on one that you find to be most helpful.

First, we recommend the simplest path – develop your own theory. How? Ignore prior theory and research and instead seek to identify as clearly as possible an explanation for some phenomena, such as variation in criminal offending, police officer suicides, court sentencing practices, implementation of drug courts, and so on. Write down the question that you want to answer. Play around with revising the question to make it more precise. Also, write down your explanation and the assumptions that underlie it, the hypotheses that you would use to test it, and different approaches that you think could be used to test the hypotheses and your theory. For example, what types of data, measures, and analyses would be best?

Then and only then consult prior literature on the topic. Why wait until this last step? The literature may be overwhelming. For some topics, a mountain of research may exist. You will want to sort through it eventually. However, if you dive in too early, you may get distracted. A mountain of research in no way means that contributions cannot be made or that some of it may be directly relevant to your goals. It simply means that a considerable amount of reading may be necessary to get a handle on what has been learned to date. As you read, you can revisit your ideas and revise and add to, or scrap them. Prior literature may bias how you think about a topic. Working through a question on your own can avoid these problems. It also can make sifting through prior work easier.

Second, develop a creative process that aids in thinking about a phenomenon. Many activities in life do not involve a single "best" way to do them. Artists, musicians, politicians, teachers, mechanics, and so on may use different strategies to do their work. Consider, then, building theory from a creative process that has been helpful to you in other arenas of your life. C. Wright Mills, for example, has written about an approach that some scholars find helpful.[48] It involves observing and reflecting on a topic, writing about it, organizing the writing, repeating that process, and seeing what comes of it. Sometimes the end result is nothing; other times, this process may create the foundation for an insight that can be transformed into a theory.

Third, develop theory from careful observation of the phenomenon that you wish to explain. This approach is one advocated by Becker and many others.[49] Sometimes referred to as "grounded theorizing," this approach includes thinking about phenomena (e.g., processes, behaviors), observing them, reflecting on how they may affect a variety of outcomes, articulating a tentative theory, and then conducting more observations to arrive at a more complete and accurate understanding of the phenomena under study.[50] One might, for example, interview gang members or spend time with them. Following the above process, the next step would be to develop the specific questions that you wish to answer and theory that can aid in doing so.[51]

Fourth, embrace middle-range theorizing.[52] Sometimes it can be tempting either to ignore thinking theoretically at all, as if somehow doing so is too difficult, or to theorize at a high level of abstraction. We thus provide no explanation for what might give rise to some phenomenon, leaving it to others to devise possible explanations. Or we provide an explanation that is so abstract – stated at such a high level of generality – that it achieves little. Consider a simplified version of rational choice theory that says that every action individuals take reflects a rational assessment. Such a theory, stated in this way, explains everything. (It also is not falsifiable; any behavior that individuals take, for example, might be found to be rational in some way.)

Middle-range theorizing can be a way out of this trap. What does such theorizing entail? Merton suggests that it entails attempting to rise above "minor but necessary working hypotheses."[53] Accordingly, we might first develop a working hypothesis or two and then proceed to go an extra step and consider how the hypothesis, and the explanation that gave rise to it, might be relevant in some broader way. A trivial but, we hope, evocative illustration: We might hypothesize that drivers get irritated by traffic delays. If asked to explain our reasoning, we say that people like to get to their destinations and that traffic delays interfere with that goal. Upon further reflection, we realize that traffic delays are but one

---

[48] See, for example, Berger (1990), Becker (1998), and Cullen and Vose (2014).
[49] Becker (1998); see, generally, Patton (2015).
[50] Corbin and Strauss (1990:10); see also Feagin *et al.* (1991); Charmaz (2014).
[51] Decker (2015).   [52] Merton (1968).   [53] Merton (1968:39).

type of interference and that driving to work is but one goal-oriented activity. We then might step back and consider the matter from a somewhat higher level of abstraction. For example, we might hypothesize that individuals are goal-seeking and that when life events (e.g., traffic) interfere with achieving these goals (e.g., getting to work on time), they become frustrated and angry.

Fifth, seek to create a "grand" theory. "Grand" theory has no single meaning. In general, it refers to efforts to create theories that seek to explain nearly all aspects of the social world. For example, Talcott Parsons sought to create a systems theory that could be used to describe and explain patterns in society or entire parts of society, such as the criminal justice system.[54] Such efforts have been criticized for being too ambitious, overly broad, and incapable of being tested empirically.[55] Even so, these theories may be useful in helping us to arrive at "middle-range" theories.[56] They also are essential if one wants to understand systems![57]

Sixth, seek to create a "general" theory. Some theories focus on specific phenomena, such as homicides, probation officer job satisfaction, prosecutorial plea-bargaining practices, and so on. A general theory seeks instead to explain a broad class of phenomena. For example, instead of seeking to explain "only" homicide, a theory might aim to explain all crime. Any such explanation must ignore the fact that some crimes appear to involve different causes. Consider petty theft and homicides. On the face of it, they seem dissimilar not only in appearance, but also in their likely causes. (That said, appearances can be deceptive.) View the matter somewhat differently – creating a general theory of all crime is similar to creating a general theory of all diseases. In the latter case, that means our theory must be equally capable of explaining and predicting hangnail, skin rashes, heart disease, and cancer. Such a theory would seem to have dubious validity. Even so, perhaps general theories can shed light on phenomena in ways that more narrowly construed theories cannot. Prominent theories of crime in fact tend to be general theories.[58] Perhaps the theories may not explain some crimes as well as others, but they nonetheless provide a unique way of thinking about and understanding crime.[59]

Seventh, use deduction or induction. Deduction tends to refer to the idea that we rely on propositions, logic, mathematical formula, or the like to derive expectations; induction tends to refer to the idea that we build up, or intuit, an explanation based on observation. A large literature in philosophy

---

[54] Parsons (1977); Mears (2017).

[55] Mills (1959) has provided one of the more trenchant critiques, but many other scholars have criticized "grand" or "systems" theories; this issue is discussed in Mears (2017).

[56] Merton (1968).   [57] Mears (2017).   [58] Akers *et al.* (2016).   [59] Gibbs (1997).

has debated what these terms actually mean.[60] Regardless, one can view each as a general approach that can be relied on to think theoretically. A deductive approach might have us starting with a general observation and then working "down" to derive a specific prediction from that observation. For example, we might begin with a theory of prison order and then seek to apply it to a particular prison riot. Alternatively, we might adopt an inductive approach in which we focus on a particular riot and seek to tease out from our observations a theory about not only that riot, but also what gives rise to prison riots in general.

Eighth, play with typologies. Typologies, like Merton's typology of deviance, provide a useful way to develop theory. These typologies might emerge from an inductive or deductive thought process and can help us to think about a phenomenon differently. However, not all typologies make sense. For example, one might cross-classify eye color and political ideology among judges. We end up with this typology: dark-eyed conservative judges, dark-eyed liberal judges, light-eyed conservative judges, and light-eyed liberal judges. Although political orientation might seem to be useful in predicting judicial sentencing practices, it seems a stretch to imagine that eye color matters. By contrast, Merton's deviance typology, which juxtaposed goals and means to goals, entails two dimensions that appear on the face of it to logically "fit" together. Developing a typology thus requires careful thought. As Kenneth Bailey has emphasized:

> One basic secret to successful classification ... is the ability to ascertain the key or fundamental characteristics on which the classification is to be based ... It is crucial that the fundamental or defining characteristics of the phenomenon be identified. Unfortunately, there is no specific formula for identifying key characteristics ... Prior knowledge and theoretical guidance are required in order to make the right decisions.[61]

Ninth, create theories that can help predict why policies may achieve their goals or undermine them. Many criminal justice policies, programs, and practices have been created with little attention to causal logic.[62] One way, therefore, to improve them – and, at the same time, to develop theory – is to imagine different causal mechanisms through which they may achieve various goals. Then repeat this process, but examine this time how the policies, programs, or practices may undermine the very goals they were designed to achieve. In creating a causal logic model, we may want to draw on existing theory and research. However, we also can first think through

[60] See, for illustration, Popper (2002), Reichertz (2014), and Lassiter and Goodman (2015).
[61] Bailey (1994:2).   [62] Mears (2010); Cooper and Worrall (2012).

the possibilities on our own. No harm comes from doing so, and we may well arrive at important theoretical insights.[63]

Tenth, seek to integrate theories.[64] Different approaches exist for doing so. There is, for example, conceptual integration (which involves identifying ways in which concepts from different theories may overlap), propositional integration (which involves linking propositions from different theories in sequences), and cross-level integration (which involves linking theories that focus on different units of analysis).[65] Integration requires familiarity with the intricacies of each theory. For that reason, it can be challenging. Also, one will encounter scholars who do not readily agree about whether integration is appropriate or how one should go about doing it. Nonetheless, the process of trying to integrate theories may shed light on avenues for developing theory that otherwise might not be apparent.

Eleventh, rely on formal theory.[66] This approach consists of using formal logic. As Gibbs has emphasized, it entails at least seven steps, which consist of describing:

> (1) major divisions or parts of a theory, (2) basic units of a theory (for example, statements in the form of empirical assertions), (3) criteria by which basic units are distinguished as to type and identified, (4) rules by which statements are derived from other statements, (5) the procedure for tests of statements derived from the theory, (6) rules for the interpretation of tests, and (7) criteria for assessing theories.[67]

This approach has the advantage of providing a more rigorous, systematic foundation for deriving hypotheses. It also allows for relevant and consistent evaluation of theory. It has the disadvantage, however, of being more difficult to undertake, and it can be difficult to present succinctly or in an accessible manner for others.

This list of recommendations is not exhaustive. It should, however, convey that there is no one best way to "do" theory. A variety of strategies exist. The variety alone underscores that science relies on the processes that are not intrinsically scientific. Rather, they entail a sort of art – the art of knowing how to relate different ideas. Productive theorizing ultimately requires a commitment to exploration and thinking through a phenomenon – whether it be crime, inequality, timely processing of cases, passage of certain types of sentencing laws, and so on – from many different perspectives. It does not entail a commitment to one or another theory or

---

[63] Rossi (1980).   [64] Messner *et al.* (1989).   [65] Akers *et al.* (2016).
[66] Gibbs (1972, 1997); Hage (1994); Reynolds (2006); Breen (2009); Ekland-Olson and Gibbs (2018).
[67] Gibbs (1972:8).

a particular way of creating theory.[68] Why? Theory should serve us, not the other way around. It should be a tool for gaining insight, nothing more.

WHAT TYPES OF CRIMINOLOGICAL AND CRIMINAL JUSTICE THEORIES EXIST?

We have discussed the uses and potential harm of theory as well as ways to "think theoretically" and to "do" theory. Here, we want to emphasize the fact that there are many types of criminological and criminal justice theories. They illustrate the range of phenomena covered by criminological and criminal justice research.

Most graduate programs in criminology and criminal justice teach a criminological theory course. In these courses, students typically will focus on crime theory. They learn, for example, about theories that seek to explain variation in why some individuals commit crime and others do not or why crime rates are higher in some communities or cities than in others.[69]

However, as we discussed earlier in the book, the causes of crime – as important as that focus may be – constitute but one of many topics of interest to scholars. They are interested as well in topics that broadly can be viewed as focused on the enactment, uses, and effects of law and on the operations and impacts of the criminal justice system and correctional system.[70] Work that focuses on such phenomena sometimes is lumped under the heading of "criminal justice theory," whereas work that focuses on crime causation is sometimes termed "criminological theory." As we discussed in Chapter 2, this terminology is not especially helpful. For example, prominent criminological theory books discuss theories about law-making or court sentencing.

What, then, does criminological and criminal justice research seek to explain? The topics run the gamut (see, for example, Chapter 9). To review, they include theories on the causes of: crime in general or specific types of crimes; why certain types of laws are passed, the role of different groups in creating these laws, and the implementation and effects of these laws; police decision-making; how law enforcement agencies are organized and how the culture within them can influence their actions and effectiveness; courtroom communities and court decision-making, including the causes of disparities in sentencing; jail and prison culture and programming, officer and inmate relations, and riots; probation and parole practices, including what shapes

---

[68] See, generally, Mills (1959), Homans (1964), Merton (1968), and Becker (1998).
[69] Cullen and Wilcox (2012); Akers *et al.* 2016).
[70] Duffee (2015); Akers *et al.* (2016); Mears (2017).

them, their implementation, and their effects; public views about crime and justice; criminal justice systems and correctional systems, including how they are administered and the effects of this administration on inmates and public safety; and more.[71]

For these and other topics, different theories exist. For example, there are specific theories that focus narrowly on a particular phenomenon, such as violent offending, sentencing disparities, prison riots, or terrorist events.[72] General theories exist as well. Minority threat theory, for example, has been used to explain sentencing laws, court decisions, prison administration practices, and more.[73] In addition, criminological and criminal justice theories can be "micro-level" (e.g., they focus on individuals), "macro-level" (e.g., they focus on groups, organizations, communities, cities, states, or even countries), or "multilevel" (e.g., they focus on several levels of analysis at once). Not least, criminological and criminal justice theory can be viewed as reflecting differing theoretical orientations. Peter Kraska has argued that at least eight distinct orientations guide criminological and criminal justice research.[74] These include: rationalism-legalism, system, crime control vs. due process, politics, social construction of reality, growth complex, oppression, and late modernity.[75] In addition to these orientations, there exist theories that specifically seek to account for the systems nature of criminal justice.[76] We have, then, a wealth of criminological and criminal justice theory!

WHAT IS THE RELEVANCE OF THEORY FOR DATA AND ANALYSIS?

For many people, including researchers, theory can seem like an activity that is divorced from data and analysis. It exists as a general guide to anticipate some relationship, but beyond that can be ignored. But theory can and should provide guidance about how we think about the data and analyses that we need to conduct to test for a relationship.[77] Without such guidance, we have no clear basis for knowing how to derive hypotheses,

---

[71] See, for example, Hagan (1989), Bernard and Engel (2001), Bernard *et al.* (2005), Kraska (2006), Maier-Katkin *et al.* (2009), Tonry (2009), Cooper and Worrall (2012), Thistlewaite and Wooldredge (2014), Duffee (2015), Akers *et al.* (2016), and Mears (2017).

[72] Useem and Piehl (2008); Dugan and Chenoweth (2012); Wooldredge *et al.* (2015).

[73] Stults and Baumer (2007).

[74] Kraska (2006) actually classifies them as "criminal justice theoretical orientations," to "criminological and criminal justice." However, the orientations that he identifies are ones that scholars have used to examine a wide array of phenomena that do not only fit into the conceptual category of "criminal justice." And, as we have emphasized, there is little consistent use in the terms "criminology" and "criminal justice"; the two can be viewed as encompassing each other.

[75] Kraska (2006:178).   [76] Mears (2017).   [77] Gibbs (1972, 1997).

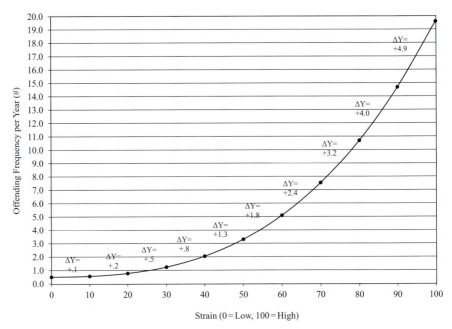

Figure 4.4 Theory as a guide to curvilinear causal relationships
Note: Adapted from Mears (2010:104).

measure key concepts, or model the relationship between a causal variable and an outcome.[78]

Consider a theory that argues that lack of self-control causes offending and, in particular, that individuals low in self-control are more likely to offend than are individuals who have high self-control.[79] How, though, exactly is self-control associated with offending? Is the relationship linear, such that each additional unit increase in self-control creates a proportionate decrease in the probability of offending? Or is the relationship curvilinear, such that each additional unit increase exerts less and less of an effect?

Consider a related idea: Perhaps greater strain causes more offending. However, at lower levels of strain, increased strain may exert little effect, while at higher levels it may greatly elevate the amount of offending committed by an individual.[80] Figure 4.4 illustrates this idea. We can see that as an individual moves from almost no strain (0) to some strain (e.g., 10, on a 100-point strain scale), the chance of more offending per year increases ever so slightly. More strain increases this chance. However, each increase of 10 points on the strain scale does not really increase the amount of

---

[78] Gibbs (1972, 1997).   [79] Gottfredson and Hirschi (1990).

[80] Agnew (1992) did not specify a curvilinear relationship between strain and offending. See, however, Agnew (2005) for a discussion of curvilinear and other nonlinear relationships that may characterize how various crime-causing factors are associated with offending.

offending much until strain hits 50 or 60. At that point, each increase of 10 points in strain results in many more acts of crime, and this effect keeps increasing. An increase from 90 to 100 in strain, for example, results in almost five additional crimes.

We have made up these numbers, but the point should be clear – a curvilinear relationship anticipated by a theory would require that we model that relationship. Otherwise, we risk assuming that the relationship is linear. In so doing, we misconstrue the causal effect of a given factor.[81] That can lead to misunderstanding. It also can greatly mislead policy. Consider, again, Figure 4.4. A program that targets high-risk offenders might reduce offending by reducing strain among participants. If the program participants all have highly elevated levels of strain, the effectiveness of the program stems from the fact that even modest reductions in strain among such individuals likely will return large dividends in criminal risk reduction. That does not mean, though, that the same would hold if the program were expanded to include low-risk, low-strain individuals! Here, even if we reduced their strain, we would see little reduction in offending given that the association between strain and offending is relatively weak at the lower end of the strain spectrum. A reduction from 30 to 20 on the strain scale, for example, only achieves 0.5 fewer crimes, whereas a reduction from 90 to 80 achieves four fewer crimes.

A theory may provide no explicit guidance about how precisely a causal force and outcome are related.[82] In this case, the researcher must think carefully about the theory's logic and whether it can be viewed as anticipating a linear or curvilinear effect. Nonlinear relationships may be common and so we should reflect carefully about the theoretical possibilities.[83] If it does provide guidance – for example, Hubert Blalock's theory of minority relationships anticipated a curvilinear relationship between the presence of minorities and the exercise of social control (as their presence increases, the effect on social control increasingly diminishes) – then we can use that guidance to develop hypotheses and analyses that test them.[84] In testing Blalock's theory, we would know to use statistical approaches that model curvilinear effects. In fact, failing to model such effects would not provide an appropriate test of the theory.

The development of hypotheses that help us test a theory is critical. Scientific progress occurs in large part through empirical tests of

---

[81] Ellenberg (2014) has provided a nice discussion of the perils of assuming linearity when reality involves nonlinear relationships.

[82] Mears *et al.* (2013a).

[83] See, generally, Agnew (2005), Mears *et al.* (2013a), and Ellenberg (2014).

[84] Blalock (1967); see, generally, Wang and Mears (2010a, 2010b).

hypotheses. If we test hypotheses that do not directly flow from a particular theory, then we are not actually testing that theory. The results of the hypothesis testing may be interesting, of course. However, they would have little relevance for helping to determine whether greater or lesser support for the theory exists.

Theory is also directly relevant for guiding measurement of core constructs. For example, self-control can be measured in a wide variety of ways.[85] Without guidance, researchers who test hypotheses about self-control may use different measures. They then create study results that are not comparable or perhaps may even be irrelevant as tests of self-control theory.[86]

Such issues are far from academic. Consider the many laws that target legal or illegal drug use as a cause of crime.[87] Some are quite specific. There might be law, for example, that calls for lengthy prison terms for manufacturing or distributing cocaine. Such a law would be premised in part on a theory about incarceration and its effect on crime rates or individual offending. We thus would want to use data that focuses on the manufacturing and distribution of cocaine and includes information about community crime rates or the recidivism of sentenced cocaine-manufacturing or cocaine-distributing offenders. Other drug laws are general. They target a wide class of behaviors, including drug "use." In this case, we need data on all drug offenders, not just those who manufactured or distributed cocaine. Theories, once again, dictate the kinds of data and outcomes that we should use to test them.

This process can work in reverse. That is, we might begin with data or analyses and work our way "up" to a theory. But exploring data can be risky. For example, we might "mine" data for possible patterns and weave a theory around what we observe. That amounts to fishing for results and can lead to explaining spurious (non-causal) associations.[88] The solution? Be cautious when "discovering" a pattern that may simply be a quirk of the data that we are using.

CONCLUSION

Theory is integral to the criminological and criminal justice research enterprise. Its role is simple – we use theory to understand the world around us. Using theory, however, can be a complex affair, not least because scholars do not all agree about the necessary ingredients that go into making a theory. That complexity should not deter researchers or those who consume

---

[85] Hassin *et al.* (2010).   [86] Goode (2008).
[87] Caulkins and Reuter (2017); Pollack (2017).   [88] Merton (1968); Gartner *et al.* (2012).

or use research from thinking in a theoretically informed manner. There is, though, no best approach to theory. What, then, to do?

We recommended different strategies that can be used to think theoretically. We recommended as well not relying exclusively on one. Instead, adopt different approaches and see which ones work best for you. In so doing, it will be clear that there is as much art as science to learning to think theoretically and, in turn, in evaluating or using theory.[89] The "art" lies in recognizing the salience of theory, that no one "best" way exists to creating theory, and that one should adopt theoretical accounts with a good dose of skepticism unless they have been subjected to considerable empirical scrutiny. The "science" lies in assessing the logical coherence of theories, the basis for deriving hypotheses or applying theories to empirical phenomena, and the most appropriate methodologies and data for testing them.

Criminological and criminal justice research entails a focus on a large universe of topics. There ultimately is room for many types of theories – "grand," general, middle-range, formal, and so on – that examine phenomena at many levels of analysis. In all such cases, theory ideally does not simply provide us with compelling explanations. It also guides us in developing empirical tests that can be used to adjudicate the veracity of these explanations. Theory is critical for developing hypotheses and for distinguishing scientific explanations from guesses, hunches, philosophies, and the like. To test hypotheses, though, we need data, as we discuss in Chapter 5, and then we must analyze the data, as we discuss in Chapter 6. Data and analysis thus are tied directly to theory. We therefore turn to discussion of data and then to discussion of analysis.

---

[89] Swedberg (2014).

5 The Role of Data in Research

INTRODUCTION

To this point, we have argued that answering any research question – as well as evaluating and using it effectively and appropriately – requires both science and art. Put differently, it requires familiarity with the "nuts and bolts" of research (the science) and the experience-driven, creative side of research (the art). This observation holds true with data as well.

Whether using data from surveys, focus groups, interviews, ethnographies, agencies, or the like, the science lies in knowing how to gather and use data in scientifically credible ways. The art lies in knowing how to leverage available data in ways that generate new and important insights. There is art in identifying the type of data one needs to answer a research question. There also is art in learning to think around corners. That includes anticipating challenges in data collection and pitfalls that can stem from reliance on certain types of data.

In keeping with the chef-in-the-kitchen analogy, data provide some of the core ingredients for research. The success of any chef's cuisine relies on an ability to understand the preferences of patrons, the types and amounts of different vegetables, meats, grains, and spices required for the recipes on the menu, how to identify high-quality products when purchasing them, and how to improvise as needed. Science contributes to successful cooking – one must know what tastes and textures result from combining certain ingredients. One must know, too, how cooking or baking conditions can affect dishes. The temperature and humidity in one's house, for example, can affect the chemistry involved in making bread.[1] But there is art as well.

---

[1] "The details of the physical mechanisms and chemical changes occurring inside the dough during its various processing states are extremely complex and only comparatively recently has it been possible to argue that breadmaking has become more of a science than an art" (Cauvain 2015:147).

A chef must be able to imagine new ways of combining ingredients that amaze and educate customers.

Credible research stems from similar processes. It entails familiarity with the types of data needed to answer certain questions. It requires knowledge about how to collect new data or organize existing data in ways that pass scientific muster. It involves understanding the strengths and limitations of information sources. And it flows from an ability to think imaginatively, to see possibilities in existing data or data that one might be able to collect. The art in doing so comes with experience, but it also comes from a sensibility, a willingness to envision different ways to answer questions.

The goal of this chapter is to describe the role of data in research and the importance of developing a researcher sensibility in thinking about data. To this end, we discuss first the importance of data. Second, we discuss the notion of "best" data (and, spoiler alert, how they do not exist, at least not in the way in which some may think). Third, we discuss strategies for obtaining useful data. Not least, we discuss nuts-and-bolts data considerations, such as preparing data for analysis, creating measures, documenting and describing coding decisions, and undertaking diagnostic checks of data prior to analysis.

We address, in short, a series of questions: What is the importance of data to the research enterprise? What are the "best" data? More precisely, what makes data useful? What types of data can be used in research? What strategies can be used to obtain the "best," most useful data? And what must be done with data prior to undertaking analyses?

THE IMPORTANCE OF DATA FOR RESEARCH

A one-sentence version of this chapter might read as follows: *A study is scientific because it answers a question with evidence from analysis of relevant high-quality data and not from anecdotes, non-systematic observations, extreme cases, or speculation.* Anything that uses the latter instead of the former may be useful, but it generally does not amount to science.

Table 5.1 provides a simple way to distinguish between data that flows from a scientific approach and data that reflects a non-scientific – or "pseudo-scientific" – approach. A scientific approach relies on theory and prior research to guide development of study questions and hypotheses. It employs credible research designs for generating useful and valid data. It uses sampling plans that flow directly from consideration of the research questions and knowledge about how to obtain the most representative sources of information. Scientific studies use valid measures of constructs,

Table 5.1 Scientific vs. non-scientific approaches to data	
Scientific approach	**Non-scientific approach**
• Theory and research guide questions	• Ignore prior theory and research
• Rely on credible research designs	• Rely on poorly designed research designs
• Rely on relevant and valid data	• Use anecdotes or no data at all
• Sampling plan reflects research questions	• Select anecdotes that confirm bias
• Employ valid measures identified in research	• Employ only measures that reflect bias
• Use methods to establish validity of measures	• Do not evaluate validity of measures
• Clearly state limitations	• Gloss over, ignore, or downplay limitations
• Rely on peer review to judge quality of data	• Assume that data are relevant and accurate

that is, the forces or phenomena that we want to examine. They use methodologies that can assist in assessing and improving the validity of measures. The studies explicitly identify limitations that may affect the generalizability or accuracy of the results. And, not least, the study data, as well as the research design and analyses, are subject to peer review by other scientists. In short, for science, data is central to creating knowledge.

A non-scientific, or pseudo-scientific, approach differs along each of these dimensions. Prior theory and research are ignored, anecdotes substitute for credible data and are employed to confirm preconceived biases, measures may reflect biases (e.g., only patterns that reflect one's preconceptions get reported), no accepted methodologies are used to assess the validity of measures, limitations are glossed over or ignored, and no scientific peer-review process is used.

Imagine, for example, a newspaper article with the headline, "Racial Bias in Criminal Sentencing Decisions." In the article, the writer recounts observations of a local judge. Two cases are examined. Both look identical except that one crime was committed by a white person and the other by an African-American person. The judge sentenced the white person to probation and the black defendant to a ten-year prison sentence, leading the reporter to describe the two cases as evidence of racial bias in sentencing. As compelling as the juxtaposition of the two cases might be, there is no science here. There is, for example, no systematic sampling of cases or collection of information that would allow us to identify the presence of bias.

What type of data *could* be used to identify on scientific grounds whether racial bias in sentencing occurs? There are numerous possibilities.

One option would be to seek court processing data from a county or state and randomly sample from a population of convicted felons. The random sample ensures that we can more safely generalize to the population (convicted felons). We then would want court information on sentencing outcomes. But we also would want information about the particular cases, especially information that might reveal how the cases differ in important ways. For example, perhaps all cases involving black felons tend to involve more serious crimes. If so, we can anticipate that black felons will be more likely to receive tougher sanctions. In a situation where no bias exists, we should find that when we examine black felons and white felons, respectively, *whose crimes involved offenses of similar severity*, no difference in punishment arises. In a situation where bias does exist, we may find that black felons who commit offenses of the same severity as that of whites receive tougher sanctions. An investigation of bias thus requires not only that we identify potential differences in sentencing outcomes, but also that we examine information – data – that will help us to determine whether the outcomes reflect bias or something else. We know that many non-random dynamics can give rise to differences in sentencing. Some may reflect bias, but others may not.[2] We need information that can help untangle which is which.

Analysis of data relevant for assessing bias results in a scientific study that differs from journalism. However, the mere fact of having some kind of data does not suffice. Other factors matter. For example, the representativeness or validity of data affect the quality of a study.

The use of data undergirds the scientific enterprise. No data, though are perfect. All data have strengths and weaknesses. Consider the example above. It involved a random sample of court records, which increases the likelihood that subsequent findings from analyses are generalizable to, or represent, all felons in the particular jurisdiction. Use of a sample creates the chance that it does not represent the population. (Alternatively, we could use all cases and avoid some of the inferential error that arises from sampling.) There also might be a problem with missingness in the data. That could affect the validity of our analyses. Reliance on electronic records might help to reduce this problem. But that holds true only if the court consistently and accurately enters information on each case. Our data also might include information that measures our outcome of interest (court sentencing decisions), our independent (explanatory) variable of interest (race), and other factors, such as offense severity and prior criminal record. This information would enable us to conduct analyses that increase our ability to identify potential bias in sentencing. The data might not include

---

[2] Mears *et al.* (2016b).

other information, though, that we would want. For example, it might not include information on plea-bargaining decisions.

Like any data, court records have weaknesses that need to be considered in evaluating the findings. These should be articulated along with corresponding statements about the uncertainty in our estimates. Uncertainty is part and parcel of the scientific enterprise. By identifying sources of uncertainty, we allow others to evaluate the generalizability and validity of our study results. For example, the court data in a given study might come from one jurisdiction; findings from the study therefore may not be generalizable to other jurisdictions. Also, the data likely would not provide information on prosecutors' views toward racial minorities; we thus would be unable to identify how their views influence sentencing decisions. The data also may not provide information on the quality of defense representation among whites and blacks, respectively. These limitations can make it difficult to determine how to interpret the causes of racial differences in sentencing, even ones that persist after controlling for offense severity or prior record.[3] Overcoming this limitation likely would require additional data, such as manually coding information from case files or from interviewing or surveying prosecutors or judges.

Other examples exist. This one, though, serves to highlight why data are critical to the research enterprise. It also highlights a related point – we do not just want *any* data for a scientific study. Rather, we want data that are *relevant* for our study questions. We want data that are representative, that accurately measure the outcomes (dependent variables) and explanatory factors (independent variables) of interest to us, and that address other theoretical concerns, such as whether associations among outcomes and explanatory factors are spurious. That said, as we discussed in Chapter 3, researchers pursue different goals (e.g., empirical description, identifying socially meaningful descriptions of phenomena and their causes, testing causal relationships, and answering policy-focused questions). A variety of considerations can come into play in selecting the "best" data for specific research goals and questions. In all cases, however, data constitute the critical platform on which to provide insights about crime and criminal justice that rise above personal beliefs or the merely anecdotal.

OBTAINING THE "BEST" DATA

Data do not just exist. They must be created. When researchers access already existing data, the information in the data set typically will have

---

[3] Mears *et al.* (2016b).

been collected by someone else for a different purpose. In either case – whether researchers collect their own (primary) data or use already collected (secondary) data – the quality of the research depends on the quality of the data. As the saying goes, "Garbage in, garbage out."

What data, then, are "best"? It is a trick question. No clear-cut answer exists. Much depends on the research questions involved.[4] Some questions may require certain types of data; others may be possible to answer with a variety of data sources. Ethical or cost constraints preclude certain study designs, thus forcing researchers to identify what may be best given such constraints. Experimental designs, for example, which are often considered to be the "gold standard" in research, sometimes cannot be ethically undertaken. Even when an experimental design would be ideal, it may be impossible or cost-prohibitive to implement.

Data options thus must be evaluated on a study-by-study basis. The evaluation should be based on analysis of many considerations. There is both science and art in this process. Here, we identify five overarching considerations that should inform one's thinking about the "best" – or most useful – data for scientific studies of crime and criminal justice.

Understand First that Data Are Not Intrinsically Meaningful

Many people, researchers included, endow data with some magical power, as if data have intrinsic meaning. They do not. We need theory or some set of broader research questions to bring them to life.

Consider research on the idea that a culture of violence exists that causes people to commit crime. In 1967, Marvin Wolfgang and Franco Ferracuti argued for just such a possibility.[5] Researchers subsequently undertook many studies to investigate if a violent culture caused, or at least was associated with, crime.[6] Many accounts of state-level variation in crime used the "South" as a measure of this "culture." Others used "percent Black." These measures, though, do not necessarily reflect anything about culture. They could be viewed as measures of other constructs. That does not mean that the studies that employed "South" or "percent Black" as indicators of a culture of violence were flawed; it does mean that the measures only made sense within the context of a theoretically framed study. Indeed, without the theoretical framing, it would be unclear how to interpret the "South" or "percent Black" associations with crime rates. Researchers do not generally prefer such crude indicators. They would prefer to have more direct measures of constructs.

[4] Khan and Fisher (2013).   [5] Wolfgang and Ferracuti (1967).
[6] See, e.g., Gastil (1971) and Messner (1983).

Consider another example – self-control research. Studies suggest that low self-control causes crime. We have, though, no objective direct measure of self-control. We cannot simply ask respondents in a survey if they have low self-control. (Actually, we can, but we might not be able to trust the accuracy of the self-assessments.) Rather, we can ask a range of questions that we hope taps into the construct, "self-control." We might ask respondents questions about how frequently they make impulsive decisions and then give them scenarios to consider when answering the questions. We also might collect responses to laboratory experimental conditions, such as the accuracy of recall after mentally taxing puzzles or exercises.[7]

There is, though, no direct measure of self-control that exists. It constitutes a theoretical construct – a phenomenon that we cannot directly observe. When we create a measure, we should remember that the construct cannot be directly measured and that its meaning stems from theory. We might liken a measure to someone's name – it may reflect their personality, but it is not a direct measure of their personality. The very idea of a personality itself only makes sense from some theoretical or conceptual framework. The problem lies in the fact that we all too frequently reify the meaning of a given measure. That is a mistake. A measure is just that, a piece of information – drawn from observations, survey questionnaires, administrative records from the police, courts, or prisons, and so on – that we hope accurately reflects a construct.

Table 5.2 illustrates this idea. In the first column, we have constructs across varying domains (e.g., crime, policing, courts, jails and prisons, and public opinion). In the second are sub-constructs – phenomena that still are not directly tangible, but collectively comprise a more general construct, in much the same way in which a set of objectives may collectively comprise a more general goal.[8] For each sub-construct, we need measures that accurately gauge the construct or sub-constructs. In turn, for any given measure, we need data. It should be evident that we might find ourselves in situations where data are not ideal. Our measures may only partially represent our sub-constructs and, in turn, our more general construct of interest.

Think about one of the most central areas of study in criminology and criminal justice – crime. It may seem odd to say it at first, but there is no objective measure of offending or crime rates. Crime is a construct, something that we never directly observe. We instead infer it from pieces of information. For example, even if a police officer witnesses a crime, such as a bank robbery or homicide, information is needed beyond what the officer sees to establish that a crime occurred. (Movies and television series

---

[7] Vohs and Baumeister (2016).   [8] Mears (2010).

	Construct	Sub-Construct	Measure	Data
Table 5.2 Data do not speak for themselves: Constructs, measures, and data				
Crime	Crime	Violent crime, property crime, public order crime	Assault, robbery, arson, rape, burglary, destruction of property, etc.	Survey; administrative records (police, court)
Policing	Police legitimacy	Procedural fairness, substantive fairness, responsivity to citizens, officer bias	Citizens' perceived satisfaction with the police during calls or interactions, response timeliness, racial proportionalities in traffic stops, searches, use of force, etc.	Survey; administrative records (police); interviews; ethnography
Courts	Punitive sanctioning	Punishments that emphasize retribution and control more so than rehabilitation	Incarceration rate, average duration of prison sentences, etc.	Survey; administrative records (court); interviews; ethnography
Jails and Prisons	Order	Compliance with rules, adherence to routines, physical order, quiet	Inmate misconduct rates, inmate victimization, officer use-of-force, deteriorating physical plant, noise levels, etc.	Survey; administrative records (court); interviews; ethnography
Public Opinion	Punitive vs. rehabilitative sentiment	Support for retribution as compared to support for rehabilitation	Extent of support for death penalty, prison sentences, longer prison sentences, rehabilitative treatment, vocational training, re-entry preparation, etc.	Survey; interviews; focus groups

mine this fact endlessly.) Similarly, conceptual issues come into play. Are we interested in someone's "criminality"? If so, what do we mean by that term? Is "criminality" a biological trait? If so, not everyone has a propensity toward crime. Perhaps, though, we view criminality as resulting from a cluster of criminogenic forces. If so, then everyone has some level of criminality. Let us assume that we agree with that statement. How, then, do we best measure "criminality"? It may vary. Why? Criminality amounts to a theoretical construct, one whose meaning reflects one's conceptualization of crime and its causes.[9]

The challenge here goes well beyond this example. Researchers measure individual-level offending in diverse ways. They may use data on past-year self-reported offending of any crime or multiple crimes, frequency of offending, diversity of offending, and so on. Or they may use court records data, which allow for measures such as past-year or any prior record of arrest or perhaps number of prior convictions. In each instance, we might use the measures to tap different constructs. Prior convictions, for example, might be viewed as a measure of criminal propensity *or* of police aggressiveness in enforcing the law in certain communities. In short, a measure only makes sense when viewed as a gauge of some more general construct, and the construct only makes sense within the context of a theory or particular question.

Theory and Research Questions Should Drive Data Decisions

Theory and research questions provide the foundation for studies. They determine what data are most relevant and useful. Researchers might begin a study with a particular set of data and imagine the possible studies that could be pursued. Even here, though, the researcher ultimately must arrive at a set of research questions. These ideally are grounded in descriptions of the theoretical logic that motivates them and the context that renders them important. That context typically consists of a gap in prior theory and research that one seeks to fill. It also can be a policy question that must be addressed to satisfy statutory requirements or that will contribute to debates about the merits of existing or proposed policies.

Proceeding without clarity about one's research questions typically results in a great deal of analysis and "facts" that have little clear import. Relevant and useful data must be directly related to answering well-articulated research questions. Consider the earlier sentencing study example. Official court records data in that case were useful in determining if racial bias in court sentencing exists. However, their usefulness in

---

[9] Sweeten (2012); see also Gottfredson and Hirschi (1990).

determining the precise cause of any identified bias was limited. The study could identify *whether* racial differences exist, but could tell us little about *why* they exist. If a study used the data and showed racial differences in sentencing persisted after controlling for various factors, we still would be left wondering what produced those differences. Variation in how law enforcement officers describe, in their written reports, their interactions with blacks? Racist prosecutorial views toward blacks? Inadequate defense counsel among black defendants? These and other explanations are anticipated by prior theory and research. If the study sought to identify what precisely gave rise to racial differences in sentencing, it would fall short because the data would not permit answering that question. Other data likely would be necessary. To illustrate, we might collect data from surveys of court actors and ask questions designed to gauge the extent to which prosecutors and judges hold stereotypical views of blacks as being more criminal.

Questions, in short, determine what data we need. If we want to know whether prosecutors' views about blacks affect their charging practices, then we need data that measure these views. If a data source does not provide that information, then it likely cannot be appropriately used to answer our research question. This issue is absolutely central to research. Confusion about it is why many studies do not provide credible insights for advancing knowledge or policy.[10]

Rely on Accurate Data

Data are useful when they are accurate. They can help us arrive at important insights. When inaccurate, data can generate "insights" that mislead science and policy. That statement may sound like a truism, but ensuring accuracy in data collection can be challenging. Recall the first consideration – data do not have intrinsic or objective meaning. Researchers refer to data accuracy as "validity." We need to have confidence that our data measure what we say they measure. That takes careful planning and analysis.

Different approaches in fact exist to gauging validity. For example, a measure might have "face validity" – that is, on the face of it, the measure seems to reflect or capture the construct that we wish to examine. "Content validity" gauges how well a measure, or set of measures, captures the diversity of the construct that we wish to study. We sometimes can increase the validity of our measures, depending on the type of data. For example, the science of survey research requires adherence to guidelines and

---

[10] Mills (1959); Merton (1968); Becker (1998).

principles for survey design to ensure accurate responses to questions. That includes attention to protocols for question wording and ordering.[11] A classic illustration is social desirability bias. If respondents feel that they should answer a question a certain way, they will tend to do so even when their true sentiment differs. We thus want to ask questions in ways that minimize this problem.[12]

Whatever data are used, one should consult the proper methodological literature before moving forward.[13] For example, precise guidance exists about measuring recidivism, and so one would want to consult relevant sources in estimating it.[14] Similarly, guidance exists for diagnosing and addressing missingness in data, a problem that can greatly undermine the validity of particular measures and analyses.[15]

Create or Use Data that Are Representative or Allow for Generalizable Statements

The "generalizability" of data refers to the extent to which we can draw conclusions from data. Generalizability can refer to how representative the data may be. A random sample, for example, should provide estimates of the prevalence of various phenomena that should more accurately reflect the true prevalence of these phenomena than would a non-random sample. It can refer as well to whether we can trust a causal estimate. One that we have more trust in has higher "internal validity." It also can refer to whether the results may be applicable to or represent other populations or areas. The technical term for this idea is "external validity"; studies that produce results that generalize quite well to other populations or areas have high external validity. For example, if a study examined policing attitudes among rural law enforcement agencies in the South, we might question whether the findings would accurately reflect what exists in urban northeastern cities.

One of the reasons that replication features prominently in the scientific enterprise stems from the fact that we cannot always trust that a study accurately represents a given population or area (external validity) or accurately estimates a causal effect (internal validity). For example, an evaluation of a community-policing program in a socially and economically disadvantaged area might find that the program fails to reduce crime. However, that does not mean that the program would be ineffective in more advantaged areas.[16] Observe, here, that our selection of data must

---

[11] Bradburn *et al.* (2004).   [12] *Ibid.*

[13] For guidance on how to do so, see Maxfield and Babbie (2015), Bachman and Schutt (2018), or Dantzker *et al.* (2018).

[14] Maltz (1984); Nagin *et al.* (2009); Villettaz *et al.* (2014); see also Sweeten (2012).

[15] Allison (2000); Horton and Kleinman (2007).   [16] Reisig (2010).

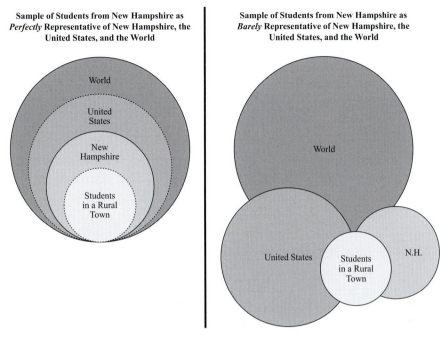

Figure 5.1 Sample representativeness

drive the focus of the study. If prior research establishes that community-policing benefits arise in all communities, we might want to turn our attention to other questions. If, however, the studies have focused only on disadvantaged communities, we might want to investigate why community policing is not effective in these places or to consider whether these effects generalize to all communities. Each focus requires a different sampling design and set of information.

Generalizability is no small matter. It stands at the center of the scientific enterprise. Consider the illustration in Figure 5.1, which depicts a situation where we take a random sample from a rural town. The sample might consist of children, adults, businesses, schools, churches, state legislators, or any other group. Let us assume that we sample high school students. We then seek to generalize from this sample. Perhaps we inquire about death penalty support. Our sample was randomly selected, but how well would it represent death penalty views among other groups in the rural town? In turn, how well would it represent the views of high school students in rural towns in general? Or high school students in New Hampshire? Or in the United States? Or, not least, in the world? In each instance, we can revisit the questions and extend our scope more broadly. For example, how well would the sample represent the views of citizens (not just students) in the rural town? Or in rural towns in New Hampshire or nationwide? Or the views of New Hampshire citizens or those of citizens throughout the United States or the world?

We have two options. First, we can assume that the sample of students perfectly represents almost any group that we can imagine. That, however, is implausible. For example, students' views can vary greatly from that of adults' views. Likewise, the views of those who live in rural areas can differ greatly from the views of citizens who reside in urban areas. It also is implausible to imagine that the views of New Hampshire citizens perfectly mirror those of people throughout the United States or the world. Assuming that the study generalizes to other groups and places, then, carries significant risk. Unfortunately, many popularized accounts of research ignore this risk. They report on a single study, one that relied on a sample from a specific group, then describe it in ways that suggest that somehow the findings generalize to the entire universe.

Our second option is the more realistic one: Assume that the sample, even if random, may barely, if at all, accurately reflect death penalty views among other groups in other places. The approach may feel less satisfying. It is, however, likely to be the more accurate one. To have confidence in any finding, we typically need a large number of studies. How many? There is no simple answer. One, though, is that we should continue conducting studies with diverse samples from different groups and areas to develop a thorough understanding of the consistency (or inconsistency) in a given estimate. This approach has the virtue of providing us with empirical information about estimates. Rather than guess or assume, we can rely on these estimates to describe the range of possibilities.

Although representativeness and generalizability provide important guideposts for researchers, they do not dictate the design of every study. If we are interested in a new area of inquiry for which little theoretical or research guidance exists, we might select samples or other sources of data with an eye toward developing theory or insights that then provide the foundation for a study that seeks to be generalizable.

Once again, no best way exists for proceeding. If there is one, it consists of seeking to clarify as precisely as possible a study's goals and its potential generalizability. Another consists of thinking clearly about what data sources best allow one to answer a study's questions. Still another consists of thinking carefully about sampling, which requires close consideration about the kinds of generalizations one seeks to make. And it consists of applying a healthy dose of skepticism. Many researchers, for example, may be prone to view secondary data as useful for their purposes simply because the data are readily available. That may lead them to overlook limitations in the data that at the least should be mentioned when describing study results.

Create and Use Trustworthy Data

Science involves trust. Can we trust that researchers did not simply make up data? That they reported all relevant limitations? That they conducted diagnostic checks to ensure the validity of their data? These and other questions frequently lurk in the background "behind" data. Consider an experiment. Room exists for researchers to ever-so-subtly influence enrollment, such that respondents most likely to have favorable outcomes wind up in the treatment group. That can happen unintentionally, or not. Either way, the possibility of it occurring means that we need to be careful when evaluating and using other research.

The risk of error in studies also means that we want to be careful in our own work. That can include any of a variety of steps, such as being organized, documenting decisions about which sources of data were used, explaining why some measures were used and others were not, investigating how much missingness exists for the measures, noting protocols that were followed when judgement calls needed to be made, and so on. Consider "offense severity." Many studies use some measure of this construct. However, disagreement exists about how to proceed. For example, do we use the most serious charge in an incident that involved multiple offenses? Or do we use some weighted average of the severity of all charges? Or do we use the most serious charge that led to a conviction? In these scenarios, the best that we can do, after consulting prior research for guidance, is to document how we proceeded and why.

TYPES OF DATA

Data almost always have flaws or limitations and sometimes extant data do not permit a credible empirical study. That means that researchers face tough decisions about data. Determining how best to proceed can be informed by an awareness of the types of data that exist, potential advantages and disadvantages of the data, and how the data might be used. Such an awareness is part and parcel of developing a researcher sensibility, which can help in making judgement calls about how to proceed.

Data do not, we want to again emphasize, somehow "speak for themselves." Decisions about data implicate decisions about related considerations, such as research design, questions, theory, analysis, and study goals.[17] These considerations frequently shape decisions about the types of data we should use and how to adjust our approach when we encounter pitfalls. For example, we may have built a study around the assumption that

---

[17] Mills (1959); Merton (1973); Becker (1998); Khan and Fisher (2013).

a particular data set would have a rich set of information about prisoner experiences. We might discover, though, after months of data preparation, that the information has been inconsistently entered. A researcher sensibility, including a willingness to think "outside the box," can help to address such challenges. For example, perhaps the prison system would allow us to administer an inmate survey. The resulting information might not be as representative of the overall prison population as we would like, but it nonetheless could help shed light on the questions that we wish to address.

Below, we discuss several data sources frequently used in criminological and criminal justice research. The discussion is not meant to substitute for comprehensive accounts.[18] These can readily be found in books on research methods and on special topics, such as surveys, interviews, and focus groups. Instead, we seek to highlight several points: (1) Many types of data exist; (2) advantages and limitations attend each of them; and (3) the best research selects data in ways that most directly answer a study's questions. As we then discuss in the next section, different strategies exist for obtaining data. Selecting such strategies, though, presumes an awareness of the types of data that exist for conducting criminological and criminal justice research.

Surveys

Survey questionnaires are a staple of the social sciences and may be the most commonly used type of data in criminology and criminal justice.[19] They provide data by asking individuals to answer questions. These questions can ask about almost any topic. For example, we might ask survey participants to express their opinions about a given issue – such as how strongly they agree or disagree with a statement or stance – or to answer questions about themselves or their experiences. We might also present respondents with hypothetical scenarios or vignettes. After doing so, we could ask them to answer questions about what they would do in those scenarios.

Surveys are helpful because we can use them to collect data on a wide range of phenomena relevant to addressing diverse research goals (see Chapter 3). For example, surveys can be used for empirical description. The US Census collects data in part for this purpose – it conducts a large-scale survey to describe people and places. The Bureau of Justice Statistics conducts a similar survey focused on inmates and prison facilities.[20] Surveys can also be used to identify socially meaningful descriptions. Consider a

[18] For an excellent overview of criminological and criminal justice data, see Huebner and Bynum (2016).
[19] Kleck *et al.* (2006).   [20] See, for example, Mumola (2000).

study of how race affects police officer decisions to make a traffic stop. You may first want to survey police officers to understand differences in how traffic stops are used and viewed. What a stop means to a police officer, for example, may vary greatly from what it means to a citizen.

We also can use surveys to test causal relationships. Many criminological and criminal justice phenomena can be measured with a carefully crafted survey. The surveys can include particular questions designed to measure such constructs as intelligence, criminal propensity, racial bias, and more. The measures then can be used to test hypotheses about the causes of crime or other phenomena. Not least, surveys can be used to answer policy questions. For example, a policy evaluation of solitary confinement might investigate when and why this housing is used, how frequently it is misused and why, as well as views about its effectiveness.[21] One special kind of survey, the factorial survey approach, can be especially useful in policy research. We present respondents with vignettes. Dimensions of the vignettes vary in ways that respondents may not readily discern, but that nonetheless influence their decisions.[22] That allows us to obtain a potentially more accurate assessment of how some factor, such as a defendant's race, affects respondents' views, such as how they would punish someone.

Other advantages of surveys exist. They allow researchers to hone in on specific attitudes or behaviors that would otherwise take a great deal of time to observe or gauge via other methods. In addition, surveys can be conducted highly efficiently. It costs little, for example, to administer questionnaires online, and responses can be readily compiled into a database. With that said, not all surveys can be conducted online. An illustration of that can be seen with surveying children – they may not be able to read and so would need the questions read to them. (We would want first to obtain parental consent to do so.)

There are important limitations of surveys to consider. For one thing, surveys can be expensive to do well. Much of the cost depends on the sample of interest. For example, for a few thousand dollars, researchers can contract with online survey companies to identify random, nationally representative samples and administer a web-based questionnaire. It is a different matter altogether to survey special populations, such as inmates or judges. We would need more time and money to interview such groups and to obtain high response rates. (Without high response rates, the concern arises that those who responded do not accurately reflect the views of the full sample. That said, the precise threshold for a response rate to yield accurate estimates of prevalence or the association among variables is

---

[21] See, for example, Riveland (1999) and Mears and Castro (2006).
[22] Wallander (2009).

complicated, and typically is much lower than many textbooks and journals suggest.[23])

In addition, surveys can be limited by the number of questions we can ask.[24] Prior research on effective survey design indicates that questionnaires that are too long have worse response rates than shorter questionnaires. Cost constraints come into play as well. A ten-minute survey allows for more questions than will a five-minute survey, but it also will cost more.

One of the central limitations of surveys is the risk of obtaining inaccurate information. Individuals are – you will not be shocked to hear! – not always entirely truthful or consistent in their views. In addition, they have different reading abilities and cultural backgrounds. These factors can affect how they interpret particular questions. Care, therefore, must be given to ensuring that questions are reliable, that is, that all respondents interpret the questions in the same way. We also need to ask questions in ways that will be more likely to garner accurate (valid) responses. We need questions not least that reduce the likelihood that respondents answer according to what they think is the ideal answer or that reflects well on them; put differently, the questions need to reduce the problem of social desirability bias or lying.

Sometimes, inaccurate responses happen because survey questions are poorly designed. For example, we may be interested in understanding the extent to which individuals prefer the death penalty, as opposed to life without parole, for convicted murderers. We have a theory that suggests that individuals hold more tempered views when they believe that multiple options exist. A survey is useful here. We could ask a sample of citizens the following question: "Do you support the death penalty?" We then could tally the responses, right? Not exactly. This particular question wording is problematic given our research question. It does not identify convicted murderers as the focus of the policy and it does not present respondents with the counterfactual scenario (life without parole) that was part of our research question. A better approach might be to ask, "On a scale of 1 to 5, where '1' is 'do not strongly support' and '5' is 'strongly support,' to what extent do you support use of the death penalty for convicted murderers?" We then could use the same scale and ask elsewhere in the survey, "To what extent do you support use of the death penalty for convicted murderers when life without parole is an option?" These questions align better with the research question and the theory we seek to test.

A key challenge of surveys – as with most any data collection or creation – involves effective planning. A solid plan can result in a

---

[23] Pickett (2017).   [24] See, generally, Dillman et al. (2014).

well-designed survey that elicits accurate responses and provides credible insights; a poor one can result in mush. The planning should include careful tailoring of survey length, question wording, strategies to boost respondents' confidence that their responses will be anonymous, and even consideration of the setting in which a survey is administered, such as in a crowded classroom or in the privacy of one's home. Fortunately, a substantial body of guidance exists to help with planning surveys.[25] In the end, though, there is no substitute for independently thinking through, on one's own – researcher sensibility in tow – the precise goals of a study and the options that exist given available resources.

Interviews

Interview data provide a foundation for obtaining rich information about particular phenomena. Why? Interviews typically involve a more intensive version of questioning than surveys.[26] (Some surveys entail in-person administration of a questionnaire, but typically do not include questions of an open-ended nature.) Qualitative studies that use interviews, however, do not use questionnaires or, if they do, the questions tend to be open-ended. For example, instead of being asked to answer a closed-ended question ("How much do you support sex offender residency restrictions?") on a scale from "1" (strongly agree) to "5" (strongly disagree), a respondent instead might be asked, "How do you feel about sex offender residency restrictions?" This approach means that researchers may have to rely on non-random samples and to allow for more time for listening to and exploring responses.

The interview format itself will fall along a continuum of structured to non-structured, the selection of which depends entirely on one's research needs. Some research questions require structured interviews. Here, all respondents are asked a consistent set of specific questions. Other studies may require leeway to let respondents guide the direction of an interview.

As with surveys, interviews can serve different research goals. They can be used for description. For example, we might use a more unstructured, open-ended interview process to gather information about a particular phenomenon. For example, we might interview prison officials and officers about their views of solitary confinement and the potential benefits and problems with its use.[27] In so doing, we might learn about a range of

---

[25] See, for example, Dillman *et al.* (2014).

[26] See, generally, Patton (2015) for a discussion of interviews, focus groups, and other qualitative methods.

[27] See, for example, Mears and Watson (2006).

potential benefits and problems. We would not know much about their prevalence, but we would know to study them. We also could use the interviews to gain insight into how prison officials view the meaning of solitary confinement. That is, what counts as solitary confinement? For example, how many hours in isolation would be viewed as "solitary confinement"? What does a stay in solitary signify to officers about an inmate? We also might use the interviews to glean insight into the causal mechanisms through which solitary confinement might contribute to various outcomes (e.g., misconduct, recidivism). Not least, the interviews might allow us to investigate policy questions. These could include a focus on how solitary confinement is used, what impacts it may have, and what options prisons can use to manage prisoners.

The advantages of interview data stem from the open-ended approach to questioning. A good interviewer can improvise as needed to elicit responses from participants and will allow the interviewee to take the conversation in different directions. This approach can provide opportunities for discovery that surveys or other data collection strategies do not allow. Consider a survey-based approach to studying community policing. A top-down approach by the researcher might lead to a questionnaire that focuses on residents' views about whether crime has gone down. That makes sense – policing generally entails a focus on public safety. However, interviews with residents might reveal that they tend to prioritize other benefits. Perhaps they report that they feel reassured that the police will respond if called or that officers will treat residents respectfully. Such information would illuminate the need for a large-scale study that included questions that tapped these possibilities.[28]

Interview data allow for in-depth understanding of phenomena. But there are trade-offs. What we learn from interviews from small, non-random samples may not reflect what the broader population thinks. Researchers, like anyone, can be prone to believe what they think must be true. That may lead them to discount some observations made by interview subjects and to prioritize other observations, especially those that accord with their own biases. (The problem can be reduced through the use of multiple coders and assessing interrater reliability.[29]) Another limitation: collecting, recording, and coding interview data can take a great deal of time. Whereas survey data may be readily analyzed, interview data cannot.

"Quantitative" researchers – those who rely on analysis of survey, administrative record, or experimental data – sometimes view qualitative research as non-quantitative and less rigorous. That view is incorrect.[30]

---

[28] Reisig (2010); Lum and Nagin (2017).
[29] See, for example, Kurasaki (2000); Campbell *et al.* (2013).   [30] Feagin *et al.* (1991).

Qualitative studies are quantitative. They use samples and data. Their lack of representativeness can mean, though, that analysis of them can lead to inaccurate statements about the social world, causal relationships, and policy impacts. The same can be said of quantitative studies. For example, a national survey is but a reflection of a country at one point in time. The survey data may provide an inaccurate portrayal of society over time or even at the time the survey was conducted. To illustrate, if it includes only questions about support for punishing offenders, it will not accurately reflect the fact that the public might well report support for rehabilitation as well as punishment.[31]

In the end, a study's questions should dictate the methodology followed. That methodology then should be clearly justified and limitations should be described. This axiom applies to virtually any study and is what contributes to making a study scientific.

Focus Groups

Focus groups are similar to interviews except here researchers hold discussions with groups of individuals.[32] As with interviews, focus groups can vary in their structure. They might be tightly focused around one question or loosely structured to explore several. That said, the typical focus group approach begins with a list of guiding questions, which encompass the range of topics the researcher wants the group to consider. Initial broad-based questions provide a "warm up" to help participants feel comfortable sharing their perspectives. The questions then can turn to more specific or potentially contentious issues.[33]

Conducting effective focus groups requires experience and skill in making participants feel comfortable, designing a set of questions that directly relate to a study's goals, and ensuring that these questions can be sufficiently explored in the time allowed. It also requires "art" – one must be able to "read" group dynamics and find ways to put individuals at ease. In addition, one must be able to listen carefully, ask nuanced questions that build on unexpected statements, and nudge conversations in new directions when comments begin to become repetitive.

Focus groups offer several advantages. First, in a group setting, participants may be more willing to share and express their views. There is "safety in numbers." In addition, groups can provide a setting in which participants can fuel each other's thinking, helping them to recall or consider nuances that, on their own, they might miss. Many studies examine how a given causal force, X, contributes to some outcome, Y. The accounts tend to focus

[31] Cullen *et al.* (2000).   [32] Patton (2015).   [33] Stewart and Shamdasani (2015).

on direct effects, that is, whether X causes Y. Focus groups, like interviews, can be useful for identifying contingent, or interactional, relationships. An individual might think that a court defendant's demeanor can greatly affect judicial leniency, but then another focus group participant highlights that for some "get-tough" judges, demeanor seems to be largely irrelevant. Others in the group might echo that view (or not), or identify other such examples. These more complicated relationships sometimes can be more readily identified in focus groups than through statistical analyses.

Of course, groups can push individuals into views that they really do not share. A good focus group facilitator will take steps to avoid this problem. In addition, the insights from focus groups may not be representative or accurate. Participants may make observations that are untrue or, if true, may be so only for a small subset of a larger population. For example, focus groups with gang members might reveal that they like to terrorize homeless citizens. Perhaps. But out of boredom a prominent gang member might flippantly shift the focus group discussion to a made-up story about harassing a homeless man. Other members join in to show support to that member. In the end, we end up with an account that does not well reflect this particular gang's activities or those of others in the community. In addition to this type of problem, there is, not least, a pragmatic consideration: It can take a considerable amount of time to arrange for focus groups, to transcribe all observations, and to analyze the resulting information.

Ethnographies

An ethnographic study requires a researcher to become immersed within a setting, such as a police department, court, prison, or community.[34] The ethnographer might be an active or a non-active participant. Regardless, the goal typically is to absorb and describe as much as possible about the day-to-day interactions among individuals or groups, the social meanings attached to particular actions or expressions, and the social forces that shape these interactions and their meaning. The data consist of extensive descriptive notes and reflections on what one observes.[35]

In Chapter 6, we discuss "units of analysis," or the level at which observations tend to accumulate. For example, many studies use individuals as the unit of analysis; information about each individual in the study is used to gain insight into variation in behaviors among individuals. Interviews and focus groups can lead us down the road of placing individuals at

[34] See, for example, Kupchik (2006); see, generally, Goffman (1989) and Patton (2015).
[35] For example, Mills (1959).

the center of the action – somehow it must be characteristics of individuals that most matter. By contrast, ethnographies can help us to focus not only on individuals, but also on groups, organizations, institutions, and the like. To illustrate, an ethnography of juvenile court decision-making might lead us to consider judges, prosecutors, defense attorneys, probation officers, juveniles, or, more likely, how all of these groups interact with one another.[36] It also might lead us to consider the role of families and school representatives in juvenile court decisions. We would likely focus, too, on caseload pressures and the larger political context in which the court operates.

Ethnographic research provides an opportunity to gain insights that could never be captured by surveys, interviews, or focus groups. For example, it allows researchers to observe first-hand the day-to-day lives of urban drug dealers,[37] how severely disadvantaged groups navigate interactions with police,[38] how asylums treat mental patients and inmates,[39] and the work and operations of thieves and "fences" (i.e., those who help to sell stolen goods).[40] One of the most famous ethnographies in criminology and criminal justice is Gresham Sykes' *The Society of Captives*.[41] Sykes spent three years observing a maximum-security prison in Trenton, New Jersey. During this time, he collected numerous observations, inmate and officer accounts, corrections officials' views, and more. His intensive data collection enabled him to describe and explain the social system within prisons. He identifies different types of characters – such as "real men" (who do their time with dignity), "ball busters," "punks," and so on. He identifies, too, how these characters respond differently to the deprivations that attend to imprisonment. More than that, he identifies how social order in prison stems from a dynamic interplay between officers and inmates. All of that complexity would be difficult, if not impossible, to establish through other types of data.

With ethnographic research, we obtain what Clifford Geertz has described as "thick description."[42] Whereas some research studies provide the equivalent of a black-and-white depiction of a narrow part of a neighborhood, ethnographies provide the equivalent of a color photograph of the entire area. This description can include empirical details about particular situations, events, or the like, the social meaning of various activities and interactions, and the causal forces that give rise to them. In so doing, it can provide fodder for theories about these situations, events, or the communities within which they occur.

---

[36] Emerson (1969); Cicourel (1976); Kupchik (2006). [37] Contreras (2013).
[38] Goffman (2014). [39] Goffman (1962). [40] Steffensmeier (1986).
[41] Sykes (1958). [42] Geertz (1973).

There is, alas, nothing free in life. Ethnography requires the ability to develop rapport with subjects and to "fit in." Without it, researchers cannot gain entrée to some groups, organizations, or communities. In addition, the people they observe may change their behavior because they know that they are being watched by someone whom they do not trust. Ethnographies also require considerably more time than other data collection strategies. It may take many months to gain access to a particular group or setting, and many more months of residing in it before the study "subjects" come to trust the researcher and before the researcher can begin to make sense of what they observe. There is, too, the question of when the study should stop. The open-ended nature of an ethnography means that there may be no natural end point. One can never really "fully" describe social patterns and dynamics. An additional challenge: The data – notes, recordings, photographs, videos, and more – do not readily lend themselves to simple tabulation. To the contrary, one typically must employ non-statistical approaches to reviewing the data to discern patterns. There is the problem that researchers may significantly misinterpret what they see and hear. And, not least, a number of moral challenges arise. For example, what is the role of a researcher in instances when they observe or are even pushed to take part in the actions of the group being studied? What to do when these actions may endanger others? Such questions assume particular salience for studies of crime. One can hardly become embedded within a criminal gang, for example, and not witness crime.

Administrative Records

Some research questions can be answered by collecting data from administrative records, which consist of data routinely collected by agencies, departments, and organizations. These records may be useful for many research questions. For example, police departments collect and archive data on arrests. Courts do the same for processing and sentencing decisions. Jails, prisons, and probation and parole departments do the same for inmates or individuals on supervision. To illustrate, most state prison systems maintain electronic databases that systematically record inmate movements between facilities, program participation, behavioral problems, visitation, physical and mental health status, and more.

If an organization consistently records accurate information, and if they make it available for study, researchers can quickly have access to rich data. The data sometimes may span many years and otherwise would have been impossible to collect independently. With the data, we can develop and test theories or seek to inform policy discussions. The advent of computers has allowed for automated, electronic databases that not only collect enormous amounts of information, but also make the information readily available for analysis to researchers. Criminological and criminal justice research has greatly advanced in recent decades precisely because of this situation. As one illustration, much more now is known about prisoners, what they experience during their confinement, and how incarceration may influence recidivism.[43]

An added advantage of administrative records data can be that one has access to an entire population. In many research studies, scientists must rely on random samples because it may be the most cost-efficient option. That situation can create error, especially if one wants generalizable information about relatively rare events or for groups, facilities, or areas that constitute a relatively small proportion of the larger population of study. Access to data for all groups, facilities, or the like can avoid this problem.

Juxtaposed against such benefits are some challenges and limitations. A simple problem is that researchers may not know that such data exist. Only those who archive data know all the ins and outs of the data, and they do not necessarily communicate regularly with individuals outside their agency. Sometimes agencies or organizations do not want to share data or cannot do so. Government agencies, for example, may have strict rules and restrictions about sharing data and some organizations may have concerns about how the data will be used. Sometimes agencies may not embrace research or they may even resist it. That will be likely if a researcher previously undertook a "Gotcha" study that unfairly cast the agency in a bad light. It can take work, then, to create trust and understanding before it will be possible to access administrative records data. That may include identifying research questions of mutual interest. It may also include creating ground rules for which data may be used, the right of an agency to review any results, and the right of the researcher to publish them.

A central limitation of administrative records data is that they generally will not have been collected with the goal of answering a particular research question. Thus, relevant measures may not be available. For example, we could use traffic stop data from state police departments to examine how demographic characteristics of individuals stopped by police affect decisions to search a vehicle. We could even geocode those stops to examine how demographic characteristics interact with contextual characteristics to affect officer decisions. If, however, our research question required something more specific about the officer or the stop, we would be out of luck. Perhaps we hypothesize that racist views influence officer decisions to stop a driver.

---

[43] Mears and Cochran (2015).

Administrative records data almost assuredly will not include information on such views.

Other limitations warrant mention as well. For example, administrative records data may suffer from missing information. To illustrate, mental health assessments might have been conducted of all inmates at intake, but, for some reason, half or more of the assessments may never have been entered into the database. Also, administrative records data can be confusing. Researchers tend to think in terms of measures and samples that can be used for analysis. By contrast, agency records frequently are created more for case-by-case decision-making. Accordingly, they allow for ready access to reams of information about a particular individual or case. Transforming that information into a useable research data file can be time-consuming. A responsive and reliable data expert from a source agency can greatly reduce this problem. However, even when these individuals exist, they may not have the time to provide extensive training on using the data.

Still Other Data Sources: Content Analyses, "Big Data," and More

Data sources are constrained mainly by our imagination. Creative researchers find ways to develop new data, access existing information, conduct experiments, discern naturally occurring experiments, and so on. Precisely for that reason, we cannot here discuss all possible sources of data. That said, there are two additional ones that we want to highlight – content analyses and so-called "big data" – along with the catch-all category of "other."[44]

We emphasize content analyses and "big" data analyses because of the advent of the Internet. Content analysis entails extracting data from already existing sources, whether in text, visual, or auditory form.[45] The data can include collection of news stories over time, historical documents, government records, and information from websites.[46] Data can be culled from social media accounts to obtain insights into members' opinions, reactions, and behaviors.[47] These data can even be geocoded to examine how views or behaviors may vary across place or time.[48] Content analysis constitutes a time-honored research methodology. It is especially useful for gaining insight into how different groups view certain phenomena. Rather than examine what people report in a survey or interview, content analysis entails examination of what people or groups have expressed as they go

[44] Many discussions of data exist – see, for example, Piquero and Weisburd (2010).
[45] Krippendorff (2004).
[46] Gerstenfeld *et al.* (2003); Taylor (2009); Rubin (2012); Campbell (2014).
[47] See, for example, Williams and Burnap (2016).
[48] See, for example, Takhteyev *et al.* (2012).

about their day-to-day lives. Media accounts of criminals, for example, can be examined for how journalists typify white criminals versus black criminals to discern if subtle differences arise in the characterizations of the two groups.[49]

The Internet has enabled far more than the ability to widen the spectrum of possible data sources for content analyses. It, along with computers, has allowed for the emergence of "big data."[50] "Big data" refers simply to data sets that are large. No widely agreed upon definition exists for knowing when data are "big."[51] Even so, when companies and government agencies can collect a diverse amount of information for thousands and millions of individuals, we might comfortably refer to the resulting data as "big." The data not only are "big," they also frequently can be readily accessed, downloaded to a laptop, tablet, computer, or any other device that allows for statistical analysis, and then analyzed.

These data provide unprecedented opportunities to conduct research. For example, researchers might leverage social media data to gauge citizens' perceptions about policing and public safety.[52] Police arrest records data, when examined in "real time," can provide up-to-the-minute insights into the evolving nature of crime across places.[53] If these data are merged with Census data or other information about neighborhoods, it becomes possible to identify how community characteristics may be associated with crime trends or the effects of interventions, such as "hot spots" policing. Such examples barely scratch the surface. Several others illustrate the point: There now exist large data repositories of genomic and DNA data that researchers can use.[54] This advance occurred only in recent decades. It has created new opportunities for research that have only begun to be investigated. Similarly, correctional systems frequently archive electronic data that enable one to track trajectories of an individual's behavior over time. Court data allow much the same. They also allow one to examine processing decisions of individuals.[55] Such data enable scholars to use machine learning algorithms – what is essentially a continuously updated prediction model – that can improve recidivism or court-processing predictions as more data accumulate about individuals.[56]

"Big data" provide a powerful foundation for research, but they do not magically generate important insights. Like all data, they are not intrinsically meaningful. They require theory and conceptual designs to inform

---

[49] Entman and Rojecki (2000); Dixon (2008).   [50] Brayne (2017); Završnik (2017).
[51] Chan and Moses (2016).   [52] See, generally, Lum and Nagin (2017).
[53] Brayne (2017).   [54] Liu and Guo (2016).
[55] Mears and Cochran (2015); Cochran and Mears (2017).
[56] See Berk (2008, 2012) and Berk and Bleich (2013); see, generally, Ridgeway (2013), Ridgeway and MacDonald (2014), Mears and Cochran (2015), and Mears (2017).

analysis of them.[57] Despite the large scale of the data, they can often be limited in scope. Any given "big data" source will not necessarily include all information relevant to one's particular research questions. In fact, it is not uncommon for especially large "big data" collections to be primarily focused on the accumulation of a single measure (e.g., arrest, an opinion on one issue). That means that research may be limited to simple empirical description rather than prediction or evaluation of policy. Findings from analyses of typical "big data" sources may also be limited in their generalizability. Social media data, for example, represent only those individuals or groups who use such media. Not least, just because the data are "big" does not mean they are accurate or that they cannot be examined in ways that reflect researcher or organizational biases. Sarah Brayne's analysis of how a large urban police department used "big data" for surveillance purposes illustrates that discretion still governs the process of selecting analyses and interpreting the results.[58] Size may matter, but it does not dictate that research will generate more accurate or relevant information.

We have only skimmed the surface of data possibilities. Theory can help guide us in seeing the possibilities, and so can awareness of different analytic approaches (discussed in Chapter 6) and causal relationships (discussed in Chapter 8). Explorations of extant research – studying what others have used to investigate crime and criminal justice – can help as well. Biosocial researchers, for example, have made great strides in the types of data that they collect. These data allow for much more advanced, nuanced approaches to understanding the biological foundations of criminal behavior.[59] The advances have been so rapid in recent decades that it would be folly to pursue research without first canvasing the literature to see what data already exist. Insights about data possibilities can come, too, from examining different data collection approaches. To illustrate, life-course researchers increasingly have used life-event calendars, in which study participants document activities and events in their day-to-day lives, to guide data collection aimed at understanding the onset and persistence of, and desistance from, offending.[60] This method opens the door to creating more dynamic portraits of individuals and the factors that influence their lives. A final illustration – although experiments occur more rarely in the social sciences than in other fields, they have become increasingly common in criminological and criminal justice research.[61] Investigating opportunities for experiments thus should be part of any researcher's toolkit.

---

[57] Chan and Moses (2016).   [58] Brayne (2017).
[59] Pratt *et al.* (2016); Theall *et al.* (2013).   [60] See, for example, Horney *et al.* (1995).
[61] Farrington and Welsh (2005).

Mixed-Methods Data Collection

For many research questions, multiple sources of data can be helpful. Scholars refer to the use of two or more types of data in a study as a "mixed-methods" approach.[62] The data might come from administrative records, surveys, interviews, focus groups, ethnographies, or the like, or any combination of them. The analyses one uses necessarily will vary by type of data.

To illustrate, we might be interested in understanding variation in how prisons use solitary confinement. If a large literature on the topic exists, we can draw on it to test competing ideas about what drives the variation. One theory might argue that the culture of some prison facilities drives placements in solitary confinement. Another might argue that administrative pressures drive up placements. Yet another might argue that a decline in rehabilitative programming is to blame. And still another might argue that changes in the types of inmates placed in prisons accounts for increased use of solitary confinement. What, though, if little to no prior research exists? We then have little basis for knowing what differences might exist or what data we should collect or examine to explain the differences. A mixed-methods approach might be helpful here. We might first conduct focus groups with staff or inmates to learn from them differences that they think we should expect and what factors would explain the differences. We might also examine administrative records data to explore how frequently solitary confinement occurs and whether some groups, such as younger inmates or racial or ethnic minorities, are placed in it more than other groups.

Together, the two methods allow for a more credible set of findings. The focus groups enable us to investigate possible differences that we might not have anticipated. The administrative data allow us to check empirically whether the differences actually exist, and possibly to test some of the suggested reasons for any differences. The two approaches can complement each other in other ways, too. For example, preliminary analysis of the records data might reveal that young inmates disproportionately experience solitary confinement. We might then use the focus groups to explore reasons for why that difference exists. Perhaps younger inmates face a high risk of victimization from older inmates and so are segregated not as punishment, but to protect them from victimization. Such an insight would not readily arise purely from analysis of the administrative records.

Studies that utilize mixed methods will typically require substantially more time and resources. Each separate data collection effort carries unique costs and challenges. In addition, the study will require multiple areas of

---

[62] See, for example, Creswell and Clark (2011).

expertise to navigate each type of data and the analyses that each requires. The trade-off? Mixed-methods studies can provide potentially more powerful insights and conclusions. They provide researchers with the ability to use multiple sources to describe the contours of a problem, the social meaning or way of referring to it, its causes, and factors that might shape policy implementation or impacts.[63] That said, mixed-methods studies that rely on poor data and analyses simply produce poor – untrustworthy – results. If they cannot be done well, it generally is better not to do them at all.

One prominent illustration of a mixed-methods approach can be seen in Jerome Skolnick's 1966 study, *Justice without Trial*.[64] Skolnick sought to understand how justice unfolds, and he began with the observation that the police make many decisions about how to handle cases and that most cases get pled out before reaching trial. As a result, Skolnick observed, "the system of administering criminal justice in the United States is a system of justice *without* trial."[65] In an effort to understand this system, he drew on a wide range of data sources. He selected one large city as a case study and immersed himself in charting the organizational structure of the criminal justice system there, collecting reports that quantified case flows through the courts. Skolnick then observed public defenders as they interviewed defendants and walked the defendants' cases through arraignment, preliminary hearings, and so on. With several months of such observation – with attendant handwritten notes about what he saw – Skolnick then repeated this process with the police to understand the "law enforcement side of the criminal courts system," and did the same with the District Attorney's office.[66] Observations, interviews, ride-alongs with police officers, and review of agency reports all merged together in his comprehensive analysis that highlighted the central role of the police in shaping justice.

STRATEGIES FOR OBTAINING THE "BEST" DATA

The "best" data are ephemeral – we never have the data that would be perfect for illuminating some phenomenon. We can, though, rely on strategies for obtaining the best data possible given time, resources, and ethical constraints. Familiarity with these strategies can help create options. Which options should be pursued ultimately requires judgement calls about the importance of different research goals and the constraints one faces. A researcher sensibility entails being aware of the various options. It entails, too, the ability to balance a number of scientific, but also pragmatic, considerations. Here, we describe several strategies that can

---

[63] Mears (2010).   [64] Skolnick (1966).
[65] Skolnick (1966:13; emphasis in the original).   [66] Skolnick (1966:31).

be used and that serve indirectly to underscore that research entails as much art as science.

Existing Data: Use It When Appropriate and When You Can!

There is no need to reinvent the wheel. That axiom applies in life and to research as well – if a set of data exists that can help us to answer a question, we should use it, not collect more. In the last several decades, this option has become increasingly available because many agencies record information electronically. It also has become more available because of data repositories in university or institute centers, government agencies, and foundations. The National Archive of Criminal Justice Data (NACJD), which is part of the University of Michigan's Interuniversity Consortium for Political and Social Research (ICPSR), is an example of one such archive. Sometimes the data may be freely accessed. Other times, permission may be needed to use them. Although existing data can be helpful, it of course does not make sense to use them when they do not permit us to answer the questions that interest us.

Don't Just Work through "Gatekeepers" to Obtain Data – Engage Them for Insights

Researchers can be like anyone else – selfish. They want to pursue their own interests. However, this approach does not mean that others will support our research projects. Individuals typically participate in studies because they benefit in some way, not because they have to do so (when the studies are ethically conducted). Much the same holds for organizations. They will be more likely to help researchers if they see a benefit to doing so. There is therefore a need to find ways to enlist the support of others and ensure real benefits to them of helping with a study.

This way of framing the matter sees individuals as "gatekeepers" who must be traversed. They may well be gatekeepers, reluctant ones at that. As with many things in life, diplomacy and courtesy go a long way to gaining cooperation. Agency officials or research staff will be more likely to help if a researcher respectfully approaches them. Sometimes little effort is required. Other times, agencies may resist. But they might be willing to help out if the specifics of the request, including the time demands on them and the uses to which the data will be put, are clarified. For scientists, learning to communicate research requests in a straightforward language is a must. A somewhat similar axiom holds for policymakers and criminal justice administrators. For them, an awareness of what research entails can be critical for encouraging relevant research.

Gatekeepers are not, however, just individuals who provide access to data. They can provide critical insights into the questions that motivate a particular study. That is yet another reason to work on building professional relationships with them and their employers. It is a reason, too, for proceeding with an open mind and a willingness to seek insights from those with "boots on the ground" insights. Corrections agency officials or research staff, for example, might be able to identify unique issues with their data or possibilities for investigating interesting questions.[67]

Think Clearly about Samples and Sampling

Many people – researchers included – do not always think clearly about the samples, or sampling approaches, used in studies. For example, a scholar might use a secondary data set from an archive, publish frequently using these data, and never really think much about how the data were generated. They also may never have collected their own data.

Sampling is, though, another central part of research. It can refer to taking a random selection of individuals, groups, organizations, or the like, collecting data, analyzing it, and then using the results to generalize to the population from which the sample was drawn. But sampling entails more than that. A great deal of research involves sampling from specific groups or populations because our research questions demand it. To illustrate, we might seek to test a theory about minority members' perceptions of police. If minorities represent a relatively small amount of a population in a given community, we may need to oversample minority citizens so that we have a large enough sample to test the theory. This oversampling will ensure that we have enough individuals to detect substantively important differences that are statistically significant.[68] Similarly, if a research question calls for comparisons of twins to account for potential heritability in criminal behavior, we will need a sample that contains twins.[69]

In these cases, we ideally have random samples. Many times, though, we cannot obtain random samples. Or such samples may not be relevant for a particular type of study. For example, a case study typically consists of just one person, organization, neighborhood, event, or the like. It is justified by what it may teach us about that case and possibly about others.[70] It is an approach that helps to create theory, not establish cause-and-effect.

---

[67] See discussions in Farabee (2005) and Mears (2010).
[68] Lipsey (1998); Ellenberg (2014).   [69] Beaver *et al.* (2009); Beaver (2016).
[70] Feagin *et al.* (1991).

Whether the sample is random or non-random, it needs to be justified based on careful consideration of a study's goals, prior research, and what ethically can be undertaken with available resources. Perhaps no studies have ever examined why police chiefs tend to be men.[71] What is our goal? If we want to identify how many female police chiefs exist nationally, we would need to find data that permit that assessment. If our goal is to understand why women are underrepresented as executives in law enforcement agencies, we could develop theories that provide plausible accounts. That would be a good start. We might, however, interview police chiefs to tap them for possible insights. They would be uniquely positioned to shed light on possible explanations. We likely would want to interview men and women who are police chiefs. However, logistical challenges might restrict us to focusing on a few jurisdictions near to where we live or work. The latter approach would be understandable, but it also would raise flags. We therefore would want to consider ways in which our sample might be unique that would limit the relevance of any insights to other law enforcement agencies or contexts.[72] That observation holds as much for experimental designs as it does for studies that rely on non-random samples.[73]

Whether producing, evaluating, or consuming research, we should understand the precise justification for a given sample. Consider "old" survey data. One might criticize a study for relying on national survey data from fifty years earlier. However, if the study seeks to test an argument about a general causal relationship – such as the effect of intelligence on offending or of court culture on sentencing decisions – the age of the data does not matter. What does is that the data have relevant measures. What matters even more is that the design of the study from which the data came permits a rigorous analysis of whether a causal effect exists. If contemporary data permit such an analysis, then we might want to use the more recent data. No clear scientific reason exists to do so, though. We could of course examine both sets of data. Doing so might provide a more robust test of the hypothesized relationship.

Virtually any sample is just that – a selection, whether representative or not, of some population. Even when we have random samples or an entire population, they are, as we have emphasized, but samples at particular places and times.[74] For example, data collected on every person in

---

[71] The nexus of gender and law enforcement in fact constitutes a rich area of study (see, e.g., Scarborough and Collins 2002).

[72] See, for example, Berk's (1983) discussion of sample selection bias in social science and strategies to account for it.

[73] Mears (2010); Harris (2017).   [74] Feagin *et al.* (1991).

the United States in 1900 would represent individuals in America at that time, not individuals in 2000 or any other year. The science and art in research consist in part of being aware of how data were generated, as well as the ways in which they constitute samples.

The importance of this issue bears emphasis and can be illustrated with two examples. First, policymakers and practitioners may tout the putative effectiveness of some policy from another jurisdiction to justify adoption of it in their own. Perhaps they read a study about a new specialized court or approach to policing that achieved wonderful results. However, the policy may not be possible to implement effectively in other places. And its effectiveness might well be overstated or specific to the original jurisdiction. Whether the study sample provides a credible basis for generalizing results to other places would have to be carefully defended. It should not willy-nilly be assumed to provide a sound basis for generalization.[75]

Second, studies themselves amount to samples. Consider provocative experimental results. A researcher conducts an experiment. The findings seem amazing, and news media then widely promulgate the results. However, for a variety of reasons, experiments sometimes can produce inaccurate findings or findings that may be specific to select jurisdictions.[76] The Minneapolis Domestic Violence Experiment, implemented in the early 1980s, is illustrative. Evaluators employed an experimental design and found that arrests, as a response to domestic violence calls, reduced the probability of subsequent arrest for domestic violence.[77] Policymakers quickly responded to the results by implementing a plethora of mandatory domestic violence arrest laws. The problem? Subsequent evaluations of similar efforts identified mixed results, including the potential for increased offending.[78] Additional studies suggested that mandatory arrest may be beneficial. Even so, the initial policy response proceeded from an incorrect and potentially dangerous assumption that results of one study provided sufficient grounds for a major new policy approach.[79] Among other things, the response ignored the fact that criminal justice policy responses occur within systems contexts that shape outcomes. Mandating arrests without providing a commensurate increase in prosecutorial capacity, for example, might result in delays in processing and greater victim dissatisfaction with their treatment.[80]

---

[75] Bardach (2004); for examples in the medical arena, see Harris (2017).
[76] Ioannidis (2005a, 2005b); Ellenberg (2014); Harris (2017).
[77] Sherman and Berk (1984).   [78] Mears (2010).   [79] Maxwell *et al.* (2001).
[80] Davis *et al.* (2003).

Use Prior Data Collection Efforts as a Guide to Creating Data

Creating new data collection instruments takes time to do well. If we need to create data, therefore, our starting point should be to look to prior research for guidance. Survey instruments may exist that have questions and scales that have been validated repeatedly and that may be useful for the focus of a given study. It would be far better to use these instruments than to create new survey questions from scratch. The same holds for any other type of research instrument. This point seems simple enough, but it is all too frequently ignored!

Address Missing Data – Don't Ignore It or Throw Out Information!

In quantitative analyses, such as those that examine survey or administrative records data, there may be missing data. Why? Someone may have forgotten to enter information into the electronic database system. In a survey, some respondents may refuse to answer questions. Or policy changes may have led some data fields to be eliminated for a period of time.

Such missingness creates many problems. Consider a marriage counseling session in which only one person shows up. We might well have doubts about the veracity of what the one person said about the other or the marriage. When data are missing, there is an analogous problem – it may be that bias somehow influences the analyses. Much depends on how missing data problems are addressed. For example, if we throw out every case in which a missing value arises, we could easily end up with a much smaller sample, and that sample may no longer represent our population of interest.

When cases within a data file have missing values, these values sometimes can be imputed or, in plainer language, created. Imputation involves using information about every case to estimate values for missing data fields. It can result in values that approximate what we would have obtained if the original data file was complete. Imputation can be the better way to proceed because, among other things, it allows us to retain the full sample and thus ensure that the results are more generalizable. However, imputation can result in values that are inaccurate, as compared to the hypothetical complete data file. That situation obviously should be avoided.

Debates exist about when and how to impute data.[81] Although the debates typically center on quantitative data, their relevance extends to qualitative data. For example, perhaps we intend to study how men and women view those who work in "non-traditional" occupations. Historically, for example, women have been underrepresented in the US Senate. We

---

[81] See, for example, Allison (2000, 2002) and Carpenter *et al.* (2006).

might seek to interview a select group of male senators and female senators to gauge their views about this situation and its relevance for criminal justice policy. If we only interview five male senators and no female senators, we quite likely will obtain a distorted impression. With any kind of data, then, we want to examine missingness in the data. We want to understand its causes. Then we want to take steps to address it, whether through imputation or possibly ending the study when the missingness is sufficiently large as to raise questions about the validity of the analyses. Thinking about missingness in data, then, raises questions about the quality of a study's data, the questions the study seeks to address, and the generalizability of the results. It is part and parcel of the science and art of creating credible research.

Be Pragmatic and Creative

Researchers almost never get to do the "perfect" study they want. Why? Resource constraints, data limitations, deadlines, ethical considerations, and more influence research. Pragmatism thus is necessary, as is a willingness to be creative.

That means exploring the limits of what can be done with available resources and data. It also means thinking "outside the box." Perhaps we fixate on the idea of an experimental evaluation of a new diversion program for first-time juvenile offenders. We expend time and resources thinking about how to do it. In the end, though, funding does not permit an experiment. For the time being, we probably should let go of this idea. That does not mean letting go of the topic. We could consider administering a survey to program participants to obtain feedback about their perceptions of the program's influence on them. Or we might investigate the possibility of merging juvenile court and police data to identify youth who resemble the diverted youth and who could serve as a comparison group. Each approach might help shed light on the potential effectiveness of diversion, which was our goal all along.

Thinking "outside the box" here clearly requires thinking about data. It also requires thinking about research design and the goals that we want a study to achieve. These considerations are, once again, why research cannot be a cookie-cutter affair. And they are why conducting, evaluating, or using research effectively and appropriately requires more than technical know-how. It requires a sensibility that appreciates the interrelated nature of all aspects of research.

Pragmatism and creativity can be seen in Dean MacCannell's account of how he came to undertake a study of prisons. He was on faculty at Temple University, yet was, by his account, so poor that he survived by "moonlighting" ("against the expressed will of my dean"), doing "contract research" at Holmesburg Prison. That experience in turn laid down an opportunity to conduct a study. The Law Enforcement Assistance Agency (LEAA) wanted insights into why inmates there killed the warden and his deputy. (Holmesburg, part of the Philadelphia prison system, became famous for medical experiments with inmates in the 1950s and 1960s and then, in the 1970s, for several prison riots.[82]) MacCannell and his colleagues "convinced the LEAA that an ethnographic report on living conditions might provide a more detailed understanding of the problem."[83] MacCannell simply took on more work to pay the bills, but his connections led to an opportunity to undertake a study, one that could address the questions of interest to the funder and that also might open the door to investigating other questions of interest.

A NUTS-AND-BOLTS ISSUE: PREPARING DATA FOR ANALYSIS

Most data require careful tending and preparation, but the amount of work will be highly variable. Some data may be "ready to go." (That is rare.) Some data require a considerable amount of attention before they can be used. (That is common.) And some data are the stuff of nightmares – lots of missing data, inconsistent coding, missing value labels, inaccurate identifying information needed to merge multiple data sets, and so on. (That, too, is relatively common.) Administrative records and secondary data sets present special challenges because researchers who use the data may not have been in charge of the initial data collection efforts. Getting data ready for analysis can be likened to preparing for painting a house ("paint prep") – it is an essential part of the process. Skimp on it and problems invariably surface later. Here, we describe some of the activities that go into preparing data for analysis and the need for a researcher sensibility in undertaking them and in interpreting study findings.

"Cleaning" and Preparing Data

Researchers refer to "cleaning" data. The language is odd. It brings to mind dishwashing detergent, water, and a little elbow grease as one scrubs some numbers to bright clear sheen. The better analogy would be "paint prep." Before undertaking analyses, a great deal of preparatory work typically is needed. This work entails checking for and documenting the amount of missing data. It entails checking for data entry errors (e.g., birthdates or addresses that do not exist or are inaccurate) and correct variable labels.

[82] Hornblum (1999).   [83] MacCannell (1990:185).

It entails checking that data from different sources have been correctly merged into a data analysis file. It also entails inspecting descriptive statistics (e.g., mean, median, range, and variance) for each measure to diagnose potential problems with the data. Sometimes mistakes may jump out, as when we see averages or percentages that do not make sense. For example, the average IQ (intelligence quotient) from a national survey of youth might be 80. That is well below 100, which is what we would expect if a random sample were used and the data were accurately entered.[84] Upon observing this discrepancy, we may discover a problem in the data – how it was organized, missing information, coding errors, and so on – and then can take steps to correct the problem. Visualizing data can help with some of these checks. To illustrate, a simple plot, histogram, or bar chart can provide valuable insight into the presence of outliers (i.e., extreme values). Such information can provide guidance about potential challenges with, as well as opportunities for, analyses.

In writing about his approach to teaching college math, Jordan Ellenberg has written that he gives credit in exams when the students reflect and show that they know an answer cannot be the right one. For example, "on a calculus exam you might be asked to compute the weight of water left in a jug after you punch some kind of hole and let some kind of flow take place for some amount of time. . . . If a student arrives at –4 grams and writes . . . , 'I screwed up somewhere, but I can't find my mistake,' I give them half credit."[85] Why? The student reflected, eyeballed the answer, realized that of course the water in a jug cannot have negative weight, reviewed their calculations, and were left knowing that somehow their calculations were wrong. That mindset is akin to having a researcher sensibility. The student in this example knew some of the math, but he or she also had the wherewithal to step back and *think*. Doing so led him or her to ask whether the answer made sense and to review the calculations that led to it.

That is the sensibility necessary for many parts of the research process, not least preparing data. This activity may seem like a relatively rote undertaking. But there is a science and an art even here. For example, researchers may organize their data in different ways, some of which facilitate stronger science and some of which do not.[86] A recommended approach involves retaining data in their original formats, then using detailed syntax documents to transform the data into a data analysis file. This approach requires more time, but it makes it easier to go back and diagnose instances of user error and for other researchers to replicate study results.

---

[84] Mears and Cochran (2013).   [85] Ellenberg (2014:56).
[86] For a fascinating account of these dimensions in medical research, see Harris (2017).

The science of data preparation consists of rigor and care in documenting decisions, while the art lies in organizing information about the decisions in an accessible manner. It lies more generally in knowing to undertake careful checks for missingness and errors. It lies in knowing, too, to record them in a way that encourages systematic analysis and replication. This observation holds true for quantitative data from surveys and administrative records. It also applies to qualitative data from interviews, focus groups, ethnographies, and the like. For example, ethnographies may result in an enormous amount of handwritten notes and audio and visual tapes. Without a coherent system for organizing the information and for identifying how it was coded, it is difficult to analyze it systematically or to allow for replication.

Creating Measures

In most studies, a primary component of data preparation involves creating variables with coding and software, such as statistical analysis or qualitative data analysis programs. Learning to use these programs can be relatively straightforward. They require that one select a data source and identify where measures in a given source can be found. Researchers then can use specific measures "as is," combine them with others, or recode them. For example, a survey questionnaire might ask respondents to report how many times in the past year they committed a robbery. We might use that count response as a variable in an analysis. Alternatively, we might recode the count into a binary response, where "1" equals "yes, I committed at least one robbery" and "0" equals "I committed no robberies." Or we might recode the count into a truncated or top-coded measure. Perhaps 99 percent of the respondents committed five crimes or fewer, and only 1 percent committed six or more crimes. Using the original count might be problematic because of these outliers. Consider the following situation: One individual in a sample of 10,000 committed 100 robberies. That person likely would be so different from the others as to raise questions about whether inclusion of the value of 100 would be appropriate. If we retained it, then analyses could be conducted that gave the appearance of being able to explain or predict some individuals committing ten, twenty, or fifty or more crimes. In reality, though, if 99 percent of the sample committed five crimes or fewer, the model could not make such predictions accurately. That is why in this instance it might be better to recode the count, such that 0 = 0, 1 = 1, 2 = 2, 3 = 3, 4 = 4, 5 = 5, and 6 = 6 or more robberies.

How to code a variable is not always a clear science. For example, as we discussed earlier, no consensus exists in criminological or criminal justice research on how exactly offending should be measured.[87] Should we use a binary measure? Count? Truncated count? A rate (e.g., the number of crimes committed per month)? A trajectory (e.g., a pattern of crime over time)? A diversity index (e.g., 0 = no crime, 1 = committed at least one type of crime, 2 = committed at least two types of crime, and so on)? No one approach necessarily is the most valid approach.

That is partly because theoretical and conceptual issues attend to coding. We might measure recidivism as the commission of a crime any time in the year after release. Here, presumably our interest is a rather blunt one: Did the individual commit a crime at all? Perhaps we think that probation should have an absolute effect. If so, this measure may make sense. If it is effective, an individual should cease to offend. On the other hand, perhaps its effect is relative. In that case, we should not expect to see an absolute difference, such as "no offending." Rather, we should expect to see a relative effect. There should be a decline in the probability of offending. Somehow, then, we must measure this probability. No agreed-upon way exists to do so. We might, though, at the least rely on something other than a binary measure, such as a count over a period of time. If the average number of crimes committed by probationers is lower than that of a control group, we might infer that their average propensity to offend has been lowered.[88] A propensity here differs conceptually from an absolute likelihood. That can be seen in the fact that although two groups may have identical probabilities of recidivating, using a binary measure of offending, they may have quite different average counts of offending.

Consider that all individuals have a non-zero probability of offending. The implications of that observation are intriguing. For example, it suggests that it would be a bit strange to grade a prison program on whether graduates commit no crime. Better would be to grade it on whether graduates improve in ways that lower the probability of offending. What should the threshold be? Perhaps a probability that more closely approximates that of members of the general public.[89] This image of course runs counter to what many members of the public may envision. Media accounts suggest that there are "criminals" and "non-criminals." In reality, though, everyone has a probability of offending. And almost everyone has committed some act of delinquency or crime, even if only a quite minor one. (Consider that skipping school, graffiti, and pushing someone in the hallway might all count as delinquency.) Such observations give rise to the following idea: Many individuals may have a probability of offending identical to that of individuals who have committed a crime. The sole difference may be that

---

[87] Sweeten (2012).   [88] *Ibid.*   [89] Blumstein and Nakamura (2009).

some random element occurred that led one individual to commit a crime and the other not to do so. Conceptually, then, what really do we mean by "criminal"?

The situation in fact is more complicated. Consider a question that asks if you have ever committed a crime? Does answering affirmatively mean that one is a criminal? If yes, then what is it about a crime committed in adolescence that makes a 60-year-old still a "criminal"? If no, when exactly does an individual cease to be a "criminal"? Consider also the use of typologies. A common one in criminological and criminal justice studies would be "violent" versus "non-violent" offenders. What exactly counts as a "violent" offense? What if an individual has committed both a violent crime and a non-violent crime? Are they then both a violent offender and non-violent offender, the equivalent of belonging to two teams or clubs?

Such questions can be extended in even more directions. A sentencing study might seek to examine court decisions to imprison. The dependent variable (or outcome measure) might be 1 = "imprisonment" versus 0 = "no imprisonment." However, sanctions include more than just the possibility of time in prison. They can include time in jail (i.e., short-term incarceration in or near an offender's hometown) or a stint on regular probation or intensive probation. Accordingly, we might use an ordered categorical variable coding scheme, where 1 = "probation," 2 = "intensive probation," 3 = "jail," and 4 = "prison." The variable is ordered in the sense that the sanctions appear to progress from less severe to more severe. It is categorical in the sense that each sanction does not lie on a clear quantitative continuum, such that a movement from one level to the next entails the same amount of additional severity. We also, though, might view the sanctions as non-ordered. Why? Some research suggests that punished offenders may not view prison as the most severe sanction.[90]

These examples illustrate that the creation of measures is very much an undertaking that can and should require theoretical and conceptual work as much as it does technical coding decisions. They also illustrate the importance of a researcher sensibility that allows one to question the meaning of a measure. This sensibility requires a sense of the science that goes into measurement. It requires, too, an appreciation of the art that goes into interpreting measures and their potential uses as well as limitations. The same observations hold for qualitative studies. Although they typically do not include statistical analyses, qualitative studies generate data. Decisions in turn must be made about how to code information from them to allow for analysis.

---

[90] The issue is discussed in Mears *et al.* (2016a) and Mears and Cochran (2018); see also May and Wood (2010).

Documenting and Describing Coding Decisions

Replication stands at the heart of the scientific enterprise. When repeated studies come to the same conclusion, we can better trust that some pattern or association is real and perhaps causal. When they vary, that does not mean that particular studies were done poorly. It does mean that problems may have undermined them or that certain conditions may produce variable results. Part of science consists of identifying the conditions under which effects vary.

This issue, like many discussed in this book, is far from academic. As Richard Harris has emphasized, some scholars believe there is a reproducibility crisis.[91] Harris' focus was on biomedical research. Studies increasingly have shown that many prominent research findings do not hold up in replication studies.[92] The reasons are assorted – researchers may employ sloppy approaches to their laboratory work, collect data haphazardly, select only results that confirm their biases, and so on. It also can stem from pressures to publish. That said, the inability to reproduce study findings is not a bad thing in and of itself. Many scientific ideas exist. Only through repeated study do most of the good ones rise to the top. That necessarily means that we should expect that many published study results may be contradicted by future research. However, inconsistent results that arise from shoddy adherence to protocols create the equivalent of scientific "noise" and hinder progress in generating knowledge.

Enter documentation. One of the pillars of good science consists of clear documentation of how the data were created, how coding decisions were made, and how such issues as missing data were addressed. It also includes documentation of data issues with analyses. For example, data preparation might reveal that missing data problems were highly prevalent for a subset of police departments. Perhaps rural police departments consistently failed, for whatever reason, to report on a survey of the racial profile of officers. One might therefore exclude these departments from a study of officer race and arrest practices because too few rural departments provided the necessary information. It would be important to document the empirical and logical basis for this type of decision. Such transparency can reduce the likelihood of errors, in much the same way that careful paint prep can reduce mess. It also can enable other researchers to undertake the important task of replicating studies with the same or other sets of data.

---

[91] Harris (2017).   [92] See also Ioannidis (2005a, 2005b).

CONCLUSION

Data are essential ingredients in the research enterprise. Viewed in that way, good, credible research requires "good" ingredients. A random sample should, for example, be truly random; it should accurately represent some larger population. Similarly, a non-random sample should be justified in a defensible manner. Perhaps the sample is the only one that we can obtain or, better yet, it provides a unique perspective on a particular issue. Interviews with drug dealers in rural communities, for example, might illuminate potential factors that contribute to drug offending that would not be evident if we used a national survey of crime.

Much depends on the particular research goals that guide a study. The "best" data can only be identified when we have clarity about those goals. For example, what are the questions that, if answered, would achieve the goals of the study? What measures would be best and how do they compare to what we have or were used in a publication? What samples would be appropriate? Answers to these questions can help us to conduct better research and to evaluate the pros and cons of a proposed or existing study. Invariably, we will be able to see limitations and problems. Our focus, then, should be on carefully reviewing them and determining if, on the whole, a given study provides insights that we trust.

No scholar, policymaker, or criminal justice administrator or practitioner should, in our view, accept research on the face of it. They should be adroit consumers. That entails developing a researcher sensibility, one that discerns the different ways in which data do not "speak for themselves." It is humans who create, analyze, and interpret data. They make numerous judgement calls. Some of the calls may be defensible, others less so. Virtually all study data carry with them caveats and limitations. We should appreciate them for what they are – the foundation for studies that, when coupled with credible theory and analysis, approximate truth.

6 The Role of Analysis in Research

INTRODUCTION

Theory, data, and analysis are the three main "ingredients" that go into creating credible research studies (see Figure 1.1). We discussed in Chapter 5 the fact that data do not "speak for themselves." That axiom holds true for all aspects of research. Theories are not "true" or "valid" simply because they seem compelling. Data do not have self-evident meaning. And analyses do not in any direct way reveal the "truth." Rather, theoretically informed analyses of data *approximate* the truth. Such approximations do not arise from applying analytic techniques willy-nilly to criminological and criminal justice phenomena. Rather, they arise from scientific and creative research designs that draw on theory, relevant data, and appropriate analyses.

We have emphasized this idea in the earlier chapters and revisit it here through a focus on analysis. We highlight the role of analysis as one part of the research enterprise. In addition, we discuss the use of analysis to aid in developing and assessing measures. The bulk of our attention, however, will center on how different types of analyses can aid in achieving the research goals discussed in Chapter 3. These goals include empirically describing criminological and criminal justice phenomena, identifying the social meaning of these phenomena, estimating causal effects, and evaluating policy. Causality features prominently in criminological and criminal justice research studies. Accordingly, we discuss the estimation of causal effects using experiments and a variety of statistical techniques, including qualitative analysis (see also Chapter 8). We also discuss the critical importance of accurately and effectively presenting study results.

Viewed in a different light, the chapter examines several questions. Which analyses are best? (It is a trick question – there frequently is no single best approach.) How can we develop or assess whether a measure is a "good" one? What analyses are useful for different types of research questions? Finally, how should results from studies be presented to convey them most accurately and effectively? It turns out that researchers have many tools at their disposal. These tools allow them to examine criminological and criminal justice questions. But they also allow them – and anyone in fact – to *imagine* different types of research questions. The importance of that skill cannot be overstated. Awareness of different analysis options creates opportunities to frame studies in ways that allow for more interesting and relevant questions to be asked. It also allows us to evaluate better the studies that use these different analytic tools.

MANY ANALYSIS OPTIONS – WHAT IS BEST DEPENDS ON THE QUESTION, DATA, AND MORE

In media accounts, journalists frequently report research findings with highly simplified summary assessments. The article titles, for example, tend to proclaim that X caused Y. They might say "Researchers Discover that Drug Courts Work," "Study Shows that Racism Increases Police Stops," "Angry Children Commit More Crime," and so on. Such proclamations typically flow from a number of mistakes. They assume that: (1) a complicated study boils down to a simple association between two factors; (2) associations are causal; (3) the size of an effect is substantively meaningful; (4) we can trust the study; (5) the effect can be generalized to other groups, populations, or areas; and much more.

Does that mean that studies cannot be accurately conveyed in a short news article or even a title? No. Some research may well lend itself to "sound-byte" summaries. More frequently, though, studies that seem to provide simple, easy-to-understand insights have limitations that should make us think twice before accepting the results.

One of the canons of scientific methodology consists of the notion that, all else equal, the best explanation is a parsimonious one.[1] Perhaps. But no logical requirement exists that says that complicated phenomena result from simple causal explanations. View criminological and criminal justice phenomena through the lens of a distribution. For every 100 phenomena, there may well be some that can be explained by a single cause. However, there will be others that stem from multiple causes, and still others that stem from complex interactions among these causes.[2] A lack of awareness of this possibility, or a fanatical adherence to "simple" models, can result in theories and analyses that miss the mark. How? They fail to capture the complex causal nexus contributing to outcomes.

[1] Mears and Stafford (2002).   [2] Mears (2017).

The best analytic modeling approach depends heavily on theory, carefully crafted research questions and hypotheses, what extant or to-be-collected data allow, and the nature of the data. Consider deterrence theory. Variations of the theory can be viewed as suggesting that severity, certainty, and celerity of punishment deter individuals from offending.[3] (Specific deterrence refers to the effects of punishment on sanctioned individuals; general deterrence refers to the effect of punishment on those who were not sanctioned.) How do we model this idea? For example, is the idea that severity by itself influences recidivism? If we stop and consider the question, it should be clear that severity cannot exert a "net" effect – that is, an effect that is independent of the certainty or celerity of punishment.

Why? Any punishment necessarily requires some non-zero level of certainty and some amount of time to pass. In analyses, however, researchers might seek to model each dimension separately. That is largely inappropriate. Regression analyses, which we discuss further below, provide researchers with a framework in which to estimate independent effects of particular forces. A deterrence model might look like the following: Y (recidivism) = b1(severity) + b2(certainty) + b3(celerity). This equation should look familiar – it is similar to ones that we might see in an algebra class. All it says is that the probability of recidivism is a function of – is caused by – the additive effect of punishment severity, certainty, and celerity. Each "b" represents a coefficient, which provides a quantitative estimate of how much an increase in each cause (severity, certainty, and celerity) changes the probability of recidivism.

Let us assume for the sake of argument that the coefficients look appreciably large (i.e., the effects seem to be substantively significant). What meaning does this model actually have? It is not clear. Why? It models a reality that does not exist. One never has an effect of severity that exists independent of certainty or celerity. Consider a cake. We would not say that how good it tastes is a function of sugar, net of flour, eggs, or the like. Cakes require multiple ingredients. There can be no "net" effect of one ingredient, only interactions. (More sugar might make a cake sweeter, but it does not make a cake more of a "cake.")

How, then, should one model the effect of the three dimensions of deterrence on recidivism? We can examine a three-way interaction which entails using a statistical model that allows each of the three causes to interact, such as Y(recidivism) = b1(severity) * b2(certainty) * b3(celerity).

---

[3] Deterrence theory – its history and variants – is complicated and the related literature is vast. Excellent overviews of deterrence can be found in Paternoster (2010), Nagin (2013), Lilly *et al.* (2015), and Akers *et al.* (2016).

If we allow for interactions, several interesting ideas emerge. For example, perhaps the effect of severity depends on the celerity of punishment. (Assume here that the certainty of punishment is constant.) A highly severe punishment might have a large effect whether it occurs within a few minutes or a few months of conviction. By contrast, a less severe punishment might exert a large effect if imposed immediately after conviction; it might exert little to no effect if imposed months or years later. This interaction in turn might vary depending on a third factor – the certainty of punishment. Perhaps an only modestly severe punishment exerts a considerable deterrent effect if it almost always occurs quickly (i.e., when the certainty and celerity of punishment are high).

Such possibilities are far from esoteric. For example, Mark Stafford and his colleagues demonstrated that interactive models provide a better (and logically more consistent) account of deterrence than additive models.[4] This finding should cause us to raise our eyebrows. Interactions are interesting and lead us to consider theoretical questions, such as what three-way interactions specifically we should anticipate. They also may lead to important policy implications. For example, perhaps investing in less severe punishments, but providing them consistently and quickly, can more effectively reduce crime than would investing in more severe punishments, but doing so less consistently and with significant delays?[5]

Let us explore "interactional" thinking a bit more. Is there a scenario where perhaps one of the three deterrence factors, or "ingredients," may exert an independent effect? One possibility involves the incarceration of convicted felons. Consider a study where we seek to determine if more severe prison sentences – conceptualized as longer durations of time incarcerated – reduce recidivism more than less severe (shorter) prison sentences do.[6] Our sole focus here appears to be on severity. This suggests that we are examining an independent effect of one dimension of deterrence. In reality, though, we are studying a unique instance of a three-way interaction. Specifically, we are studying the effect of severe punishment for an average level of certainty and an average level of celerity, respectively.

To illustrate, imagine that two states each have identical prison populations. Inmates in them serve the same amount of time and are clones of one another. What differs? In one state, the certainty of receiving a prison sentence is low and in the other it is high. (Assume for simplicity's sake that the celerity of punishment is the same in each state.) We might find that in the low-certainty state, prison time exerts little effect on recidivism, while in

---

[4] Stafford *et al.* (1986).
[5] For related ideas, see Stafford *et al.* (1986) and Durlauf and Nagin (2011).
[6] Mears *et al.* (2016a).

the high-certainty state it exerts a much greater effect. The potential for such a difference highlights that even in a study seemingly focused just on severity, a three-way interaction in fact lurks in the background.

Why this detour into deterrence, modeling decisions, and theory? *We do so to highlight that analysis is not something that researchers should thoughtlessly apply to a set of data.* They should think through the type of effects that may exist and then create analyses that enable them to test for such effects. No short cut exists here. This exercise requires not statistics, but rather thoughtful consideration about how different factors may cause the phenomenon that we wish to study. Statistical or various qualitative analyses flow from that process.

Analyses also flow from considering data. What if a set of court data includes no information on the celerity of punishment? Well, for one thing, we cannot take into account how the celerity of punishment influences recidivism. It also means that we therefore must assume that any identified effects exist only for some average level of celerity (i.e., the average within the context of the sampled population). What the effects would be in contexts where punishment occurs more slowly or quickly could not be determined. Consider a related question: What if the data include only individuals sentenced after a particular year? The results may not generalize to individuals sentenced prior to that year. This matters because the quality of prison programming may have changed. Perhaps it improved. That would mean that any estimated effect of time served may only apply to prison systems with higher-quality programming.

(We say "estimated" when describing effects because all social scientific studies consist of estimates. They never capture absolute reality. Use of the term "estimated" in writing can be tedious, but it provides a reminder of that fact.)

We return, then, to where we started – the journalist and news story bottom-line assessments. These accounts rarely consider the theoretical foundation of studies, the hypotheses that guided them, the limitations of data, and so on. When they do a good job of reporting on studies, problems still arise. For example, they select only those studies that lend themselves to simple summaries. They also may select only high-profile or novel findings.[7] Doing so creates the appearance to readers that scientific progress occurs in big leaps and bounds and that single studies can be trusted. Nothing could be further from the truth. Scientists tend to be hesitant about claiming too much for any given study. Why? Because a great deal of uncertainty attends even the best research.[8]

---

[7] Harris (2017).

[8] Kuhn (1962); Merton (1968); Popper (2002); Ellenberg (2014); Harris (2017).

With these observations in mind, below we discuss different analytic techniques that exist for identifying whether two or more factors may be associated and whether the associations are causal. We do so to highlight several points. First, analyses can help us to answer questions. They do nothing more or less. The questions come from theory, reflection, policy concerns, and so on. Analyses then allow us to answer them. They do not compensate for poor theory or data.

Second, awareness of different types of analyses can aid in imagining a wider range of questions. Many introductory research methods and statistics classes cover a narrow range of analytic techniques. That is understandable. One must, it seems, walk before running. Yet, this analogy really does not hold. It is possible to learn about advanced research methodologies without knowing how to do them. Consider spatial analyses. The statistical methods used for conducting them can be quite complex. Yet, the idea of examining how crime clusters may move from one area to another is simple. Consideration of that simple idea then opens the door to thinking about spatial dimensions of crime and criminal justice. For example, what is the effect of changing the distribution of crime in one community on crime in a neighboring one? Awareness of analyses creates possibilities for identifying new questions that researchers might pursue or that policymakers or practitioners might ask researchers to address.

Figure 6.1 illuminates this idea. Familiarity with only one type of analysis allows researchers to answer and to imagine a relatively narrow set of questions. For non-researchers, such familiarity imposes similar constraints. It forestalls the ability to imagine the types of research questions that might most advance policy or practice. Conversely, familiarity with many types of analyses allows researchers and non-researchers alike to imagine and answer more questions. That does not mean that they can undertake the analyses. They can, though, use awareness of the various analysis techniques as conceptual tools. Then they can collaborate with researchers with specific analytic expertise to undertake them.

In Chapter 5, we discussed the fact that analytic techniques exist for investigating and addressing missing data. As noted there, techniques exist for assessing the extent to which samples may not be representative of the populations or areas that we seek to examine. Here, our focus will center on analyses for creating better measures and addressing the four research goals discussed in Chapter 3. We submit that in all instances credible analyses flow from a researcher sensibility. That sensibility does not reduce to an ability to think theoretically, to design data, or to analyze. It comes from all three in combination. It flows from a chef-like approach to knowing how to combine research ingredients. And it requires seeing the forest and the trees, the "big picture" and the smallest of details. Credible research entails

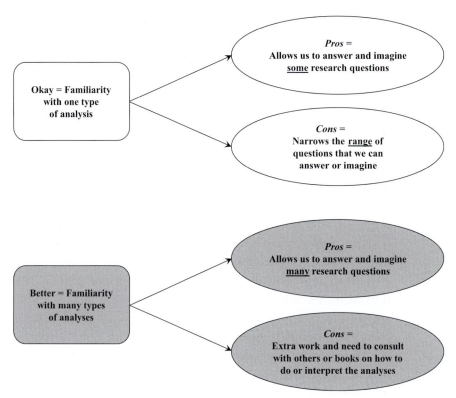

Figure 6.1 Analyses and the doors they open

careful consideration of the most appropriate analysis for a given question and set of data, the extent to which the data can be trusted, and how much we can generalize results.

ANALYSES FOR CREATING BETTER MEASURES

As we discussed in Chapter 5, good data are required to produce good measures; these in turn provide the building blocks of analyses. But even high-quality data require thoughtful attention before undertaking what might be considered the "main" analyses, such as those that seek to identify causal effects. Three considerations stand out when thinking about measures.

First, recall from the discussion in Chapter 5 that we typically have no direct measures of social phenomena, such as crime and criminal justice processes and outcomes. Instead, we rely on indirect measures that tap into some more general construct. This situation creates room for error. To measure crime in a community, for example, we might use police arrest data. Arrest data, though, are flawed measures of true crime because they only measure offenses known to the police. They therefore are biased in whatever ways arrest or policing practices may be biased or in ways that citizens' reporting of crimes to police might be biased. To illustrate, arrest data may under- or over-represent certain types of crime, especially less serious crimes.[9] They also may underestimate crime committed in areas or among groups where citizens (e.g., immigrants) are more reluctant to report crime. Or they may underestimate types of crimes that are less likely to be reported to the police (e.g., domestic violence).[10]

Researchers encounter a range of such biases and other measurement challenges. It is important, then, to develop a tool kit for addressing them. Some forms of bias can be identified via specific empirical tests. For example, survey researchers routinely engage in a series of checks, including pre-tests and interview follow-ups with respondents, to ensure that survey questions are measuring a phenomenon of interest. Qualitative methods can be used to assess the reliability of measurement from interviews or focus groups; multiple investigators may be used to interpret and code audio recordings or transcripts to ensure consistency of interpretation and coding.[11] Other types of data present different challenges, some of which cannot be addressed, but instead must be noted. For example, we may be unable to assess the extent to which ethnographic observations or administrative records data contain errors. Our only option in such instances is to be transparent about the limitations of the data.

Second, there are statistical analyses that can be used to develop better measures from data. Sometimes a single measure provides a poor indicator of a general construct. To illustrate, it would be problematic to measure peer offending with a single measure, such as responses to a question about how many of one's friends smoke. Why? A single measure of peer smoking provides only limited insight into how and to what extent one's peers engage in criminal activity. A more robust measure of peer offending might come from combining information from separate items, such as responses to questions about the extent to which one's friends engage in any of a variety of criminal acts (e.g., theft, burglary, robbery). By merging them into a single score or index, we likely arrive at a more valid (accurate) indicator of peer offending. Many statistical techniques exist, including factor analysis techniques and latent class analyses, for turning multiple measures into a unified measure of a single underlying construct.[12] Such approaches can be used in combination with others to expand domains of scientific inquiry.

---

[9] See Warren *et al.* (2006) for a discussion of police stop data, for example; see, generally, Mears *et al.* (2016b).

[10] Cohen and Land (1984); Gove *et al.* (1985); Baumer and Lauritsen (2010).

[11] Lawrence *et al.* (1984); Campbell *et al.* (2013).

[12] See, for example, Hagenaars and McCutcheon (2002) on latent class analysis and Brown (2015) on factor analysis.

We might, for example, create ratios or differences in an individual's offending relative to that of his or her peers to explore different nuances in criminal behavior.[13]

Third, analyses can be used to diagnose problems with measures; they also can be used to create new or better measures relevant for testing theories. A theory might identify factors that affect the amount of crime individuals commit. If our data contain arrest records, we need to create a measure that counts how many arrests individuals accrued over time, which might be viewed as a proxy for how much crime they undertake. Alternatively, a theory might anticipate that individuals fall into different patterns of offending. Here, our count measure of arrests will not be helpful. However, we could use the same data and some analytic techniques, like growth curve modeling or group-based trajectory analysis, to estimate the duration or consistency of offending over time. We then could move to the task of predicting which individuals fall into different trajectories of offending.[14]

Measurement is critical. Most studies therefore include analytic work that focuses on improving the measures that will be used. This work sometimes will include analyses that assess the quality of measurement. Other times they will lead to the creation of new measures. In any study, researchers should undertake "groundwork" analyses that ensure that their studies use the best possible measures for estimating prevalence, associations, effects, and the like.

ANALYSES FOR EMPIRICAL DESCRIPTION

Recall from Chapter 3 that a central goal of social scientific research entails description. Indeed, description constitutes a large part of criminological and criminal justice inquiry. Sometimes researchers move too quickly on to more advanced analyses. This approach stems, we suspect, from the false assumption that such analyses are intrinsically "better."

Without first working to describe a given phenomenon, predictive or causal analyses risk "missing the forest for the trees." For example, researchers might seek to explain variation in a phenomenon even though little variation in it exists. Consider school shootings – one might seek to predict them. That clearly constitutes an important task. An equally important undertaking, though, consists of documenting how frequently shootings occur and where they occur. Descriptive findings are powerful on their own and can be vital for informing theory and policy.

[13] McGloin (2009).   [14] Nagin (2005); Taxman (2017).

How should one go about description? Quantitative approaches for conducting a descriptive analysis often entail use of the types of statistical analyses students learn in high school and in an introduction-to-statistics course.[15] Means (i.e., averages), medians, modes, and ranges can provide a great deal of insight about a phenomenon. Percentages alone can reveal much. For example, knowing that from 3 to 17 percent of offenders are "life-course persisters" – that is, individuals who engage in offending throughout the life-course – provides a foundation for thinking about the causes of crime.[16] Why, we might ask, do some individuals persist in offending and why do others desist? It also provides a foundation for policy. Perhaps, most first-time, second-time, and third-time offenders warrant little attention given that they likely will never commit a crime again.

Use of these basic statistical measures can be useful in making comparisons. These in turn may shed light on interesting issues or causal relationships. For example, in a study of criminal punishment, we can learn about how different racial and ethnic groups may be disproportionately exposed to severe punishments simply by examining something like mean incarceration rates among whites, blacks, and Latinos, respectively. We can take the analysis further. We might disaggregate the incarceration rates within each of these groups by age and gender. Perhaps incarceration rates of young, black males, for example, turn out to be much higher than those of other groups.[17] We can go still further and create multiple measures of these rates across different places (e.g., states or countries) or over different time periods (e.g., the past five years or the past five decades). Such information then can be presented in the form of charts, figures, or tables to facilitate identification of trends and differences among groups or areas. It also can be presented in the form of maps. A researcher might create a "heat" map that plots crime rates by using darker or lighter shading to help visualize crime distributions.[18] In each instance, we arrive at a picture of the world that enables us to discern patterns that otherwise would not be evident.

Qualitative approaches for empirical description employ different types of analyses, but are similarly useful. As we discussed in Chapter 5, qualitative analyses allow researchers to observe details that quantitative analyses cannot. The trade-off consists of smaller and less representative samples. Even so, qualitative analyses can be especially useful for identifying patterns, trends, and groups that quantitative analyses might miss. Consider police and citizen encounters. Interviews might focus on understanding citizen experiences with local police. A descriptive analysis of interview

---

[15] Knoke *et al.* (2002).   [16] Jolliffe *et al.* (2017).   [17] Mears and Cochran (2015).
[18] See, for example, Yau (2011) for an overview of data visualization techniques.

data might provide insight into possible variation in how citizens perceive police encounters. It also might identify that some groups appear to be more likely to report unsatisfactory experiences with the police. And it might identify a range of possible factors that influence citizens' views.

In criminological and criminal justice research, description has long been a central avenue for illuminating important questions. Early studies in particular adopted this approach, in no small part because the study of crime and criminal justice was new. One prominent illustration comes from Clifford Shaw and Henry McKay's pioneering work. Their studies documented that juvenile delinquency occurred in a clear pattern – it surfaced more in some Chicago neighborhoods than others.[19] Gresham Sykes' famous qualitative study of prisons also was largely descriptive. He discovered different "pains" of imprisonment experienced by inmates; this discovery fueled the development of theories about how inmates adjust to prison life.[20]

Today, descriptive efforts continue to be employed and are no less important. In some cases, however, they rely on newer tools. For example, researchers can better describe crime rates across communities by using computerized spatial and mapping tools. (Shaw and McKay had to do theirs by hand!) And many advanced statistical techniques, like trajectory modeling and growth curve models, provide a foundation for describing the different groups of offenders based on patterns of offending over the life-course.[21]

ANALYSES FOR DESCRIBING SOCIAL MEANINGS AND CAUSES

Scientists seek to understand the world around us. That seems like a straightforward endeavor. Identify some phenomenon, study it, gain insight into potential causes, and test hypotheses about that insight to assess its veracity. How, though, do we identify causes of something if we cannot even recognize what that "thing" is?

Consider the example from Chapter 4 – if we wish to study conspiratorial winking rates among different groups of people, we first have to know what such winking is. We might define it as the rapid closing of one eyelid one time while looking at a fellow conspirator with a facial expression that conveys, "I'm just kidding around to see how so-and-so responds, and by winking at you I'm pulling you into my playful shenanigans." That sequence, though, does not make sense in some cultures. It therefore would not make sense to count rates of conspiratorial winking in them.

[19] Shaw and McKay (1969).   [20] Sykes (1958).   [21] Jolliffe et al. (2017).

It is an admittedly silly example. But it nonetheless captures an important dimension of research: We can only study what we can apprehend. That does not mean that we understand what *causes* a particular phenomenon. It does mean that we must be able to discern it in some way. A person from a culture where conspiratorial winking does not make sense cannot, in turn, make sense of such winking. Consider the culture within many families. There may be shorthand non-verbal expressions for describing things that only make sense within a particular family. To outsiders, these expressions may leave them bewildered or they literally may not see them. Humans are wired to see patterns, but this does not mean that they always see them.[22]

Conspiratorial winking and family-specific expressions obviously constitute relatively innocuous events (though perhaps not if you are the victim of the conspiratorial activity). But many criminological and criminal justice phenomena consist of activities or events that may not jump out at us and yet may be important for advancing knowledge or improving policy. An illustration can be found again in Chapter 4, where we discussed Elijah Anderson's work on the code of the street.[23] His interviews with neighborhood residents enabled him to apprehend a phenomenon that otherwise might have gone unnoticed. In turn, by drawing attention to the notion of a "street code," he enabled other researchers to conduct studies that collected data about the existence of this code and its potential influence on crime and victimization.[24]

Analyses of various types of qualitative data – such as information from interviews, focus groups, and ethnographies – consist of efforts like Anderson's. They enable us to discern phenomena that might go unnoticed. More generally, they enable us to gain insight into how individuals, groups, communities, or organizations act and the culture that frames the meaning of their actions. Consider a study that Gilbert Geis conducted of white-collar crime. During a Senate subcommittee hearing, a committee attorney asked one of the Allis Chalmers executives about their illegal involvement in price-fixing (a criminal violation of the Sherman Anti-Trust Act that led to over 1 billion dollars in illegal profits). When asked if he knew that "these meetings with competitors were illegal," the executive responded: "Illegal? Yes, but not criminal. I didn't find that out until I read the indictment . . . I assumed that criminal action meant endangering someone, and we did not do that . . . I thought we were more or less working on a survival basis in order to try to make enough to keep our plant and our employees."[25] Such statements showed how the price-fixing executives viewed their actions. They saw them as "illegal," but, because no one seemed to be directly

---

[22] Kahneman (2011).   [23] Anderson (1999).
[24] See, for example, Stewart and Simons (2010).   [25] Geis (1996:106).

endangered, "not criminal." And this view in turn seemed to emanate from a culture that engendered this way of thinking.

Studies like the one Geis conducted help us to understand how others see the world. Sometimes the insights that we gain may be obvious. Other times, as with the price-fixing study, the insights may be far from obvious. Who, for example, would imagine that someone could think that engaging in illegal activity was not criminal?

Such studies also enable us to develop theoretical accounts about causation. To illustrate, in the price-fixing case study, we can begin to discern the contours of a theory that emphasizes (1) the role of an individual's understanding of the law, (2) social distancing (as in, "I did something illegal, but of course I am not a criminal"), and (3) perhaps the importance of organizational culture in supporting a particular view of reality (as in, "We are doing something that may be illegal, but not criminal because everyone is doing it and so it must be an acceptable activity").

Can analyses of quantitative data allow us to discern the social meaning of various phenomena or to develop theoretical accounts of them? Yes, but it can be more difficult. For example, we cannot readily count something that we do not recognize as existing. But, one might respond, how about descriptive statistics of a particular phenomenon? For example, we might analyze data that show that 55 percent of all jail officers voted for a Republican candidate in a state election. The greater support for a Republican candidate may be interesting. Yet, in and of itself, the fact does not signify any particular meaning. For example, we do not know how officers view the act of voting or what their votes mean to them. We therefore will have difficulty developing a theoretical account of why jail officers vote as they do.

It is, of course, possible to explore quantitative data just as one might explore qualitative data. With both types of data, we can look for facts or patterns that for some reason stand out. Upon finding a pattern, we can dig deeper. We might read through interview transcripts or examine different groups of jail officers. Like detectives, we can pursue different leads, going on hunches, until we begin to see some rhyme or reason – patterns – in the data.

What types of quantitative analyses might be used? Simple descriptive statistics (e.g., percentages, averages, ranges, cross-tabulations) can be helpful. Regression analyses – which seek to explore how a variety of factors may be associated with a phenomenon of interest (see the discussion further below) – also can be helpful. Although such approaches do not readily allow us to identify the social meaning of phenomena, they can prod us into considering them and consulting scholarship, such as qualitative studies, that may help us to develop a theory.

What types of qualitative analyses might be conducted? Just as there exist many types of quantitative analyses, there also exist many approaches to analyzing qualitative data. The selected approach will depend on the type of data. Regardless, qualitative analyses typically seek to interpret the social meaning of various actions and to code data for themes. For example, an ethnography might involve residing in a place for an extended period of time, trying to fit in, and, in turn, seeking to understand how individuals or groups view themselves, their actions, others, and the world around them. One might end up with extensive written notes, recordings, pictures, and more. The researcher then might read, re-read, and think about this material. He or she identifies possible patterns, then assembles them in writing to develop a coherent account. That account typically will include a description of how individuals or groups view the world. It might also include description of the potential causes and consequences of these views.

Much the same approach arises with analysis of interviews and focus groups. The difference lies in the fact that the information, the data, all tends to be written and in response to questions. The goal remains that of learning about the social meaning of various phenomena and developing a causal theory. To this end, the researcher reads and re-reads participants' responses, looking for themes, and organizing notes about these themes to identify factors that may be related.

In general, qualitative analyses proceed through a series of steps. These include: (1) recording data (e.g., notes, observations, interview or audio transcripts); (2) developing familiarity with each data source (e.g., reading and re-reading transcripts or different historical accounts of a particular event); (3) creating a system for coding information, with an eye toward relying on either a pre-established coding system, a coding system that emerges over time through reflection, or both; (4) seeking patterns that may form the basis for a theory; (5) describing the theory; (6) applying it to the data to determine if it appears to explain the patterns; and (7) revising the theory.[26] Because qualitative data do not usually lend themselves to statistical analysis, analyses of such data benefit from relying on these steps. Why? They force researchers to "get inside the data." In much the same way that cultural immersion can help us to learn a foreign language, spending time continuously thinking about potential connections in qualitative data can lead to a greater ability to discern patterns and explanations.

---

[26] See, generally, Corbin and Strauss (1990), Feagin *et al.* (1991), Miles *et al.* (2014), Reichertz (2014), Miller and Palacios (2015), Patton (2015), and Wincup (2017).

How might researchers go about the central activity of identifying themes and possible causal explanations?[27] Following the above steps is the main way. Another, though, is simply to become immersed in the observations that one has recorded and think about them. To illustrate, researchers might interview prosecutors about their views on sentencing juvenile offenders to life without parole. As they review the typed transcripts, they see that some prosecutors tend to frame such sentencing decisions as entirely out of their hands. They view themselves as simply enforcing the law on the books. Other prosecutors wrestle with the decision. They look for any mitigating factors that might enable them to impose a less draconian sanction. This difference may interest the researchers and lead them to investigate what gives rise to it. Accordingly, they might code each instance where a respondent weighed in on this topic. They also might code each transcript for instances of responses that could explain the difference. In the end, then, the researchers end up with coded interviews that they then can organize and analyze using software. For example, they might cross-tabulate textual responses about views of life-without-parole sentences with each possible cause to see if in fact a clear association exists. Evidence of an association would not necessarily indicate a causal relationship. It would, however, provide a foundation for developing a theory that then might be tested with more representative data.

When undertaking analyses, a mixed-methods approach – as discussed in Chapter 5 – sometimes can be better than one or another approach by itself.[28] Analysis of multiple types of data can allow us to appreciate different aspects of criminological or criminal justice phenomena. In turn, we obtain a more holistic understanding of them.

As we develop an understanding of some phenomena, there is always the risk that we may allow biases to inform our analyses. For example, if we view the police as racist, we might perceive every response during an interview as evidence of racism. Research is akin to shining a light in certain directions. The mere act of illuminating one area and not others may distort our understanding. To illustrate, perhaps an officer says something racist. We select only that fact to support our belief that officers hold racist views and then to develop a theory about why they do. However, the same officer might say other things that suggest they are not racist or that their view of race is nuanced. If we fail to consider this

---

[27] It bears mention that social science approaches to historical analysis tend to emphasize not just causation, but also the identification of generalizable causal processes. The latter typically is what distinguishes such approaches from purely historical accounts (Weber 1949, 1978).

[28] George and Bennett (2004).

latter possibility, we risk creating a theoretical account that distorts reality. Although this problem may seem more likely in qualitative analyses, it can surface in quantitative analyses as well. With statistical models, a researcher selects variables that he or she thinks may influence the outcome. That may result in the inclusion of only those variables that support a particular view. No one best solution to this problem exists. Some steps to reduce the influence of bias, though, include relying on other researchers to check one's coding and analyses, seeking to examine data from diverse perspectives, and, in particular, endeavoring to counter-argue hypotheses and the results of analyses.

ANALYSES FOR IDENTIFYING OR TESTING CAUSAL RELATIONSHIPS

Criminological and criminal justice research often seeks to understand the causes of various outcomes. For example, what causes individuals to offend? What causes some communities to have higher crime rates than others? What causes some courts to punish offenders more punitively than other courts? What causes some officers or police departments to act more professionally than others? Or what causes some states to enact certain types of crime laws and implement them more successfully than other states?

Quantitative statistical techniques generally constitute the "go-to" methodology for estimating causal relationships. For that reason, we discuss them at some length here. However, the qualitative approaches to research discussed above can be used to provide insights into potential causal effects. Indeed, in some cases, as with some historical-comparative analyses, these methods provide the only way to investigate causal effects.

Undertaking advanced statistical or qualitative methods requires an investment of time. However, that is not necessary for understanding the core ideas behind the methods and when they may be useful. In what follows, we describe some of the more prominent "advanced" statistical techniques that can be used in criminological and criminal justice research. We describe, too, some of the types of questions about causal relationships that they can answer. Details about how to use these and other approaches can be found in readily available books and edited volumes, such as the *Handbook of Quantitative Criminology*.[29] Our focus here centers on illuminating the fact that diverse analytic techniques exist. We highlight that these techniques allow for imagining and answering different questions.

---

[29] Piquero and Weisburd (2010); Pratt (2012); Bachman and Paternoster (2017).

Knowledge of those techniques is an important first step for understanding research possibilities.

Experiments as a Way of Testing for Causal Effects

Experiments provide one critical avenue for testing whether a causal relationship exists. They can be implemented in many different ways, but the logic is simple. By randomizing individuals, groups, organizations, and the like to a treatment or control condition, we can be sure that any observed difference in an outcome may be due to the treatment and not some spurious factor.[30]

When experiments are done well, we can trust better that a true causal effect exists. Doing them well, however, can be difficult and costly. Many factors may adversely affect an experiment. For example, the randomization process may become compromised or attrition through death or participants moving may diminish the sample sizes to a point where we cannot trust the estimated effects.[31] Such effects can be costly to avoid. Regardless, the failure to avoid them can result in invalid causal estimates.[32]

In addition, the results of the study may not necessarily be generalizable to other groups or areas. Consider a program that staff implement carefully under the watchful eye of a funder and an evaluation team. The program might benefit from full funding and staff taking extra steps to ensure timely and quality delivery of services. A study then shows that the program is effective. However, whether this program would be effective under typical conditions – such as insufficient funding and possibly moderate to poor implementation – is another matter.

This distinction gives rise to the concept of "efficacy" studies. These identify program effects under ideal conditions. In comparison, "effectiveness" studies identify program effects under "real-world" conditions.[33] Should we be concerned that efficacy studies generate different results than effectiveness studies? Absolutely. In the "real world," many different factors may alter the relationships between causal variables and outcomes.

Experiments thus can be a wonderful tool, but they are not a panacea. In addition, they can be expensive and, in many instances, cannot ethically

[30] Many discussions of experimental designs exist. For a general discussion, see Rossi *et al.* (2004). For examples related to criminology and criminal justice, see Mears (2010) and Welsh *et al.* (2013).
[31] See, for example, Gottfredson *et al.*'s (2003) experimental design evaluation of a drug court.
[32] See Mears (2010); for interesting examples from the medical research arena, see Ioannidis (2005a, 2005b) and Harris (2017).
[33] Rossi *et al.* (2004:260).

be undertaken or are simply impossible. In such cases, "quasi-experimental" studies can be helpful. They involve strategies for approximating an experiment to investigate causal relationships. Below, we discuss several types of "quasi-experimental" approaches to estimating causal effects.

The Logic of Multivariate Analyses: Estimating Causal Effects

Multivariate analyses constitute the primary quantitative tool used by researchers when experiments are impossible or inappropriate. They are used to approximate what we would otherwise like to do with experiments – namely, to determine, or have more confidence, that some factor, X, causes another factor, Y, and is not simply "associated" with it.

Such analyses are multivariate because they include control variables. These are measures of other dimensions, characteristics, and forces that might conceivably act as confounding influences on the relationship between an X and a Y. Confounding influences are those that might explain why we identify a relationship between an X and a Y. Because any given independent variable is not randomly assigned, there may be selection bias. That means that there may be factors that determine both exposure to the independent variable and to the outcome of interest. Without controlling for these confounding forces, estimates of the effects of an X on a Y will be inaccurate.

For example, say we are interested in estimating the effect of unemployment (X) on crime (Y) across cities. In addition to examining the association between rates of unemployment and crime, we would need to account for other factors that might be linked both to unemployment and to crime. For example, poverty may affect each of them. If our analyses do not take into account – or we might say "adjust for" – poverty, then the estimated effect of unemployment on crime will be biased.[34] More simply, it will be wrong.

Accounting for any and all sources of selection biases can be challenging. Consider research that seeks to identify whether punishments have causal effects on individuals' criminality. Decisions to incarcerate are not made randomly. Judges and prosecutors assign prison sentences to a select group of people, such as those who have extensive histories of offending. These individuals will be more likely than the average person to reoffend. That is selection bias. With an experiment, we could avoid the problem by randomly assigning some convicted felons to prison and others to probation. Without it, we face the problem that the courts select higher-risk individuals for incarceration. We thus need to control for confounding factors (e.g., prior criminal record, severity of offense, demonstrated

---

[34] See, for example, Raphael and Winter-Ebmer (2001). Regarding the logic of multivariate analysis, see Knoke *et al.* (2002) or any multivariate statistics textbook.

remorse) that contribute to selection into prison *and* to offending. We then can approximate what that experiment would achieve – to wit, an estimate of the effect of prison relative to probation on recidivism.

It will not always be clear what factors confound our estimates. That problem in turn creates a related one that plagues many quasi-experimental studies – namely, we can rarely be fully confident that our estimated effects are accurate or whether unobserved confounding creates bias in them. For this reason, deciding which control variables to include constitutes a critical research decision. There are two somewhat opposing schools of thought regarding the "best" approach for selecting control variables. One advocates a "kitchen sink" approach. Here, one includes any and all variables that may possibly be related to the independent and dependent variables. If it is in the data set, "toss" it in the analytic model! The kitchen sink approach might be viewed as a conservative or can't-be-too-safe approach to multivariate modeling. However, as Stanley Lieberson has shown, careless inclusion of control variables can sometimes lead to less rather than more accurate estimates.[35] Sometimes less in fact is more!

A better approach is to rely on past research and theory. We want control variables that have been shown – through empirical studies or through theoretical analysis – to be associated with both the independent variable and the dependent variable. Measures not clearly associated with X and Y are not needed. Why? Sometimes their inclusion is not problematic. But many things can go wrong statistically when there are too many variables in a model.[36]

The goal of multivariate analysis is to estimate a causal effect. It bears emphasizing, however, that estimating causal effects is not necessarily straightforward. For example, does each additional amount of X cause an increase in Y? Or do changes in X have variable effects? For example, do they initially create large changes in Y and then, at higher values of X, do the changes exert less of an effect on Y? Consideration of such issues constitutes as much a theoretical undertaking as an analytic one. If we have reason to believe that X has variable effects, then we need to undertake the types of statistical analyses that will enable us to identify them. This idea is discussed more in Chapter 8.

Regression Analysis with Various Kinds of Outcomes

Regression analysis is a statistical approach for estimating the association between an independent and a dependent variable, net of other (control) variables. It serves as the "workhorse" multivariate tool in the social

---

[35] Lieberson (1985).   [36] *Ibid.*

sciences, including criminology and criminal justice. It is for that reason typically the first multivariate technique that graduate students are taught.

Regression analysis can be used in many creative ways. The main use, however, consists of estimating whether X and Y are related. That is, is there a statistically and substantively significant relationship between them? (Determining statistical significance involves the types of diagnostic tests discussed in introductory statistics texts. It involves determining whether, on probabilistic grounds, an estimated effect is likely to exist. Assessing substantive significance is another matter. No set formula exists. What might be a large effect or small effect depends on the phenomenon under study and the magnitude of effects of other causal forces.)

An illustration: Say that we wish to test the hypothesis that economic strain (X) leads to criminal behavior (Y). If we can measure economic strain, criminal behavior, and relevant confounding variables for a sample of individuals, a regression analysis can be used. With it, we estimate the association between economic strain and crime, net of the confounders. Perhaps the analysis identifies a statistically significant positive association, such as that increased strain leads to increased crime. We then have support for our hypothesis.[37]

There are many versions of regression analysis. The nature of one's dependent variable, among other factors, typically dictates which kind of regression technique one uses. A continuous variable, such as measures of crime rates, typically requires what is called ordinary least squares (OLS) regression. A dichotomous (1/0) outcome, such as a measure of whether someone recidivates, typically requires an approach like logistic or probit regression. If we want to examine a categorical outcome (e.g., supporter of the death penalty, opponent of the death penalty, undecided about whether the death penalty should exist), then multinomial (also called polytomous) regression should be used. Many studies examine a count variable, such as studies of the number of crimes someone has committed. Poisson regression techniques should be used in these instances or perhaps negative binomial regression if the count outcome is skewed. Still other types of regression analysis exist. In almost every instance, and regardless of their complexity, the basic goal typically is the same: We want to identify how, if at all, a potential factor or force (X) is related to, and perhaps exerts a causal effect on, an outcome (Y).

Structural-Equation Modeling

Estimating a regression model is a straightforward approach for testing hypotheses about simple causal relationships. But some causal effects may

---

[37] See, generally, Allison (1999).

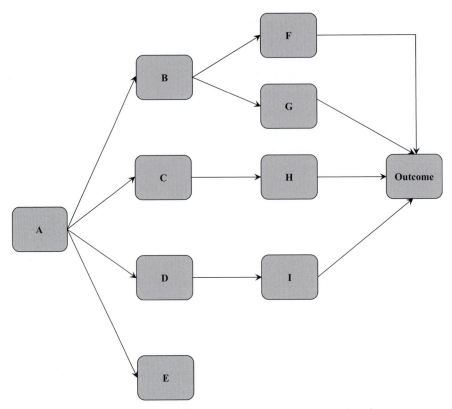

Figure 6.2 Structural equation analyses as a means of testing causal pathways

not be simple. For example, we can build on the hypothesis above by considering a range of different pathways linking economic strain to crime. Economic strain might have a direct effect on crime. The regression model above tested that possibility. There may be, however, indirect effects that interest us. We might hypothesize that economic strain leads to crime to the extent that it leads first to other outcomes (e.g., familial strain, substance abuse, mental illness). These outcomes might lead to still others, which in turn eventually contribute to crime.

Exploring these possibilities can be done using a special type of analysis termed "structural equation modelling" (SEM). SEM enables one to test different and complex causal pathways.[38] Figure 6.2 provides an abstract example. In the figure, A through I represent different factors, or forces, that eventually contribute to some outcome (crime, rates of inmate infractions, public support for the death penalty, etc.). A virtue of SEM lies in the fact that it enables us to chart a variety of causal pathways anticipated by theory.

---

[38] See, generally, Acock (2013) and Kline (2016); see also Duncan (1966) and Loehlin (1987) for information on path analysis, which follows a logic similar to that of SEM.

When little theoretical guidance exists, we can use SEM to help us think about different causal possibilities. For example, in the figure, A contributes to, or causes, four separate factors – B, C, D, and E. In turn, B contributes to F and G, each of which contributes to the outcome. C contributes to the outcome as well, but does so indirectly through H. Similarly, D contributes to the outcome, but does so indirectly through I. Not least, E contributes to the outcome directly.

Many resources exist that provide detailed, technical background of how SEM works and the various ways it can be utilized.[39] Like most multivariate models, SEM approaches rely on regression-based methods. As is the case with all of the techniques we discuss here, SEM has never been more accessible to researchers. Most mainstream statistical software packages now include modules for SEM. Understanding SEM well enough to use it can take time. But, understanding at least in concept how the tool works is a critical first step for envisioning research questions that might take advantage of it.

Multilevel Analyses

Multilevel analyses constitute a family of techniques aimed at examining causal relationships that cross between different "levels," or "units," of analysis. A typical multilevel analysis considers how context or place influences the behavior of individuals. How do community conditions affect the experiences of individuals that reside there or their views about crime or punishment? How does school environment affect children's delinquency? How do prison facility characteristics influence inmate misconduct? These are examples of questions that require multilevel analysis because they involve consideration of causal forces that may flow from at least two (or more) units of analysis.

Figure 6.3 illustrates this idea. In the figure, two levels exist: schools and students. The figure highlights that school-level characteristics may influence rates of delinquency in schools. For example, schools that have too few teachers and resources may experience higher delinquency rates.

The figure also highlights that individual-level characteristics – that is, characteristics of individual students – may contribute to delinquency among students. For example, students who are malnourished or hungry may engage in more delinquency.

Finally, the figure highlights that school-level characteristics may not only contribute to school-level rates of delinquency, but also to delinquency among individual students. For example, individual students who attend

---

[39] See, for example, Acock (2013) and Kline (2016).

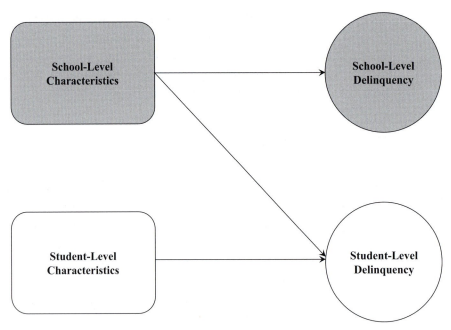

Figure 6.3 The logic of multilevel modeling

schools with too few teachers or resources may be more likely, on average, to engage in delinquency as compared to their counterparts at schools with comparatively more teachers and resources. This idea is interesting on theoretical and policy grounds. From a theoretical perspective, if we wish to understand the causes of delinquency, we may need to examine not only individual-level characteristics of youth, but also the contexts in which they reside. From a policy perspective, if we want to help individual youth to be less likely to offend, we may want to focus on ways to help them navigate the criminogenic influences that they may encounter while at school.

"Multilevel thinking" permeates criminological and criminal justice research.[40] Even so, much progress remains to be made. For example, many mainstream criminological theories of individual-level offending typically focus on individual-level characteristics of youth, not on the social contexts within which they reside. In reality, it seems likely that many factors – individual-, family-, school- or work-, and community-level – may collect-ively influence offending. Thinking about multiple levels of analysis facili-tates thinking about such possibilities.

In the era of "big data," this idea takes on special salience. With the advent of large amounts of electronically available data, researchers now can merge data from many different sources. They also may create

---

[40] Johnson (2010).

hierarchical linkages – that is, they can nest data from within one unit of analysis to another unit of analysis. At the same time, computing power and statistical software packages make it increasingly possible to access and analyze such data. An abundance of opportunities thus now exists to undertake "multilevel thinking" and analyses.

Time Series Analyses

Time series analyses help us to identify trends over time in outcomes of interest, such as crime rates, public views about the correctional system, death penalty sentences, and so on. The analyses consist of plotting outcomes on a traditional Cartesian grid, with a horizontal X-axis and vertical Y-axis. Simple descriptive time series analyses can help us to see what, if any, trends exist and whether there may be seasonal aspects to the trends. Perhaps, for example, delinquency referrals increase every summer, coinciding with the end of school. Given a trend or seasonal pattern, we then might turn our attention to explaining what gives rise to it.

One way to do so involves an interrupted time series analysis. Here, we identify a trend prior to some intervention and then determine if the trend after the intervention differs appreciably from what otherwise would have happened. Figure 6.4 illustrates the idea by showing what we hope would happen with a community policing initiative. Community policing ascended into prominence in the 1980s as a prominent new way of fighting crime through collaborations between the police and citizens. Such efforts might reduce crime and improve citizen satisfaction with the police, or they might not.[41] What we need are data on crime or citizens' views over an extended period of time. We then can plot the information and compare the trends before and after the intervention.

That alone, however, may not be sufficient. What if crime declines after the implementation of community policing, but would have done so even with no new change in policing? To address this problem, we want to compare areas that implemented community policing with similar ones that did not do so. The trick here consists of ensuring that one identifies appropriate "apples-to-apples" areas. That involves using a mix of quantitative and qualitative information. Once the intervention and comparison sites have been identified, we can plot the trends and then use statistical techniques that are designed for assessing time series and whether any differences in trends are statistically significant or substantively important.[42] For example, in the figure, we can see that in areas with community policing,

---

[41] Reisig (2010); Lum and Nagin (2017).
[42] Yaffee (2000); Berk (2008); McCleary *et al.* (2017).

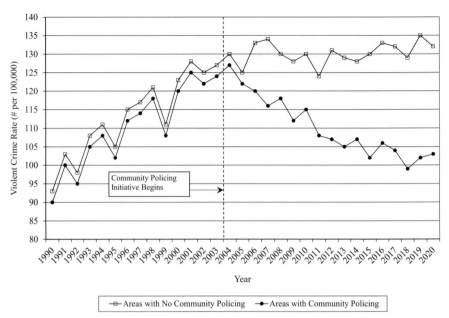

Figure 6.4 Time series analysis to assess policy or program impact
Note: Adapted from Mears (2010:178).

violent crime rates declined. Time series analytic techniques provide a statistical check on our visual impressions.

It can be easy to believe that a difference exists that really does not or, conversely, to miss subtle but important differences that do exist. In the figure, we can see that in the pre-intervention period, the trends in the two sets of areas mirror each other. That suggests that we did a credible job of selecting comparison areas that are similar to the intervention areas. After community policing began in the intervention areas, violent crime came down. It works! But, wait a minute. For the first few years, it is not fully evident that a difference exists. Crime in both areas seems to be trending downward. However, when we use a longer time horizon, we see that crime indeed steadily declined in the areas with community policing. It remained level or slightly increased in the comparison areas.

We can cull several insights from this example. First, it can be easy to assume that a trend has a ready interpretation. In fact, that rarely will be the case. Second, better data make for better assessments. Had we not had data over a relatively long period of time before and after the intervention, it would be difficult to arrive at a credible estimate of impact. Third, short-term and longer-term horizons can and frequently do provide a quite different view of policy and program impacts. Fourth, if we want to claim that an intervention produced a sustained impact, we need to demonstrate that the intervention was consistently and well implemented over the entire observation period. That observation underscores that analysis alone does not suffice. It can help us understand causal relationships. But it cannot answer all relevant questions, such as how well an intervention was implemented or what parts of it contributed to observed impacts.

Life-Course Analyses

Life-course criminological approaches emphasize the importance of considering events and causal forces in the context of an individual's developmental trajectory. The idea is that individuals may follow a certain life-course and that events can alter this path. Crime and contact with the criminal justice system are prime examples – they may be but one part in a dynamic life-course process.[43] As developmental criminological approaches have advanced, so too have statistical tools for testing hypotheses about crime over the life-course.

Here, we refer to life-course analyses as the analytic tools for identifying pathways that individuals may follow and events that may alter these pathways. Consider studies that examine trajectories of offending. This focus departs from earlier work in criminological and criminal justice research, which tended to conceptualize offending as a relatively static phenomenon – either one is or is not a criminal. This static image continues to serve as the main way in which many scholars, policymakers, and practitioners think about offenders and offending. By contrast, the focus on trajectories highlights that the potential for engaging in crime may vary as individuals age. In turn, this potential may be influenced by many different factors (e.g., individual change, family context, community conditions).

Scholars have developed statistical techniques that can identify trajectories, when they change, and what influences them. Trajectory models and related approaches are used to identify clustering of individuals based on how they change over time. There may be "flat" trajectories that change little over time – for example, someone who never offends, someone who offends often and consistently, someone who offends rarely, but consistently, and so on. There may be more dynamic trajectories. For example, there may be individuals who engage in increasingly more crime or those who suddenly experience a dramatic decrease in offending.

Other advanced analytic techniques allow for a developmental focus. Event modeling can be used to estimate how life-course events cause "within person change," by observing individuals both before and after a

---

[43] Farrington (2003a).

particular life event.[44] Other techniques include SEM, path analysis, growth curve models, and analysis of life calendar data.

Not surprisingly, a large body of work has emerged in recent decades that seeks to identify the onset and persistence of, as well as desistance from, offending. This work has led to considerable attention to the causes of each and illustrates how theory and methodology go hand-in-hand.[45] Advances in life-course theories have led to methodological innovations, and the methodological innovations have helped to promote new theories.[46] There has been, for example, increasingly greater attention to understanding recidivism through the prism of the life-course.[47] Rather than focus just on reoffending in the months and years immediately after punishment, researchers have turned to understanding how punishments may influence offending over the life-course. They examine, too, the factors, such as family or community context, that may moderate these effects.[48] Life-course theories and analyses, however, do not have to focus solely on criminal activity. One can examine many outcomes – including law enforcement careers or prosecutorial or judicial decision-making – from a life-course perspective.

Spatial Analyses

Spatial analyses consist of descriptive and predictive efforts aimed at understanding how criminological phenomena are distributed across places, as well as understanding the causes of spatial distributions of these phenomena. One prominent example involves "hot spot" analyses. With this focus, researchers seek to identify clusters of crime or other outcomes among neighborhoods and communities.[49] The trick lies in determining whether a cluster occurs randomly or represents a concentration of crime (or other outcomes) greater than what would be expected given the population in the area or other characteristics of it.

As with many analytic techniques, spatial analysis can be used purely for descriptive purposes. For example, where in a given city does crime seem to concentrate? It also can be used to examine and test ideas about the factors – such as demographic and social characteristics of residents in

---

44 Osgood (2010).
45 See, for example, Krohn and Gibson (2013), Mears *et al.* (2013b), Siennick *et al.* (2013), Copp *et al.* (2016), Mears and Siennick (2016), and Cochran and Mears (2013, 2017).
46 See, for example, Sampson and Laub (1993). See, generally, Farrington (2003a) and Gibson and Krohn (2013).
47 Laub and Sampson (2003); Mears *et al.* (2013b).
48 See, generally, Maruna and Immarigeon (2013) and Rocque (2017).
49 Ratcliffe *et al.* (2011); Braga *et al.* (2014).

communities, the amount of collective efficacy (e.g., the willingness of residents to help one another[50]), or other such dimensions – that may predict clusters.[51] It also can be used to examine whether crime interventions displace crime to other areas. And it can be used to examine whether the factors that contribute to crime in one community (e.g., concentrated social disadvantage) may contribute to crime in others.[52]

Matching Analyses

Part of the science of criminological and criminal justice research lies in examining questions from diverse angles and using as many different approaches as possible. When results are similar across the different approaches, scientists tend to trust them more. We discuss matching analyses here as one example, and then we turn to instrumental variable analyses as another. These techniques are but a few of the many different approaches that exist for providing potentially more rigorous estimates of causal effects than can be obtained with conventional methods.

Matching analyses account for potential sources of selection bias by seeking to approximate the randomization that one obtains in experiments. They do so by creating matched groups – that is, a "treated" group and a comparison group – that share similar characteristics. Compared to regression, matching can be especially useful when "treated" and comparison group members differ starkly across some characteristics. For example, say that we want to evaluate the hypothesis that participating in a prison yoga class reduces inmate recidivism.[53] Any inmate can participate in the program. Random assignment thus is not possible. We could use a traditional regression approach to estimate whether yoga reduces recidivism. But this approach does not necessarily result in an "apples-to-apples" comparison like one would obtain with an experiment.

A matching design overcomes this problem. One such approach is called propensity score matching (PSM). With PSM, we use a multivariate logistic regression model to estimate every inmate's propensity, or likelihood, of participating in yoga based on the measures in our data. We then can assign each inmate a "propensity score." In turn, we can match each yoga participant with a non-participant based on whether they have the same propensity score. If we can obtain matches for all, or nearly all, the yoga participants, then we have approximated an experiment and can

---

[50] See, for example, Pridemore and Grubesic (2013); see, generally, Sampson *et al.* (1997) and Sampson (2013).

[51] For a more detailed discussion of the development of spatial regression in criminological research, see Tita and Radil (2010a, 2010b).

[52] Mears and Bhati (2006); Braga *et al.* (2014).   [53] Auty *et al.* (2017).

compare the recidivism of the two groups.[54] If the yoga group recidivates less than the matched non-yoga group, the hypothesis is supported.

That is the basic logic of matching analyses. Although they can be useful, many conditions must be met for them to generate estimates that we can trust.[55] For example, when researchers have a large set of theoretically relevant matching variables, the estimated treatment effects will be more credible. (As with any statistical modeling approach, matching analysis does not magically solve poor sampling designs or data.) In addition, matching may be untenable when sample sizes are low or when it is difficult to identify a sufficient number of matched cases within a sample.

Instrumental Variable Analyses

Instrumental variable (IV) analysis is another tool used by researchers to estimate causal effects. IV analysis is particularly useful in non-experimental settings when researchers lack confidence that they can account for critical confounding influences. Even with great data, we cannot always account for all potential sources of selection bias. Under certain conditions, IV analysis can sidestep this problem. How? An IV analysis involves identifying an "instrument," which is a special variable that can be used to account for unobserved confounders. To be an instrument, the variable must be associated with both the independent and the dependent variables of interest. However, its association with the dependent variable must be possible only because of the instrument's association with the independent variable.[56]

IV analysis is difficult to envision in the abstract, so instead, consider an example. To assess the impact of illegal immigration on crime, one might collect data on immigration over time and pair that data with crime rate data and relevant control variables. A traditional regression analysis, using control variables, might provide an accurate estimate of an immigration effect. However, with a good instrument, we might obtain a more valid one.

The trick lies in identifying a valid instrument. We need a variable that affects the independent and dependent variables, but would have no direct effect on crime (the dependent variable). The obvious answer? Rainfall. (Just kidding – this possibility is not really obvious at all.) It seems far-fetched, but in fact researchers have explored this exact question. Aaron Chalfin explored whether rainfall serves as a viable instrument for

[54] Apel and Sweeten (2010); He *et al.* (2016); Linden *et al.* (2016).
[55] For general discussions about the benefits and technical issues related to PSM and matching, see Guo and Fraser (2010) and Apel and Sweeten (2010).
[56] Winship and Morgan (1999); Angrist (2006); Bushway and Apel (2010); Morgan and Winship (2015).

estimating the impact of Mexico-to-US immigration on crime.[57] Chalfin argued that extreme amounts of rainfall – either extremely heavy rainfall or extreme drought – in any given time period will reduce immigration rates. Thus, rainfall should directly affect immigration and thus have an indirect effect on crime rates via rainfall's influence on immigration. In this scenario, an IV analysis allows the researcher to identify and then isolate the variation in immigration (i.e., its increases or decreases over time) that is caused by extreme rainfall conditions. Since rainfall is largely random year to year, by isolating the "piece" of variation in immigration that is affected by rainfall, we can estimate the effect of the variation in immigration rates that can be explained by rainfall on crime rates, while ruling out any influences from unmeasured confounding factors. What did Chalfin find? Illegal immigration from Mexico did not appear to affect US crime rates.

IV analysis sounds complex at first and in some ways it is. But once one becomes accustomed to thinking about relationships between two variables and the possibility of instruments, IV analysis provides a potentially powerful statistical tool for answering interesting questions. For example, David Kirk used a natural disaster as an instrument to estimate the effect of housing instability on the recidivism of ex-state prisoners.[58] Other researchers have used the random variation in the assignment of judges to judicial cases (an instrument) to develop causal estimates of prison effects on recidivism.[59]

And Many Other Kinds of Quantitative Analyses

The above analyses provide a sampling of approaches that can be used both to think about and to answer research questions. It is truly a sampling. There are, for example, a host of analytic techniques in biosocial criminology that apply specifically to studies of twins.[60] These techniques take advantage of the fact that genetically similar individuals reside in different social contexts. It thus is possible to tease out different ways in which genetics and the environment may contribute to behavior. In addition, many different types of analyses exist for examining data that follow individuals or places over time. Some approaches are needed because of the unique nature of the phenomenon under study (e.g., the spatial distribution of crime). In others, they allow us to approximate experiments in a more rigorous manner. For example, regression discontinuity analyses allow researchers to take advantage of situations where a natural "break" exists. To illustrate, if sentencing guidelines use a threshold score to determine who

---

[57] Chalfin (2014); see, generally, Mears (2001b).   [58] Kirk (2009).
[59] Green and Winik (2010).   [60] Beaver (2016).

should be sent to prison, a study might compare individuals immediately above and below this score to assess the impact of incarceration on recidivism.[61]

The range of analytic techniques that exist can be a bit dizzying. We have emphasized the notion that there is a science and an art to research, and that is for good reason. Few hard and fast rules exist about which analysis one should use in any given research situation. Instead, analytic choices require having an understanding of a particular research question, goals of a study, the theory guiding it, and data limitations and opportunities. The choices also require knowing that the analysis tool kit includes many options. Will we always be able to conduct or understand these options? No. But if we know that they exist, we then can seek out others who may help us to understand them.

Qualitative Analyses

In criminology and criminal justice, and in the social sciences generally, assessments of causal relationships tend to rely on statistical analyses of quantitative data.[62] Such analyses can provide a convenient and, when done well, rigorous way to ensure that we have accurately gauged how two or more phenomena may be causally related. Analyses are not, however, magical. In particular, they do not compensate for poor theory, data, or model specification. Not least, they may not always be possible or the best option.

Qualitative analyses, discussed earlier in the chapter, can be helpful in these cases or as a way to augment statistical analyses. Historical-comparative research is illustrative. If we want to understand how a myriad of factors interact over many decades or even centuries, we will need to rely on diverse sets of data, including archival records. Similarly, if we want to understand the role of state political context in shaping imprisonment policies, we need historical works that describe changes in penal regimes.[63] Or, if we want to understand the influence of the street code on community dynamics, we likely require analyses of ethnographic data.[64] That would entail living in a community and observing individuals and groups.

For criminological or criminal justice phenomena that cover many decades or centuries or that involve complicated interactions and dynamics that unfold in complicated ways over time, qualitative analyses may be our only and best option. That means, though, that we should be cautious in accepting causal claims. Why? It is difficult to rigorously and systematically

[61] See, for example, Mitchell *et al.* (2017).   [62] Kleck *et al.* (2006).   [63] Barker (2009).
[64] Anderson (1999).

evaluate whether the many complicated causal chains actually operate as described. That is fine, though. All research must be evaluated with a skeptical, questioning eye. That axiom holds true for both qualitative *and* quantitative analyses.

ANALYSES FOR POLICY AND PROGRAM ANALYSIS

The methods that social scientists use apply not only to "basic" (science-focused) research, they also can be used for policy and program analysis. As we discuss in Chapter 7, the main difference between "basic" and "applied" research lies with the substantive focus. "Basic" research tends to focus on generating scientific knowledge about crime and justice – it refers to the idea that researchers seek to understand the core causes of phenomena. By contrast, "applied" research tends to focus on efforts to apply knowledge or research in ways to improve public safety and justice through policies and programs. It focuses, for example, on generating scientific knowledge about the need for or the theory, uses, impacts, and cost-efficiency of policies, programs, practices, laws, and the like. However, no special set of analyses exists for the exclusive purpose of examining policies and programs. Rather, researchers rely on the same box of tools for such endeavors as they use for "basic" research studies.

META-ANALYSIS AND SYSTEMATIC REVIEWS

Meta-analysis is a study of studies. Researchers seek to identify prior empirical studies that focus on the same research question and then to assess the strength of effects or a pattern of findings across those studies.[65] To do so, the researcher typically codes each individual study's estimated effect, including its magnitude and direction, along with other key characteristics of each study's research design (e.g., sample size, collection strategy, sample characteristics, methodological characteristics). The analysis then seeks to estimate the consistency and strength of an effect. It does so after taking into account – through a regression analysis that controls for the quality of each study – the characteristics of the constituent studies.

Perhaps the most significant benefit of meta-analysis lies in its ability to limit the role of subjective biases in assessments of the "state of the literature."[66] "Narrative" reviews, where a researcher reads studies and arrives at a sense of what the overall pattern of results indicates, can be

[65] See, for example, Lipsey and Wilson (2001), Lipsey (2009), and Pratt (2012).
[66] Weisburd *et al.* (2017).

problematic. Researchers might unconsciously give greater weight to studies with results that accord with what they think must be correct. They may dismiss others when the results conflict with their assumptions about what somehow must be true. Meta-analyses reduce that influence by relying on a quantitative analysis of the estimated effects from all studies and by introducing controls for the strength of different study designs. A poorly designed study, for example, generates estimates that should be given less weight than one that is well designed.

Do meta-analyses matter? Yes. Many examples exist of situations where an assumed relationship exists that a meta-analysis then reveals either not to exist or to be highly suspect. To illustrate, many evaluations of juvenile drug courts exist. These courts emerged in the early 1990s and subsequently proliferated. Some narrative reviews have concluded that they effectively reduce recidivism. However, using a meta-analysis, Emily Tanner-Smith and colleagues found that juvenile drug courts were no more successful than traditional court-processing approaches to reducing recidivism.[67]

That said, meta-analyses – like all research studies – are only as good as the data on which they rely. For example, if studies that identify null effects of a program never get published (termed the "file drawer" problem), then relying on published studies will provide a skewed assessment of program effectiveness.[68]

Another approach to assessing the state of evidence on a topic involves the use of a systematic review.[69] This approach goes beyond the narrative reviews typical of many dissertations, journal articles, and the like. It involves selection of studies that meet pre-established criteria (e.g., reliance on experiments or strong methodological designs, such as matching analyses and the use of controls to address confounding). It involves, too, efforts to quantify the potential bias in each study, data quality, and the rigor of each study based on a scoring system (e.g., "low," "medium," or "high" quality). Use of protocols for the reviews elevates their assessments above narrative reviews and provides an alternative to meta-analysis.

EFFECTIVELY DISPLAYING AND CONVEYING INFORMATION

Regardless of the analysis used, displaying or conveying information constitutes a critical part of research. When presented effectively, information is understood by the audience. When done poorly, the research is misunderstood and potentially misused.

---

[67] Tanner-Smith *et al.* (2016).   [68] Cooper (2017).   [69] Higgins and Green (2011).

The impact of any study on theory, research, or policy may well be determined by the extent to which it effectively communicates findings. Form and function go together. To convey results well, it can help to use well-organized tables and clear figures and charts.[70] Taking time to creatively present information can be the difference between people understanding or misunderstanding study findings. Simple illustrations can be far more effective than complicated or fancy figures.

In many analyses, the magnitude of an effect may be difficult to discern. For example, in regression analyses, a coefficient may not always be straightforward to interpret. Use of a figure – with values of a causal variable (X) on the x-axis and of an outcome (Y) on the y-axis – can be helpful in these situations. We then can more easily see whether an effect appears to be large (e.g., a steep slope) or small (e.g., a slope that is almost flat).

Graphical displays are especially important for policymakers and practitioners. When done right, the displays can make complicated statistical results digestible. It is commonly said that a picture is worth a thousand words. That axiom certainly holds true in research. For example, charts can far more effectively show the causal logic of a complicated theory or program than can many pages of text.[71]

A related part of the research process includes accurately conveying information. Trivial findings should not be presented in a way that suggests they are earth-shaking. Similarly, we should not bury important findings behind mountains of statistics, tables, and the like. It also is important that the limitations of studies be clearly articulated. All studies have limitations – the samples may be problematic, data may be missing for key measures, only a handful of relevant outcomes may be available, and so on. Information about them provides context for understanding the caution that should be exercised when interpreting study results.

CONCLUSION

Analyses might be seen as the final and most important part of research. They are not. As we emphasized in earlier chapters, analyses go hand in hand with study design, data considerations, and the theoretical or policy-focused questions that we seek to answer. Analyses are no more independent of these dimensions than cooking techniques are independent of the recipes, ingredients, and the social contexts for which specific dishes are intended (e.g., dinner with friends, lunch for next week, wedding reception).

[70] RAND (1996).   [71] Mears (2010).

If we are to conduct, evaluate, or use analyses well, we should be conversant with multiple aspects of research. This includes the goals, theory, and questions that guide any given study. Analyses do not solve poor research design. They also do not correct for insufficient attention to articulating the theoretical underpinnings of study hypotheses or for data of poor quality.

When done well, however, analyses can advance scientific understanding and policy. They enable us to provide representative empirical descriptions of phenomena. We can identify the social meaning of criminological and criminal justice phenomena, as well as their potential causes. And we can test hypothesized causal relationships and assess policy or program impact.

Sometimes the word "analysis" brings to mind advanced statistics. These can shed light on important questions and so have their place. But they do not substitute for analyses that directly answer a study's questions. For example, simple descriptive statistics, including averages and percentages, can provide critical insights into the prevalence of various phenomena. Consider school shootings. Media accounts convey a sense that they occur regularly. They certainly happen far too frequently. That, however, does not mean that they are increasing. A well-done descriptive study can provide us with perspective on the scope of and trends in this problem.[72] In turn, a well-done qualitative study might shed light on potential causes of school shootings. From a scientific perspective, such undertakings are as important as any study that uses sophisticated statistical modeling techniques.

We began the chapter with the question, "Which analyses are best?" The answer should be evident – none. What is best depends entirely on where our researcher sensibility carries us. That does not mean that "anything goes." To the contrary, a researcher sensibility means that we bring to the table an awareness that analyses should be evaluated in light of the questions they were designed to answer. They also should be evaluated in light of how much we can trust them. For example, a statistical analysis that fails to include controls for factors that we think might bias an estimated effect should lead us to be even more skeptical than we otherwise might be about a finding. An analysis that relies on a rich set of controls should give us greater confidence. And if the analysis focuses on a highly specific group of individuals (e.g., repeat violent sex offenders), we should question how generalizable the results may be to other groups (e.g., first-time non-violent felons or, for that matter, any other category of offender).

---

[72] Mears *et al.* (2017b).

A final note – care and caution should be exercised when presenting or interpreting study results. It can be easy to unwittingly convey the sense that a particular finding must be especially important. It also can be easy to be led into accepting research accounts that present seemingly stunning, ground breaking results. Part of a researcher sensibility entails a focus on "packaging" – that is, how a study presents results and whether it does so in ways that help or hinder an accurate interpretation of the results. The best research makes this step easy. It cautions us by identifying limitations of a study. It provides a sense of the magnitude of an effect or how much we can trust an explanation for one. When research does not make it easy, however, we should identify the limitations and potential significance of a study ourselves.

Part III

Types of Criminological and Criminal Justice Research

7 Basic (Science-Focused) vs. Applied (Policy-Focused) Research

INTRODUCTION

Research comes in different "flavors." Two broad categories can be identified. First, there is research that seeks to advance science. The goal? Generation of knowledge for knowledge's sake. Second, there is research that seeks to advance policy. We term the first "basic" research because of the focus on uncovering fundamental facts or causes about things. The second we term "applied" research because of the focus on applying research and knowledge in ways that can improve policy. This distinction warrants attention because the history of criminological and criminal justice research has involved a tension between "basic" and "applied" researchers, as discussed in Chapter 2. The tension stems from the view held by some scholars that only basic research is important. Other scholars, as well as policymakers and practitioners, may believe that only applied research is valuable. In reality, better theories and greater understanding of crime and criminal justice can come from applied research; at the same time, policy advances for reducing crime and improving justice can come from basic research.[1] Awareness of the two types of research can open doors. It allows us to imagine a much wider universe of questions than we otherwise might consider and to identify new ways to improve policy.

This chapter thus examines the question: What makes for "basic" research and "applied" research, respectively? It turns then to several related questions: What is the evaluation research hierarchy and its relevance for basic and applied research? In what ways can basic research have policy implications and in what ways can applied research have scientific implications? And, turning in particular to policy, what are the challenges faced by researchers in providing useful guidance to policymakers and practitioners?

---

[1] Rossi (1980); Petersilia (1991); Mears (2010, 2016b).

BASIC (SCIENCE-FOCUSED) RESEARCH VS. APPLIED (POLICY-FOCUSED) RESEARCH

The field of criminology and criminal justice has led to long-standing tensions between those who feel that its sole focus should be on advancing science and others who feel that the field should focus on policy and practice (see Chapter 2). As with many things in life, a distribution exists. Some researchers hew strongly to one end of the spectrum, others to the opposite end, and most likely sit near the middle and embrace both types of research. During certain eras in the history of the field of criminology and criminal justice, some parts of this spectrum have held more sway than others. But both types of research still have been and remain a central feature of criminological and criminal justice research.

What, though, is "basic" research? We briefly touched on it in Chapter 6: "Basic" does not mean "simple." It instead refers to the idea that scientists seek to understand the underlying forces that shape or govern phenomena. Basic research questions include the following: What exactly is crime? Why are some actions considered crimes, but not others? What causes crime? Why does something cause crime? Under what specific conditions does it do so?

These and other questions can lead us to deeper insight into the inner workings of some phenomena. Of course, for any question, there may be superficial answers. For example, stealing from someone is a crime because a law exists that defines such action as criminal. Right. But why does the law exist? And, regardless of whether a law exists, why and under what conditions would someone steal from someone else? Whether we focus on crime, policing, sentencing, law-making, or any other topic, our goal with "basic" research consists of unraveling deep answers regardless of whether there may be policy implications.

That does not always mean that "basic" research always identifies causes. To the contrary, as we discussed in earlier chapters, research advances on many different fronts. That can include the description of new phenomena. Descriptive efforts then might lead to speculation about causes, development of theories, tests of them, and so on.

"Applied" research differs in that it seeks insights that can contribute to policy in some way. How? Such research might assess empirically the need for a policy, the theoretical underpinnings of it, how well the policy is implemented, its impacts, or its cost-efficiency. And it would emphasize how one might translate research findings into policy, how to enhance adoption of research-based policy, or how to effectively disseminate research results.[2]

---

[2] Laub (2012).

This distinction between basic and applied research may make it seem that the basic research only advances scientific knowledge and that applied research only advances policy. That simply is not true. Basic research may seek to address a question that advances science. In so doing, though, it may well inform policy debates. Consider a study of sexting, which involves sending sexually explicit images via electronic social media, such as text messages.[3] The study might be undertaken with the motivation that underlies many studies – researchers learn about a phenomenon and begin to study it by first mapping its contours, such as where and among whom it occurs. Although the researchers may not be set on informing policy, the study might inform discussions about the prevalence of sexting. The study also might lead to discussions about what, if anything, should be done to address it.

Conversely, consider a legislative request to examine whether assistance to ex-felons in obtaining employment effectively results in job attainment and reduced offending. The focus here is avowedly on policy. There is an opportunity, though, to apply and test theory. For example, conflict, labeling, and opportunity theories can be viewed as arguing that poverty contributes to pursuit of criminal activity. By extension, they imply that efforts to reduce poverty may reduce offending. Evaluation of an employment assistance program thus could be used to test this idea and extend theoretical arguments about factors that contribute to desistance.[4] Policy studies thus can and do contribute to the development of theory.[5]

In short, and as Peter Rossi has emphasized, "the line between basic and applied work . . . is fuzzy and indeterminate."[6] We can see that in the leadership of criminology and criminal justice and in the content of scholarly association presidential addresses. Lawrence Sherman, for example, a former president of the American Society of Criminology, became famous for his participation in evaluation of a policy of mandatory arrest in cases of domestic violence and for developing defiance theory.[7] Like those made by many others in the Society, his Presidential Address called for greater interplay between science- and policy-focused research.[8] A similar dual focus on basic and applied research can also be found in the Academy of Criminal Justice Sciences' presidential addresses and publications. This focus stems from the fact that many researchers have dual interests – they want to advance both science and policy. It also stems from the "fuzzy and

[3] Mitchell et al. (2012).
[4] See the discussion in Rossi (1980:898); see also Mears et al. (2014).
[5] Rossi (1980); Cooper and Worrall (2012).   [6] Rossi (1980:893).
[7] Sherman and Berk (1984); Sherman (1993).
[8] Petersilia (1991); Mears (2010, 2016b); Laub (2012); Blomberg et al. (2016); see also Rossi's (1980) account of sociology.

indeterminate" line that differentiates basic and applied studies. One way to see the reason for this indeterminacy is to focus on the evaluation hierarchy.

THE EVALUATION RESEARCH HIERARCHY

Evaluation research emerged as a distinct type of undertaking – one focused on policy – during the 1930s and expanded during the 1950s.[9] Social science and its methods became more widely known during this time. After World War II, federal funding to reduce poverty and disease led to recognition that these methods might be used to identify whether government programs benefited society. Applied, or evaluation, research quickly took off: "By the end of the 1950s, program evaluation was commonplace. Social scientists engaged in assessments of delinquency prevention programs, psychotherapeutic and psychopharmacological treatments, public housing programs, educational activities, community organization initiatives, and numerous other initiatives."[10]

In the decades that followed, different disciplines – including criminology and criminal justice – maintained a distinct focus on the phenomena and theories of interest to them. Evaluation research developed as a distinct field as well. Its emphases overlapped with and contributed to advances across the social sciences. Federal demonstration projects, for example, provided opportunities to apply experimental and survey methods to evaluating policies. They also provided opportunities to investigate "basic" research questions in sociology, psychology, social work, and more. The timing for criminological and criminal justice scholarship was fortuitous. New theories and methods were on the rise, and so, too, was funding for a vast array of crime prevention and control policies.

What, then, exactly is evaluation research?[11] Rossi and his colleagues have defined it as follows: "[Policy] evaluation is the use of social research methods to systematically investigate the effectiveness of social intervention

---

[9] Rossi *et al.* (2004).   [10] Rossi *et al.* (2004:9).

[11] Scholars sometimes use "research" and "evaluation research" to mean different things. For example, the authors of one article on evidence-based policy noted: "We often use the word *research* to refer to all types of systematic empirical inquiry, including evaluation. We use *evaluation* to refer specifically to research that examines the processes and outcomes of social interventions" (Weiss *et al.* 2008:44; emphasis in original). We take a somewhat different view of the matter. As can be seen by reviewing the hierarchy, evaluation involves more than a focus on processes and outcomes. It also involves a focus on questions about the need for a policy, the theory, design, or conceptualization of the policy, and its cost-efficiency. It is, however, true that many research studies are not expressly designed as evaluations. Regardless, the distinction between "research" and "evaluation research" is not, in our view, especially helpful. For that reason, the terms are used interchangeably in this book.

programs in ways that are adapted to their political and organizational environments and are designed to inform social action to improve social conditions."[12] They actually used the term "program" rather than "policy" evaluation. We use the latter term because to us it seems to suggest more clearly that our interest should be with a wide spectrum of efforts – laws, rules, procedures, practices, and, of course, programs – that may influence crime and justice.[13]

Is "evaluation research" different from "research"? No. It simply constitutes research that focuses on the specific task of evaluating policy questions. That distinction is, we think, useful, though not especially consistent. It would be better to talk about "science-focused research" and "policy-focused research." That terminology underscores that research is but a tool. As such, it can be used in different ways, such as to advance science or policy.

Even then, some confusion arises. For example, we just discussed the fact that "basic" research and "applied" (evaluation) research can overlap a great deal. They both rely on theories and scientific methods. Also, pursuit of one activity frequently seems to contribute to another. The situation can seem a bit of a muddle, all the more so because some scholars and texts do not necessarily agree on terminology.[14]

Our view is that the terminology should not matter. What should matter are the ideas. And the most important one is that all kinds of research – whether used to answer "basic" or "applied" questions – can contribute to advancing science and policy. It can be hard in fact to know when a study will contribute more to one goal or the other.

Against that backdrop, then, we describe the "evaluation hierarchy." Knowledge of this hierarchy can open the door to thinking about many interesting and important policy questions. It also can open the door to advances in understanding law, crime, criminal justice, and formal and informal social control – all of which constitute domains of central interest to scholars.

This hierarchy consists of five types of evaluations: (1) needs; (2) theory; (3) implementation (or process); (4) impact; and (5) cost-efficiency. Some discussions of evaluation research may prioritize discussion of implementation and impact evaluations under the assumption that they matter more than other types.[15] That is understandable. From a policy perspective, we naturally might want to know, "Does this program or practice 'work'?"

---

[12] Rossi *et al.* (2004:16).   [13] Mears (2010:265).

[14] See, for example, Rossi *et al.* (2004), Weiss *et al.* (2008), and Mears (2010, 2017).

[15] The details of the evaluation hierarchy can be found in Rossi *et al.* (2004) and, as applied to criminological and criminal justice research, in Mears (2010).

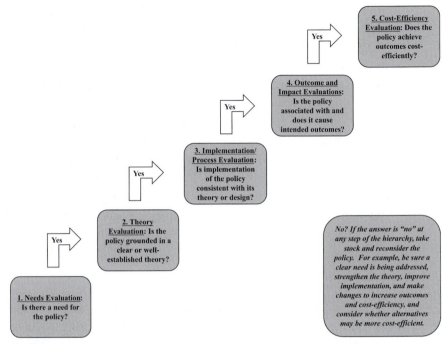

Figure 7.1 The evaluation research hierarchy
Note: Adapted from Mears (2010:10); see also Rossi *et al.* (2004:80). Used with permission from Sage Publications.

That is, is it effective in changing some outcome? No one type of evaluation merits more attention than another, though.

Figure 7.1 illustrates the hierarchy and its logic. It depicts five types of evaluations. Each answers a different question. A *needs* evaluation is just that – it examines whether a need exists for a policy that is up for consideration or that already has been adopted. A *theory* evaluation examines whether the policy rests on a credible, well-established theoretical foundation. Such a foundation includes a clear causal logic that shows how various parts of a policy work together to result in an improved outcome. An *implementation* evaluation – sometimes referred to as a process evaluation – examines whether a policy has been enacted in a way that accords with its design. An *outcome* evaluation monitors changes in an outcome that the policy seeks to change; an *impact* evaluation employs experimental or quasi-experimental research designs to determine if the policy actually caused any observed changes. And, not least, a *cost-efficiency* evaluation assesses the costs and benefits associated with the policy. Cost-efficiency evaluations come in two flavors. Cost-effectiveness evaluations examine costs relative to a particular outcome; cost–benefit studies monetize all costs and benefits.

We will elaborate more on each type of evaluation below. Here, though, we describe the logic of the hierarchy. It is simple: In developing better policy, we want to proceed through each level before proceeding to the next because doing so will help to ensure that we alleviate social problems and do so efficiently. What does "better" mean? It means investing resources and time only after first establishing that a significant social problem, such as crime or prison system graft, exists. Otherwise, why waste resources on it? It means not proceeding with a policy unless we have a clear idea of why and how it can effectively address the social problem. Otherwise, an idea that somehow seems intuitively sound may lead us astray. It also means that we should ensure full and quality implementation before assessing effectiveness. Why expect, for example, a policy to be effective if it is not well-implemented? And it means assessing cost-efficiency only after we have assessed a policy's effectiveness. A policy can hardly be cost-efficient if we spend money on it, but have no improved outcomes.

Needs Evaluation

A few observations about each type of evaluation are warranted. A *needs evaluation* consists of a study that seeks to document the prevalence, intensity, and nature of some social problem, such as crime, non-responsiveness to victims, police officer suicide, racial, ethnic, or gender disparities in punishment, and so on. Consider a situation in which a physician tells us that we should completely change our diet, exercise three hours each day, and, for good measure, quit our jobs and meditate as often as possible. Some of those steps might be healthy. However, embracing the recommendations might change our lives for the worse. Quitting work, for example, would likely leave us in a precarious financial position. The doctor responds by saying that we look a bit "stressed." Okay. But simply "looking stressed" hardly amounts to a need of such magnitude as to call for such a significant life change. Just as importantly, we can take other steps besides quitting work to reduce stress.

This idea undergirds policy assessments of need. Without a sufficient need for intervention, and without a comparison of the relative need for different policies, we lack a basis for effectively investing resources. For example, probation departments might adopt new training approaches that are not warranted or states might enact laws that address rare problems. An axiom in legal arenas states that "bad cases make bad law." One example consists of isolated incidents. Perhaps a school shooting occurs and the perpetrators texted each other to coordinate their efforts. Legislators then consider passage of a law that prohibits students from carrying phones onto school grounds. That almost seems to make sense. If the shooters had not texted each other, no shooting would have occurred. From a needs evaluation perspective, though, a few questions surface. For example, exactly how often do school shootings involve multiple shooters who coordinated their efforts via text messaging? Among those who did, how many would just as easily have undertaken an attack without the use of smart phones? Not least, is it really the case that the shooting would not have occurred without student access to phones? We might find compelling, empirical research that leads us to believe that a significant problem exists. We might find research, too, that suggests warrant for the phone ban. Just as likely is the possibility that we determine that no clear need exists for one.

Theory Evaluation

A *theory evaluation* examines a policy's causal logic. That is, how exactly might the policy produce particular outcomes? We discussed in Chapter 4 the causal logic of a drug court. Timely sentencing, close supervision, and frequent check-ins with a judge may produce a specific deterrent effect. Drug treatment might reduce addiction and the criminogenic effects that addiction can have, such as eroding social bonds and creating incentives to steal to support a drug habit. Rehabilitative programming might improve employment prospects, which in turn could reduce strain. Collectively, these activities and theoretical mechanisms might combine to reduce recidivism. In cases where a policy has a clear causal logic and it incorporates established theories or credible assumptions, there is a fighting chance that it will be effective. In addition, the logic provides guidance to those responsible for implementing a policy or program on what they should do. However, many times, the logic goes unarticulated except in the most bare-bones way. A policy is not likely to be effective in such cases.

Theory evaluations include several elements. They identify: (1) the organizational plan for implementing a policy (e.g., Who will do what?); (2) the service delivery or utilization plan (e.g., What services will be given to or required of certain groups?); and (3) the impact theory (e.g., How exactly will each organizational activity and service ultimately achieve the policy's goals?). The impact theory typically will identify short-, intermediate-, and longer-term goals. For example, drug treatment might be anticipated to result in reduced addiction in the short term, improved relationships at home and work in the intermediate term, and employment and less offending in the longer term. We can see here the critical importance of theory. For every part of a causal chain, we need to identify the theoretical grounds for anticipating how one activity or outcome may influence another. That includes specifying the types of causal relationships that may exist. Do we expect drug treatment sessions to have an instantaneous and cumulative effect? Or do we anticipate some type of threshold effect, such that significant improvements only arise after a certain number of treatment sessions? Policies can involve complicated causal chains. That is one reason why policy-focused research provides numerous opportunities for developing, applying, and testing theory.

Another important aspect of theory evaluations involves the assumptions on which policies are built. These frequently can be examined empirically. An illustration: Observing that truancy seems to be increasing, a policymaker advocates a law that requires revocation of the driver's license of any student who skips school. Other policymakers agree and enact the law. They learn a year later that no impact on truancy occurred. Why? After studying more closely the students who skipped, it becomes clear that almost none of the truants had driver's licenses. Perhaps, then, a need to address truancy existed. But the need for this particular policy did not because the theory on which it rested made an incorrect assumption. Had the officials undertaken a theory evaluation first – one that developed a clear causal logic and examined its empirical underpinnings – they might well have charted a different path toward addressing truancy.[16]

Needs and theory evaluations go hand in hand. We not only want to identify the amount and nature of a problem, we also want to know what causes it. In addition, we want to identify which causes can be influenced by policy. Then we want to know which, among those causes, might result in the largest benefits.

Policies frequently arise that violate these axioms. They address a problem whose prevalence is unknown. At the same time, they address a cause that cannot readily be changed and ignore those that can be and that, if addressed, might have a greater impact.

Implementation (or "Process") Evaluation

An *implementation – or "process" – evaluation* constitutes the logical next step after a theory evaluation. Given a need for a policy and the development of one that rests on a credible theoretical, logical, and empirical foundation, we want to determine how well the policy is implemented. To illustrate the importance of this type of evaluation, consider a medical intervention for a serious bacterial infection. A physician tells us to rest in bed for seven days and then slowly, over another week, resume a normal routine, drink ten to twelve cups of water each day, and take antibiotics with food four times a day. If we follow the instructions, then hopefully we will be healthy at the end of the two weeks. What will happen, though, if we

---

[16] Professor Robert O. Dawson, who served on Mears' doctoral dissertation committee, offered this real-life example to illustrate one of the ways in which policies can proceed on questionable empirical or logical grounds.

ignore them entirely? Or only follow some of the instructions? For example, what if we do not rest at home, but instead work full-time, drink minimal amounts of water, and only take half of the medicine? Why only half? Perhaps we are forgetful. Or we take the antibiotics without food, get an upset stomach, and then develop an aversion to taking the medicine. The end result? We do not get better and perhaps our condition worsens. The implication should be clear: If researchers test a new treatment protocol and do not monitor adherence to it, they might conclude that the treatment is ineffective. In reality, it may be that the treatment never had a chance to be effective because participants in the study did not actually take the medicine.

Policies can be quite complicated and involve many moving parts. Community policing, assessment protocols for whom to detain in jail, a legislative mandate to privatize a certain percentage of corrections spending, a family-focused rehabilitative treatment intervention for delinquent youth – these and a myriad of other policies rarely consist of just one activity. This creates enormous room for poor implementation. Police officers may not be trained in community policing and so act in ways contrary to the spirit of this approach to reducing crime. A local court may lack sufficient staffing to undertake high-quality mental health assessments of youth in detention. Prison system officials may struggle with monitoring what exactly occurs inside private prison facilities. And staff in family-focused treatment programs may act in ways that antagonize families of delinquent youth. In every instance, we can anticipate a failure to achieve desired goals or outcomes.

Poor implementation plagues many criminal justice policies.[17] The reasons are numerous: insufficient staffing, poor leadership, little to no oversight, ambiguity about which activities or services to prioritize, and so on.[18] The end result is the same – policies fail to produce appreciable gains. Money gets spent, but we will not see improvements in outcomes.

These observations point to three benefits that can result from implementation evaluations. First, we can obtain critical information about the amount and quality of implementation; in so doing, the results can be used to increase accountability. They do not magically create it. Rather, the results provide information that policymakers, administrators, and the public can use to judge performance. They then can make decisions about how to proceed. When used in this way, such research is called a

---

[17] Lipsey *et al.* (2005); Mears (2007, 2010).
[18] Farrington (2003b); Bardach (2004, 2012).

"summative evaluation."[19] (Performance monitoring is frequently used in this manner; it amounts to an ongoing, rather than one-time, evaluation.[20])

Second, an implementation study can be used as a "formative evaluation." It provides information about how well a policy has been implemented. It also provides information about what causes any shortfalls in implementation and what might be done to make improvements.[21] A formative evaluation thus helps to "form" the policy. Here, again, we can see the evaluation hierarchy's logic. Few policies achieve perfect implementation from the start. They encounter unexpected problems. Before evaluating their impact, then, we should make adjustments to improve the quality of implementation. If the adjustments require major changes, we may even want to alter the design of the policy. For example, perhaps it is unrealistic to expect that a drug court provide weekly check-ins with a judge. We might need to reconsider whether the frequency of the check-ins is viable. That in turn might lead us to reassess whether the court has the resources to support judicial monitoring as a part of the overall drug court design.

Third, implementation evaluations can be used to help make sense of impact evaluations. Perhaps we find that a drug court greatly reduced offending. Drawing on an implementation evaluation, we learn that check-ins with the judge rarely occurred. By contrast, drug treatment services occurred frequently and with a high degree of fidelity to protocol. We have some basis, then, for believing that the drug courts can be effective without relying on frequent judicial oversight. Of course, we also have a basis for wondering whether the results might have been even more beneficial if more frequent judicial check-ins had occurred. These interpretations enable us to provide a more accurate appraisal of the impact evaluation. They enable us, too, to point to important questions that future research and policy would want to consider.

Outcome and Impact Evaluations

Outcome and impact evaluations come next in the hierarchy. With *outcome evaluations*, we want to identify whether a policy is associated with expected outcomes. For example, lawmakers might enact sentencing guidelines in the hopes that the guidelines reduce inconsistency in sentencing. An outcome evaluation could entail developing a measure of inconsistency and then determining whether inconsistency actually declined after

---

[19] McDavid and Hawthorn (2006:21); see also Rossi *et al.* (2004:36).
[20] General Accounting Office (1998); Hatry (2006).
[21] McDavid and Hawthorn (2006:21); see also Rossi *et al.* (2004:34).

enactment of the guidelines. Outcome evaluations can be useful as part of an overall performance monitoring process. They provide information that can guide policy. For example, if inconsistency in sentencing increased, we then would know to look more closely at the implementation of the guidelines to understand what would create this effect.

Although helpful, outcome evaluations do not establish causality. That means that they cannot establish whether a policy is effective. To assess effectiveness, we want *impact evaluations*. Experiments constitute one approach to assessing impact. As discussed in Chapter 6, however, many quasi-experimental research designs and statistical methodologies exist for achieving the same goal. Regardless of approach, an impact evaluation relies on a comparison group or place to determine if a policy produces changes in one or more outcomes.

Making inferences about causality without a point of comparison can be problematic. To illustrate, I might run a juvenile court diversion program and identify a 98 percent "success rate." That is, only 2 percent of the participants commit an offense that results in new referrals to juvenile court. By contrast, perhaps 30 percent of all other juvenile court referrals recidivate. We have a comparison group in this instance. It is not, though, the same as the diversion group. It includes youth who may have committed many prior and serious offenses. By contrast, my diversion program might allow in only youth who have no prior offenses and then committed a misdemeanor. The problem is one of selection bias. My program has selectively identified the "best" youth, that is, youth with the lowest chance of committing a crime again. (The problem sometimes is described as one of "creaming" the "best" cases.) In turn, we are left with an "apples-to-oranges" rather than an "apples-to-apples" comparison. Another way of describing the situation is to say that selection effects undermine the validity of the comparison. We need some way to arrive at an "apples-to-apples" comparison that would produce valid causal estimates. Experiments and various quasi-experimental designs and statistical methods provide the tools for doing so. What would we find if first-time misdemeanants had been randomly assigned to my diversion program and others to "business as usual"? Who knows, but the betting money is that both groups would have low recidivism rates because of the focus on low-risk youth.

Impact evaluations provide a foundation for assessing policy and they are greatly needed in criminal justice. The effectiveness of many criminal justice policies frequently is unknown. Why? They have not been subject to rigorous impact evaluations.[22] Such evaluations provide opportunities to

---

[22] General Accounting Office (2003); Sherman (2003a, 2004); Lipsey *et al.* (2005); Mears (2010, 2017).

evaluate effectiveness and to investigate interesting theoretical questions. Perhaps, for example, a program produces greater reductions in offending for one group than another. Why? In seeking to answer that question, we may shed light both on ways to improve the program's effectiveness and on ways in which punishment may influence behavior. To illustrate, we might discover that minorities who participate in a diversion program appear to be more likely to offend, whereas whites appear to be less likely to do so. In digging more deeply, we may discover that program staff issued community service conditions that required youth to be transported to and from the service area. Minority parents may have had fewer resources to provide the transportation or less access to public transportation. The impact evaluation thus prompted collection of information that could help improve the program. (For example, program staff might assign community service conditions in places where youth can actually fulfill them.) It also led to insights of interest to scholars, such as how community context can influence the experience and consequences of punishment. Not least, it led to insight into one way in which racial or ethnic disparities may arise in the juvenile or criminal justice systems. Scholars and policymakers alike would be interested in this phenomenon.

Cost-Efficiency (Cost-Effectiveness or Cost–Benefit) Evaluation

Finally, a *cost-efficiency evaluation* enables us to put a dollar value on the impact of a policy. Of course, without knowledge of the magnitude of the impact, we cannot assess a policy's cost-efficiency. That is why the hierarchy requires that an impact evaluation first occur, or that some body of research provide a credible estimate of assumed impact. With one, we can proceed to estimate the "bang for the buck" associated with a policy. Sometimes that can consist of identification of the monetary costs of a crime prevention program relative to improved outcome. We might show, for example, that for every $100 spent, we obtain five fewer crimes. That would be a cost-effectiveness study – we monetize everything but the outcome. This approach can be helpful when comparing two policies that both seek to achieve the same goal.

What do we do, though, if we want to compare two policies with *different* goals? One policy might seek to reduce crime and the other might seek to reduce teen pregnancies. We need a common metric to create a comparison. Cost–benefit analyses do that by monetizing costs and benefits, including the outcomes.[23] In this example, we would need to develop monetary values for each averted crime and teen pregnancy. We would

---

[23] Welsh and Farrington (2000); Nagin (2001); Kee (2004); Roman *et al.* (2010).

want to estimate operational costs as well. Armed with such information, we can compute for each policy net benefits (e.g., a given policy creates a net benefit of $100,000) or cost–benefit ratios (e.g., for each $1 spent, the policy creates $5 in benefits). Then policymakers can decide which one warrants greater support.

Of course, it can be a challenge to arrive at accurate estimates of the monetary value to assign to outcomes. What monetary value should be placed on an averted burglary, assault, rape, or murder? To even ask the question seems off-putting. Yet, without an answer, we lack a foundation for determining where to allocate a finite amount of resources in a situation of competing demands. Researchers thus have developed creative ways of monetizing various social phenomena. For example, citizens can be surveyed about how much they would be willing to pay to avert each of several different types of crimes.

Other challenges exist. For example, which perspective should we adopt in evaluating cost-efficiency? The importance of this question can be seen in the fact that what may be cost-efficient from one perspective may not be so from another. Consider a community policing program. Perhaps it reduces crime in one town by displacing it to another. For the town with the program, we might determine that the program is cost-efficient. But for the one without it, the program is harmful. And for society as a whole? There may be a net gain or loss.

These types of considerations highlight why cost-efficiency evaluations are no panacea. They do not substitute for rigorous impact evaluations. They say nothing about the factors that influence implementation. They can rest on questionable assumptions about the monetary value of various outcomes. And they can fail to include information about unintended costs or benefits if studies do not first identify them. At the same time, they can illuminate the assumptions on which policy preferences rest. Consider supermax prison housing. Many states have invested heavily in it. Because the housing costs a great deal to build and operate, it needs to achieve substantial benefits simply to "break even" – that is, for the benefits to at least offset the costs. A cost–benefit analysis, even one without information on impacts, can be helpful in determining whether investing in this housing makes financial sense.[24] To illustrate, we could seek to estimate costs as accurately as possible and speculate about different potential benefits and their magnitude. We then could conduct break-even analyses that seek to identify just how large the benefits would have to be to justify the costs. In so doing, we may discover that the anticipated benefits would have to be

[24] Lawrence and Mears (2004).

unrealistically large to achieve this goal. Such information need not dictate the final policy decision. It can, though, provide useful insights that can further productive deliberation about the policy and possible alternatives.

Benefits of Evaluation Research

As we can see, each step in the evaluation hierarchy logically leads to the next. If the hierarchy is used, several benefits can arise. First, if policymakers and criminal justice administrators follow it when making decisions, they can ensure that policies address real needs, they are designed and implemented well, adjustments occur to improve implementation, desired impacts are achieved, and policies with the greatest efficiency are identified.

Second, the hierarchy can be useful for thinking about "evidence-based" policy. Recall that in Chapter 2, we highlighted that this term has no objective meaning and is used to mean different things. Policymakers and criminal justice administrators tend to use "evidence-based" to refer to the idea that scientific studies have shown that a policy or program is effective – that is, it improves some outcome, such as public safety or justice. "Scientific" studies, though, do not consist solely of those that assess policy impact. There can be, for example, scientific studies that investigate the prevalence of social problems and theoretical explanations for them. In addition, "science" itself can entail reliance on many different methods, research designs, data sources, and the like. It does not consist solely of experimental or quasi-experimental studies. Against that context, a simple way to use the hierarchy is to view policies as evidence-based if rigorous research approaches demonstrate policy need, a credible policy theory, high-quality implementation, substantial impact, and appreciable cost-efficiency.

Third, and as we have already discussed, use of the hierarchy can lead to a more systematic approach to viewing criminological and criminal justice topics. It also can enable us to gain insights into questions that we otherwise might fail to consider. These questions then might become central to developing new theories or exploring new avenues of inquiry.

The evaluation hierarchy might seem like a tool primarily for applied research; it is not. Each step in the hierarchy examines questions that, if answered, certainly *can* inform policy. Yet, these questions feature prominently in basic research as well. Consider a needs evaluation. In seeking to assess need, we could undertake a prevalence study of crime, citizen dissatisfaction, sentencing disparities, and so on. We might simultaneously seek to understand how different groups perceive a given social problem. That is precisely what basic research entails – identifying the prevalence of phenomena and seeking to uncover how various groups or organizations characterize the phenomena and causes. Similarly, we might assess the theoretical foundation or impact of a policy. Here, again, basic research does the same.

One difference is that a basic research focus might lead us to study criminological or criminal justice phenomena that have little clear relevance for policy. True. Yet, even the most avowedly "basic" research study may have implications for policy. Consider a famous study conducted by Howard Becker that examined deviance. He showed how there is nothing straightforward about using or enjoying marijuana.[25] Instead, individuals learn through social interactions how to use and enjoy marijuana. The study sought to contribute to sociological understanding of deviance. It had, though, implications for policy. How? Any insight into the causes of crime simultaneously sheds light on potential ways to reduce it.

Finally, the hierarchy should be seen for what it is – a heuristic device for helping us to see possibilities for research and the way in which different types of questions are related. It is not itself a methodology. It instead provides a set of logically sequenced questions that various methods can be used to address. Familiarity with the hierarchy in turn provides another way to undertake research creatively to advance science and policy.

BASIC RESEARCH CAN HAVE POLICY IMPLICATIONS AND POLICY RESEARCH CAN ADVANCE SCIENCE

Given how basic and applied research can seemingly blend into each other, one might ask if a distinction between the two is warranted. No correct answer exists. We would say, though, "Yes." The motivation for a study may help us to understand why a study was framed in a certain way. To illustrate, it may lead us to focus on whether a funding source perhaps shaped the study in some way. Consider a situation where Democrats request evaluation of a policy that they do not like. They push for a study that, even if seemingly neutral on the face of it, serves to identify problems with the policy. The assignment to the researcher: Assess whether get-tough sentencing laws create harms. The researcher might objectively answer the question. In so doing, though, an equally important question will not have been investigated: How effective are such laws in reducing recidivism or crime? By focusing only on possible harms, the researcher will be unable to identify whether the policy is effective. The same observation holds for any type of ideologically slanted research question. For example, Republicans

---

[25] Becker (1991).

might request a study that provides a similarly skewed evaluation of a particular policy. Think tanks with liberal or conservative leanings may do the same as well.

The distinction between basic and applied research also can be helpful in thinking about the relevance of a study. Perhaps scholars know that a type of re-entry program effectively reduces recidivism and they know how it does so. A city implements a version of the program and then evaluates it. Given that we have considerable insight into this type of program, there may be little scientific gain from the evaluation. A study still is warranted, though, if no advance occurs for science. The study could be used to inform policymaker decisions about support for the program. It also might provide guidance about how to improve the program's implementation.

These benefits may be modest, but are, we think, important. It can be helpful to recognize that the two types of research differ in their avowed goals, but that the difference reduces to one of relative emphasis. Basic research primarily advances science, but it secondarily helps to inform policy decisions. If one were an investor in knowledge or better policy, the most consistent and largest returns on investment likely would come from investing in both types of research.[26]

We want to emphasize that for scholars interested only in advancing science, the evaluation hierarchy provides a framework for discovering new lines of inquiry. For example, a scholar might undertake a theoretical analysis of political and cultural forces that give rise to get-tough sentencing laws.[27] That would entail a causal analysis akin to undertaking a theory evaluation.

More relevant, though, is that the hierarchy can lead us to ask new, equally interesting questions. For example, what need existed for these policies? Was there in fact an objective need? Or was there simply the perception of need with no objective foundation to support it? Or was a need fabricated in part to enable lawmakers to justify legislation that would garner them political capital? If policymakers truly felt that a need for tougher policies existed, what exactly drove their perceptions? In what ways did they think that punitive sanctions somehow would be effective, and why? To illustrate, was the intent to increase retributive responses to crime or to reduce crime? Was it perhaps something different, such as seeking to gain political capital? Or to control groups perceived as threatening by the powerful?

It also might lead us to consider the implementation of these laws. Such a focus could reveal to us many dimensions of relevance to understanding

---

[26] Weinberg (2015).
[27] Garland (2001, 2013); Gottschalk (2006, 2011, 2013); Barker (2009).

contemporary society. For example, what if get-tough laws are enforced more strongly with minorities or immigrants?[28] Documenting differential implementation of the laws would be of interest in its own right. It would be of interest, too, in thinking about theoretical explanations for variation in sentencing. (A large literature in fact examines the variable application of sentencing laws to different groups.[29])

The hierarchy would also lead us to think about impacts. That is, drawing on insights from a needs evaluation, what effects if any do these laws have on a variety of outcomes? Here, the applied research focus overlaps substantially with the focus of basic research. We are interested in both instances in identifying impacts and how they arise.

Not least, the hierarchy would lead us to consider interesting theoretical questions about the cost-efficiency of get-tough sentencing laws. For example, to the extent that these laws are effective, how cost-efficient are they? What conditions influence the cost-efficiency of the laws? How do lawmakers weigh and balance the uncertainty that attends cost-efficiency estimates? Why do they prioritize some types of uncertainty and ignore others?

CHALLENGES IN PROVIDING USEFUL GUIDANCE TO POLICYMAKERS AND ADMINISTRATORS

Policymakers and criminal justice and correctional administrators may face challenges in obtaining the information they want or need. Here, we discuss several of these challenges.

First, scholars may not want to contribute to policy discussions. That is fine. However, their knowledge of a particular body of work may be salient to a particular policy issue. If they contribute their insights, scholars may feel that they will compromise their values. But if they refrain from weighing in, they may inadvertently allow less knowledgeable experts to inform discussions about the policy. No clear solution here exists save for scholars or researchers in non-academic settings to abide by what they view as appropriate.

That said, we are not suggesting that research should dictate any specific policies. Basic and applied research may inform policies in various ways, but they do not indicate what should happen. Why? Many other considerations go into the decisions that legislators, criminal justice administrators, and those who work in the criminal justice arena make. Political

---

[28] Kubrin *et al.* (2012).
[29] Mears (1998); Mitchell (2005); Johnson (2010); Rodriguez (2010); Feldmeyer *et al.* (2015); Wang and Mears (2015); Mears *et al.* (2016b); Ulmer and Laskorunsky (2016).

considerations may weigh heavily in such decisions. Available resources will be another consideration. And ethical concerns may enter into the equation. Research constitutes but one part of an overall assessment that decision-makers undertake when determining what they should do.[30]

Second, policymakers and administrators may be confronted by "experts" who are more than willing to contribute their insights. Whose views, though, should decision-makers trust? Self-avowed "experts"? If so, which ones? Researchers from left-leaning, right-leaning, or non-partisan research organizations? These individuals all might undertake excellent research, but how can one know when one can trust particular studies from them? Here, again, no simple solution exists except for policymakers and practitioners to develop their own researcher sensibility in requesting and interpreting studies. They should also consider obtaining information about research primarily from individuals with no clear vested interest in a particular policy outcome. For researchers, there is the need to convey any research evidence in ways that accurately convey the state of knowledge. Chapter 10 discusses some of the considerations that both groups should weigh when requesting, evaluating, and using research.

Third, uncertainty can create problems. Those who must make decisions about policy or practice typically do not like uncertainty – they want definitive answers.[31] But uncertainty attends most things in life, and it definitely exists in the research universe. For good reason, scientists are trained to be careful in going too far in generalizing findings or identifying implications for policy. Studies can provide distorted views of the social world. Only with repeated investigation over many years using a wide variety of data and methods can we be confident (not certain) in an assessment. In the policy arena, the landscape is littered with interventions touted as effective after one or two studies only to be shown later to be ineffective.[32] The solution: Research should always be conveyed as accurately as possible and in ways that highlight uncertainty about findings and their relevance for policy need, theory, implementation, effectiveness, or efficiency. What should be resisted is the temptation to say what one thinks decision-makers want to hear or to speak in "sound bytes" that distort research.

Fourth, researchers may consciously or unconsciously seek to lend support to the views held by legislators. Why? One reason may be that it creates an opportunity to be heard and to receive media attention. Regardless of the reason, it can lead to a mistaken belief that scientific "evidence" exists for particular policies. This situation can be especially problematic

[30] Bardach (2012); Mears (2016b).   [31] Ellenberg (2014).   [32] Mears (2010).

when lawmakers seek support for dramatic policy shifts. Political discourse sometimes results in an emphasis on extremes. That can lead to the notion that only extreme options exist. When researchers respond to questions about these extremes, they reinforce the impression that extremes alone constitute the available options. Alfred Blumstein has highlighted how scholars – in responding to numerous calls by legislators in the 1980s to study deterrence – indirectly reinforced the notion that there existed an "either/or" situation, that is, either invest in punitive, deterrence-based policies or in ineffective rehabilitative programs.[33] The more complicated reality? Extreme responses may not be the only options, and they likely are not always effective or ineffective. Researchers should not ignore requests for the state of evidence on some policy issue. Rather, they should – if they choose to weigh in – provide responses that convey the range of options that exist and the evidence for them. They should also highlight uncertainty in what research tells us about the conditions under which effects may arise.

Fifth, researchers rarely receive training in distilling research in ways that help decision-makers, which can create misunderstanding or a situation where research gets ignored.[34] Lawmakers and criminal justice officials have little time to sit through lectures on the intricacies of research design. When confronted with them, they may choose simply not to ask for research guidance. Or they may listen only to those who have honed their presentation skills. The solution is simple – researchers must receive better training in presenting information effectively to a policy-focused audience. Fortunately, considerable guidance exists for doing so. For example, the RAND Corporation, a prominent "think tank" research organization, long ago developed materials for how researchers can effectively present information in written or oral form.[35] Many other sources – federal and state agencies, foundations, books, and more – provide similar information. Much of the guidance boils down to knowing one's audience, tailoring the amount and type of information to the time allotted, packaging material in an accessible manner (e.g., if using slides, use large font and make only one point per slide), and using visual graphics to convey points.

Sixth, it can be difficult to get research into the hands of legislators and criminal justice administrators and practitioners. These groups sometimes critique researchers, especially those in university or college settings, for not focusing on the "real world." They also critique them for providing little actionable insight. Both assessments have some validity. For example, researchers sometimes act as if a theory or the results of a particular study have obvious relevance for policy. All too often, there is in fact nothing

---

[33] Blumstein (1997).   [34] Petersilia (1991).   [35] RAND (1996).

obvious about their relevance. For example, a study that finds that low self-control can increase offending does not provide any insight into *how* one might improve self-control.

That said, it simply is not the case that little credible scientific guidance exists on ways to improve policy and practice.[36] To illustrate, David Weisburd and colleagues reviewed a large set of systematic reviews of research. They found that strong empirical evidence existed that interventions across many domains can be and are effective. These included developmental prevention programs, community prevention, situational prevention, policing, sentencing and deterrence, correctional interventions, and drug treatment interventions.[37] Francis Cullen, a former President of the American Society of Criminology and of the Academy of Criminal Justice Sciences, has written about the many ways in which criminological and criminal justice science has productively guided policy.[38] Many other accounts also document the myriad of ways in which researchers have undertaken studies with "real-world" relevance.[39]

The problem is one of awareness and communication – good and relevant research exists that can productively inform policy and practice. Getting that research into the hands of those who need it is where problems arise.[40] As we have suggested, a researcher sensibility can help to inform requests for studies as well as the ability to sift through the good and the bad. Channels of communication must be created, too. Without them, research results will not find their way to legislatures, agencies, the courts, or other stakeholder groups. As we will discuss, investing in research infrastructure can help to increase the amount and quality of research. It also can create channels of communication that would provide decision-makers with access to credible research.

Finally, one of the central challenges policymakers and administrators may face is not only access to credible research, but also the dearth of relevant research. There is plenty of research that may be relevant to informing policy and practice. However, for many critical decisions that lawmakers and officials must make, information is lacking. Researchers can be called on to testify or offer their views. But the research community cannot provide information that does not exist. What contributes to this situation? Most states and local communities have few resources to allocate to research. Researchers cannot willy-nilly create credible scientific

---

[36] See, generally, Lipsey *et al.* (2005), Mears (2010, 2017), and Weisburd *et al.* (2017).
[37] Weisburd *et al.* (2017).
[38] Cullen (2005); see also Lipsey and Cullen (2007) and Cullen and Gilbert (2013).
[39] See, generally, Petersilia (1991), MacKenzie (2006), Welsh *et al.* (2013), MacKenzie and Farrington (2015), Maguire and Duffee (2015), and Blomberg *et al.* (2016).
[40] Laub (2012).

information out of thin air. What happens? Without research, hunches and philosophical or political ideology drive decision-making.[41] At the federal level, the situation is not much better. Spending on basic or applied research in criminology and criminal justice traditionally has paled in comparison to investment in other policy arenas, such as health care.[42] The solution? Federal, state, and local agencies will need to invest more resources into research if they want information that can help them to create greater accountability and more cost-efficient policy.

CONCLUSION

We end with an illustration – prosecution. In many criminal justice systems, prosecutors hold sway. They have more power than any other system actors, including judges. When, on behalf of citizens, they wield their power well, society benefits from greater accountability, public order, and justice. When they abuse their power, the opposite may occur. It is notable, then, that during the get-tough era in America, throughout the 1980s and in subsequent decades, prosecutors accumulated even more power. Legislators provided more funding for prosecutors than for the judiciary. They enacted laws that provided prosecutors with more authority. And they called on prosecutors to impose tougher sanctions on individuals convicted of crimes. Not surprisingly, scholars attribute part of the historically unprecedented increase in probation and incarceration during this period to prosecutorial aggressiveness in punishment.[43]

Whether this experiment was warranted or effective can be debated. For our purposes here what stands out is the limited research on prosecutorial decision-making.[44] Many sentencing studies do exist.[45] They document flows of cases through the courts or the percentages of cases that prosecutors take to trial that result in convictions. Sometimes they identify factors associated with court outcomes, but do so with minimal, if any, information about prosecutors. However, such studies by and large tell us little about prosecutors and their performance.

Why? One reason is that trials occur infrequently. Plea bargaining decides most cases. Estimates suggest that 90 percent or more of federal felony convictions result from plea bargains and 97 percent of state felony

---

[41] Mears (2017).
[42] Blumstein (1997); Sherman (2004); Mears (2010, 2017); Vito and Higgins (2015).
[43] Corbett (2015); Mears and Cochran (2015); Wright (2017).   [44] Wright (2017).
[45] See, generally, Mears (1998) and Ulmer (2012).

convictions in large urban courts result from them.[46] Far more useful, then, would be a focus on how prosecutors handle *all* cases that come before them. Typical studies only examine the final outcomes, such as convictions, that result from prosecutors' decisions and they ignore plea-bargaining processes. In addition, they tell us little about the performance of prosecutors.

How might we go about evaluating their performance? We could look at conviction rates. However, these can be influenced by too-aggressive plea-bargaining strategies. Individuals tend to be risk-averse. When facing a possible prison sentence, for example, they may admit guilt – even when innocent – to avoid this more severe punishment.[47] A high conviction rate might mean success in establishing the guilt of those who actually committed crime. Alternatively, it might mean success in coercing guilty pleas among the innocent! Accordingly, as Ronald Wright and Marc Miller have suggested, a better measure might be the convicted-as-charged ratio:

> The higher the ratio of "as charged convictions" to "convictions," the more readily a prosecutor should be praised and reelected. A ratio near one – where most convictions are "as charged," whether they result from guilty pleas or trials – is the best sign of a healthy, honest, and tough system. The lower the ratio of "as charged convictions" to "convictions" (approaching zero), the more the prosecutor should be criticized for sloppiness, injustice, and obfuscation. A lower ratio might also reflect a prosecutor's undue leniency.[48]

This measure enables monitoring of plea-bargaining outcomes and allows for more transparency in prosecutorial decision-making.[49] That in turn might reduce errors of justice.[50]

From a policy perspective, it should be evident that the public has an interest in knowing something useful about prosecutorial performance. Prosecutors have a stake as well. Some might want to hide behind success in a few high-profile cases. Many, though, likely would embrace information that could help them to improve case processing. Why, then, as one review found, is "information about [prosecutor] office performance . . . difficult to find"?[51] Answering that question involves its own study. Perhaps prosecutors prefer operating with little oversight. Perhaps they feel that they can be more effective that way. Perhaps they have few resources to allocate

[46] Johnson *et al.* (2016:480); see generally, Skolnick (1966), Altschuler (1975, 2015), Heilbroner (1990), Reaves (2013), Bushway *et al.* (2014), Yoffe (2017), and Spohn (2018).
[47] Blumberg (1967); Altschuler (1975, 2015).
[48] Wright and Miller (2002:35); see also Piehl and Bushway (2007).
[49] Wright (2017:424).   [50] Forst (2004).   [51] Wright (2017:422).

to research or do not know how research might be useful. Or perhaps legislatures and the courts have not historically viewed research as integral to criminal justice operations.[52]

Whatever the reasons, we can see where applied research could be extremely helpful. It could help to determine the need for changes to prosecutorial decision-making practices or hiring more prosecutors. It could help identify the theory guiding some decisions (e.g., a policy of overcharging defendants in the belief that doing so will result in quicker, and more, plea bargains). It could help to assess the amount and quality of case decision-making. And it could establish a foundation for assessing impact and efficiency. All of these dimensions arise from thinking about the evaluation hierarchy as it applies to prosecutors' offices.

We also can see the relevance of basic research. For example, many court-processing studies and theories – such as the "shadow of the trial," focal concerns, courtroom community perspectives – testify to the potential for plea bargaining to help or undermine accountability and justice.[53] They highlight how prosecutors and defendants may negotiate a deal based on predictions about what likely would result from a trial.[54] They point to the potential for some groups, such as minorities, to be processed differently. In addition, they illuminate ways in which courtroom workgroups and context may influence case dispositions.[55] All of this work can be used to identify ways to evaluate and improve prosecutors' performance. At the same time, research aimed at evaluating dimensions of performance can create opportunities for testing and revising theory, developing theories, and identifying new avenues of inquiry.

Part of the art of research stems from awareness of the questions that one might ask. That can, we hope, be seen in thinking about basic and applied research and in the example above involving prosecutors. If we begin with basic research and consider its implications for policy, we may arrive at insights that we otherwise might miss. Similarly, if we begin with applied research questions – such as those that the evaluation hierarchy leads us to ask – and consider the implications for science, we may well find opportunities to create greater understanding.

---

[52] Mears (2017).   [53] Johnson *et al.* (2016).
[54] Bibas (2004); Bushway *et al.* (2014); Johnson *et al.* (2016).
[55] See, for example, von Hirsch and Ashworth (1992), Mears (1998), Johnson (2010), Ulmer (2012), Baumer (2013), Spohn (2013), and Johnson *et al.* (2016).

8 Identifying Causal Effects

INTRODUCTION

The goal of many scientific studies is to understand the causes of phenomena. Causation in fact stands as perhaps the most prominent goal of research. It features prominently as an end goal of descriptive accounts and efforts to understand the social meaning of criminological and criminal justice phenomena. And policy and practice typically build on the idea that various actions will result in improved social outcomes, such as greater public safety or justice.

The concept of causation seems simple – some force, X (e.g., tougher punishments), causes some outcome, Y (e.g., lower crime rates). Causation is far more complex than that, however. Awareness of that complexity can be critical for science and policy. Why? Consider an example of a community policing study. It might show that this approach makes the public feel more willing to call the police for assistance. It also might show that the effect arises primarily through police interactions that citizens view as demonstrating respect for them and their community. Further, it might show that citizens value this benefit more than rapid response times to calls for help. Such information would raise questions about the theoretical mechanisms through which community policing programs achieve their effects. And it could help police chiefs or sheriffs. How? They would know to emphasize respectful interactions as a way of engendering greater citizen willingness to report crime and assist officers.[1] Clarity about causation is not a nicety – it can lead to better science and policy.[2]

We turn, therefore, to causation. Or, more precisely, we revisit it. As the earlier chapters identified, assessment of causality occurs through many steps. These include consideration of research design, the types of data to be

---

[1] See, generally, Reisig (2010) and Lum and Nagin (2017).
[2] This discussion of causation draws on Mears (2017).

used, and analyses. Much of this discussion, however, provided a too-fleeting account of causal relationships. We thus expand on the concept of causation and discuss its relevance for criminological and criminal justice research and policy.

The chapter seeks to answer several questions. What is causality? What are different causal effects that may characterize diverse criminological and criminal justice phenomena? What is the difference between linear and nonlinear effects? What are examples of nonlinear effects? And what are other causal effects that may be relevant for theory, research, and policy? Our central contention is that awareness of diverse causal effects can provide a foundation for improving theory and policy. Awareness of them is part and parcel of developing a researcher sensibility that can guide one in conducting, evaluating, or using research.

WHAT IS CAUSALITY?

Philosophers have long debated the nature of causality.[3] The complexity of the concept is remarkable. A few examples illustrate the point. Consider that some things in life happen by chance. Here, there can be no clear causal force. When we consider crime and criminal justice, we might well find that some phenomena appear to be inexplicable. A sudden rise and fall in crime, for example, might occur randomly. Other things result from a mix of chance *and* one or more causal forces. It might be chance that led a particular person to be hungry (he or she skipped lunch because of a meeting). The hunger may trigger the person's low self-control and lead to an altercation at a restaurant. We would view self-control as the causal force that led to the altercation. The hunger was a random event. Here, then, the altercation stems from a mix of chance and predictable causation. (Of course, the person's low self-control might have contributed to skipping lunch. If so, the altercation is more predictable than we surmise!)

Still other things might be completely determined by one or more forces. We can think of no criminological or criminal justice phenomena where that holds true, but perhaps examples exist. The point is simply that we can view criminological and criminal justice causation as lying along a continuum ranging from pure chance to pure determinism. That idea alone introduces complexity into our discussion. For example, crimes or criminal justice phenomena that occur more by chance will be more difficult to explain through theory or research.

---

[3] Beebee *et al.* (2017).

A. Assumed Causal Relationship Is Real

B. Assumed Causal Relationship Is Spurious

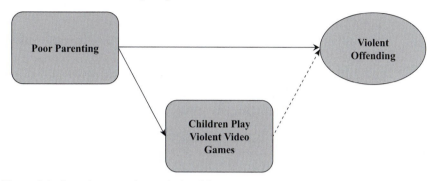

Figure 8.1 Causal vs. spurious relationships

Complexity also arises in the identification of causation. In general, we cannot see a causal force unfold before our very eyes. Consider getting hit in the arm. That might lead one to become angry. However, no one, including the person who was hit, can see the precise sequence of neurological and psychological forces that creates the anger. In addition, they cannot see the anger directly. It can only be inferred from various verbal or physical cues. As with the self-control example, further complications arise because of the potential for interactions. For example, not all hits in the arm cause anger. Much depends on social context, one's pain tolerance, the intention of the "hitter," and so on.

Causal complexity surfaces in still other ways. Consider the following scenario: What if we can provide a convincing explanation for why a prison riot occurred, but we cannot predict with any accuracy when *future* riots will occur? The accuracy of the causal explanation might seem questionable even though it seems compelling and "fits the facts."

This idea raises one of the most critical causal issues in the social sciences – identification of a causal effect. Consider Figure 8.1. It contrasts two situations. In one, shown in panel A, children who play violent video games commit more violent crime, and this relationship is causal. Put differently, the effect is real – among children who play violent video games, there will be a tendency, on average, to engage in more violent offending than otherwise would occur. Parents and policymakers have been concerned about this issue for decades. The concern flows from a belief that (1) an association exists and (2) it is causal.

In panel B, a different reality is shown. Here, poor parenting is the cause of children playing violent video games and of violent offending. The dashed line from children playing video games to violent offending serves to identify a spurious association. In this scenario, violent video games play no causal role in violent offending. (The fact of an association may make it seem like a causal effect exists, though.) It is, of course, possible that video games *do* cause violent offending. Panel B then would be depicting a mediating relationship, one where poor parenting causes children to play violent video games and, in turn, where playing such games causes violent offending. A mix of spuriousness and causation can also occur. In that case, the observed association overstates the amount of causal effect between video games and offending.

Research to date has identified no clear causal relationship between violent video game-playing and offending.[4] Of more relevance to our discussion, though, is that causal complexity goes well beyond establishing that one factor causes another. The complexity may be daunting. That is the glass-half-empty view. The glass-half-full view? Causal complexity opens the door to thinking more clearly about crime and criminal justice.

Our goal in what follows is not to chart philosophical debates about causation. Nor do we seek to summarize ways of estimating causal effects (see Chapter 6). Rather, we want to draw attention to the fact that causation underlies theoretical accounts of criminological and criminal justice phenomena.[5] Causation matters greatly for policy evaluation as well. Social scientists are trained to be cautious about claiming to demonstrate causation. Accordingly, they may use euphemistic phrasing. For example, a research study might refer to "relationships," "associations," or "correlations" among variables. Or it might refer to causal effects and do so using tempered language, such as, "X appears to contribute to Y." Such tentative phrasing may be appropriate. However, it can obscure the fact that scientists actually do seek to identify causal effects.[6] In what follows, we thus use the term "causal" with the understanding that this goal exists *and* that one should be careful about accepting causal claims.

TYPES OF CAUSAL EFFECTS

When developing or evaluating a theory about a phenomenon, such as crime, we should consider different types of causal effects. Failure to do so

---

[4] Smith *et al.* (2018).   [5] Stafford and Mears (2015).   [6] Mears and Stafford (2002).

means that we likely default to what perhaps may be the simplest of all types – a linear effect. Here, more of X gives rise to more of Y. Such a relationship, however, barely scratches the surface of the range of ways in which X and Y may be causally related. If a theory provides guidance about the precise nature of the relationship, that will help us when undertaking analyses. For example, a theory might tell us that X and Y are related in a curvilinear manner (which we discuss below). If so, we can use that information to provide a set of analyses that can provide a more accurate assessment of whether in fact X and Y are related in that way.

If the theory fails to provide such guidance, then we should consider a variety of possible causal relationships. To some scholars, that might seem like hearsay. They would say that we should test only for what a theory tells us to do. They also would instruct us to default to the simplest causal relationship – a linear one – if a theory fails to provide clear instruction. However, theories may not tell us exactly how causal forces relate to one another. And, as will become evident, just because two factors are "related" does not mean that the relationship is linear. Many other possibilities exist.

One of the central challenges in conducting, evaluating, or using research well stems from a failure to imagine differing types of causal relationships. This problem can affect anyone, even scholars who have studied particular criminological or criminal justice topics for decades. It is unfortunate because opportunities to advance science and to devise effective policies go missed. We argue that awareness of different types of causal effects can guide imagination. They can lead us to consider possibilities that otherwise would be unrecognized. For this reason, we turn to a discussion of linear, nonlinear, and other types of causal effects.

LINEAR EFFECTS – THE ASSUMED CAUSAL RELATIONSHIP IN MANY THEORIES AND POLICIES

As shown in Table 8.1, many types of causal effects exist.[7] The most common one found in criminological and criminal justice theories and policies is a linear one. A higher level (or an increase) in some causal force, X, is anticipated to result in a higher level (or a fixed amount of change) in an outcome, Y. This effect typically is assumed to be additive – each additional increase in X keeps adding up to a larger effect.

Assuming that linearity governs various phenomena can be problematic.[8] Consider the physical world first. Water does not turn to ice until it hits a certain temperature; a threshold, not a linear, effect exists here.

---

[7] This table builds on a version in Mears (2017:68, figure 3.1).   [8] Ellenberg (2014).

Table 8.1 Types of causal relationships

- **Linear (additive).** Changes in X (a causal force) result in the same change in Y (an outcome) regardless of the level of X. Thus, changes in X result in additive effects on Y. For example, three unit changes in X produce three times as much change in Y as does one unit of X.
- **Nonlinear.** Change in X results in different changes in Y depending on the level of X or the presence of other factors. Different types of nonlinear relationships exist.
  — *Curvilinear.* Change in X results in different amounts of change in Y depending on the level of X. For example, an increase in X at low values of X may have little effect on Y, but the same increase at high values of X may have large effects on Y.
  — *Tipping point (threshold).* Change in X may not affect Y until X reaches a certain level.
  — *Interactive (moderating).* X interacts with another factor, Z, such that X's effect on Y varies depending on the level of Z. Alternatively stated, X's effect on Y is moderated, that is, it is increased or decreased, by Z.
  — *Dose.* A specific change in X achieves a particular change in Y. Dose effects may be variable or involve thresholds or interactions.
  — *Reciprocal or self-reinforcing causation and feedback loops.* Change in X may affect Y, and a change in Y may affect X. There may be *stabilizing feedback loops* (i.e., the feedbacks tend toward stabilization of X at a certain level) and *amplification feedback loops* (i.e., the feedbacks tend toward continually increasing X).
- **Other**
  — *Direct vs. indirect (mediating).* Change in X may directly affect Y or it may do so indirectly through (i.e., be mediated by) intervening causal mechanisms.
  — *Proximate vs. distal.* Effects of X on Y may occur over different time spans or areas. Those that occur sooner in time or space may be said to be temporally or spatially proximate; those that occur later in time may be said to be temporally or spatially distal.
  — *Reversible vs. irreversible.* Change caused by X might be reversible (e.g., an increase in X increases Y and a decrease in X decreases Y) or irreversible (e.g., a decrease in X does not decrease Y).
  — *Multiple.* Many factors may cause Y.

Note: Adapted from Mears (2017:68).

Or consider bread – it results not from any one ingredient or even the addition of ingredients on top of one another. It results from the combination of several ingredients, as well as a duration of exposure to a set temperature. If we fail to combine the ingredients and bake them for a sufficient duration and at a sufficient temperature, we will have something – a mess perhaps – but no bread. There is no linear effect here, but rather an interaction effect. Nonlinearity arises in many medical illnesses as well. For example, some illnesses, including cancers, will not emerge unless a unique set of conditions exists.[9]

Linearity can exist for many crime and criminal justice phenomena. Perhaps each additional day in a drug treatment court reduces offending by a set amount. Or perhaps each additional increase in social disadvantage increases by a set amount the number of crimes in a community. Or perhaps fixed increases in law enforcement training decreases by a set amount the quality of officer interactions with citizens.

However, we should not assume that linearity constitutes the rule. It may well be, as we discuss below, that many causal forces involve non-linearities. Theory should help us determine when to anticipate one or the other. However, many criminological and criminal justice theories do not formally articulate precise causal relationships. Leading crime theories, for example, frequently posit simply that one causal force is positively or negatively associated with offending or crime rates. They do not specify a linear or nonlinear relationship.[10] Researchers may assume a linear relationship by default. But doing so does not provide a more accurate test of a theory unless the theory explicitly argues for such a relationship. Interestingly, tests of theories may assume any functional form (e.g., a linear association between X and Y or any of a wide variety of nonlinear associations) that they want and claim that they have provided a test of a given theory. Yet, the theorist can always claim that the test was not valid. Why? The test assumed a functional form not anticipated by the theory. Of course, when no such form is articulated, the researcher has no choice but to specify some type of relationship!

Functional form refers to the precise way in which causal forces are related. Does it matter? Yes. To illustrate, imagine that the plotted association between two forces looks like an inverted U. An increase in the causal force leads to an increase in the outcome, until the outcome reaches a certain peak. At that point the associated effect reverses, causing a decrease in the outcome. If we do not know to conduct analyses that allow for such a difference – if we assume linearity – we would find little to no association between the two forces. Why? In a model that assumes a linear relationship, the positive and negative effects would cancel each other out. Functional form matters for another reason – accuracy. If a curvilinear relationship exists, we should develop a theory about it. Our understanding of chemistry is enhanced when we explain why water freezes only below a

---

[9] Mukherjee (2016).

[10] See, for example, discussions in Agnew (2005), Lilly *et al.* (2015), Maguire and Duffee (2015), and Akers *et al.* (2016).

certain temperature. Similarly, our understanding of the causes of crime and criminal justice phenomena is enhanced when we explain why nonlinearities exist.

NONLINEAR EFFECTS – THE REALITY THAT MAY UNDERLIE MANY CAUSAL RELATIONSHIPS

A nonlinear effect is easy to describe – it is any relationship that is not linear. A straight line is just that, a straight line. Anything that departs from it can be termed "nonlinear." Although linear relationships are easier to understand, they may constitute the exception rather than the rule in describing how the natural or social worlds operate.[11] As Donella Meadows has observed, "the world is full of nonlinearities."[12] Unfortunately, assuming linearity in a nonlinear world can distort our understanding and policies. Meadows has aptly observed, for example:

> The world often surprises our linear-thinking minds. If we've learned that a small push produces a small response, we think that twice as big a push will produce twice as big a response. But in a nonlinear system, twice the push could produce one-sixth the response, or the response squared, or no response at all.[13]

If we want to be able to understand crime and criminal justice, and if we want to improve public safety and justice outcomes, awareness of such possibilities is critical, as we illustrate below.

Curvilinear

A curvilinear relationship exists when each additional change in X produces a different effect on Y. Consider the concept of marginal returns – our first pair of shoes provides a large benefit, but each additional pair thereafter provides less and less of a benefit. This type of causal effect can be seen with recidivism and time served in prison. A study that we conducted suggested that for the first twelve months or so of incarceration, each additional month of incarceration increased the probability of recidivism. Thereafter, each additional month reduced the probability of recidivism, until about thirty-six months, at which point each additional month appeared to exert little appreciable effect. Interestingly, the probability of recidivism typically was lowest for those individuals who served the least amount of time.[14]

Now, this study might have been a fluke. Only with more research can we know the true relationship between recidivism and time served. The

[11] Ellenberg (2014).   [12] Meadows (2008:91).   [13] *Ibid.*   [14] Mears *et al.* (2016a).

underlying point should be clear, however: Assuming, as many accounts of deterrence or get-tough sentencing policies do, that additional time in prison will necessarily reduce recidivism is far from a safe bet.

From an analytic perspective, the study's findings stand out for a clear reason – had we tested only for a linear effect, we would have identified that time served was not associated with recidivism. Only by estimating statistical models that allowed for a curvilinear functional form could we identify what arguably was the true relationship in the data. The study's findings also stand out for another reason. We knew to test for them only by drawing on theoretical arguments hinted at in prior research that had not been systematically tested.

Curvilinear relationships can vary.[15] For example, there might be a slight causal association initially between X and Y, and then the effect might escalate rapidly. Conversely, there might initially be a strong causal effect that, with each additional increase in X, diminishes. These possibilities raise theoretical questions, such as why the effect of X varies. In addition, they raise implications for policy. To illustrate, it might be that initial efforts to engage citizens in community policing initiatives garner little public support. With continued effort, however, citizen support may increasingly emerge. If so, this suggests that community policing effectiveness likely follows a curvilinear path – initially, it reduces crime rates only a little, and then increasingly produces markedly greater reductions in crime.

Tipping Point (Threshold)

Tipping, or threshold, points constitute a related type of nonlinear relationship. A linear or curvilinear effect may exist, but past a certain point no relationship exists or it substantially changes. In one study, we argued that self-control effects operate in this way: Up to a certain point, increases in low self-control may influence offending, but after a certain threshold, the effect may accelerate and then, at still a higher threshold, the effect may flatten.[16] This possibility emerged not directly from self-control theory, but from a broader literature on self-control. Even so, it had not been tested. We found evidence to support the hypothesized effect, but of course many more studies would be needed before one could be confident that self-control's effect on offending involves threshold effects. There also is the corresponding need for research that tests theoretical arguments for why thresholds exist.

[15] See Allison (1999) for a number of examples.
[16] Mears *et al.* (2013a); see, generally, Hassin *et al.* (2010).

Once one looks for tipping points, they can start to seem ubiquitous. Consider children: They may only begin to cry once they have reached a certain level of hunger or fatigue. Or consider policymakers: Only once a certain critical mass of problems in criminal justice arises, such as police shootings, do they then enact large-scale reforms.[17] In personal relationships, sometimes we wait for underlying tensions to reach a certain break point before we then address them. Such possibilities barely scratch the surface and illustrate the importance of not only looking for tipping points, but also of developing explanations for their existence.

Interactive (Moderating)

Interactions occur when the effect of one causal variable, such as X1, moderates or amplifies the effect of another variable, X2, on an outcome, Y. In a linear view of the universe, one factor, such as strain, causes crime. What, though, if crime may be caused not only by strain, but by many factors? And what if – when these factors are jointly present – a disproportionately greater likelihood of offending arises? For example, perhaps more strain increases the probability of offending. Association with criminals might also do so as well, but the effect of strain may be even greater when someone has many peers who commit crime. Why? Strain may impel us toward crime, and association with criminals may channel or "fast-track" that tendency.

Interaction effects occur in many ways and can be found throughout criminal justice.[18] Consider get-tough sentencing laws. Alone, they might increase prison populations. When, however, they are combined with funding to expand law enforcement and correctional system capacity, they might produce exponentially greater increases in imprisonment. Mass incarceration provides another illustration. It can be argued to have resulted from the interaction of these and other forces, such as decreases in rehabilitative programming for those in prisons or on probation.[19]

In statistical models, an interaction of two variables means that one variable's effect on an outcome is greater (or lesser) depending on the level of or change in some other variable. Perhaps, for example, higher unemployment rates (X1) contribute to higher crime rates (Y), but this effect may be greater among areas that have higher levels of mistrust among the police and community residents (X2).

A three-way interaction is even more complicated. Here, we have three forces – X1, X2, and X3. They combine in ways that generate effects that differ from simply adding up the "net" effects of each force by itself. Many

---

[17] Mears (2017).   [18] Mears (2017).   [19] Mears and Cochran (2015).

studies do not examine two-way interactions, much less three-way or four-way interactions. Even so, such interactions exist and warrant study if we want to improve scientific understanding and policy.[20]

Interestingly, whereas quantitative studies typically eschew interactions – in part because of the complexity of the models – qualitative studies frequently work from the opposite direction. They assume an interactional universe. For example, qualitative studies may identify a myriad of forces and how unique combinations of them give rise to certain outcomes.[21] The methods may differ, but the logic – that of interactive forces – is similar.

Dose

When examining dose effects, our interest centers on how exactly a given outcome responds to varying levels of or changes in a causal variable. A threshold effect with medicine provides an illustration of this idea – only with a certain amount of medicine for a certain number of days do we see improvement in reducing an illness. Below that threshold, little to no benefit arises. Dose effects can take many different forms. They may be curvilinear – too little or too much and no effect arises. Perhaps a "Goldilocks" effect exists. Only at a "just right" dose does the benefit that we want arise. Consider, again, community policing. It seems self-evident that token gestures at community policing would engender little citizen support. However, and perhaps less self-evident, if officers take too commanding a role in implementing community policing, they might well undermine one of the cornerstones of this approach – empowering citizens to take ownership of their neighborhoods. There may well be a "just right" level of community policing that is most effective. Similarly, there may be specific doses of many causal forces that achieve maximum effects on offending, crime rates, prosecutorial decision-making, public support for policies, the effectiveness of probation or prison, and so on.

One of the interesting issues with dose effects is the possibility that level effects may not correspond to change effects. For example, when we study whether varying levels of some potential causal force are associated with an outcome, we typically assume that some process occurs at a given level.

---

[20] Agnew (2005); Mears *et al.* (2013a).

[21] As Becker (1998:190) has written in describing the approach taken by Boolean analysis researchers, many social science "explanations are typically 'multiple conjunctural': conjunctural in that causes are understood as combinations of factors, and multiple in that many such combinations might produce the same result." See, generally, Feagin *et al.* (1991), Garland (2001, 2013), Gottschalk (2006, 2011, 2013), Barker (2009), and Campbell (2014).

The process results in a change that either arises immediately or some time thereafter. Change effects differ. The logic here is that some amount of change – a small amount or a large amount, however we wish to measure "small" or "large" – creates a change in some outcome. Many studies of level effects assume that they are estimating change effects, but they are not. Conversely, a study of change effects does not provide an estimate of level effects. They are two distinct causal possibilities. Each must be assessed as a distinct process. They also may interact. Change at one level may exert a different effect than change at another level.[22]

Reciprocal or Self-Reinforcing Effects and Feedback Loops

Reciprocal effects arise when X causes Y and Y then causes X. Different terms capture this idea. For example, we can view reciprocal causation as a type of self-reinforcing or feedback loop. To illustrate, perhaps political liberalism leads a policymaker to support rehabilitative programs. The policymaker focuses primarily on these programs and sees that they can be effective. (Perhaps, too, he or she unconsciously ignores evidence about ineffective programs.) Their effectiveness then might be construed as lending support to the validity of a liberal political philosophy. The policymaker's support for rehabilitation then grows even more.

Or consider crime. Some scholars, such as Robert Agnew, have suggested that crime may cause more crime.[23] How? An individual commits a crime. Others label him or her as a "criminal." The individual comes to accept this label, and then commits even more crime. Once, again, the individual gets labeled and he or or she again accepts it as reflecting their intrinsic character. They engage in more offending, and the cycle continues.

Feedback loops involve these possibilities. They also involve the possibility of systems forces that counterbalance or build off changes in other forces. Edward Humes' description of the operations of one large juvenile court system captures this idea. An errant judge, whom public defenders viewed as becoming increasingly too harsh, "papered" him with court filings. The judge then adopted a more tempered approach – still tough, but in line with the more typical approach to handling juvenile court cases.[24] This type of effect might be termed a stabilizing feedback loop because it involves one force initiating when another reaches a certain point, causing some outcome (e.g., rates of juvenile court detention) to resume its usual level.

---

[22] See, for example, Wang and Mears (2010b) and Mears *et al.* (2013a).
[23] Agnew (2005:87).   [24] Humes (1996).

Amplification effects exist, too. Consider the illustration above of a state that has greatly increased prison capacity. This increase might lead policymakers to feel emboldened to take a logical next step – to increase investment in law enforcement and court capacity. That step then generates much greater increases in incarceration. Eventually, policymakers become concerned about prison overcrowding. They push for expanding prison capacity. The process then repeats itself. Indeed, it might create a self-perpetuating amplification effect because it simultaneously reduces the ability of policymakers to divert resources to crime prevention programs or other approaches to increasing public safety.

STILL OTHER CAUSAL EFFECTS

To this point, we have discussed linear and nonlinear causal effects. Other types of causation exist, too. Awareness of them can provide avenues for developing and testing theories as well as for devising policies, programs, and practices that may be more effective.

Direct vs. Indirect

Many times, a theory – one that we read about or that we create – contemplates a situation involving a causal chain. For example, A causes B and then B causes C (A → B → C). Here, the A → B and B → C linkages are "direct" effects. That is, the effects of a variable directly cause an outcome. By contrast, the A → B → C sequence points to an indirect effect, one in which the A → C effect arises through the indirect, or mediating, pathway through B.

Scientists frequently posit such causal chains without knowing if they are correct. Research then seeks to test the whole sequence or parts. In policy research, "black box" evaluations focus only on the beginning and end of the causal chain (A → C). Experiments frequently take this approach, too. They randomize subjects into an intervention group and separately a control group. We then learn if the program effectively improved some outcome, such as recidivism. However, we may learn little about exactly what produced this effect.

If a clearly articulated theory guided the intervention, we might assume that the effect arose through the mechanisms anticipated by the theory. However, without an empirical study that documents the "how," we are left only knowing that A causes C, not whether the effect arises through B. For example, drug court evaluations have been conducted that document potential beneficial effects on recidivism. However, the evaluations frequently do not include empirical assessment of the causal pathways that produced these benefits.[25]

Fortunately, many studies seek to understand other parts of the process. One might study the A → B relationship and another might study the B → C relationship. Still another might try to examine the entire sequence. Eventually, a body of work emerges that hopefully provides clear guidance about the precise causal pathway that gives rise to the A → C relationship.

Proximity in Time or Space

Effects can occur *proximately or distally in time*. Lag effects are illustrative. Consider the impact of an insult made in passing. We hear it, but do not fully comprehend it. Later in the evening, when perhaps the dust from the day has settled, we reflect. We suddenly realize the depth of the insult. What happens next, of course, may depend greatly on one's personality. Those of us with a retributivist bent might seek some type of payback. We might even plot the payback at great length! The point is that the causal effect did not arise immediately; instead, it took time. The effect arose distally from the time of the causal force. Other forces may result in near-instantaneous effects. In studies of the code of the street, for example, insults require that an individual respond in a retaliatory and public manner. Doing so immediately would be more likely to garner the respect that the retaliation is intended to achieve.[26]

Causal effects may not necessarily arise in the place where they occur – that is, the effects can be *spatially proximate or distal*. Consider "hot spots" policing, an approach in which law enforcement officers target high-crime areas. This approach might reduce crime in one area. That should make the residents there happy. But the approach might push crime into adjoining areas. Would-be offenders might simply migrate to these areas to commit crime. Evaluating the crime reduction in the intervention site without investigating crime displacement would provide a highly distorted appraisal of the policy's effectiveness. It also would mean that we miss an opportunity to understand better the theoretical mechanisms through which crime occurs. Studies have in fact investigated the potential for such displacement effects and identified that spatial effects of "hot spots" policing exist. The effects appear to be beneficial. As Anthony Braga and his colleagues found in a meta-analysis, "hot spots policing programs generate modest crime control gains and are likely to produce a diffusion of crime control benefits into areas immediately surrounding targeted high-activity crime places."[27]

[25] Gottfredson *et al.* (2003); Wilson *et al.* (2006); Mears (2010); Rossman *et al.* (2011).
[26] Anderson (1999).   [27] Braga *et al.* (2014:658).

Spatial effects may include a form of lag as well – for example, community disadvantage in one area might produce diffusion effects that extend not only to adjacent areas, but also to non-adjacent ones.[28]

Reversible vs. Irreversible

Although some effects may be reversible, others may be irreversible. Reversible causation means that a change in some causal force, X, works in two directions. For example, an increase in it may increase an outcome, Y, and a decrease in X may decrease Y. Irreversible causation means that this process works only in one direction – an increase in X may increase Y, but a decrease in X may not exert any influence on Y.[29]

The distinction may seem at first blush to be one of splitting hairs, but it is not. Consider tooth brushing. An increase in tooth brushing (X) may decrease the amount of cavities that we get (Y), and a decrease in brushing may increase them. Here, we have a reversible process. Observe, though, that irreversible causation also may come into play. The existence of a cavity (Y), for example, cannot be undone by more tooth brushing (X).

The concept of reversibility can allow us to appreciate nuances in causal relationships. Recall the study of Shai Danziger and his colleagues discussed in Chapter 2: Judges became tougher in their parole decisions throughout each morning. Why? They were fatigued from making decisions and resorted to the cognitively less demanding option of denying prisoner requests for parole. After lunch, judges became more lenient.[30] Why? They were refreshed and ready for more cognitively demanding decision-making. There was a reversible causal process at play.

Consider now a possible irreversible, or not easily reversible, process. We increase law enforcement, court, and prison system capacity (X), which then gives rise to increased incarceration rates (Y). We then seek to reduce incarceration rates by decreasing the number of law enforcement officers. Several interesting possibilities exist that may interfere with reverse caus-ation. First, if we cut the number of officers by, say, 10 percent, we may do little to nothing to affect the incarceration rate. The reason is simple – the remaining officers still make plenty of arrests to fuel the conviction–incarceration pipeline. Second, prosecutors might pursue incarceration for increasingly less serious crimes. Third, the causes themselves may be largely irreversible. Policymakers, for example, may risk their careers if they slash budgets for law enforcement, the courts, or prison systems.

---

[28] Mears and Bhati (2006).   [29] Lieberson (1985).   [30] Danziger *et al.* (2011).

Multiple

Theories of crime and justice often zero in on a single causal factor. Many policies do the same thing. We can see that with a great deal of legislation and programs. To illustrate, lawmakers might enact a get-tough sentencing statute in the belief that it will independently – net of all else that occurs in the lives of offenders and in society – reduce recidivism or crime rates. Or they might require police to wear body cameras in the belief that it will reduce officer abuse of citizens. Implicit in such beliefs are the notions that (1) the effect exists, (2) it exists independently of other individual- or contextual-level forces, (3) it is substantial, and (4) it exerts an effect that is substantially greater than that of other factors.

Such beliefs rest on a questionable foundation. Many putative effects are not in fact causal. Illegal drug use, for example, is associated with incarceration – disproportionately more individuals in prison have used illegal drugs as compared to what one finds in the general population.[31] That effect may be causal; illegal drug use may cause offending. Or it may be that illegal drug use and offending stem from similar causes; here, then, drug use does not cause offending. Its relation to offending would be said to be spurious.

Effects may also be contingent. Much of life results from complicated additions and interactions of many factors. That insight served as a foundation of the Chicago school of sociology, which has infused scholarship in criminology and criminal justice. As Andrew Abbott has emphasized, "The Chicago view was that the concept of net effect was social scientific nonsense. Nothing that ever occurs in the social world occurs 'net of other variables.' All social facts are located in contexts. So why bother to pretend that they are not?"[32]

In developing greater understanding about the world, social scientists may focus on one causal force. A study might test whether a theory about self-control is supported empirically. Another might test a theory about the effects of unemployment rates. And another might test a theory about how childhood abuse may cause future violence. These and other theories or hypotheses pursue a time-honored tradition in science: They use study designs that enable them to isolate one effect. This approach creates insight into causes of various phenomena. But it has the decidedly negative effect of leading us to view particular causes as universal, as if somehow they exist within a vacuum where personal, family, organizational, community, and societal characteristics do not matter or do not condition the influence of the identified cause.

---

[31] Mears and Cochran (2015).   [32] Abbott (1997:1152).

Single-variable theories and policies tend to ignore this latter possibility. They also tend to assume that single variables, or forces, have large effects. However, to say that two factors are causally related does not mean that a strong causal effect exists. It might be trivial. Perhaps a drug treatment program reduces recidivism by 1 percent, from 50 percent to 49 percent. The effect might be a real one. But it would not likely lead us to invest more taxpayer dollars in the program. We should not confuse statistical significance with substantive significance.

Not least, a focus on particular causal forces can lead us to lose sight of the fact that many phenomena in life stem from multiple causes. Is being hungry at the end of the day a potential cause of irritability? Sure. But so, too, is a bad day at the office, a cold, an argument with a friend, a delay in getting to an appointment, and so on. The headline, though, in the newspaper reads: "Study Shows that Staving Off Hunger Can Make You Less Irritable." In so doing, it creates the appearance that hunger is a significant cause of irritability. It might be. Yet, it might exert no effect if other factors counterbalance it.

CONCLUSION

The types of causal effects that we have discussed are not the only ones that exist. But they suffice for our purposes – they illustrate that causation goes far beyond the idea that a single factor produces a clear and uniform effect on another.[33] Even with the simplest of scenarios, a linear effect, we face the challenge of identifying mediating effects that explain the causal mechanism that produces this effect.[34]

Knowing to think about and look for causal complexity is part and parcel of a researcher sensibility. This sensibility, as we have emphasized, entails awareness of how theory, data, and analysis contribute to creating good, credible research. It entails more than that, though. It requires a willingness and ability to draw on one's imagination.

Perhaps the most important part of research is imagination – being able to conceptualize, discern, or somehow see questions, patterns, explanations, opportunities to collect or use data, and analyses that can illuminate some criminological or criminal justice topic. Imagination guides good research. It helps in creating theories, devising useful data, and thinking about appropriate analytic strategies. Imagination also enables us to better evaluate studies and their possible uses.

[33] See, generally, Lieberson (1985), Marini and Singer (1988), Stafford and Mears (2015), and Mears (2017).
[34] McDowall (2002).

How, then, can we tap into or activate our imaginative abilities? One way is to consider different types of causal effects. Knowledge of curvilinear effects makes us aware that a study that focused only on linear effects of time served and recidivism and found none might have missed the boat. A relationship might well have been identified had the researcher tested for a curvilinear association. Similarly, knowledge of interaction effects allows us to consider how crime-causing factors might exert greater or lesser effects for some groups, and in turn to consider why. If we know to look for feedback loops, we may identify ways in which policies have unintended effects because of the systems context within which they occur. And if we are aware of the possibility of lag effects, we know to consider that a study that identifies short-term effects of, say, parental incarceration on children's development might miss out on longer-term effects that unfold over many years and possibly decades.[35]

Consideration of different types of causal effects also forces us to expand our theoretical horizons. If community policing only reduces crime once residents reach a certain threshold of trust in the police, what is that threshold and, as importantly, why does it exist? That is a fundamentally theoretical question. To answer it, we can look to extant theory for guidance or we can seek to develop our own theory. Either way, we arrive at a much richer, more nuanced, and, hopefully, more complete understanding of crime and criminal justice.

Not least, the potential for diverse causal effects also forces us to expand our methodological horizons. Testing for feedback loops requires, for example, that we have data that cover multiple time periods. Then we can determine if a phenomenon, such as criminal offending, can contribute to itself.[36] To do so requires that we push ourselves to develop the analytic skills to test for the existence of such effects, or to work with others who can help us do so.

Imagination might be viewed as the glue that binds together the science and art of research. It allows one to be inspired to see possibilities in all of the different activities that go into the "science" of research. The "art" of research thus consists of knowing to leverage imagination and these activities in ways that lead to greater insight.

---

[35] Mears and Siennick (2016).   [36] Agnew (2005).

9 Criminological and Criminal Justice Research Areas and Topics

INTRODUCTION

For a book focused on criminological and criminal justice research, it may seem odd to have waited until now to describe areas and topics of study specific to this field. However, the discussions to this point provide the foundation for appreciating the diversity of phenomena that fall under the rubric of "criminological and criminal justice research." The history of the field, for example, points to the varying emphasis placed on different areas (e.g., policing, causes of crime, mass incarceration) over the decades (Chapter 2). The variety of research goals that exist illuminate that any one topic might be examined through different prisms (Chapter 3). Theory fundamentally shapes how we conceptualize research questions and understand crime and justice phenomena (Chapter 4). Data types and considerations (Chapter 5) and analysis possibilities (Chapter 6) do so as well. There also is the distinction between basic (science-focused) research and applied (policy-focused) research, which can determine the types of studies relevant for our particular goals (Chapter 7). Not least, a variety of causal effects can exist; awareness of them can shape what we study and how we do so (Chapter 8).

That backdrop thus provides a foundation for discerning and appreciating the diversity of phenomena examined in criminological and criminal justice research. Even so, some truth in advertising warrants mention: The range of phenomena covers too much territory to describe adequately in one chapter, book, or even many volumes. What we seek to do here, then, is portray a *sense* of the criminological and criminal justice research landscape. In so doing, we seek to highlight the broader context under which any given study falls, as well as opportunities for thinking about research. To this end, we present what we describe as the "research matrix" and discuss its relevance for theory, research, and policy. We argue the idea that awareness of this research matrix can be instrumental to developing a researcher sensibility for informing efforts to conduct, evaluate, or use research in a useful and appropriate manner. In short, the chapter examines several questions: What areas or topics constitute the field of criminological and criminal justice research? Put differently, what kinds of research areas and questions exist? What relevance does awareness of them have for advancing science or policy? And what relevance does it have, not least, for developing a researcher sensibility?

THE RESEARCH MATRIX OF CRIMINOLOGICAL AND CRIMINAL JUSTICE RESEARCH

The Partial Research Matrix: Research Goals and Topics

Many readers may never have taken a criminology or criminal justice course. Those who have may not have taken courses that covered the spectrum of areas examined in criminology and criminal justice as a field. For example, they may have taken a course on the police, prisons, or crime theory, but not on the courts or the sociology of law. This situation is understandable. But it also can result in an unnecessarily too-narrow view of what criminological and criminal justice research can entail. That view then can limit one's ability to imagine possible research studies and to put existing ones into context.

Our goal is to avoid this problem by illuminating the vast landscape of research possibilities. Table 9.1 provides a simple way to do so. It presents a partial matrix of research possibilities. (In the next section, we discuss a fuller matrix that identifies even more possibilities.) This matrix stems from cross-classifying the four research goals discussed in Chapter 3 with different topical areas and specific topics within these areas; the checkmarks serve to demarcate a category of research. The areas and topics are not set in stone. We simply have identified some of the most prominent ones. No doubt, one could rearrange them in other ways and identify more areas or topics. For many of the areas, such as victimization, the media, public opinion, and measurement and methods, we have identified no sub-areas or specific topics. We have done so purposely to draw attention to the fact that these areas truly represent broad categories of research; within any one of them, diverse avenues of inquiry exist. The same holds equally true of those areas where we have identified sub-areas or specific topics.

As can be seen in Table 9.1, the mere existence of different areas alone testifies to the diversity of topics that criminological and criminal justice research covers. The existence of sub-areas further underscores this idea. To illustrate, a study of offending might focus on crime in general. Or it might zero in on just one type of crime, such as fraud or cybercrime (i.e., offenses

	Goal 1: Empirical description	Goal 2: Understand social meanings and causes of criminological and CJ phenomena	Goal 3: Identify and test causal relationships and theory	Goal 4: Answer criminal justice policy questions
Offending	√	√	√	√
Types				
Trajectories				
Correlates				
Causes				
Life-course/development				
contexts				
Crime rates	√	√	√	√
Types				
Trends				
Correlates				
Causes				
Contexts				
Informal social control	√	√	√	√
Collective efficacy				
Friends/family/other				
Punishments/sanctions				
Restorative sanctions				
Shame				
Formal social control	√	√	√	√
Law-making				
Law enforcement				
Courts/sentencing				
Punishments/sanctions				
Corrections	√	√	√	√
Jails and prisons				
Duration				
Experiences				
Rehabilitative				
Programs				
Re-entry				
Community supervision				
Criminal justice system	√	√	√	√
Juvenile justice system	√	√	√	√
Victimization	√	√	√	√
Media	√	√	√	√
Public opinion	√	√	√	√
Philosophy and ethics	√	√	√	√

Table 9.1 The research matrix of criminological and criminal justice research

Table 9.1 (cont.)

	Goal 1: Empirical description	Goal 2: Understand social meanings and causes of criminological and CJ phenomena	Goal 3: Identify and test causal relationships and theory	Goal 4: Answer criminal justice policy questions
Measurement and methods	√	√	√	√
Demographic dimensions	√	√	√	√
Age				
Race				
Ethnicity				
Sex				
Biological dimensions	√	√	√	√
Brain structure				
Evolutionary processes				
Genetic				
Gene-environment				
Hormones				
Neurophysiology				
Psychological dimensions	√	√	√	√
Intelligence				
Mental illness				
Personality type				
Resilience				
Self-control				
Social dimensions	√	√	√	√
Economic conditions				
Employment				
Education				
Environmental contexts				
Health				
Immigration				
Inequality				
Families and households				
Neighborhoods				
Political orientation				
Religious orientation				
Sexual orientation				
Situational contexts				
Social networks				
Socio-economic status				

The research matrix: The matrix of research possibilities in the table emerges from considering research goals and topics. However, the matrix is considerably larger than the cross-tabulation of these two dimensions. It includes the potential for the diverse array of studies that stem from the cross-tabulation of five dimensions. These include studies that focus on: (1) one or more research goals; (2) multiple topics or their interaction; (3) one or more units of analysis (e.g., micro-level, such as a focus on individuals; macro-level, such as a focus on families, schools, or neighborhoods; or multiple units of analysis); (4) one or more types of data (e.g., administrative records, survey, interviews, ethnographies, archival records); and (5) one or more analytic techniques or methods.

committed through the Internet).[1] In one step, then, we have greatly expanded the domain of possible study (i.e., all crime or any number of specific types of crime).

The research possibilities proliferate from there depending on the goal one has for a study. For example, as reflected by the checkmarks next to "Offending," there are four goals of research, each of which leads to different questions and the need to consider different research designs. Consider the following. A study of cybercrime might be focused purely on empirical description (goal 1). Perhaps little to nothing is known about cybercrime. Here, we might use snowball sampling techniques to identify cybercriminals and learn something about their characteristics, such as their age, sex, race, ethnicity, education, and more. If such research already exists, we might conduct a study focused on identifying what cybercrime means to those who engage in it and to those who are affected by it (goal 2). In so doing, we might develop a tentative understanding of possible causes of cyber offending. If, however, prior work already has covered this terrain, we might instead identify a causal model or hypothesis and test it empirically (goal 3). Finally, we might focus on answering policy questions about cybercrime, such as its prevalence, the likely effectiveness of a policy, how well a particular anti-cybercrime initiative is implemented, the effectiveness of the initiative, or its cost-efficiency (goal 4).

Such possibilities exist for all crime or for the study of any one particular type of crime. Yet, they barely scratch the surface of the variety of topics that exist. They also ignore entirely other areas that criminological and criminal justice research investigates. To highlight this fact, below we briefly describe each of the areas identified in Table 9.1. We cannot describe all questions that arise from considering all four goals that might be investigated for the areas and sub-areas. To do so would be impossible. It also is unnecessary. We seek simply to convey a sense of the research that can be undertaken. Our approach can be likened to that of sampling ice cream flavors at a store that literally has thousands of options.

Offending

Criminal behavior is, of course, central to the field of criminological and criminal justice research. The study of it involves proceeding from the four broad research goals – that is, estimating the amount, meaning, and causes of offending, as well as how to reduce it. Studies can branch out in all sorts of directions. For example, they can examine specific types of criminal

---

[1] Holtfreter *et al.* (2008); Holtfreter and Meyers (2015).

activity (e.g., gun crime, domestic violence, sexual offending, murder).[2] They can study – typically from a life-course or developmental perspective – trajectories of offending, including the onset of, persistence in, and desistance from offending.[3] In each instance, they can examine correlates of offending (i.e., the association of various factors with offending, under the assumption that the correlates might have a causal effect on crime). They also can examine the relative contribution of different causes, such as drug use, mental illness, or contextual factors (e.g., family or school characteristics) of offending. And they can examine how to reduce offending, whether by targeting these causes or others.[4] These varied lines of inquiry can entail descriptive studies, efforts to understand the meaning of crime to individuals or others, development and testing of different theories, and program and policy evaluations.

Crime Rates

Instead of focusing on individuals, research can focus on variation in crime rates among groups, neighborhoods, towns, cities, states, and countries, or trends over time in crime rates in one or more areas. For example, one might examine why crime rates declined in many Western countries from the Middle Ages to the mid 1900s or why crime rates increased more rapidly in some countries than in others during the 1980s and 1990s.[5] One might examine types of crime as well. Why, for example, did property crime steadily decline throughout the 1980s and 1990s at a time when violent crime temporarily spiked upwards?[6] Studies of crime rates might focus on variation among social or demographic groups (e.g., homicide rates among different racial or ethnic groups).[7] Correlational or causal studies might examine the characteristics of groups or contextual dimensions of areas that may contribute to lower or higher crime rates. And policy studies might seek to understand how we can reduce crime rates. In such cases, the policies typically will focus on areas, as opposed to programs, which typically focus on individuals.

Informal Social Control

Informal social control refers to efforts to steer individuals, groups, communities, and others in directions that accord with a particular cultural tradition. Peers may push their friends to act in certain ways, families may

---

[2] Tonry (2009).   [3] Laub and Sampson (2003); Carlson and Sarnecki (2015).
[4] Mears (2001a, 2004); Caulkins and Reuter (2017); Mulvey and Schubert (2017); Pollack (2017).
[5] Tonry (2014).   [6] Mears (2010).   [7] Parker (2008).

do so, and so, too, may religious groups, communities, and organizations.[8] Social control in such instances is exerted through "informal" – that is, non-legal – means. Families might shame members who violate the codes or rules that govern how one ought to behave. Neighbors may do the same thing. Informal control need not be punishment-focused, however. It can include support and assistance during difficult times. A prominent theory of crime argues, for example, that in communities where residents are more willing to monitor what happens in their neighborhood and to cooperate with one another, crime will be lower.[9] Similarly, restorative justice sanctions build on the idea that informal social control may be more effective than formal sanctions for reducing crime and for increasing victim satisfaction.[10] Informal social control can extend in many directions. It may influence how prison officers interact with inmates, prosecutors handle plea bargains, courts process cases, and more. In each instance, studies may focus on documenting the existence of informal social control mechanisms as well as their causes and effects. They also can focus on ways in which different social contexts may play a role in the effectiveness of formal social control efforts.[11]

Formal Social Control

Almost all societies have some system of informal and also formal social control.[12] Formal social control entails the enforcement of rules, policies, or laws by those officially designated to do so (e.g., law enforcement or courts). These efforts may be undertaken for a variety of reasons, such as the meting out of justice or the prevention of crime. Research on formal social control examines law-making, such as differences in laws across states, what affects their implementation, and what societal forces lead to the creation of some laws or the greater application of them toward certain groups.[13] It examines law enforcement – who joins, what influences police stops, why some law enforcement departments or agencies have higher or lower rates of citizen complaints, the implementation and effectiveness of hot spots and community policing efforts, and so on.[14] It also examines the courts. Research might focus on such topics as racial and ethnic disparities in sanctioning, the role of prosecutorial discretion, the influence of defense counsel on plea

---

[8] Anderson (1999).   [9] Sampson *et al.* (1997).   [10] Van Ness and Strong (2015).
[11] Fagan and Lindsey (2015).
[12] Durkheim (1933); Parsons *et al.* (1961); Weber (1978); Starr and Collier (1989); Gertz (2017).
[13] Gibbs (1989); Liska (1992); Garland (2001); Black (2010).
[14] Johnson (2010); Johnson *et al.* (2016); Lum and Nagin (2017).

bargains, and ways in which individual, court, and community characteristics may affect sentencing.[15] Not least, research might examine the use and effects of sanctions, such as the death penalty, as well as alternative ways to approach sentencing. Restorative justice provides one example. It emphasizes reintegrative sanctioning and inclusion of victims in the process of identifying punishments that may more effectively reduce offending, create justice, and help victims.[16] Under what conditions does it do so? Similar lines of research arise when considering any system of crime control and punishment.

Corrections

Although corrections – including incarceration and community supervision – constitutes a sub-area of formal social control, its growth has led it to become a central area of inquiry in criminological and criminal justice research.[17] Society uses incarceration to obtain some measure of retribution or justice, to educate citizens about the existence of laws, and to deter those who have been sanctioned (specific deterrence) or those who might consider offending (general deterrence).[18] It also may be used as a vehicle for controlling groups who perhaps are seen as threatening.[19] With the rise of mass incarceration during the 1980s and in subsequent decades came interest in understanding the factors that gave rise to this change. Scholars wanted to know why some states and countries embraced prison-as-punishment more so than others, how incarceration was being used, and what its effects were.[20] The questions that can be asked are far-ranging. For example, to what extent does incarceration influence recidivism and other outcomes (e.g., homelessness, employment, outcomes among family members)? How does incarceration affect family members and communities?[21] What collateral consequences, such as not being able to vote (disenfranchisement) or difficulty finding employment, arise from incarceration?[22] What factors – such as the duration and conditions of confinement, the amount and quality of rehabilitative programming, and re-entry preparation – influence its effectiveness?[23] How can jail be used more efficiently when deciding who

---

[15] Heilbroner (1990); Wright (2017).
[16] Braithwaite (1989); Van Ness and Strong (2015).   [17] Mears and Cochran (2015).
[18] Gibbs (1975); Mears and Cochran (2015).   [19] Liska (1992); Alexander (2012).
[20] Garland (2001); Petersilia (2003); Gottschalk (2006); Barker (2009); Travis et al. (2014); Mears and Cochran (2015).
[21] Turanovic and Rodriguez (2017); see, generally, Travis et al. (2014), Uggen and McElrath (2014), and Mears and Cochran (2015).
[22] Manza and Uggen (2006); Denver et al. (2017).
[23] Mears et al. (2015); Mears et al. (2016a).

should be held in custody prior to court proceedings? What happens inside jails and prisons and what are the implications of those experiences?[24] For example, how do officers and inmates navigate life in prison, and what contributes to their respective experiences?

Community supervision – including probation, parole, and a variety of intermediate sanctions – is used more than prisons and so warrants distinct mention if only because of issues of scale. For example, in a given year, there typically are three to four times more individuals on probation or parole than in prison.[25] Why? It is less expensive. Joan Petersilia estimated that it cost about $3 annually to supervise one parolee versus the $29,000 it cost annually to house one inmate in prison.[26] What, though, is the effect of community supervision of various types?[27] How much does the amount or quality of supervision or support influence the effects of community supervision? How might society obtain more, or less, justice through community supervision and intermediate sanctions, such as house arrest and fines? Why do supervision practices vary over time and by jurisdiction? To what extent do community supervision and various intermediate sanctions, including many diversion programs, result in "net-widening"? (Net-widening is the unintended expansion of formal social control that can occur when someone struggles to navigate the challenges of stricter supervision practices.[28]) What can we learn about offending or public views about punishment through the study of community sanctions?

Such questions illustrate the many avenues of inquiry that can be and are addressed in corrections research. They may derive from an interest in shedding light on policy. Or they may derive from an interest in developing or applying theory.[29] Regardless, either emphasis can result in greater knowledge and improved policy.

Criminal Justice System

Criminal justice can be viewed as encompassing all formal social control efforts, including law-making, law enforcement, courts (e.g., defense, prosecution, and judges, as well as court decisions on the constitutionality of various policies or practices), and the correctional system (e.g., jails, prisons, community supervision).[30] Above, we illuminated one aspect of criminal justice – corrections – because of its prominent growth in recent

---

[24] Mears (2008a, 2012b).   [25] Mears and Cochran (2015); Cullen *et al.* (2017).
[26] Petersilia (2011:499).   [27] Piehl and LoBuglio (2005).   [28] Mears *et al.* (2016c).
[29] Sparks *et al.* (1996) have provided an excellent illustration of this point in their focus on prisons and social order.
[30] Mears (2010).

decades. The reality, though, is that all aspects of criminal justice have expanded greatly. To support the growth in corrections, many countries, especially the United States, implemented get-tough laws and expanded law enforcement and court capacity. All of these areas constitute distinct avenues along which research can and is undertaken.

Another important avenue of inquiry is the study of this system as a whole.[31] Criminal justice may not operate like a Swiss watch. It nonetheless consists of components that can influence one another. When they do, the effects may not always or even typically arise in ways that policymakers, administrators, or the public would like. Research on how criminal justice operates like a system represents an important and distinct line of inquiry. For example, when legislators enact laws that allow for longer stays in prison, that can create a need for more incarceration capacity or greater reliance on parole. Similarly, when such laws occur alongside greater funding of police or policies that toughen court responses to supervision violations, even more pressure on prisons and parole can result.

Juvenile Justice System

In America, the first juvenile court opened in 1899 in Cook County, Illinois. The idea took hold. In a span of but a few decades, all states created their own version of a juvenile justice system.[32] Many other countries also rely on entirely separate systems of justice for juveniles.[33] Why? Juveniles may seem more deserving of specialized attention. Perhaps they are more amenable to rehabilitation. And perhaps more informal modes of punishment are more effective with them. These and other claims rest on problematic assumptions.[34] For example, the public does not necessarily value the lives of juveniles more than that of other groups. And many adults may be amenable to rehabilitation and benefit from informal punishments. Members of the public, though, do seem to feel especially strongly about protecting young people. Also, evidence has accumulated that adolescents, and even young adults, in fact differ from adults along a number of developmental dimensions. They may be less developed psychologically, emotionally, socially, neurobiologically, and so on.[35] Such differences clearly can or may have implications for justice. To illustrate, if youth lack the capacity or competence to waive their rights, then policies may need to be in place to protect them.

---

[31] Feeley (1973, 1979); Mears (2017).   [32] Mears (2012a).
[33] Feld and Bishop (2012).   [34] Hirschi and Gottfredson (1993).
[35] Feld and Bishop (2012); Feld (2017).

This situation creates innumerable opportunities to investigate questions that cannot be investigated through a focus on criminal justice. Consider boundary issues, such as the age thresholds used to establish the lower and upper ages of juvenile court jurisdiction. These vary greatly across states. Why? What are the effects of these different boundaries? Such questions clearly are specific to a focus on juvenile justice. That said, the avenues of inquiry can run in many directions, some of which may be unique to juvenile justice and some of which may parallel criminal justice. They include questions about law enforcement, the use of police in schools, court decisions, how to balance an emphasis on punishment and rehabilitation, the effectiveness of diverse sanctions, the role of communities in delinquency and crime prevention, and more.

Victimization

It may seem odd to think that a field of study focused on crime would neglect victimization. Yet, that is what happened. Scholars tended to focus on criminals and how to punish or intervene with them. That has changed. In the mid 1900s, a sub-field, victimology, emerged that focused on "the etiology (of causes) of victimization, its consequences, how the criminal justice system accommodates and assists victims, and how other elements of society, such as the media, deal with crime victims."[36] Even so, change is slow. For example, crime policy efforts still tend to focus primarily on catching, punishing, or intervening in some way with those who commit crime. This emphasis can be seen in the focus on "criminal justice" and the "criminal justice system" rather than "victim justice" or an equivalent "victim justice system."[37]

Victimology has highlighted the problems with this approach. From a policy perspective, it is short-sighted and can result in less justice. A simple illustration of that can be seen in the fact that victims do not always or necessarily feel better simply because an offender was punished. From a scientific perspective, it needlessly delimits what gets studied. For example, many important and fascinating questions exist about victimization. Which individuals are most likely to be victimized and what aspects of situations, organizations, or communities may increase victimization in general or among certain groups? There also are many questions about the consequences of victimization. In what ways do different types of victimization affect individuals over the life-course? What facilitates or impedes recovery from victimization? There are many

---

[36] Daigle and Muftic (2016:1).   [37] Herman (2010).

questions, too, about how society views victims and what contributes to changes in these views. It is not an overstatement to say that victimology has greatly expanded the horizon of criminological and criminal justice research. It also has expanded the focus of policy.

Media

Media studies draw attention to the way in which television, the news, the Internet, and more reflect and shape society's understanding of crime and justice.[38] One of the most famous axioms in sociology is the "Thomas theorem," named after W. I. Thomas: "If [people] define situations as real, they are real in their consequences."[39] This idea – one anticipated by the Greek philosopher Protagoras in the fifth century BCE in his statement that "Man is the measure of all things" – forms a cornerstone of research aimed at understanding the meaning of social action.[40] It includes a focus on the "social construction" of reality. This is the notion that, in many instances, no one fixed or absolute reality exists. Instead, there simply are different ways of viewing phenomena, with no one view necessarily more "real" than another.[41] Criminological and criminal justice research on the media builds on this idea. It examines how the media characterize criminals and crime and criminal justice, including law-making, law enforcement, the courts, and corrections. It also examines how the media shape public perception of these different areas, such as views about the amount of crime or the effectiveness or professionalism of the police, as well as contributing to crime and policy. A focus on the media thus provides numerous opportunities to understand crime and criminal justice and how and why society responds to it in different ways.

Public Opinion

Crime policy, especially in democracies, frequently rests on claims about what "the public" wants.[42] Yet, it is not always clear what the public wants or how it views crime and justice. How, then, can policymakers accurately justify any claims about public mandates without knowing how the public views particular issues? The answer is that they cannot. Data on public views therefore are needed. However, as usual, data alone tell us little. We need theories and analyses that identify relevant dimensions of public views.

---

[38] Surette (2015).
[39] Thomas and Thomas (1928:572); the original formulation used "men" instead of "people." The history of the original formulation is interesting and a bit murky (see Merton 1995).
[40] Burnyeat (1976:44).   [41] Berger and Luckmann (1967).   [42] Burstein (2014).

Public opinion research examines these dimensions and their causes.[43] It involves, for example, studies of the accuracy of views about crime and punishment,[44] how certain groups, such as sex offenders, should be punished,[45] ways in which race may influence views about crime and justice,[46] perceptions about the integrity or effectiveness of corrections,[47] support for various laws,[48] community contextual influences on public views,[49] public views about sentencing,[50] and many other such topics.

As with almost all criminological and criminal justice research, public opinion studies may have an "applied," or policy-focused, bent. But it can be justified as being of scientific interest in its own right. For example, if the public supports a more rehabilitative-focused approach to sanctioning juveniles, why does it do so?[51] An answer to that question may not necessarily inform policy, yet still it would shed light on how society views children and youth. Similarly, what factors explain why some individuals support the death penalty or why support for capital punishment varies over time?[52] What, if any, are the effects of changing public support for the death penalty on actual policy? Answers to these questions are relevant for theory *and* policy.

Philosophy and Ethics

There are many philosophical and ethical dimensions to criminal justice. Consider the goals of sentencing. We can justify punishment as a means of achieving retribution, that is, punishment for punishment's sake.[53] On what philosophical basis, though, should this goal be given greater or lesser weight than the goal of improving public safety? Should we punish at all? Or, more specifically, should we rely on specific types of punishment? Corporal punishment illustrates the salience of the question. Many countries have abolished it. Why? Concerns exist that the deterrent benefits do not offset potential harms, including the moral price of contravening the "conscience of a civilized community."[54]

We can explore the philosophical aspects of corporal punishment as they relate to retribution or public safety. But we also can explore them empirically. To illustrate, corporal punishment arguments rest in part on the notion that physical pain, such as that caused through beatings, has a

---

[43] See, generally, Flanagan and Longmire (1996), Cullen *et al.* (2000), Roberts and Stalans (2000), Roberts and Hough (2005), and Roberts (2008).
[44] Pickett *et al.* (2015).   [45] Mancini and Mears (2010); Pickett *et al.* (2013).
[46] Unnever (2014).   [47] Mancini and Mears (2013).   [48] Mancini *et al.* (2013).
[49] Stults and Baumer (2007).   [50] Berk and Rossi (1997).   [51] Mears *et al.* (2007).
[52] Cullen *et al.* (2000).   [53] See, generally, von Hirsch and Ashworth (1992).
[54] Scarre (2003:301).

specific or general deterrent effect. Whether it does so is, however, an empirical, not a philosophical, issue. The nature of corporal punishment is also as much an empirical as philosophical question. For example, incarceration can affect the body indirectly in various ways, such as through victimization, sleep deprivation, or the physical discomfort of prison life.[55] Any assessment of how "corporal" a given punishment is thus requires empirical research on the effects of various punishments on a person's body.

Philosophical and empirical considerations come into play for other goals of punishment. Some philosophers argue that morally just sanctions require proportionate punishment.[56] Why, though, should punishments be "proportional" to a crime? What would proportionality look like empirically? Consider community sanctions. On what basis can such sanctions be scaled to be "proportional" to prison stays? Consider next a different goal – incapacitation. In pursuing incapacitation, how do we determine the length of punishment, such as incarceration or intensive probation, for different individuals? Or consider rehabilitation. It may seem like a straightforward benevolent act. However, rehabilitation can include intrusion into the lives of individuals that goes well beyond what many may see as warranted for a particular crime.[57] In virtually every instance, empirical issues come into play. How? Debates about punishment involve assumptions about the severity of crimes, the moral weight to be assigned to various goals, public views about the morality of various punishments, the effectiveness of punishment, the appropriateness of relying on uncertain predictions about future behavior among the punished or the effects of various sanctions on the public, and so on.

Discussions of crime and punishment clearly implicate ethical considerations as well. The existence of a journal, *Criminal Justice Ethics*, devoted purely to them attests to their importance and scope. Indeed, ethical considerations arise throughout all aspects of criminal justice. A few examples follow. For example, what is the ethical basis of implementing a law that may appear to be neutral on its face, but that in reality may disproportionately affect one group? Or a punishment that may result in harms to families or communities? Or a policy that prioritizes criminals and largely ignores victims? Or law-making processes that reflect various lobbying interests and thus those groups with greater power? What, too, is the ethical basis of calling for greater government accountability and reliance on "evidence-based" policy, but not creating the infrastructure to ensure that both occur?

---

[55] Scarre (2003:298).   [56] See, generally, von Hirsch and Ashworth (1992).   [57] *Ibid.*

Measurement and Methods

Credible research rests on "good" data and methods of analyzing them. Understandably, then, scholars invest considerable time examining the best ways to measure various crime and justice phenomena, the forces thought to influence them, and the outcomes affected by them. A simple example illustrates the point: Criminological and criminal justice researchers frequently study offending. Ironically, though, no consensus exists about how best to measure it.

The issue here is not simply whether self-report, police, court, or other data should be used. It also is how we conceptualize and quantify offending, as we discussed in Chapter 5. For example, should we treat it as a binary phenomenon? That is, one is, or is not, an "offender" by dint of ever having committed any crime. (If we count delinquency and include status offenses, that would mean that almost everybody – except a small handful of deviant ritualists who have never broken any rule – can be classified as an "offender.") Or should we view offending in scalar terms? For example, one is more of an "offender" the more one has committed multiple crimes. What, though, should be scaled? The frequency of offending or the severity of offending? Some scholars, such as Gary Sweeten, have advocated use of a variety index, which measures the total number of different crimes that one has committed.[58] Compelling arguments exist for such an approach. Even so, no agreement yet exists about the best way to proceed.

Much the same can be said for measurement of almost everything that criminological and criminal justice research examines. That includes crime types, victimization, police, court, and correctional system operations and outcomes, public attitudes, community citizens' views of crime and justice, the costs of crime, and more.[59] There is, then, more than enough basis for ongoing efforts to improve measurement.

The same can be said for methods. Social science methods have advanced tremendously in recent decades and show no sign of stopping. Consider some of the topics from an edited volume on *quantitative* methods in criminological and criminal justice research: Crime-mapping, spatial analyses, methods for visualizing data, trajectory modeling, cost-estimation, matching and other approaches (e.g., instrumental variable and regression-discontinuity techniques) to estimating causal effects, meta-analysis, social network analysis, addressing missingness in data, use of life-event calendars, use of experimental designs, gauging statistical power, and so on.[60] Consider as well some topics from an edited volume on *qualitative* methods

---

[58] Sweeten (2012); for a different approach, see Osgood *et al.* (2002).
[59] See Huebner and Bynum (2016).   [60] Piquero and Weisburd (2010).

in criminological and criminal justice research: use of mixed-methods approaches, analysis of offenders' stories, comparison of active versus incarcerated offenders, examining online data, ethnographical approaches to studying crime and justice, physical and ethical risks of ethnography, and how to teach fieldwork.[61] The very existence of such diverse approaches testifies to the different approaches to research that exist. It also testifies to the need for at least passing familiarity with them to make informed decisions about conducting, evaluating, or using research.

Demographic Dimensions

We turn now to four dimensions along which many studies proceed. The first focuses on demography, which refers to what might be termed "core" population characteristics, such as the age, race, ethnicity, or sex of a group. Those are among the most common demographic dimensions examined by researchers, but many others exist. Further below, for example, we discuss social dimensions. When combined with the "core" characteristics, these sometimes are referred to as "socio-demographic" or "socio-economic" variables. The "core" characteristics receive special attention for a number of reasons. One is that a myriad of differences exists among individuals as they age across the life-course, among racial and ethnic groups, and between men and women. If one wanted to identify a basis for dividing society into groups that most differ from one another, demography would provide a good starting point.

A second and related reason is that these groups may vary greatly in their experiences, including those that may contribute to offending, victimization, informal and formal social control, and more. The variation can be of interest in its own right. It also can signal that mixing the groups together in studies may amount to mixing apples and oranges. The groups differ so greatly that including them together in analyses would create misleading accounts. Indeed, the differences can be so large and varied that controlling for demographic measures in many analyses amounts to simultaneously controlling for a wide range of other unmeasured factors.

Demography also can be of interest for policy reasons. Laws may stipulate that there can be no discriminatory treatment of demographic groups. The laws may seek to ameliorate past or contemporary discrimination. For example, concern may exist that discrimination prevents women from rising to executive positions within criminal justice agencies. They may seek as well to prioritize some groups. The juvenile justice system, as

---

[61] Copes (2012).

discussed above, illustrates the point – it exists in no small part because of a societal view that younger people warrant special treatment.

Biological Dimensions

Biology can play a prominent role – either directly or in interaction with social environmental factors – in many criminological and criminal justice phenomena. The range of possibilities is vast. There may be dimensions of brain structure, evolution, genetics, hormones, and neurophysiology that can influence human behavior. That can include, not least, criminal activity, victimization, the actions of those who work in criminal justice, and more.[62] In the past, debates centered on assumptions about whether biology matters. Contemporary scholarship, however, is grounded in empirical research and the availability of new and better sources of data on which to examine the contribution of biology to behavior.[63] As but one example, methods now exist to assess the neurobiology of resilience, a topic of central relevance not only for studying offending, but also how others, such as police officers, cope with stress.[64] Similarly, an accumulation of different sources of data have provided the groundwork for identifying the developmental dimensions of adolescence. It points to the potential importance of developmental differences for understanding delinquency and informing juvenile justice policy.[65] One of the more intriguing aspects of biosocial scholarship lies in its emphasis on interactions. Research frequently seeks to isolate unique effects of this or that factor; policies often follow suit in targeting a single "silver bullet" solution to a problem. By contrast, biosocial research illuminates the conditional nature of many aspects of behavior. This view in turn highlights that much of social life includes complicated interactions among a wide range of individual, family, community, societal, and other factors.

Psychological Dimensions

Crime and justice can also be systematically examined from a psychological perspective. For example, we can study the potential contribution of intelligence, mental illness, personality type, resilience, self-control, and

---

[62] DeLisi and Vaughn (2015); Beaver (2016).

[63] Critiques of biosocial perspectives nonetheless have persisted. See, for example, a prominent criticism of biosocial criminological research, especially heritability studies, in *Criminology* (Burt and Simons (2014)) and the response to it (Barnes *et al.* (2014)). The exchange focused on genetics, which is but one area of biosocial research.

[64] See, for example, van der Werff *et al.* (2017).

[65] See, for example, Feld and Bishop (2012), Kelly (2015, 2016), Feld (2017), and Kelly *et al.* (2017).

other such dimensions to criminal behavior in general or to specific types of crimes.[66] In so doing, we might examine other dimensions. These might include the role of peers and family, developmental aspects of criminal behavior, such as the influence of early childhood experiences (e.g., victimization, maltreatment) and the transition into and out of adolescence, and mental illness (e.g., psychopathy, bipolar disorder, schizophrenia). A focus on psychology need not dictate attention only to crime. For example, a large literature exists that examines the psychology of court and trial decision-making, interrogations, and, more generally, the criminal justice process.[67] Research also examines the "environmental psychology" of prisons and jails. It investigates the justification for specific facility and cell designs. In addition, it evaluates the effects of these designs, as well as prison crowding, isolation, and other aspects of prison life, on inmates as well as on officers and the staff who work in custodial settings.[68] A psychological approach can be adopted to examine many more areas or topics. For example, how do victims cope in the aftermath of crime? What is the psychology underlying the stigmatization of or the sympathy given to victims?[69] Also, what influences how some individuals or groups view the legitimacy or fairness of the criminal justice system?[70] Different racial and ethnic groups may hold different views of the prevalence or causes of bias.[71] What informs these views and how individuals or groups respond to them? There is, in truth, an endless number of ways to examine criminological and criminal justice phenomena through the prism of a psychological perspective.

Social Dimensions

For almost any area or topic of study and for any of the four primary research goals, one can examine the social dimensions of it. The focus might be descriptive. For example, what is the difference between offending among religious groups?[72] It might be focused on investigating social meaning, such as differences in how some courtroom communities view use of illegal substances (e.g., as a health problem or a criminal justice problem).[73] It might focus on causation, such as how situational factors may contribute to victimization.[74] Or it might focus on policy. How, for example, do neighborhood characteristics influence the effectiveness of community

---

[66] Bartol and Bartol (2017).
[67] Simon (2012); Benforado (2016); Lieberman and Krauss (2016).   [68] Wener (2012).
[69] Lyons (2006).   [70] Tyler (2006).   [71] Peffley and Hurwitz (2010).
[72] Ellis (2002).   [73] Forer (1994).   [74] Turanovic and Pratt (2014).

policing efforts or supervision of probationers?[75] In every instance, the social dimensions vary greatly. They include economic conditions, employment, education, environmental contexts, health, immigration, inequality, families and households, neighborhoods, political parties or affiliation, religious groups or affiliation, sexual orientation, situational contexts, social networks, socio-economic status measures, and more.

Each dimension provides a different lens through which we can examine various areas and topics. To illustrate, one might examine how the different dimensions relate to citizen–police encounters.[76] For example, what effect does race or social class have on the extent to which citizens or the police perceive each other as threatening or supportive? How might social networks amplify perceptions of police bias? What influence does policing have on officers' families, and for which groups (e.g., men or women, minorities, street officers or detectives) are the effects the greatest? In a similar vein, a myriad of questions surface when we start with a given social dimension and then ask about its implications for some topic, such as domestic violence. For example, do changes in economic conditions influence rates of such violence? Or to what extent do certain groups, such as immigrants, under-report spousal abuse?

The Full Research Matrix: Goals × Topics × Units of Analysis × Data × Analyses

We have focused to this point on what we have termed a "partial research matrix" of research possibilities. It stemmed from cross-classifying four research goals with a range of research areas and topics. Here, we focus on the "full research matrix."

As highlighted at the bottom of Table 9.1, the full matrix is much more elaborate. Why? Whereas the partial matrix involves cross-classifying two dimensions, the full matrix involves cross-classifying five. These include: (1) research goals; (2) topics; (3) units of analysis; (4) types of data; and (5) types of analyses.

We start with the first: A study of any given area or topic can be undertaken with an eye toward achieving multiple goals. In these cases, a study will have questions that reflect these different goals and need to employ data and methods specific to answering these questions.

In addition, instead of focusing on just one area or topic, a study might examine several at once. We might study the intersection of race, prior victimization experiences, and law enforcement officer professionalism on

[75] Reisig (2010); Schaefer *et al.* (2016).   [76] Mears *et al.* (2017a).

police–citizen interactions. Similarly, we might examine the ways in which both biology and social environments influence any of a range of outcomes.[77] In these cases, a study might contribute to multiple areas of scholarship.

Many research areas or topics also can be investigated through the vantage point of one or more units of analysis (see Chapter 6). For example, one might examine parental incarceration effects on life outcomes of children. Such a study would be at the individual-level unit of analysis. Alternatively, one might examine whether communities with higher rates of parental incarceration differ in the outcomes of all children, not just those with incarcerated parents. This type of study would be at the community-level unit of analysis. Or one might combine both types of studies and undertake "multilevel" analyses.

Any given study might use one or more sources of data (see Chapter 5). A study of prosecutorial decision-making, for example, might rely on analysis of observations of prosecutors during courtroom proceedings, interviews, court administrative records data, case-file notes, or information from a survey of prosecutors. Sometimes the data may illuminate different aspects of a phenomenon. Other times they may provide a way of validating whether results using one source of data appear to be valid. If analysis of multiple types of data identifies similar patterns, we might be more confident in viewing the patterns as reflecting reality. Of course, many times, we do not have data that would be ideal. For example, reliable and accurate crime data do not exist for all countries, thus making cross-national comparisons difficult.[78]

Finally, we can employ more than one quantitative or qualitative analytic technique with a given set of data. The different approaches may reflect an interest in answering slightly different questions. For example, we might be interested in predicting whether or not someone will offend. Our interest here is in a binary outcome and so we would want to use a statistical approach suitable for such an outcome. But we instead might be interested in predicting who will commit the highest number of crimes. Here, we would want to use a slightly different statistical modeling approach, one suitable for predicting count outcomes. The different approaches enable us to answer different questions. Sometimes, though, we might use multiple approaches to investigate the same question, and do so to determine if identified patterns are "robust." That is, do we find the same type of pattern regardless of how we analyze the data?

---

[77] DeLisi and Vaughn (2015).   [78] Tonry (2014).

RESEARCH OPPORTUNITIES AND THEIR IMPLICATIONS

Several implications for criminological and criminal justice research flow from this seemingly dizzying set of research possibilities. The first is that the five dimensions – when cross-classified with one another – give rise to a tremendous number of avenues for research. That is how science advances, along many different avenues. Some turn out to be rabbit holes that lead to nowhere interesting or scientifically important. Others surprise us. Sometimes they greatly shape our understanding of crime and criminal justice. A "research matrix" way of thinking provides a convenient way to discern these possibilities.

Consider a focus on gun-related crime. If we follow the full matrix, many research possibilities emerge. We might be interested in identifying the social meaning associated with use of guns in general or among gangs specifically. We also might be interested in testing a theoretical model of gun-related offending. There may be multiple topics that we seek to investigate (e.g., gun offending, gun-related crime rates, laws for reducing illegal gun use, and so on). We could investigate these topics at different units of analysis. For example, a study might focus on variation among individual prosecutors in the implementation of gun laws or variation among counties, cities, or states in gun-law implementation. For any given study, we might rely on several sources of data; each might provide a different vantage point for shedding light on our questions. Similarly, for each data source, we might rely on multiple analytic techniques to gain a sense of how robust our findings are across the different approaches.

Second, when pursuing any one of the many possibilities, one should of course begin with reviewing what already is known. That means drawing on prior empirical studies. It also means drawing on prior theory. For some topics, an abundance of theories exists. Marcus Felson, in reviewing different theories of crime found, for example, over forty theories and many sub-theories.[79] At the same time, theories of criminal justice also abound.[80] Even so, one might well stumble into areas or topics where relatively little guidance exists. A researcher sensibility in these cases can be helpful in determining how to proceed. The matrix illuminates, for example, some of the directions along which one would want to conduct a literature review.

Third, awareness of these different possibilities also helps in placing studies in context. It is clear that one can examine one or more topics in

---

[79] Felson (2017).
[80] Kraska (2004, 2006); Manning (2005); Cooper and Worrall (2012); Maguire and Duffee (2015).

different ways. By extension, it is evident that any one study provides only a narrow slice of insight into a particular phenomenon. Awareness of research possibilities and the context within which they lie can help when thinking about what type of study one might want to conduct. It also can help us to evaluate existing studies. To illustrate, it should be clear that one study, no matter how well done, provides a weak basis for establishing a causal relationship or for guiding significant policy changes.

Fourth, consideration of the matrix suggests that no one area of research somehow possesses more importance than another. They simply differ from one another. Some topics may be more popular among researchers. And some may be more relevant for informing policy decisions. However, no clear foundation exists for privileging one line of research over another. Only in retrospect do we typically discern what lines of inquiry most advance science or policy.

Fifth, the matrix is not the only way to organize or gain a sense of the criminological and criminal justice research landscape. Scholars carve up this landscape in different ways. For example, one might categorize research based on (1) whether it focuses on crime, public views about crime and justice, and parts of the criminal justice system it examines, (2) theories or the theoretical assumptions, (3) dependent variables, (4) independent variables, or (5) units of analysis.[81] The matrix in fact encompasses all of these different approaches. For some individuals, though, a more parsimonious approach to categorizing research possibilities may be more helpful. One prominent series of edited volumes, for example, builds around topical areas, such as "crime and criminal justice," "crime prevention," "sentencing and corrections," "police and policing," and "prisons and imprisonment."[82]

There is no "right" or "wrong" here. Indeed, from a scientific perspective, no consensus exists about how to categorize research. There is also no consensus about what approach to doing so may somehow best lead to scientific progress or the accumulation of knowledge.[83] Proceed, therefore, with the approach that best works for you.

A closing and related observation – as we argued in Chapter 2 and have suggested throughout the book – no clean dividing line exists that separates "criminological" from "criminal justice" research. Indeed, when one considers either the partial or full matrix, it can be difficult to identify any

---

[81] See, generally, Hagan (1989), Messner *et al.* (1989), Bernard and Engel (2001), Kraska (2006), and Akers *et al.* (2016).

[82] Tonry (2011); Farrington and Welsh (2012); Petersilia and Reitz (2012); Reisig and Kane (2014); Wooldredge and Smith (2016).

[83] Mears and Stafford (2002).

logical basis for classifying one area or topic as purely "criminological" or "criminal justice" in focus. Consider the above-mentioned series: It included a volume focused on "criminological theory." This volume primarily examines theories of offending and crime. The series also included another on "criminology." It focuses on crime *and* criminal justice![84] The matrix thus illustrates in part why we have argued for viewing "criminological" research and "criminal justice" research as one and the same thing. They describe a field that investigates an enormous array of phenomena, many of which intersect with one another.

CONCLUSION

We set out with this chapter to convey the criminological and criminal justice research landscape. To this end, we described a "research matrix" of research possibilities that come from considering research goals, a range of specific areas and topics, and different units of analysis, types of data, and analytic approaches. The possibilities for research are seemingly endless.

Awareness of this landscape is, we submit, part of developing a researcher sensibility. How? It helps one to see the potential possibilities for research. When we open a pantry door, we may see lots of ingredients. Without a chef-like awareness, we will not see the different dishes that can be made, though. We simply see ingredients. Discerning research possibilities can be likened to possessing a chef-like ability to imagine many different cooking or baking options.

At the same time, awareness of this landscape can help one to better appreciate that any given study constitutes a narrow window into a given topic. This means that caution is indicated in inferring too much from one study. It does not mean that the study lacks credibility or importance. Sometimes one study can matter a great deal. Perhaps a study emerges that identifies a better way to measure self-control. The one study might throw into stark relief the possibility that many prior studies of the effects of self-control may have arrived at questionable conclusions, at least in so far as their measure of self-control was problematic. Still, we should exercise caution when imbuing any one study with too much significance.

The ability to discern research possibilities not only flows from considering the research matrix. It also flows from familiarity with the different considerations that go into the research enterprise. That includes, as we have discussed in earlier chapters, familiarity with "basic" versus "applied"

---

[84] Cullen and Wilcox (2012); Liebling *et al.* (2017).

research. More than that, it includes familiarity with how research goals drive research questions, how these questions drive the theories that we develop, apply, or test, and how theory, data, and analyses go hand in hand with one another. A researcher sensibility thus involves awareness of possible research avenues and familiarity with all aspects of the research process.

Part IV

Chefs in the Kitchen

10 Criteria for Conducting, Evaluating, and Using Research

INTRODUCTION

We turn finally to being a "chef in the kitchen." By that we mean the ability to imagine research possibilities, including ways to conduct, evaluate, or use research. One step in developing this ability comes from familiarity with the topics discussed in Parts I, II, and III of the book. Two final steps are involved. One, which we discuss here, consists of being aware of criteria for conducting, evaluating, and using research. A second, which we briefly discuss here and revisit in the final chapter, involves pragmatic activities that can be useful in pulling together aspects of the research process in a creative manner that works best for you.

We begin first with a question: What criteria should be used to judge how well a study is conducted or to evaluate or use its results effectively and appropriately? We wish that we could point to a cookie-cutter checklist of objective criteria, but there is no such list. Instead, diverse criteria exist. Some may be more relevant to conducting research, while others may be more relevant to evaluating or using it. In addition, relevance itself will depend on context. Consider a situation where we know almost nothing about some phenomenon. In this situation, an exploratory study with a non-representative sample might advance our understanding. It might even be viewed as groundbreaking because it illuminates something that previously went unnoticed. The study of course may provide weak grounds for demonstrating cause-and-effect, and its generalizability may be questionable. However, given the context – limited knowledge about a particular phenomenon – the research may be quite important.

The ability to discern context and its relevance is part and parcel of a researcher sensibility. In this chapter, we seek to convey this idea by identifying criteria that can be relevant to conducting, evaluating, or using research. We seek not least to highlight that the criteria should not be applied thoughtlessly. They instead should be applied with awareness of context. That includes consideration of a study's goals, the possibilities and limits of research, and ethics.

In short, the chapter addresses a series of related questions. What criteria can be used to guide researchers in undertaking credible studies? What criteria can be used for evaluating research? What criteria can be used to guide the use of it? Not least, what are the ethical issues that may bear on conducting, evaluating, or using research?

CRITERIA FOR CONDUCTING RESEARCH

One way to think about research is to view it like one might a house. We can all readily appreciate that a number of factors go into creating a solid home – that is, one that we might want to occupy. As shown in Table 10.1, one factor consists of reliance on architectural designs that meet the needs of homeowners (see Chapter 3). That is a pretty clear-cut consideration. A family with five children will need more space than a family with one

Table 10.1 An analogy – how credible research resembles building strong homes

Strong homes rely on …	Credible research relies on …
• Architectural designs that meet the needs of homeowners	• Research designs that meet the needs of scientists, policymakers, or practitioners
• Sufficient number of skilled workers	• Sufficient number of skilled researchers
• Established "best practices," based on industry standards, to steer all aspects of construction, from layout to types of materials used throughout the home	• Established "best practices," based on existing literature, to steer all aspects of research, from research design to theory and types of data and analyses used
• Integration of structural layout, materials, and colors, within constraints set by budget and timeline, to achieve goals	• Integration of theory, data, and analyses, within constraints set by budget and timeline, to achieve goals
• Thorough checks of all parts of the home, including roof, wiring, plumbing, drywall, paint, doors, furnace, air conditioning, windows, and more	• Thorough checks of all parts of study, including sampling, measures, missing data, analyses, accurate portrayal of findings and limitations, and more
• Features that enhance comfort and fuel efficiency	• Findings speak to particular goals, such as description or estimating causal effects
• Inspections to assess quality	• Peer review to assess quality

child. Someone who needs wheelchair access will need a specific configuration for means of egress.

To build a house obviously requires that there be a sufficient number of workers with the skills necessary to tackle various parts of construction. That includes plumbers, electricians, drywall installers, and more. In each instance, we want workers who adopt industry-established "best practices." Following all federal, state, and local building requirements would be essential.

From a design perspective, the different parts of the house need to come together "just so" if we are to view it favorably and for it to be functional. The layout needs to match our needs, materials must be placed appropriately (e.g., patio stones would not work well in the bedroom), colors should be as envisioned, and so on. Most importantly, this integration and the overall home design and construction must accord with our budget and timeline.

When building a house from scratch, there is the need to check that all installations have been done correctly. We would want to check for any mistakes, imperfections, omissions, and so on. We also would want to ensure that any and all features that would promote comfort and fuel efficiency have been included.

Finally, before inhabiting the home, we would want it checked thoroughly. Inspectors provide this service and ensure that the construction meets building codes.

Creating or identifying credible research is akin to this process. Indeed, the parallels are striking. For example, the research design should meet the needs of the groups – such as scientists, policymakers, or practitioners – who want it. It requires sufficient staffing, including reliance on skilled research teams. Those teams should rely on "best practices' for undertaking specific activities, such as designing the sampling frame, drawing on theory, creating appropriate measures, applying appropriate analytic techniques, and so on. None of these activities happens in isolation. To create credible research, they all must be considered in conjunction with one another. Findings should be subjected to careful scrutiny, with limitations duly noted, and they should respond directly to the study's goals. Not least, they should be subject to peer review.

Such parallels should make clear that developing the ability to appraise research does not require special abilities that only scientists possess. At bottom, it requires simply an ability to think about all of the dimensions that go into research.

What, though, are the specific criteria that should be considered when evaluating the credibility of research findings? In fact, no single criterion matters most. Instead, when assessing how well a study was conducted or in thinking through the best approach to a study that one is contemplating, many criteria are relevant. In certain contexts, some may be more important than others. Much depends on a study's particular goals and the state of prior research. Much also depends on constraints (e.g., data availability, resources for the study).

Here, then, we discuss some of the criteria that go into assessing how well a study was conducted or the likely contribution, validity, or usefulness of a proposed one. We discuss these criteria under the heading of "conducting" research because they are part of the nuts and bolts of doing research. However, these same criteria can be used to inform evaluation of a study's results as well, which we highlight in the next section.

Research Infrastructure and Staffing

Proposed or completed studies can be judged in part on the extent to which sufficient research infrastructure and staffing exist to execute the various research activities. Larger-scale studies in particular may require experts on sampling, survey or interview instrument design, and analyses. They may require many staff to collect data, administer surveys, coordinate focus groups, and so on. All research activities can be implemented with varying degrees of quality. Well-conducted studies depend on having adequate organizational capabilities. That includes having staff with expertise in relevant areas. It also includes having appropriate physical and technological capacity, such as office space, computers, and software. Funders typically require that research proposals include a description of an organization's capabilities precisely because of the importance of research infrastructure for undertaking quality work. However, completed studies also can be judged with such considerations in mind. Studies that rely on experts and state-of-the-art data collection and analysis approaches should generally engender more trust.

Prior Relevant Literature

From a scientific or policy perspective, research should build on what has come before. Replication for the sake of replication serves no one. The best proposals and completed studies build on extant theory and research; they state clearly how exactly they advance prior scientific studies. What counts as "relevant" varies. For example, a study of public views about different sentencing options might benefit from drawing on insights from scholars whose work falls outside the criminological and criminal justice literature.

"Relevance" cannot be precisely identified or quantified. That is where a researcher sensibility enters. One must take stock of prior work and reflect on how it does, or does not, inform efforts to shed light on a particular study's questions. Creative researchers find ways to apply prior work in new ways or to see avenues for addressing research gaps. Even then, the relevance of a study may take decades to become clear.[1] That does not absolve researchers from carefully describing the contribution of their research as they see it. It does mean that some humility is in order when assessing the relevance of a study for science or policy.

Appropriate Theory, Data, and Analyses

The axiom "don't reinvent the wheel" applies to research. Research should draw on the best and most appropriate theories, data, and analytic techniques. If new ones need to be invented, so be it. Efficiency alone, however, dictates reliance on accumulated knowledge. How can one select the "best" techniques? It is difficult! One strategy involves canvassing prior work. Another involves consulting with experts. That can mean talking with those who have done pioneering theoretical work, others who have familiarity with an array of data sources and their relative strengths and weaknesses, and still others with expertise in analytic methodologies. There is no short cut here. Skimping on a review of prior work or consultation ultimately leads to proposed or actual research findings of questionable validity or policy relevance.

Accuracy and Trustworthiness

Research should be accurate and trustworthy. Accuracy can mean many different things. For example, we can view accuracy as a prevalence estimate of some phenomenon, such as crime, that we can trust. Homicide counts typically can be trusted because most deaths get reported. By contrast, police reports do not provide an accurate reflection of the total amount of actual burglaries because homeowners may not call the police after a burglary. We can also view accuracy as a situation where we can trust that a causal estimate provides a true reflection of the direction and magnitude of force that one factor exerts on another. This idea is reflected in the concept of "internal validity"; studies with high internal validity can be trusted to more accurately have estimated a causal effect. Here, again, we may be unable to trust such estimates for the reasons, such as weak methodological designs, enumerated in prior chapters. Accuracy also might be viewed as the extent to which a study's effect represents what one would find in a study of other populations and places. "External validity" captures

---

[1] Kuhn (1962); Merton (1973); Mears and Stafford (2002).

this idea. Studies with high external validity provide estimates that we can reasonably anticipate finding in many populations and places. Accuracy can mean more than that, though. For example, we want measures that accurately reflect the constructs they are supposed to capture. A single question about whether 2 + 2 = 4 would not, for example, tell us much about an adult's intelligence.

Trustworthiness is part and parcel of the accuracy of studies. When researchers draw on the best available theory, data, and analytic methods, when they demonstrate care in how they combine these different research ingredients, when they explicitly identify limitations – when these and all aspects of a study have been undertaken with precision, we have greater trust in the results of the study. That does not mean that a trustworthy study necessarily provides an accurate depiction of the "truth." It also does not mean that reliance on an accurate measure necessarily results in an accurate causal estimate. It means simply that we typically will have greater confidence in studies that have been undertaken with due care and attention to detail.

Consistent vs. Inconsistent Results

Uncertainty attends all research.[2] Policymakers and criminal justice administrators may want more certainty. They may want concrete recommendations. That is understandable, and when such can be provided, researchers should do so. Scientists also want certainty. They want to know that a pattern or causal effect somehow is real or true.

Yet, uncertainty pervades most research and should be acknowledged. Consider a typical published research study. Readers might be presented with two to three tables of results. A page or so of findings may accompany these tables. The conclusion then discusses the "central" findings. These typically involve a small handful of causal estimates, claims about a theory, or ideas about how the world operates. However, to arrive at those few tables, researchers might conduct hundreds of analyses. They select those that they believe best represent the "truth." That is necessary because otherwise readers would be buried in hundreds of pages of tables, many of which the researcher dismissed because they identified problems with the modeling. Even so, it creates a misleading impression. It suggests more consistency in the results than would be the case were one to see the hundreds of other analyses.

In the end, we should view any one study as a sample from hundreds of studies. And the results within any one study may be but one sample among

---

[2] Ellenberg (2014:430).

many analyses. Accordingly, one way to evaluate how well a study was or will be conducted lies with explicit statements about the consistency of the results. When research studies provide forthright discussions of consistency, or inconsistency, in the results, we can trust them more.

This issue assumes particular importance when those who undertake studies have a vested interest in the outcomes. For example, we can rightfully be concerned that an advocacy organization or lobbying group will highlight only those results that they want to believe represent reality. From the hundreds of possibilities, they may select only those that advance their cause. In these cases, and, indeed, with all studies, explicit statements about the consistency of all analyses helps to bolster our confidence in the veracity of the results.

Hypothesis Testing

One of the central methods used in science consists of the derivation and tests of hypotheses.[3] This approach frequently involves recourse to using statistical analyses to detect if an observed relationship is "statistically significant." Hypotheses can be advantageous in testing parts of theories. They can clarify our ideas about how the world operates. There is, though, considerable debate about how best to derive hypotheses. For example, advocates of formal theory highlight that conventional theories lead to ad hoc hypotheses that provide no clear insight about a theory's accuracy.[4] There are other issues as well. For example, hypothesis testing with qualitative research does not readily lend itself to precise quantitative estimates of differences or associations. And testing with quantitative data can lead to more confusion than not.

Why? One reason has to do with the difference between *substantive* significance and *statistical* significance. Suppose a study shows that 56 percent of youth with authoritarian parents engage in delinquency and that 44 percent of youth without authoritarian parents do so.[5] This difference seems substantively large. Such a determination, however, lies outside the realm of statistics. Whether some effect is sufficiently large to be of scientific or policy interest depends on many other considerations. Even so, when we hear the word "significant," we tend to think that it means that a study finding is "real," large, or important in some way.

That is why the phrase "statistical significance" causes many problems. Statistical significance does not equate to substantive significance. It refers to our confidence in the probability that observed differences in samples correspond to what we think are true. The standard for feeling confident

[3] Ellenberg (2014). [4] Gibbs (1972). [5] Hoeve *et al.* (2009:762).

has been set, by convention, to a probability – a "p-value" – of less than 0.05 (i.e., a 1 in 20 chance). The researcher approach to hypothesis testing involves identifying a null hypothesis, that is, a statement that no statistical difference in some outcome exists between, say, two populations. A conventional p-value threshold of 0.05 means that "if the null hypothesis is true for some particular experiment, then the chance that experiment will nonetheless return a statistically significant result is only 1 in 20."[6]

Researchers can and do stray from this bar and debates exist about how to go about hypothesis testing.[7] In addition, with a 0.05 or lower bar, we still end up with thousands of studies that identify "statistically significant" results. Many of these studies – including those that rely on experimental designs – identify results that are incorrect. They constitute "false positives."[8] Another problematic aspect of hypothesis testing is the fact that many studies that achieve statistical significance lack substantive significance. They do so by relying on larger samples. With such samples, differences or associations can emerge as statistically significant even when they are trivial in magnitude. In addition, studies can produce statistically significant differences or associations by mining data for any possible one that can be found in a set of data. They do so in part because statistical significance frequently constitutes a minimum bar for a study to be published, regardless of whether any sound theoretical basis exists to anticipate some difference between groups or an association between two variables.

What relevance does this issue have for assessing how well a proposed or completed study is conducted? We should look for clear statements about exactly why a relationship can be anticipated. We should look for clear articulation of hypotheses and how they were derived. We should look as well for evidence that the researchers did not or, for proposed work, will not engage in p-value hacking or hunting. P-hacking consists of looking for any statistically significant association (by running many different analyses) and building a seemingly credible scientific explanation around it.[9] It may not always be obvious when p-hacking occurs. However, credible research makes it easy for us to feel more confident in it by relying on theory and articulating clearly the study's contributions and limitations, which we discuss below.

Specific Contributions and Limitations of a Study

Good researchers make it easy to understand the relevance of their study. They show how the results of their study address (or will address) particular

---

[6] Ellenberg (2014:146).   [7] Kringen *et al.* (2018).   [8] Ioannidis (2005a, 2005b).
[9] Chawla (2017); see also Kringen *et al.* (2018).

gaps in research. The gaps may center on estimates of the effect of some variable, explanations for the effects, the need for more accurate measures of phenomena or better methods for estimating certain types of relationships, and so on. Sometimes researchers obscure their contributions behind "scholarly" verbiage or technical jargon. That does not mean that we should dismiss study results. It does, though, raise questions about whether the authors seek to spruce up substantively insignificant findings.

In addition, studies that we can trust more highlight their limitations. Sometimes description of the limitations involves delimiting the precise contribution that research makes. For example, a study might credibly establish that probation in a particular state reduces recidivism more so than does incarceration. This effect, though, may well arise from unique aspects of probation and prisons in that state. Accordingly, it may not be one that would arise in others. Here, the study contributes to efforts to understand the relative effectiveness of probation and prison, respectively. But the contribution is limited by the fact that its results may only generalize to states that have similar approaches to probation and prison.

For researchers, identifying limitations should come easily. However, many forces conspire against complete and accurate depiction of limitations. Journals, and the reviewers on which they rely, might balk at publishing studies that have too many problems. Listing too many limitations would seem to imply that a study lacked credibility. Also, journals impose strict page limits on papers. It can be difficult to provide a full account of limitations and caveats when one struggles simply to convey the main theoretical arguments, study design, and analyses.

The fact is that all studies have not one but many limitations. Some studies are under-powered or rely on samples that are so small, they cannot reveal anything but large effects.[10] Here, then, the honest approach in reporting null results is to identify just how large an effect would have to have been to identify a statistically significant effect. Studies may rely on data or methods that may be defensible, but that nonetheless result in estimates with considerable uncertainty. The samples may not be representative. Measures may not accurately reflect the intended constructs. Potential confounding variables may have been omitted because they were unavailable. Only some outcomes relevant to testing a theory or evaluating a policy may be examined. The list goes on and on. That is why studies that clearly identify their limitations should increase rather than decrease our confidence in them. Of course, some limitations may be

---

[10] Lipsey (1998).

"deal-breakers" – they completely undermine the integrity of a study. If so, it is best for other researchers to make that determination rather than to make it for them by hiding problems.

Efficiency

Resources consumed by a study can be important for evaluating how well it was conducted. Labor, and associated costs, go into collecting and analyzing data and then crafting scholarly journals, agency reports, congressional briefs, or the like. Accordingly, all else equal, the better study is one that incurs fewer financial or labor time costs. This idea assumes even greater importance in situations where study results, if made available quickly, could help prevent crime, assist victims, or improve society in some tangible way.

CRITERIA FOR EVALUATING RESEARCH – ALL OF THE ABOVE PLUS SEVERAL OTHERS

The above criteria can be useful for assessing how well a study was conducted or the plans for a proposed study. These criteria can also be useful for evaluating study results. Several additional criteria come into play, though, when evaluating studies, their results, and their implications. We discuss three: (1) the predictive power of theories; (2) the extent to which replication studies exist; and (3) the relevance of one or more studies for science or policy.

Predictive Power of Theories

Theories in criminology and criminal justice rarely get rejected. Instead, they live on, get modified, or are reincarnated under a different name. All the while, new theories surface. Why? Almost any theory can be found to have some level of empirical support from at least a few studies. That makes it possible to report something like, "Studies suggest mixed evidence for the theory, but several lend support to it." Some theories seem to attract more attention than others. That may be due to a large number of studies that lend support to them. It is possible, though, that the theories are popular because they seem intuitive, emerged at just the right time to garner attention, or have been marketed well.[11] This popularity does not mean that a particular theory is somehow better than others in scientific terms. It does

---

[11] Many accounts of the influences on science exist. Kuhn's (1962) and Merton's (1973) still provide some of the most trenchant insights on what can be termed the "sociology of knowledge."

mean that a large number of studies may lend support to the theory even though an equally large number may not.

The ever-increasing amount of theories significantly undercuts the ability of scientific knowledge to accumulate.[12] Theories provide insights. They explain. However, even when they do so convincingly – through appeals to logic and intuition – they actually may fall far short of providing an explanation that empirical research *consistently* supports. They also may fall short relative to other theories. Alternatively, although they may fall short in some ways in comparison with such theories, they may do better in other ways.

What would help? One solution consists of applying a set of criteria to theories of crime or criminal justice. Jack Gibbs has provided one such set that can help us to situate the status of any one theory relative to others.[13] Specifically, he argued that "predictive power" should provide the ultimate criterion for comparing which theories perform better than others. In turn, predictive power consists of seven criteria:

(1) *Testability* – the extent to which a theory includes testable statements and the theory's constituent variables can be measured.
(2) *Predictive accuracy* – the ability to make accurate predictions about the direction, magnitude, and consistency of associations between putative causes and their effects.
(3) *Range* – the number of units of analysis (e.g., individuals, neighborhoods, cities, states) to which a theory can be applied.
(4) *Scope* – the number of dependent variables to which a theory can be applied.
(5) *Intensity* – the number of space–time relations predicted by a theory, such as the number of synchronic predictions (e.g., cross-sectional associations, such as correlations between levels of one variable and another) and diachronic predictions (e.g., over-time associations, such as correlations between changes in one variable and changes in another).
(6) *Discriminatory power* – the ability to predict the relative strengths of different anticipated relationships in a theory.
(7) *Parsimony* – the ability of a theory to generate many predictions with few premises and, in particular, to generate more theorems (or conclusions) relative to premises.[14]

---

[12] See Gibbs (1972, 1985, 1997); see, generally, Mears and Stafford (2002).
[13] Gibbs (1985, 1989, 1997); see also Ekland-Olson and Gibbs (2018).
[14] Gibbs (1997); Ekland-Olson and Gibbs (2018).

Another criterion might include "fertility," namely, the idea that one theory is better than another to the extent that, all else equal, it generates more new lines of research.[15] A thought-provoking theoretical investigation sometimes can lead to new ways of understanding even if the theory did not accurately account for a particular phenomenon.[16] In that way, such a theory may be better than others that enjoy more empirical support.

These criteria can be useful in assessing the relative strength of different theories. More importantly, they highlight that no theory likely exceeds all others across all dimensions. Instead, some theories may have greater predictive power along one or two dimensions. For example, they might predict a greater number of dependent variables, but only for one unit of analysis, while another theory might explain fewer dependent variables, but do so across multiple units of analysis. In addition, the criteria illuminate that science cannot advance appreciably if no basis exists for judging when one theory is better than another.

The criteria also can be useful in judging the relative significance of particular empirical studies. For example, a study might demonstrate that a prisoner re-entry program reduced recidivism. That is certainly one indicator of successful re-entry. When, however, we consider "scope," we instantly realize that other outcomes, such as homelessness and employment, may be relevant to evaluating the program. We thus can apply the different criteria to contextualize the importance of any given study for theory or policy.

Replication

Science advances by gaining ever-greater certainty about explanations or relationships. It rarely if ever achieves absolute certainty. That is the nature of science. Provisional truth emerges until some study comes along and highlights an error in prior understanding. Replication thus constitutes a central platform for evaluating a body of research. Without it, we are left with a small handful of studies, or perhaps only one or two, on which to base our assessments about presumed relationships. That can be risky.

One example that illustrates this point comes from a classic study in the field of corrections, the Stanford Prison Experiment (SPE). Undertaken in 1971, Philip Zimbardo recruited Stanford University students to participate in a study where they were told to pretend to be inmates or guards and were given guidance in how to act. In the study, the student "guards" became so

[15] Mears and Stafford (2002:19).
[16] Kulig *et al.* (2017) have provided an illuminating example of that in their appraisal of the Stanford Prison Experiment.

abusive and student "inmates" became so submissive that the experiment had to be terminated.[17] As Teresa Kulig and her colleagues have written, a seemingly clear lesson, one anticipated by Gresham Sykes' inmate deprivation theory, could be gleaned: "Prison is an inherently destructive institution, one that is capable of turning otherwise good people into evil-doers, and of turning otherwise well-adjusted people into cowering balls of anxiety."[18] Their review highlighted a problem, though – this claim went largely unevaluated. Few replications occurred. Over time, the work became a "classic," one whose insight many scholars and publications accepted on faith. This development occurred with minimal replication of the study, and the few replications that did occur failed to obtain similar results. The lesson? Replication is essential for gaining confidence in "findings." That axiom holds all the more so if study results accord with our preconceived notions of truth.

Another example is the Minneapolis Domestic Violence Experiment, which occurred in the 1980s.[19] The study randomly assigned officers to a treatment condition, which consisted of mandating an arrest in cases of domestic violence calls for service, and two control conditions. One consisted of separating the abuser and victim for several hours, and the other consisted of advising them to seek recourse through mediation. The researchers reported lower levels of recidivism among the arrested abusers. In response – and despite cautions by the researchers to proceed carefully on the basis of just one study – many states enacted "mandatory arrest" policies.[20] What happened? Subsequent evaluations reported mixed results. Some found no effect of the laws, others found beneficial effects only for some groups, such as the married or employed, and still others found potential harmful effects (e.g., increased recidivism).[21] Replication avoids such problems and enables science to separate the wheat from the chaff.

Still another example involves a prominent policy change in the 1990s – the proliferation of drug courts. Built on the idea that speedier processing, drug treatment, and imposition of tougher supervision conditions would be effective, these courts appealed to political conservatives and liberals alike. Why? They seemed to promote accountability and punishment and simultaneously to be smart on crime. It also zeroed in on a causal force, drug addiction, that many policymakers felt substantially contributed to offending. Although some studies have found that drug courts may reduce recidivism, some assessments suggest warrant for caution. Few drug

---

[17] Haney *et al.* (1973); Zimbardo *et al.* (1973).   [18] Kulig *et al.* (2017:76).
[19] Sherman and Berk (1984).
[20] Maxwell *et al.* (2002); Bridges *et al.* (2008); Hines (2009); Iyengar (2009).
[21] Hines (2009:125); see also Maxwell *et al.* (2002).

courts ever get evaluated, for example, and some studies have found null effects of drug courts. In addition, many studies document numerous challenges in implementing the courts. These challenges diminish the potential effectiveness of drug courts.[22]

Replication is, in short, the lifeblood of science. It is no less important for improving policies. We can see in the above illustrations, for example, that "evidence-based" policy lacks much in the way of "evidence" when it relies on only a few studies (or sometimes just one).

Relevance for Science or Policy

Another way of evaluating research involves appraising its relevance for science or policy. That is easier said than done. As the "predictive power" criteria highlight, we might invoke one criterion or many to evaluate which theories fare better than others. That is well and fine. But we still are left wondering about which theories most advance science or policy.

The problem here is that scientists typically have little idea about which studies or lines of inquiry will lead to the "biggest" advances. What in fact counts as "bigger" or "biggest"? Such assessments usually emerge over time, and they stem from historians or communities of scientists collectively reflecting at length about the contribution of particular lines of work.

To make matters more confusing, science in fact progresses along many different fronts.[23] Sometimes the advance seems somewhat trivial – a better measure of some phenomenon, for example. But better measures can lead to tremendous strides in understanding the social world. Advances also might consist of developing new methodologies, assessing associations across multiple units of analysis, investigating different causal mechanisms that account for a well-established association, and so on. How can we know what amounts to a significant contribution or leap in knowledge?

There seems to us to be no solution here, save one: Identify the criteria for why one thinks that particular studies advance science or hold special relevance for policy. The relevance of studies for policy is, we should emphasize, a no-less-important consideration than is the relevance of them for science. As with theories, the evaluative criteria may vary. For example, if prison officials want information on how well a vocational training program was implemented, they need research on program implementation, not impacts. Similarly, if they want information on program impacts, an implementation evaluation may prove to be a waste of time. Still other

---

[22] See, generally, Roman and DeStefano (2004), Wilson *et al.* (2006), Huddleston *et al.* (2008), and Tanner-Smith *et al.* (2016).

[23] Mears and Stafford (2002).

considerations go into assessing policy relevance. Lawmakers or criminal justice administrators might want information about the magnitude of benefit that they can anticipate from a particular intervention. That is, they may need the intervention to achieve a sizable improvement, one that greatly exceeds the intervention's costs. Not least, we typically want policies to achieve their goals and not to cause harms. Another criterion to consider, then, involves the extent to which a law, program, or practice has adverse effects and the trade-off between benefits and harms.

CRITERIA FOR USING RESEARCH

As we have discussed, criteria exist for how research should be conducted and evaluated. These criteria can also inform the appropriate use of research for science or policy. There are, though, several others that should be considered.

For researchers, there is first and foremost the need to draw on prior research in an appropriate manner. That includes accurately characterizing findings from prior studies when proposing or undertaking research. Researchers should carefully consider which studies to include in their own work. Consider traditional narrative reviews. They can be colored by researcher bias. For example, a researcher might examine hundreds of studies and give greater weight to those that obtained results that accord with their preconceptions of what must be true, and discount those that do not. Meta-analyses help to reduce such bias.[24] The larger issue, though, is that when framing the significance of a study or how it contributes to science, we want to be sure that we have accurately represented the state of knowledge. Journal peer-review processes can help to ensure that researchers do just that. However, that process cannot and does not weed out all instances of researchers failing to accurately depict prior work.

Researchers also should try to state precisely the way in which results of their study might credibly be used. It is commonplace to suggest that its findings have implications for research and for policy. That can be inappropriate sometimes. For example, a study might find that minority felons receive more severe sanctions than white felons. It then might suggest that funding should be targeted toward efforts to reduce discriminatory attitudes of prosecutors. However, let us assume that the study never sought to explain what produced the differences in punishment. How, then, could it possibly provide insight into what caused them *or* which ones might be amenable to policy influence?[25] The answer: It cannot. Should potential

---

[24] Lipsey and Wilson (2001).   [25] Mears *et al.* (2016b).

policy implications be articulated when possible? Sure, but with all due precision about what the study examined, the study's limitations, and the need for caution in generalizing from it.

For policymakers, one of the most important criteria for using research to inform policy deliberations or decisions is the study's relevance. Research that only tangentially bears on a policy issue provides a questionable basis for taking action. To illustrate, in the above example, it may be both unnecessary and ineffective to call for oversight of a prosecutor's decision-making. The oversight might reduce racial differences in sentencing. However, it is unlikely given that the differences might stem from a myriad of other causes.

*Another criterion for appropriate use of research consists of drawing on **all** relevant studies, not just those that accord with our notions of what somehow must be effective.* This criterion seems like common sense, but policymakers and criminal justice officials are human and so may be prone to accept research "evidence" that supports what they think.

Yet another criterion to consider is not relying on only one or few studies to guide decision-making. Why? The studies may have been poorly done. They may have identified patterns or effects specific to the location where they were conducted. The effects identified in the studies might depend on certain conditions that were not identified in the original studies. And the studies tell us nothing about factors that might be more important to address. By way of illustration, consider a study of a diversion program that seems to reduce recidivism. The study might have relied on an experimental design that was poorly implemented. It might have relied on a non-experimental research design that included no comparison group. The program might have been effective only because it operated within a community that had resources to provide quality services, treatment, and supervision. It also is possible that the program's potential effectiveness may be largely irrelevant. Far more pressing may be the possibility that the jurisdiction that adopted the diversion program was, at the same time, ignoring a wide range of systems problems. Addressing such problems might achieve far more than implementing a diversion program that modestly reduces recidivism for a relatively small number of youths.

ETHICS AND RESEARCH

Finally, we turn to several ethical dimensions that also warrant consideration when conducting, evaluating, or using research. Many detailed accounts of ethics and research exist.[26] In addition, scientific associations – such as the

---

[26] See, for example, Elliott and Stern (1997), Israel and Hay (2006), Macrina (2014), and Cowburn *et al.* (2017).

American Society of Criminology and the Academy of Criminal Justice Sciences – provide codes of ethics that can guide researchers and those who fund or request research.[27] We therefore touch only on a few critical dimensions to illuminate the fact that ethical questions and judgement calls attend to the research enterprise.

Political Influences on Research

Politics can influence research, which is not necessarily a bad thing. Indeed, from an ethical standpoint, it would seem incumbent on legislators to call for research on the need for and implementation, effects, and cost-efficiency of the laws they enact.

What, though, when funding for science gets determined by legislatures? What if, in turn, legislatures dictate the directions in which research goes? Even here, the problem is not clear. For example, without federal funding for science, there likely would be far fewer scientific advances. Advances instead would likely center on a narrow spectrum of questions that interest businesses because answers to them might increase profits.

Federal funding does not, however, come free of strings. Those who fund research typically shape what gets studied. That means that they push scientific progress in different directions. This type of "push" has occurred in criminology and criminal justice. For example, during eras in which policymakers emphasized rehabilitation, funding typically has focused on evaluating the implementation and effects of rehabilitative programs. During get-tough eras, such as occurred during the 1980s and 1990s, funding has tended to emphasize the study of deterrence.[28] In recent decades, large-scale growth in incarceration has led to funding aimed at understanding prisoner re-entry and how to promote desistance from offending.[29]

Similar "pushes" come from state and local agencies. These agencies typically seek answers to particular policy-focused questions, not necessarily those that will most advance science. The "pushes" also come from foundations and businesses, which may seek to promote knowledge in particular areas. Such "pushes" can be seen as a form of political influence.

When, then, might political influence on research become a concern? There are many possible scenarios. First, there is the possibility that the

---

[27] The ASC Code of Ethics can be found online at www.asc41.com/code_of_ethics_copies/ASC_Code_of_Ethics.pdf, as can the ACJS Code of Ethics at www.acjs.org/page/Code_Of_Ethics.

[28] Blumstein (1997).

[29] Cullen (2005); Clear and Frost (2013); Mears and Cochran (2015).

political orientations of funders shape the topics that get studied. Second, funders may seek to dictate which research findings can be published. How? They might dictate that all published research must first be reviewed and approved by them. Third, they may dictate that only certain findings be published. Fourth, they may ensure that research proposal review panels consist only of individuals who they know will support certain lines of research. The proposal process begins with producing a written narrative with many elements, such as the statement of the research gap to be addressed, research objectives, data and methods, organizational and researcher capacity to undertake the work, budget, and timeline. Those are the dimensions that should most influence a decision to fund. However, reviewers' assessments of any given proposal might be shaped by their political leanings. That, in turn, can mean that a scientifically sound study does not get funded and one that may be not as strong does. Fifth, researchers themselves may undertake research that reflects their political leanings. They also may allow these leanings to color how they interpret their results. Perhaps, for example, they unconsciously tend to dismiss "unfavorable" findings as reflecting a methodological problem and to accept "favorable" ones uncritically.

These and other potential political influences do not have to affect research. Indeed, when one reviews the wide range of topics and questions addressed in scholarly journals, quite the opposite appears to be the case. That may reflect the fact that universities tend to promote science-for-science's-sake research and so provide a buffer against political influences. Or it may reflect the sincere attempt by many funders to promote scientific knowledge. That said, political influences do exist. When they occur, they can distort or waylay scientific progress.

Institutional Review Boards (IRBs) and Potential Harms to Human Subjects

In medicine, physicians learn the adage, "first, do no harm."[30] The same principle guides research – when conducting a study and collecting data, there should be no harm to humans. In addition, human subjects should be cognizant of the risks and benefits of participating in the research. If they are not, the studies should not proceed. Human subjects also should not be coerced into participating in a study or providing data. Instead, they should be given relevant information for deciding whether to participate. This

---

[30] The precise phrase does not appear in, but generally is attributed to, Inman (1860) (see Sokol 2013).

means informing them of potential harms that may arise. Then the individuals can consent or not to participate.

Such principles seem simple, but they can be complicated in practice. For example, just how much detail suffices to convey what exactly involvement in a study will entail? What exactly constitutes coercion? Which groups are capable of providing informed consent? Consider a situation where a college professor wants to administer a questionnaire to students in his or her class. Students are told only that completing it will aid in a study on crime. That provides too little detail for an individual to understand the study's goals, how long it will take to complete the questionnaire, or what the benefits or risks of participation will be. Also, some students may be under the age of 18 and so are considered a "child"; as such, they cannot provide informed consent. Not least, students may feel coerced into participating out of a fear that, if they do not complete the questionnaire, they will receive lower grades in the class.

In many countries, laws exist that dictate or provide guidance on how to conduct research in ways that advance science, but that also protect human subjects. For example, in the United States, Part 46 of Title 45 of the Code of Federal Regulations (45 CFR 46) lays out the Department of Health and Human Services' policy for such protection.[31] Research institutions may impose additional stipulations for how research must be conducted. They also may have Institutional Review Boards (IRBs). The IRBs assess each proposed study to ensure that it complies with law and their own criteria for what passes muster in protecting individuals. The basic elements that researchers are expected to follow include clear explanation to potential subjects about the purpose of a study, the duration of participation and exactly what participants will be asked to do, foreseeable risks and benefits, whether and to what extent confidentiality will be maintained, emphasis on the fact that participation is voluntary, and who to contact with questions about a study. With vulnerable populations, such as children, additional steps must be followed and generally entail requesting permission from legal guardians.

Researchers sometimes may feel that IRBs serve primarily to interfere with research. There is, no doubt, a layer of bureaucracy involved in submitting applications and in following protocols to ensure the protection of human subjects. However, the bureaucracy and protocols exist for an excellent reason. Science should not advance at the expense of individuals. Some studies might contribute to scientific knowledge, yet violate that axiom. Even seemingly benign studies can cause potential harms. Consider

---

[31] The 45 CFR 46 is available online at the Department's website: www.hhs.gov/ohrp/ regulations-and-policy/regulations/45-cfr-46/index.html.

criminological and criminal justice questionnaires, which frequently include questions about past offending and victimization. Answering such questions may be traumatic for some individuals. IRBs exist not to block science, but rather to help ensure that researchers take steps to prevent such possibilities.

Objective Research and Ethical Considerations

Scholars disagree about what makes for "objective" research. All studies involve reference to particular conceptual frameworks or points of view. That does not have to mean an embrace of relativism, though. For example, from one perspective, a car is an example of a vehicle that can be used to get from one place to another. From another, it serves as a weapon for killing people. It is, admittedly, not the intention of manufacturers that cars be used in that way. Even so, if someone uses a car to drive over a group of people, it would be accurate to characterize the car as a type of weapon. Both perspectives involve description of the same object, and both descriptions are accurate in their own way.

When, though, we think about objective research, we may think more about the notion that a researcher or an organization that funds research seeks to slant facts – to present an inaccurate depiction of the social world. There are no hard and fast ways to identify when a deliberate effort to skew study findings occurs. Researchers are human. They have biases that may color how they see and study crime and justice. Consider the selection of a topic. By focusing on, say, officer professionalism, one may draw attention to the positive aspects of policing. Conversely, by focusing on officer abuse of citizens, one may draw attention to the negative aspect. In each instance, a researcher might rely on well-established theories, credible research designs, data, and analyses, and present results in a balanced way, including discussion of the study's limitations. Yet, each study by itself may provide a distorted sense of law enforcement.

The easier situations are when researchers rely on weak study designs, distort facts by not placing them in context, cherry-pick only information that comports with their viewpoint, and so on. Consider a liberal advocacy organization that draws attention to the terrible performance of public defenders. They may do so based on a study in one metropolitan area that relied on interviews with a handful of individuals convicted of felonies. Alternatively, a conservative advocacy organization may point to crimes committed by several immigrants. They then might call for immigration reform to address out-of-control immigrant crime. These constitute pretty clear-cut cases of making claims on research of questionable validity. The more difficult-to-discern biases arise when these types of organizations take reputable studies, but emphasize only one part of them. They may inappropriately generalize the results or they may ignore the larger numbers of better-done studies that find conflicting results. A researcher sensibility is, in our view, the main path toward adjudicating when one can or cannot trust a study. That sensibility includes thinking about the motivations of the researchers or funding organizations. It includes, too, using different perspectives or criteria to evaluate the research.

One question that frequently arises is whether organizations can conduct credible studies of themselves and their activities. On the face of it, the answer would seem to be, "No." For example, we might be hard-pressed to trust that a department of corrections would provide an accurate evaluation of its use of solitary confinement. Why? There is an inherent conflict of interest. If the department reports about misuse of such confinement, it risks the legislature calling for an inquiry. Funding might be affected, administrators might lose their jobs, and there would be the risk of considerable negative publicity.

An independent research organization may be the better bet in such situations. That said, independent researchers may not necessarily be truly independent. For example, if a university researcher wants to collaborate with an organization in the future, he or she may downplay some findings to avoid casting a negative light on it. Still, we might feel more confident that the "independent" researcher's study was a little more objective.

There is a related consideration. Law enforcement departments, court systems, corrections agencies, and the like in fact may actively seek to illuminate as accurately as possible how the organization operates. They also may have specialized knowledge about their data and be uniquely positioned to use it appropriately. Outside researchers may have their own agendas and may not understand the intricacies of the data.[32]

Accordingly, when seeking to obtain the most objective and accurate study of some phenomenon, no specific guideline exists on whether to proceed with an agency or an independent researcher. One helpful quality-control check, though, is to ensure that any study results get reviewed by several independent researchers. This layer of review can help to weed out biased or inaccurate results and thus enhance a study's credibility.

Other Considerations

There are many other ethical considerations that bear on research. Several others that warrant mention include the following. First, researchers should seek to present results in as balanced a way as they can. That means

[32] Farabee (2005); Mears (2010).

presenting clearly any significant study limitations and conflicts of interest. This step not only helps to ensure accuracy, it can inhibit the misuse or distortion of a study's findings. Second, when publishing research, studies should focus on advancing science or policy, not on producing publications for the sake of it. Piecemeal publishing does not advance science or policy, and so, as we discuss in the next chapter, should be avoided. Third, authorship "credit" should be accurately apportioned. Frank discussions at the beginning of a study and throughout can help to avoid such problems as a contributor being omitted or given limited credit when he or she played a critical instrumental role in a publication. Fourth, there exists an entirely separate ethical problem – pursuing policies that will use large amounts of taxpayer dollars without first relying on credible empirical research. The issue here differs from the misuse of research, but it presents no less of an ethical concern.

CONCLUSION

"Criteria" and "ethics" may seem like dry concepts, ones far removed from the "action" that goes into undertaking a study or developing a policy. In fact, though, they constitute core parts of the research process. Without criteria, scientific knowledge cannot accumulate and policymakers cannot evaluate the credibility of a given study. Science instead devolves into a chaotic potpourri of new theories and facts with little clarity about their accuracy or relevance. And policy proceeds from ignorance or, worse than that, inaccurate or distorted information.

At the same time, ethical issues permeate all aspects of research. They enter into decisions about what types of research to fund or undertake. They come into play in efforts to describe research accurately and to evaluate research appropriately. They arise whenever potential conflicts of interest exist. And they must be considered when risks to human subjects exist.

There is no single "best" way to evaluate a study. There instead exist diverse criteria and ethical considerations. Sorting through them requires careful reflection. As we have argued, no checklist will do. Rather, what is needed is a researcher sensibility, one that involves awareness of different criteria and considerations, as well as a commitment to credible and ethical research.

11 The Science and Art of Conducting, Evaluating, and Using Research: Practical Steps

INTRODUCTION

Throughout the book, we have argued that development of a researcher sensibility is critical for three distinct but related activities: conducting, evaluating, and using research. This sensibility can help researchers and, indeed, anyone with an interest in information about crime and justice. We also have argued that this sensibility hinges on the ability to appreciate the science and the art of research. It requires, for example, understanding the different considerations, activities, and constraints that intersect in research on crime and justice.

Developing this sensibility does not demand extensive training in statistics, survey sampling, experimental designs, or the like. These are valuable tools and they may be required for certain kinds of studies. We believe, though, that anyone can develop a researcher sensibility without necessarily knowing how to undertake particular types of studies. Jordan Ellenberg has made a similar point about profound ideas in math – an understanding of complicated types of math is not needed to appreciate them.[1] So, too, with a researcher sensibility – it can be acquired without training in advanced statistics or various research methodologies.

There is, of course, no substitute for experience. Conducting research can greatly improve one's ability to understand what it can and cannot do. Such experience does not always lead to a researcher sensibility, however. Plenty of researchers conduct poor research. They may not do so consciously, but it happens nonetheless. Indeed, almost any researcher who looks back on their prior work can think of innumerable ways in which they could have improved what they did.

With this chapter, we revisit the core theme of the book – the idea that a researcher sensibility is important, it can be acquired, and there is a science

---

[1] Ellenberg (2014:15).

and art to research. In what follows, we offer guidance to researchers about approaches and activities they may find useful in developing a researcher sensibility. We also offer additional guidance to policymakers and criminal justice administrators and practitioners, as well as members of the public. These groups play a prominent role in requesting and shaping research. They frequently need to evaluate it. Lawmakers and criminal justice administrators especially need research when making decisions that affect public safety, justice, and taxpayers. A researcher sensibility can be instrumental, more broadly, for anyone with an interest in helping society to advance science and policy.

The chapter seeks specifically to answer the following questions: In what ways do criminological and criminal justice studies benefit from a researcher sensibility? What steps, strategies, or approaches can be taken to improve or strengthen this sensibility? What strategies or approaches can policymakers, criminal justice administrators and practitioners, and members of the public use to develop it? For example, what can these groups do to increase their ability to request information and, in particular, research that addresses questions of interest and importance to them? And what can these groups do to improve their ability to consume, evaluate, and effectively and appropriately use research?

SCIENCE AND ART – THERE IS NO SINGLE BEST WAY TO CONDUCT, EVALUATE, OR USE RESEARCH

A researcher sensibility entails, as we have argued, a mixture of science and art. One can see this mixture across the history of science. Siddhartha Mukherjee's description of progress in understanding cancer powerfully illuminates this idea.[2] Medical researchers have stumbled into insights, persevered into others, followed dead ends (no pun intended), confronted political and bureaucratic constraints, and more along the way to developing better ways of detecting, understanding, and treating cancer. Dan Fagin has provided a similarly intriguing account of the stumbling and myriad steps that have advanced our understanding of environmental pollution.[3] Thomas Kuhn, Robert K. Merton, and other historians of science have documented other quirky roads to scientific knowledge across numerous fields.[4]

Equally quirky can be the steps and missteps that arise in the interface between science and policy. Sometimes science gets ahead of policy –

---

[2] Mukherjee (2010).   [3] Fagin (2013).
[4] See, for example, Kuhn (1962) and Merton (1968, 1973). Stephen Jay Gould's many books provide evocative examples of the science and art of research (see, e.g., Gould 2002).

advances occur that cannot easily be translated into policies. Or scientists convey the advances poorly. Conversely, policymakers and agency officials sometimes shape research in good ways or in bad ways. They may help to fund important, groundbreaking studies. They also may unduly narrow the scope of what gets examined, leading to a form of scientific myopia. Or they simply ignore research.

Part of the quirkiness of scientific progress – and of the misuse of science in policy – stems from the inherent complexity of research. Consider the powerful role of measures. Perhaps a local jurisdiction has identified gangs as a central cause of crime. That would not be hard to do. Many criminal acts involve gangs. The police and prosecutors often target gang activity. In this jurisdiction, then, heightened attention to gangs might lead to more arrests and convictions. Based on increased rates of gang-related arrests and convictions, it thus appears that the "gang problem" has escalated. However, if we conducted a survey of residents, we might well find – using this better source of data – that gang crime occurs rarely and even may have decreased. The survey might also reveal that other types of crime, such as domestic violence, may be far more prevalent than arrest data suggest.

In this example, no new theory was developed. No new principle or axiom about criminal activity emerged. Yet, a critical insight arose about the nature of crime in this one community. This insight resulted from use of a more accurate measure of gang-related crime and could be used by community leaders to develop a potentially more effective intervention to reduce crime. At the same time, the data would give researchers an opportunity to advance theory. For example, as local leaders push to better understand the domestic violence problem, they may find that such violence occurs more frequently in certain parts of the community. Why? Researchers might apply existing theory to see if it could help to explain patterns of violence. They might then find that a "tweak" to the theory can provide a better account of the patterns.

This theoretical account may point to strategies that local leaders could employ to reduce domestic violence. In addition, it might suggest the need to dig further. Perhaps the theory anticipates that domestic violence will occur more when abusers know that victims and bystanders will not call the police. The survey may not have collected information on victim or citizen willingness to call the police, however. At this point, local leaders could ignore that fact and fund a new program that encourages victims and others to report domestic violence. One leader pauses, though, and reflects on the possibility that the program would be more effective if it built on information about *why* reporting patterns in certain areas were low. What causes under-reporting? He or she convinces the others to conduct interviews with local residents and treatment providers to explore explanations.

The research shows that many residents feel that the police ignore them. This evidence leads to discussion about the need for better training of and responses from the police in cases of domestic violence. We have here a more precise policy response that addresses the underlying cause of the problem.

We can see science and art at work here. An awareness existed about the limitations of arrest data for accurately inferring crime prevalence and distributions. Methodologies from the researchers' tool kit allowed for developing a more accurate, empirically based depiction of crime and responses to it. Yet, there was art in knowing to question the premise that gang-related crime is the most important problem. There was art, too, in knowing that a response to citizen under-reporting of domestic violence should focus on victims or residents and their experiences with the police. There also was an art to knowing that interviews might productively be paired with self-report data to glean information about *why* under-reporting occurred. A creative researcher might participate in this process and both apply and develop theory.

Such examples are endless and could be identified for many other topics: enactment of laws, variation in court decisions, community crime prevention programs, crime increases or decreases and their causes, offender specialization, victim reporting, reactions to victimization, law enforcement organization and activities, court operations, prisons and jails, and probation and parole practices. The possibilities go on and on, as can be seen in the examples in Chapter 9.

When researchers try to contribute to knowledge about crime and justice, they must be able to scan the landscape and zero in on research gaps and questions that matter most. But what matters "most"? No clear answer exists save for recourse to the views of other researchers about frontiers – theory, facts, methods, and so on – that seem most critical to advancing science. Researchers therefore must have a tool kit on which they can draw to devise studies appropriate for addressing critical gaps and questions. They must be able, in scanning the landscape, to readily appreciate the strengths and limitations of different studies. They also must be able to build on prior work by using the theories, data, and methods that have created the foundation for this work. Not least, they must be able to make adjustments that take into account real-world limitations, such as the amount of time available to conduct a study, the accessibility of data, their ability to analyze the data with sufficient rigor to pass scientific muster, and so on.

There is no simple avenue to creating this ability. Rather, one can at most take steps to continuously develop more awareness about theory, data, analysis, and topic-specific knowledge. We discuss some of these steps below. Here, though, we emphasize that continuous effort helps, much as it does in becoming linguistically conversant in a new language. What also helps is to be aware that there is science and art in creating insight.

In our view, that statement holds true equally for "non-researchers." Criminal justice lawmakers, administrators, practitioners, and the public at large all play a tremendous role in dictating the types of research that happens. Lawmakers, for example, allocate funding to research organizations and agencies. They consume large amounts of information about diverse aspects of criminal justice. They demand such information and have the ability to fund, or not, creation of better information. In the end, the usefulness of the information depends heavily on how savvy lawmakers are in making research requests. Similar observations hold for heads of criminal justice and correctional agencies. When they make educated, reasonable requests, they receive useful information. When they ignore research altogether, they create policies that likely miss the mark. When they ask for information that only tangentially relates to the social problem they wish to address, they again miss the mark. And when they misinterpret the accuracy and generalizability of studies, they miss the mark by an even wider margin.[5]

The cure? For researchers and non-researchers alike, it is, we submit, the development of a "researcher sensibility." We believe that to be true and have tried to illustrate why in the preceding chapters. This sensibility cannot be reduced to rote formulas any more than learning to ride a bike can be reduced to memorizing each step in the process (move feet, look ahead, watch out for cars, balance, brake, etc.). And it cannot be achieved by learning particular theories or statistical techniques. It instead requires ongoing effort to learn about different aspects of the research process and to think carefully about them. It requires flexibility and a willingness to see crime and justice from different perspectives. It also requires skepticism about what we know.

Each chapter illuminates some of the science and art specific to different dimensions. The range of dimensions alone illuminates why a researcher sensibility is needed. One needs to be able to juggle consideration of them when thinking about specific research problems. How, though, can this sensibility be acquired? How can one learn to cook like a chef or, to extend the analogy above, to put all the pieces together that go into riding a bike?

Although we have no one best solution, we do have a few suggestions for researchers and non-researchers alike. We offer the guidance with the

[5] See, generally, Mears and Bacon (2009).

awareness that what works for some individuals may not work for others. The suggestions may help, though, in developing a researcher sensibility and in conveying the science and art of research.

Alongside this guidance is one that bears special emphasis: Consult published accounts that describe the craft of research. Table 11.1 provides a small sampling from criminological and criminal justice researchers and from social scientists more broadly. A common thread running throughout these sources is the fact that research rarely proceeds in a linear manner. Much of the time it occurs through fits and starts, happenstance, and being prepared to seize on research possibilities when they arise. It can arise, for example, when facing publication biases that force one to consider whether to pursue publication in other disciplines.[6] That might seem to be an extreme reaction. But it might result from careful consideration of how best to proceed, and it might create interdisciplinary connections that end up advancing several disciplines at once. Being able to see or capitalize on such vagaries is itself part of the art that goes into research.

There are also excellent introductions to research methods in criminology and criminal justice that can be consulted. These include James Lasley's *Essentials of Criminal Justice and Criminology Research*, Pamela Davies and colleagues' *Doing Criminological Research*, John Chamberlain's *Understanding Criminological Research*, Michael Maxfield and Earl Babbie's *Research Methods for Criminal Justice and Criminology*, Ronet Bachman and Russell Schutt's *Fundamentals of Research in Criminology and Criminal Justice*, and Mark Dantzker, Ronald Hunter, and Susan Quinn's *Research Methods for Criminology and Criminal Justice*.[7] They introduce a wide spectrum of core concepts and methods used in research. Our focus here, though, and for most of the sources in the table, lies with the science and art of research.

GUIDANCE FOR RESEARCHERS

Let your Interests and Questions Drive the Research

To create studies that contribute significantly to science, follow your own interests and the questions that most intrigue you. Doing so provides an excellent path toward conducting research that addresses important gaps in knowledge. All too often, students, policymakers, practitioners – indeed,

---

[6] Wright and Beaver (2014).
[7] Lasley (1998); Davies *et al.* (2011); Chamberlain (2013); Maxfield and Babbie (2015); Bachman and Schutt (2018); Dantzker *et al.* (2018).

Table 11.1 Sources for learning the criminological and criminal justice research craft

Academy of Criminal Justice Sciences History Site (www.acjs.org/page/Historian). The site provides information about the history of the Academy; the Academy's website provides information about its publications and research by members of the Academy.

American Society of Criminology Oral History Project (www.asc41.com/videos/Oral_History). The site provides videos that involved interviews with leading scholars; the Society's website provides information about its publications and research by members of the Society.

Authors of their own Lives (1990), a volume edited by Bennett M. Berger and published by the University of California Press (Berkeley). The account describes experiences of many scholars in developing their research focus and approach.

The Craft of Social Research (1964), a volume edited by Phillip E. Hammond and published by Basic Books (New York). This book, like Becker's (1998), provides insight from scholars about how research unfolds in the "real world."

The Craft of Research (2005), by Wayne C. Booth, Gregory G. Colomb, and Joseph M. Williams and published by the University of Chicago Press. This account describes different ways in which research is a craft and how research unfolds in the "real world."

Criminology in the Making: An Oral History (1983), by John Laub and published by Northeastern University Press (Boston). Interviews with leading criminologists provide insight into how they approached theory and research on crime.

Delinquency Research: An Appraisal of Analytic Methods (1996), by Travis Hirschi and Hanan C. Selvin and published by Transaction (Piscataway, NJ). This classic account describes many of the twists and turns involved in conducting and interpreting research.

How to Be a Successful Graduate Student (2014), an article by Francis T. Cullen and Brenda Vose and published in the *Journal of Contemporary Criminal Justice* (vol. 30, pp. 362–377). This essay provides insights relevant to anyone interested in developing a research career.

Methods of Discovery: Heuristics for the Social Sciences (2004), by Andrew Abbott and published by W. W. Norton. This book describes strategies and habits that can help in creating and imagining theory and different approaches to empirical research.

The Origins of American Criminology (2011), a volume edited by Francis T. Cullen, Cheryl L. Jonson, Andrew J. Myer, and Freda Adler and published by Transaction (New Brunswick, NJ). This volume consists of many essays that describe leading intellectual traditions in criminology and criminal justice and how they unfolded.

Science as a Vocation (1946), an essay by Max Weber, published in *From Max Weber: Essays in Sociology* (pp. 129–156), edited and translated by H. H. Gerth and C. Wright Mills, and published by Oxford University Press (New York). This essay highlights the nature of science and what being a researcher entails.

The Sociological Imagination (1959), by C. Wright Mills and published by Oxford University Press (New York). This series of essays provides insights into how to conceptualize research that is interesting and that may be more likely to contribute to scientific progress.

Tricks of the Trade: How to Think about your Research while You're Doing It (1998), by Howard S. Becker and published by the University of Chicago Press. This highly entertaining book describes the craft of research and some tricks for doing it well.

most of us – let others frame questions for us. We then may miss what is most interesting or relevant to us and, quite possibly, to others.

One example from our own research involves super-maximum, or "supermax," housing, which entails up to twenty-four-hour-per-day confinement for indefinite periods in isolation.[8] Both of us have toured supermax facilities in various states. In each instance, inmates peered out through small window slits. It was often noisy – inmates yelled constantly. We learned that inmate problems still existed even in this highly controlled environment. Inmates might refuse to follow an order, or they might throw a "cocktail" of excrement through the slit in the door. A cell extraction team then would have to enter the cell to control the inmate and enforce "order." Such a situation highlighted to us a fundamentally interesting aspect of prison order – no matter what degree of control correctional systems exert, inmates can find ways to challenge it.[9] This situation arises for many reasons, but one is the fact that all social order depends on the perceived legitimacy of authorities. Without it, individuals typically will not conform with societal or institutional rules. Emile Durkheim long ago emphasized that the non-contractual elements of contract – that is, unspoken values and norms – contribute to whether individuals abide by a contract.[10] Much the same can be said of prisons. Punishment may deter some individuals from misconduct. If, though, inmates perceive prison authorities as wielding power in an unfair manner, they will be less likely to conform and more likely to act out.

After my (Dan's) first tour of a supermax prison in Texas in the late 1990s, I began to read everything I could find on supermax prisons. As I did so, I repeatedly encountered phrasing that suggested that supermaxes serve to control the "worst of the worst." That made sense. Yet, as I thought more about the housing, questions popped up. What exactly does it mean to "control" an inmate? That question made sense to me because I knew that even in supermax housing inmates could act out in many ways. Where, then, was the "control"? Also, who exactly counted as the "worst of the worst"? We are, of course, talking about people who committed crimes sufficiently serious to land them in prison. So, among prisoners, who counts as "worst of the worst"? It dawned on me one day that the statement – "to house the worst of the worst" – never actually answered my question about the goals of supermax housing. Why? Placing the "worst of the worst" in such housing is not a goal, it is a strategy for achieving a goal.

This ambiguity about the goals of supermax housing fascinated me and led to more and more questions about it. Eventually, I was fortunate to

---

[8] Mears (2016a).   [9] Bottoms (1999).   [10] Durkheim (1933).

receive federal funding to conduct a study of supermax housing. A central focus of the study involved a focus on goals.[11] Specifically, I designed the study in such a way that it would shed light on the diverse range of possible goals associated with supermax housing. By that time, I learned enough to know that the housing might well produce many unintended effects, some beneficial and some harmful. Accordingly, the study included methods, including interviews with corrections officials and a survey of wardens, aimed at gleaning insight into these potential effects.

At the time, I was pushed both by what I read in the research literature and by colleagues to focus on an important question: To wit, do supermax prisons work? Are they effective? I agreed that this focus warranted attention. Yet, I could not help but feel that such a study would be premature. How do you study the impacts of a policy if you do not know its goals?

The scientific relevance of the resulting study can be debated.[12] Here, the point simply is that the close read of the literature and the experience of touring a supermax facility led to questions that I pursued because, quite frankly, they interested me. The added bonus, however, was that the questions addressed several significant gaps and questions in the research literature. For example, what are the goals of supermax housing? What unintended benefits and harms might result from supermax prisons? What theory or theories guide them? That is, by what theoretical logic do they achieve any of their goals? The relevance of these questions would not likely have been apparent to me had I not focused on my interests first.

This detour serves to highlight that a researcher sensibility can flow in part from immersing yourself in a topic and thinking about it from many different angles. The more you care about the topic, the easier it becomes to adopt these angles and gain insights. Some of those insights may duplicate what others have already established in prior research. That is fine. You learn to appreciate better what others have done. At the same time, some of the insights may be new. They may even seem sufficiently important to warrant further attention.

Following your own interests can be helpful in another way – it can help to avoid what might be called the "glazed eye" problem. That occurs when we do not see why something is important to what we are doing. An illustration – many graduate students cannot differentiate between the concept of "internal validity" and "external validity." This problem is not trivial. The two concepts are central to research. (Internal validity generally refers to the idea that a study's design produces a cause–effect estimate that

---

[11] Mears (2006).
[12] See Mears (2005, 2006, 2008b, 2013, 2016a), Mears and Castro (2006), Mears and Reisig (2006), and Mears and Watson (2006).

we can trust. External validity refers to the idea that we can generalize a cause–effect estimate to other areas, groups, or populations.) In fact, the problem runs deeper. Students may understand the concepts well enough to answer questions in an exam. Weeks later, though, they may have no recollection of them and no ability to discern the relevance of these concepts in their own work or that of others.

This problem can arise for many reasons. One, though, is the disconnect between the concepts and student interests. Students typically learn about various types of validity in a research methods class. In that same class, they learn about many other concepts and ideas. It is a lot to learn. To make matters worse, they may have limited opportunities in such a class to tie the concepts and ideas back to their own interests and research projects. Some teachers may help to convey these ideas in ways that "stick" with students. But the nature of many courses frequently precludes that possibility – too much must be covered in them. Accordingly, it becomes incumbent on students to work continuously to tie what they learn to real-world examples, especially those that most interest them.

Attend to the Craft of Research

Research is a craft. It requires many different skills. They can be acquired in many different ways – participating in research projects, practicing different methodologies, reading, talking with other researchers, attending conferences, and so on. The common denominator in each instance consists of viewing research as a craft, as something that must be learned and continuously refined. With that said, we recommend two specific approaches to developing the craft of research or, as we have characterized it, a researcher sensibility.

First, we echo C. Wright Mills in advocating that you "use your life experience in your intellectual work: continually to examine and interpret it. In this sense craftsmanship is the center of yourself and you are personally involved in every intellectual product upon which you may work."[13] That does not mean that one should allow biases to rule the day. Rather, it simply means that all of us should seek to identify patterns and relationships in our own lives and of the world around us. As Mills observed, this strategy has many benefits, including the possibility of catching "'fringe thoughts': various ideas which may be byproducts of everyday life, snatches of conversation overheard on the street, or, for that matter, dreams. Once noted, these may lead to more systematic thinking."[14]

[13] Mills (1959:196).   [14] Ibid.

What is "systematic thinking"? It consists of the mix of research skills and tools that go into the craft of research. For example, much of life entails distributions. Consider continuous distributions – virtually everyone has some probability of offending. For some, that probability is near zero and for others it is near to 100 percent. Once we think about that idea, the world looks different. What, for example, is the likely probability of my neighbor, uncle, friend, mayor, or so on, committing a crime? It cannot be zero. So, what is it? Distributions in turn make us think differently about our experiences. Perhaps an officer pulls us over for speeding. Was that random? Was it not just because I was speeding, but also because I was driving a sports car? Is that how officers make decisions? That is, do they get influenced by such factors as car color or the race or ethnicity of the driver?

Thinking about distributions also can lead us to realize that any phenomenon we see may constitute an exception. Or it may be typical. For example, if smoking on average contributes to cancer, that does not mean that it does so for everyone. Perhaps some individuals smoke for years and do not get cancer. That fact would not be exceptional. Should, though, we generalize from a few cases in which we know someone who smoked and did not get cancer? No. Neither should we assume that smoking always causes cancer. We can think about it, though, and consider whether it does. We can think about possible studies that would be needed to determine if such an effect exists. In so doing, we can learn (or re-learn) that exceptions may actually represent typical cases. Or sometimes they may be just that, exceptions to a rule. In the case of smoking, for example, research clearly points to smoking as a cause of cancer. The fact of an exception would not alter that finding.[15]

Once we embark upon viewing our own lives and that of the world around us as a source of insight about possible social patterns and relationships, that world becomes a richer place. It becomes a source of insight. Drawing on our own personal experiences provides a simple and convenient way to tap into such discovery. When, then, we pair this approach with thinking like a researcher – such as thinking about distributions, possible relationships, and why the relationships may or may not exist – we begin to see more and more research possibilities. We also learn to evaluate and use research in a more sophisticated manner.

A second and much more down-to-earth recommendation is to write out research ideas. Brainstorm and then write two statements. First, write a "context statement," which is a brief but specific description of why a

---

[15] Mukherjee (2010); Oreskes and Conway (2010).

particular research question may be interesting or important. Why is it relevant to you? Why might it be relevant to others? Or for theory or policy?

Second, then imagine some type of study that would answer the question. Contemplate different approaches. Imagine that the study is complete and someone asks, "Why was your study important?" Write out an answer. For example, does it advance theory or scholarship in a particular field or sub-field? Does it resolve an ongoing scientific debate? The implications of any study typically go beyond specific empirical results, so think broadly. For example, a study might find that minorities may be more likely than a majority group to be arrested for similar offenses. This finding might be relevant for informing research on policing, the use of formal social control, racial and ethnic disparities in punishment, and theories of power and social order.

This strategy may feel cumbersome at first. Over time, however, it can help in developing greater skill in framing research questions. It can also help in identifying different ways to answer them. It can help as well in discerning research possibilities and how to evaluate and use research. And, not least, it can help to ensure that your interests continue to drive your work.

Let Prior Research Inform your Research

This recommendation seems obvious, but it is no less important. Researchers may fail to read important works. We may skim these works without fully understanding them. In addition, we may focus our reading too narrowly and miss out on relevant works that may seem tangential, but that actually may help to illuminate our topic.

Prior research can be useful in many ways. It helps to establish promising lines of inquiry. It points to areas of dispute. It provides guidance on data sources and analytic techniques. And it provides the context for situating any given study's relevance. More often than not, a study that we might want to undertake may be relevant to multiple literatures. Consulting prior research thus both serves to guide our research endeavors and to identify the scholarly landscapes within which our research may be relevant.

Keeping up with the ever-growing bodies of prior research can be a challenge, so consider a few tricks of the trade. First, sign up for tables of contents from a core set of journals relevant to your research area. When the emails arrive, quickly scroll through them. If something is relevant, take ten minutes to click on the link, skim through the paper, and decide whether it deserves a closer look. You may be surprised by how much you recall from these quick reading sessions.

Second, maintain and update databases (with spreadsheets or tags using notes software) of specific research questions and studies that address them. Keep these topics specific (e.g., studies of the effects of visitation on prisoner re-entry). That will make maintaining lists of studies manageable and useful to you as you continue to work in a particular research area.

Third, do not allow a literature review or background discussion to meander. We have all read boring, tedious, or monotonous reviews. Tie any given discussion of a prior study to its implications for *your* study. Work to ensure readers see the forest through the trees. For example, if you mention specific details, it should be clear *why* those details matter. After summarizing prior studies, identify clearly the important discussion points and their salience for your study. What specifically are the research gaps that you are going to address?

Other approaches exist as well, but the main point remains – virtually any study benefits from building on work that has come before it. Researchers should not reinvent the wheel. Rather, they should seek to build on the theories, data designs or sources, methods, and so on, that are viewed as credible foundations for other studies.

Consult and Collaborate

One image of science envisions the lone scientist. He or she works in a lab or sits staring off into space, contemplating the universe. Late-night lucubration eventually leads to a masterful stroke of insight that transforms our understanding of some phenomenon.

That model of science occurs. It seems to us to be atypical, however. We are unaware of empirical studies that document the percentage of science that occurs by individuals who work alone and publish only solo articles. What we can say is that a considerable amount of science comes from individuals working in teams. In that way, science resembles most human endeavors. Groups of individuals coordinate their efforts to achieve various goals.

The benefits of consulting and collaborating with other researchers are many. We learn about new theoretical perspectives, data, methodologies, and more. Sometimes, other researchers can do in a day what might take weeks or months for us to do. In such cases, collaborations can enable studies both to occur and to get completed in a timely manner.

Each new collaboration opens new vistas and possibilities. This approach can be likened to traveling to many different places. Each new destination exposes you to new cultures and, in turn, to new possibilities for future travels. You become an increasingly savvier traveler in picking destinations and structuring your time. So, too, collaborations can foster a researcher sensibility that allows you to see opportunities for interesting and relevant studies.

An indication of the importance of collaboration can be seen in the individuals who have been appointed fellows of prominent criminology and criminal justice organizations. It can be seen, too, in individuals who have received book awards and outstanding article awards. The awards frequently involve collaborative efforts. In addition, the individuals who receive these awards typically have extensive records of collaborating with other scholars.

Enjoy the Benefits of Multidisciplinary Research

Collaborations do not necessarily require that we break out of a given field. That is unfortunate. When researchers work with others in different disciplines, the possibility opens, yet again, for new ways of viewing and understanding social phenomena. Fortunately, many criminology and criminal justice programs have faculty who come from diverse academic backgrounds. These include sociology, psychology, political science, social work, public health, biology, public policy, and more. This means that multidisciplinary research can occur within such programs. Even so, a mindful approach to seeking out scholars in different disciplines can help protect against the insularity that comes from rubbing elbows with individuals who may hold similar views and have similar experiences to you. Put differently, it can open the door to new ways of understanding crime and justice and to new lines of investigation.

Enjoy the Benefits of Multimethods Research

Two observations about multimethods research bear mention. First, most researchers are not methodologists. They are generalists – they develop an expertise in one or more "topical" areas (e.g., juvenile justice, prisons, public opinion about crime and justice, causes of crime among communities). Methodology serves as a means to an end. Accordingly, this means that most researchers operate with only a moderately sophisticated understanding of various research designs, extant data sets, how to create and conduct surveys, how and when to use any of a myriad of statistical techniques, and so on.

The generalist orientation is critical for undertaking research. To be a "chef," one must know how to combine different ingredients – the types, amounts, sequence, and so on – to create a dish. Similarly, to conduct, evaluate, or use research requires an ability to appreciate the salience of different considerations, or dimensions of research, and how to combine them.

Unfortunately, this situation hamstrings researchers. It means that they may not always know when or how to use different data and methodologies to answer research questions. Working with other researchers can offset this problem. They may know about better approaches that could be pursued, and they may be able to undertake them. If one is fortunate to have different types of specialists nearby – substantive area specialists, theorists, methodologists, statisticians, etc. – they can be especially instrumental in approaching studies in the most rigorous way.

This point bears emphasizing because many scholars frame questions in ways that reflect their ability. If they work with others, then the questions they can contemplate open up. Similarly, the possible approaches to answering them open up as well.

Consider spatial analyses. Most researchers learn about logistic regression analysis (for binary outcomes) or ordinary least squares regression analysis (for continuous outcomes). One might use these approaches to explain how support for the death penalty (support or not) is associated with education or how variation in crime rates (a continuous variable) is related to, and perhaps caused by, poverty. That is well and fine. A researcher who knows these two regression techniques may think about many interesting research studies. But they may not even know to contemplate others, such as how crime is spatially patterned. Why, for example, does crime appear to be concentrated in some neighborhoods of Chicago more so than others?[16] Such a question seems immediately obvious if we think about crime and place. If we know how to conduct spatial regression analyses, the question is even more obvious.

The blinders imposed by certain methodologies can create this type of problem. One "cure," then, consists of having many methodologies in one's tool kit. Or, as we have emphasized, it can help to have many individuals with whom we can collaborate and who collectively know about a much broader range of methods that could be employed.

Second, mixed-methods research goes beyond using different analytic techniques. It involves use of different data collection strategies and approaches to theorizing. Consider a situation in which we learn that crime may be concentrated along city waterfronts. We want to know why. A theory might help point to some factor or another. But perhaps we can find no such theory, or the theory seems incomplete. We might have a few ideas about what may be relevant. Perhaps the large amount of commerce that occurs along the waterfront attracts would-be offenders. That idea

---

[16] See Sampson (2012, 2013).

leads us to consider a study in which we seek to determine if a statistical association exists between waterfront crime rates and the amount of business activity in them. This study seems interesting. However, given, in this example, our limited understanding about waterfront crime, it might be helpful to draw on additional approaches. For example, we might survey waterfront business owners or pedestrians about the factors that we suspect contribute to the association. We also might conduct focus groups with the business owners and local law enforcement, or interview them individually, to identify a broader array of possible explanations. As a result, we discover that several explanations consistently show up in the survey, focus group, and interview analyses. We then might see if we can collect data about these explanations that enables us to test hypothesized explanations for why crime is higher in waterfront areas.

Mixed-methods studies can be fun – they allow for a much more colorful examination of crime and justice. They create opportunities for developing and testing hypotheses. They allow us to identify patterns and explanations that we otherwise might miss entirely. And they allow us to "avoid the fetishism of method and technique," Mills' characterization of research that seems important simply because it relies on advanced methods.[17]

Know and Leverage your Personality

We all have unique personalities. For some people, spontaneous extended work sessions may be most effective. For others, a fixed schedule is better. Some individuals find it more effective to read a great deal before then developing a research idea. Others are more comfortable writing out their own ideas before having their views influenced by other work. Some of us need another person to serve as taskmaster to keep focused, while others work better proceeding at our own pace. Such possibilities barely scratch the surface.

Here is the point – problems arise when you do not know the conditions under which you work best, and when you instead march to someone else's beat. We all face limits in how much we can control our work schedules and approaches. To the extent that some flexibility is possible, however, identify ways to structure your work time, space, and activities to maximal effect. Build in clear expectations and ways to motivate yourself. It sounds trite, but the relevance of "self-managing" is no less important for it.

[17] Mills (1959:224).

Balance Being a Specialist and a Generalist

Researchers frequently are pushed to specialize. Many graduate programs, for example, may push the notion that students should do so. To be fair, there is warrant for it. One cannot specialize in everything. However, part of developing expertise entails broadening one's horizons to learn about new topics, theories, methods, and more.

Accordingly, we here echo Francis Cullen and Brenda Vose who, in an essay that sought to provide guidance on being a successful criminology and criminal justice graduate student, recommended that students become hedgehogs with fox tendencies.[18] The expression, as Cullen and Vose noted, comes from a 1953 essay by Isaiah Berlin entitled, "The Hedgehog and the Fox," in which he quotes Archilochus, a Greek poet: "The fox knows many things, but the hedgehog knows one big thing."[19]

What does that mean? Become a specialist in one topic, but seek opportunities to learn about new areas and methods. Emphasize depth in one area and breadth through exposure to many others. The two approaches can reinforce each other and help us to develop as researchers.

Look for and Seize Opportunities

Research rarely plays out in the straightforward manner depicted in many textbooks and media accounts. That can contribute to specialization. It may take many years to create data suitable for answering one's research questions. As a result, researchers may want to mine these data for as many insights as possible. Then, when they move on, they may seek similar types of data or pursue a similar avenue of inquiry. It makes sense to do so. However, some of the biggest advances in science can come from embracing serendipity rather than fending it off through a commitment to specialization or a particular way of approaching a topic. What does that mean? Look for and embrace research opportunities. Collaborate with someone new. Accept an invitation to tackle a question that may lie outside your comfort zone. One especially useful strategy – keep an eye out for research possibilities that arise from naturally occurring experiments. For example, a prison system might offer a new rehabilitation program for inmates; it may screen all inmates and end up with a waiting list. The existence of the waiting list creates the possibility for undertaking a quasi-experimental research design, one with a strong control group as a basis for estimating program effects.

---

[18] Cullen and Vose (2014:367).
[19] Berlin (1953:1), as cited in Cullen and Vose (2014:367).

Serendipity can be seen throughout the criminological and criminal justice literature. One of the most famous examples can be seen in the development of Robert Sampson and John Laub's age-graded theory of informal social control. In the mid 1980s, they learned about "dusty cartons of data in the basement of the Harvard Law School Library."[20] It turned out that the more than fifty cartons contained case files from Sheldon and Eleanor Glueck's 1950 study, *Unraveling Juvenile Delinquency.*[21] One unique opportunity afforded by the data was the possibility of following up with the individuals in the original study. Doing so would create longitudinal data that would allow for investigation of the causes of crime as people age. Despite the tremendous challenges of sorting through the material to create useable data analysis files, Sampson and Laub proceeded. The end result was an award-winning book and a prod to the field to understand how crime unfolds over the life-course.

Avoid Piecemeal Publishing

For researchers who seek to publish their research, avoid publishing studies of little import. Put differently, be cautious about pursuing studies that are doable but trivial, what some have termed "piecemeal publishing." Concern about this issue surfaced when the editors of *Criminology*, a prominent criminological journal, sought to provide guidance to authors.[22] The idea is that researchers may avoid doing one "big" article and instead break it into three or four or more "smaller" articles. Why? Perhaps they might do so to appear more productive by having a more impressive publication record (to the extent that the number of articles that one publishes may be viewed – appropriately or not – as a marker of what constitutes "impressive").

The concern is, in our view, legitimate. Science advances through good, thoughtful studies, not a business-like approach to slicing and dicing studies in ways that produce more journal articles. Yet, many scholars may seek to publish more "thin" studies than "thick" ones to pad their academic record. Universities and colleges contribute to the situation by emphasizing the number of articles scholars have and the number of times the articles get cited. Indeed, "savvy" researchers may seek to game their citation counts by publishing many "piecemeal" articles and aggressively encouraging others to cite their works.

However, the issue is complicated. Science advances through small and big steps. Frequently, we mistakenly view small steps as big ones and, vice versa, we view big steps as small ones. Only with hindsight do we typically

---

[20] Sampson and Laub (1993:1).   [21] Glueck and Glueck (1950).
[22] Gartner *et al.* (2012).

obtain clarity about what amounts to a breakthrough. Small advances are worthy goals in their own right. They help contribute to progress in gaining deeper insight into the social world. What, then, amounts to an article that is "piecemeal"? Many scholars disagree.

How, then, can researchers proceed? One way is to proceed thoughtfully and with a moral compass focused on improving science. A second is to be guided by a researcher sensibility. With it, one can think through the potential merits of creating one "big" paper or several "small" ones. In our experience, some topics have nuances that one paper alone cannot address. Several separate, but related, studies then make sense. In others, we can see how separate papers could be undertaken, but choose a "big" paper because it strikes us as the way to make a larger impact.

There is no silver-bullet solution. Use judgement and consider how any given study will be used to inform future theory, research, and policy. Take stock of these considerations and determine what the best path may be toward advancing science.

Be a "Renaissance" Person: Read Widely

It can be a bit tedious to do just one thing. And doing so can make for boring conversations. For these reasons alone, being a "Renaissance" person can be fun. Technically, to be a Renaissance person means to be good or clever at many different things. Perhaps that is too high a bar for many of us. But we can aspire to reach it! That can include reading widely about many topics, including those that have little obvious relevance to criminology and criminal justice.

Historical accounts of science provide innumerable examples of ways in which researchers arrived at ideas through highly circuitous paths. Television shows and movies showcase this idea. They frequently show a scientist at a party, taking a walk, observing nature, and then something suddenly happens and a lightbulb goes off in the scientist's head. Off they run to their office to write up some brilliant insight!

There is some truth to that idea. When any of us spends time in different activities and pursuits, we see the world differently. This can lead to new ideas or approaches to research.

One example from our own work is criminal justice decision-making. I (Dan) had become interested in medical decision-making because of several articles that I had read in popular press magazines. The articles intrigued me, so I kept looking for similar ones. I am not sure how or why, but at some point it occurred to me that many of the types of decision-making errors that researchers have documented among physicians have clear counterparts to decision-making in the criminal justice system. For example, recency bias occurs when we interpret or view a person as if he or she is similar to someone we just met. To illustrate, if a physician sees a patient who has delirium tremens – cognitive confusion that occurs when alcoholics go into withdrawal – he or she then may assume that the next patient who exhibits similar symptoms necessarily has the same problem.[23] It is not a stretch to imagine that recency effects may influence criminal justice practitioners. Judges, for example, may be irritated with a defendant who slumps in their chair and acts defiantly. The next defendant who comes in who slumps then may be viewed by the judge as defiant. The insight that parallels exist between the types of decision-making errors that occur in medicine and in criminal justice led then to a more systematic exploration of this idea that eventually resulted in an article.[24] It highlighted that numerous opportunities for cognitive bias exist across the entire criminal justice system.

Whether the article constitutes an important contribution to science remains to be seen. The point here is that it never would have happened if not for reading research from outside the criminological and criminal justice arena. In the end, the suggestion to read widely may not greatly improve your research. We are confident, though, that it will not hurt!

Be a "Renaissance" Researcher: Do Everything (Ideas, Theory, Data, Analysis, Writing)

It can be easy to slip into a particular role when undertaking research studies, especially collaborative efforts. One person is the "theorist," another is the "data person," another is the "analyst," and still another is the "writer." That can be efficient, but also deadly. It can close off developing insights about research that can only come from being involved in all aspects of research. Accessing data from a prison administration database, for example, entails may different challenges and conceptual issues. To illustrate, the database may include several hundred categories for classifying an offense. How should these offenses be categorized? Which ones count as "violent" or "property" offenses? When conducting analyses, similar conceptual issues arise. For example, should one examine a binary measure of recidivism? The number of times someone recidivates? The number and types of crimes committed?[25] Statistical answers can be had. They do not, though, resolve the issue because the questions are as much conceptual as they are statistical. Similar observations can be made about developing or applying theory and about writing all aspects of a research study. If you find yourself getting locked in to a particular role, push to do

---

[23] Groopman (2007).   [24] Mears and Bacon (2009).   [25] See Sweeten (2012).

something different. Your other skills will diminish without upkeep and practice, when really those skills should continue to mature and improve over time.

Take Charge of your Research Career

In their essay, Cullen and Vose listed the following as their number-one lesson for those who seek to become researchers: "You are the architect of your career."[26] The lesson, of course, applies to many walks of life, not just research careers, but its importance is no less relevant.

Researchers can be found in all walks of life: businesses, non-profit organizations, research institutes, local, state, and federal governmental agencies, colleges, universities, and more. In every instance, there is a need for individuals who can shape research to good effect. This will happen more frequently if these individuals find the work that they do interesting and if they have a tool kit that enables them to imagine the diverse possibilities for improving research.

For those who want to pursue a successful research career, no single silver-bullet solution exists for "success." Indeed, the notion of "success" depends greatly on one's definition of it. That said, one will not go too far wrong in seeking, as Cullen and Vose emphasized, to be the "architect of your career."[27] That can mean many things. For doctoral students specifically, it can entail adherence to a number of specific axioms, or lessons, which Cullen and Vose identify. Their first lesson is, in fact, to embrace being in charge of your career. They view that first step as foundational. Without it, few others likely matter.

The full set of lessons include the following: (1) You are the architect of your career; (2) practice cumulative advantage (i.e., get off on the "right foot" and take advantage of opportunities as they arise); (3) make yourself useful (develop skills); (4) become a hedgehog (with considerable knowledge of one topic) with fox tendencies (i.e., with a little bit of knowledge about many things); (5) prepare for your comprehensive exams from day 1; (6) learn how to teach; (7) become a scholar; (8) mate (not literally) with your advisor; (9) work on your dissertation; and (10) always have a plan.[28]

These lessons include ones specific to doctoral students, but they also include ones that are useful to any researcher. Making oneself useful to others and being a hedgehog with fox tendencies, for example, are strategies that can help in many different research settings.

There are still other strategies for taking charge of your career. C. Wright Mills and Howard Becker, for example, have written wonderful

---

[26] Cullen and Vose (2014:364).   [27] *Ibid.*   [28] Cullen and Vose (2014).

accounts about a variety of strategies for approaching research or, in Becker's words, learning the "tricks of the trade."[29] To illustrate, Mills recommended creating a filing system for organizing thoughts and observations about one's personal life experiences, the world around you, and what you read. Revisit this filing system and associated notes. Seek to make sense of what you read and see. Brainstorm. Talk with others about your ideas and speculations. Ask them for their thoughts. Question supposed "facts." Frame a question and keep reframing it until the question clearly makes sense and fits within a broader context. In so doing, think about different factors and how they may be related to one another. Revisit the questions and theory that you are developing again and again.

Mills also recommended developing a "sociological imagination." This imagination is similar to, but also differs from, what we have termed a "researcher sensibility." Mills was interested in building up what he termed "an adequate view of a total society and its components."[30] That is a worthy goal. In our view, however, Mills needlessly diminished the role of many aspects of the research process, such as conducting empirical research, in generating insights.[31] That can be seen in part by comparing his discussion with that of Howard Becker's.

His book, *Tricks of the Trade*, describes a diverse array of "tricks," that is, techniques for thinking about research. It discusses the use of imagery, sampling, concepts, and logic to, as the subtitle to his book states, "think about research while you're doing it."[32] What do these terms mean? *Imagery* refers to "how we think about what we are going to study before we actually start our research"; *sampling* refers to "how we choose what we actually look at, the cases we will have in mind when we formulate our general ideas explicitly"; *concepts* refers to "the making of our ideas . . . [and how] we put together what we learn from our samples in the form of more general ideas"; and *logic* refers to "ways of manipulating ideas through methods or more or less (mostly less) formal logic."[33] The "tricks" relate to many aspects of the research process. Indeed, "serious researchers repeatedly move back and forth among these four areas of thought, and each area affects the others."[34] Use of them, then, means that one ends up thinking about all aspects of research and their interrelatedness with one another.

The lesson? No one activity – theory, data, analysis, and so on – is more important than any other in arriving at insights. One can start with

[29] Mills (1959); Becker (1998).   [30] Mills (1959:211).
[31] Consider, for example, his statement: "Now I do not like to do empirical work if I can possibly avoid it" (Mills 1959:205).
[32] Becker (1998).   [33] Becker (1998:8).   [34] Becker (1998:9).

any aspect of the research process and find one's way to potentially interesting and important insights about these different phenomena. If you practice thinking about research in your personal and professional life, then thinking with a "sociological imagination" (Mills' phrase) or "thinking social science" (Becker's phrase) – or thinking with a "researcher sensibility" (our phrase) – will be "as natural as breathing."[35]

We have, finally, a more pragmatic recommendation – avoid "going with the flow." Letting a research career path "just happen" can be great. Some of the greatest advances in research have come from the serendipity that occurs when we allow for it.[36] Even so, it creates the risk that we fail to grow and to see new ways of generating insights. Being the "architect of your career" can help to avoid such problems.

Use a "Due Diligence" Research Checklist

We end on one final pragmatic recommendation – use a "due diligence" researcher checklist, such as the one in Table 11.2. We call it a "due diligence" checklist because each item on the checklist consists of the steps that good, or credible, research typically should follow. Why use a checklist? With any complicated undertaking, the risk of mistakes arises. That holds for airplane pilots, medicine, and certainly not least, research. Checklists can be quite simple. Even so, using them can help to reduce mistakes, such as conducting surgery on the wrong body part![37] Conducting credible research entails the management of many different activities, any of which can entail potential error. This results in mistakes that can undermine the integrity of our studies. (This problem arises in the natural and social sciences alike.[38]) Accordingly, the use of checklists can help to reduce errors and simultaneously may strengthen studies.

Many of the problems with research studies stem from not clearly describing why they were done. The studies might not include clear statements of the research questions, discussion of prior research, or the research gap to be addressed. Accordingly, the checklist begins with these initial considerations. Many studies also do not clearly articulate the theoretical foundation that guides them. They may omit mention of the specific hypotheses to be tested. In some cases, as with exploratory studies, there may be no hypotheses. Even then, there should be a justification for what the study explores. Another shortfall in studies, one that undermines the ability to replicate them, consists of insufficient description of the sample or the way in which it was collected. Without such details, replication cannot occur.

---

[35] Becker (1998:217).   [36] Berger (1990).   [37] Gawande (2009); Mears (2017).
[38] Harris (2017).

Table 11.2 A "due diligence" research checklist
☑ *Main topic presented clearly?*
☑ *Research questions presented?*
☑ *Relevant prior research discussed?*
☑ *Research gap described?*
☑ *Theoretical foundation for hypotheses articulated?*
☑ *Hypotheses and basis for them stated? (Or exploratory analyses justified?)*
☑ *Sampling process described and justified?*
☑ *Sample characteristics described well?*
☑ *Validated measures used, or reasons provided if not using them?*
☑ *Diagnostic checks conducted to ensure reliability and validity of results?*
☑ *Analyses conducted to check how robust the results are with different approaches?*
☑ *If presenting statistical analyses, appropriate statistical significance levels used?*
☑ *Magnitude of effects (substantive significance) conveyed accurately?*
☑ *Results discussed clearly and accurately?*
☑ *Uncertainty about results (e.g., confidence in effects, external validity) discussed?*
☑ *Limitations and funding sources, as well as conflicts of interest, identified?*
☑ *Implications of study for theory, research, or policy described?*
☑ *Relevant cautions emphasized if discussing policy implications?*

Or, when one study replicates another, it entails an "apples-to-oranges" comparison that provides, in fact, no replication. Studies also should rely on past research, including use of well-validated measures. If these do not exist, then the studies should carefully justify why the measures they use can be trusted.

Whether a study examines quantitative or qualitative data, diagnostic checks should be undertaken to ensure that one understands quirks and problems in the data. Such checks are described in detail in research methods and statistics textbooks. For example, one should inspect the data for missingness. The greater the missingness, the more likely it is that we should employ strategies for addressing it and for highlighting the issue as a potential limitation of the study.

One of the big risks with statistical analyses consists of elevating minor (but statistically significant) results into prominence and downplaying non-statistically significant findings. Accordingly, a diverse array of analyses should be conducted to assess the robustness of a study's results. When a particular finding consistently emerges across different approaches, we can have greater confidence in the results. When it does not, we should proceed with caution. We also should avoid confusing statistical significance (i.e., a situation where an association between two variables may, probabilistically speaking, exist) and substantive significance (i.e., a situation where an association is sufficiently large to warrant attention). All results should be discussed clearly and accurately. That includes identifying the uncertainty of the estimated effects. It includes, more generally, discussion of the study's limitations as well as funding sources, given that the latter may be viewed as potentially introducing bias into a study. Not least, the concluding discussion should include a description of the study's implications for theory, research, and policy. In the event that the study may have implications for policy, relevant cautions should be described to reduce the likelihood that others may inadvertently base policy on results of questionable generalizability.

Adherence to a checklist is not a cure-all. However, there is no downside to using one. The upside is the potential for studies to be stronger, for research to progress in a more productive manner, and for policy to be grounded on a more credible research foundation.

GUIDANCE FOR THOSE WHO REQUEST AND NEED TO EVALUATE AND USE RESEARCH

Researchers by trade conduct, evaluate, and use research. But they are far from the only individuals for whom research is relevant. To the contrary, many people use research. Citizens do so as they seek to understand policy issues to arrive at their own view about them. Policymakers do so as they consider policies they want to enact, continue, or modify. And criminal justice administrators do so as they consider programs, practices, procedures, and the like for improving agency effectiveness and efficiency.

The latter two groups may not only consume research, they may drive it. Legislators, for example, may dictate the types of research conducted by research agencies. The US Government Accountability Office (GAO) is a case in point. Congress requests that the GAO undertake studies to answer questions they have about various agencies' performance.[39] Many states have similar counterparts to the GAO. Agency officials also may request studies. Other groups may do so as well, such as those who oversee crime prevention efforts, court operations, prison programming, and other such efforts.

In the ideal scenario, their requests reflect informed understanding of the research that would best situate them to make better decisions. Unfortunately, they may not fully appreciate what goes into research. They then fail to ask important research questions or, alternatively, may ask questions that cannot be realistically answered. Many officials, for example, want to know if a specific law or program is effective and will save money. That sounds reasonable. However, some laws and programs cannot be easily

---

[39] Basu *et al.* (1999); Mears (2010).

evaluated without considerable time and expense. The general axiom is that almost any policy or program can be evaluated, but the rigor, or credibility, of the evaluation will vary greatly depending on the available resources and time.

These different groups – especially policymakers and criminal justice administrators – not only request research, but they invariably must consume and use it. This entails evaluating the information they receive. It then entails determining how to act on it. Here, again, that is easier said than done. Even with extensive training in research, it may not always be clear how to proceed. Consider the large body of research on the death penalty. A National Research Council report convened a panel of experts to discuss the state of evidence on the deterrent effects of capital punishment on homicide rates.[40] Many complicated nuances attend research on the death penalty. In the end, the panel concluded that extant research by and large shed little light on whether capital punishment deters would-be murderers and whether it does so more than such alternatives as life sentences or other forms of punishment.

Familiarity with research can, though, provide a critical buffer against misinterpreting studies and their putative relevance for policy or practice. There is no other good alternative. Anything less puts key decision-makers in the position of unquestioningly trusting the information they receive or ignoring research altogether and going with their gut instincts. Neither option bodes well for making good decisions.[41]

What can they do to improve their requests for research and their ability to evaluate and use research effectively and appropriately? Many strategies exist. Here, we identify several that may be useful in acquiring a researcher sensibility. This sensibility allows policymakers and criminal justice administrators and practitioners to improve their ability to request, evaluate, and use research.

Read Research

Make reading research a hobby, and zero in on research related to your area of interest. Read popular accounts in the media and in books, but also peruse journal articles, as well as reports from research institutes. (Fortunately, the availability of this information on the Internet makes this approach practical.) Doing so can create a sensibility or awareness that only comes with repeated exposure and practice, much as language acquisition requires repetition.

---

[40] Nagin and Pepper (2012); Nagin (2013).   [41] Mears (2010, 2017).

Here, though, we also have a somewhat counterintuitive recommendation: When reading, stop once you have a sense of what the study sought to do. Do not read what the study found or what the authors report as implications. Instead, reflect for a moment on what kind of study you would ideally have to achieve the goals – or to answer the questions posed – in what you just read. For example, what kind of sample and data would you want? What would be relevant outcomes? How might a particular factor be related to the outcomes? What problems might interfere with your effort to document the prevalence of some phenomenon (e.g., crime, victimization, prosecutor abuse of discretion, inconsistency in sentencing)? What problems might interfere with your study's ability to show how various factors (e.g., individual, family, community, or organizational characteristics) are related to or cause a particular outcome? What limitations of your study might be important to emphasize?

In short, think like a researcher. Be comfortable doing so. The worst that happens is that you may not have thought as incisively about the issue as did the authors of the study that you read. However, it is far more likely that you will have thought about nuances that may be highly significant to evaluating the credibility and usefulness of a study.

The next step then consists of returning to the article, report, or book that prompted this process and continuing to read. What approach was taken in the study? How did it differ from the ideas that you had when you considered how you would try to answer the study's questions?

One example may illustrate the point. I (Dan) once lived near Baltimore, Maryland, and so took notice when I read about an experiment that randomized convicted felons to a drug court or to "business as usual."[42] Drug courts offer more intensive supervision and treatment to drug-involved offenders. Both may help to reduce recidivism more than would typical court sanctions, such as probation. The findings? Participants recidivated at a lower rate than did control-group subjects. This assessment stood out because relatively few high-quality experimental-design studies of drug courts existed at the time (or since). Yet, what caught my eye was the fact that almost 90 percent of the participants were black.[43] That led me to zero in on the fact that this study reflected the nature of the population of individuals likely to end up in the Baltimore criminal justice system.

One question, then, that seemed natural to ask was how generalizable the results would be to other places in America? On the one hand, the fact that the results stemmed from an experiment suggested warrant for the

---

[42] Gottfredson *et al.* (2003).   [43] Gottfredson *et al.* (2003:180).

notion that drug courts effectively reduce recidivism. On the other hand, Baltimore might have had an especially ineffective business-as-usual response to drug offenders. If that were true, it might not take much for *any* intervention to create an improvement. The implication of that observation should be evident – a similar drug court in a criminal justice system with a panoply of effective interventions for drug offenders might not produce any appreciable benefit over and above the business-as-usual "control" condition. Put differently, the Baltimore study had high internal validity (i.e., we could trust that drug courts likely produced the observed reduction in recidivism). But it might have had weak external validity (i.e., we could not be sure that a similar effect would arise in other areas).[44]

That insight did not come from a careful reading of the study. Rather, it came from stepping back and reflecting on the goals of the study, then wondering about whether the sample and site provided a credible basis for generalizing about identified benefits. When I went back and read the article carefully, many more of the study's strengths and limitations became apparent. (It helped that the authors nicely summarized them at the end of their study!)

In our experience, most students in the classes we teach have little familiarity with research. Yet, within a few weeks of walking through a few studies, some diligent students start to develop a sense of different perspectives they can adopt in evaluating a study. It is not magic and it certainly does not require an advanced degree. What it does require is a willingness to read and think about research.

The benefit of a regular "diet" of research articles, reports, books, and the like goes well beyond developing an ability to evaluate the results. It includes an ability to frame questions in a way that may be more useful for the legislature, a criminal justice agency, or organizations interested in advancing scholarship or policy on crime and justice. It also includes an ability to appreciate better the potential uses or misuses of research. For example, the Baltimore drug court study clearly provides a sound foundation for considering adopting a drug court. But it provides almost no foundation for anticipating that a similar drug court would achieve comparable benefits in other places. We would need much more information about the precise conditions under which drug courts achieve benefits. A local jurisdiction might well want to explore whether a drug court would be appropriate and helpful. But it would be foolish to adopt one without first assessing how well its "business-as-usual" practices achieve their goals

---

[44] Mears *et al.* (2011). See Eck's (2010) discussion of the relevance of external validity for policy.

and whether perhaps minor tweaks to them could produce significant improvements.[45]

Think Carefully about Generalizability and Truth

Many studies identify patterns and associations. A critical question that we all face when conducting or reading about research is whether the patterns or associations are "real" and whether they generalize to other populations or areas. For example, a news article might report, based on interviews with a few students at a campus rally, that college students in America think that the death penalty should not be allowed for children. But these students may not represent all students at the campus, much less students nationwide. And, most importantly, they may differ from such students in ways that affect their views about the death penalty. The news story might also report that the cause of this view stems from a sense that children in contemporary America increasingly have no moral compass due to permissive parenting. This inference would go well beyond what a few interviews could establish.

Many such examples exist. So many exist that one cannot really rely on a checklist of items that must be met to trust a study or a reported finding. Our view, then, is that a researcher sensibility – including a healthy dose of skepticism – serves as the best guide for interpreting studies and media accounts of research. That begins with thoughtfully reflecting on what exactly a given study sought to achieve and what would be the best way to answer its questions. For example, if the goal was to gauge students' views about the death penalty, then a national survey might be the way to go. What, though, if the goal was to identify the crimes for which "the public" thinks the death penalty may be appropriate? We would want a survey of all citizens, not just students at one university. Just as importantly, the survey would need to inquire about the appropriateness of capital punishment for each of a range of distinct crimes.

Questions should be asked as well about the implications of studies. For example, a study may find that low self-control contributes to offending. But that does not imply that we should invest in a particular program aimed at improving the self-control of convicted felons. That program may or may not do a good job at its stated task; the only way to know would be to evaluate that program, not to point to studies that have identified an association between self-control and criminal behavior. In addition, we would want to consider other issues. For example, the self-control of felons may not be the most important contributor to offending among a group of offenders in a given community. Other factors, such as

---

[45] Mears (2010).

poverty, unemployment, drug abuse, and the like – or any other factors that increase criminogenic risk – may warrant more attention. In short, what really is the implication of a given study for other lines of research or for policy? Careful reflection about that question can serve as a buffer against adopting or accepting knee-jerk assumptions about the implications of any study.

This observation holds special relevance for policy efforts that build on "what works" in other places. Lawmakers might learn that some legislation "worked" in another state. They then push to adopt similar legislation. All too frequently, the only evidence that the legislation worked came from nothing more than claims that it did so. Perhaps a state created a new law that mandated arrest of offenders in domestic violence disputes. Subsequently, calls about domestic violence go down. Lawmakers nationwide then seek to adopt a similar policy.[46] The problem, however, is that, absent credible studies, we have no scientific basis to know whether or not the policy "worked."[47] To illustrate, it may be that mandatory arrest laws inhibit domestic violence victims from calling the police. This may have reduced calls for domestic violence, but, of course, not violence itself. This situation clearly would be highly problematic. Instead of reducing domestic violence, the law in fact might allow it to continue or even to increase.

Many states and local jurisdictions lack the research infrastructure for systematically evaluating their own policies and programs or for assessing the evidence from efforts elsewhere.[48] That can contribute to a greater willingness to accept on faith that some law, program, or practice somehow "works." This willingness should be resisted because it amounts to a willingness to base policy on belief rather than scientific evidence.

Another way of thinking about generalizability is to view research as always involving an approximation of truth. No single study captures "reality," but instead approximates. The trick, one grounded in a researcher sensibility, lies in appreciating both the veracity and the limits of the insights a study or body of research may offer.

Take Charge of Driving the Research Questions

It should not be surprising that researchers, when consulted by policy-makers and practitioners, will have many opinions about the research questions that should be asked and how to answer them. A careful researcher will first listen to policymakers, administrators, and others before

---

[46] See, for example, Sherman and Berk (1984).   [47] See, generally, Mears (2010).
[48] Sherman (2003a, 2003b, 2004); Mears (2010, 2017).

offering suggestions. Many, though, will not do that. Even when they may be willing to listen, agencies may want the researcher to commandeer the entire process. Why? They view research as amounting to a specialized language that they cannot readily understand.

The end result? A government agency or private organization or business pays for a study that they do not need or that will not help them. Whatever the reason, the outcome almost always will be undesirable. There simply is no substitute for policymakers and criminal justice administrators taking charge of the research question process. Just as a good physician listens carefully to patients before jumping to a diagnosis, good policy-making and decision-making entails listening carefully first and foremost to one's own interests and needs and then asking questions. The act of driving the research questions is very much central to the act of *conducting* research. If done well, money is well spent and any subsequent research will help inform policy. If done poorly, money is wasted and the study may produce results of limited use.

Listen to Researchers

The logical corollary to the above recommendation consists of listening to researchers. Typically, one would hire an architecture firm to oversee the design and construction of a building. Similarly, if you want research done, then there is no substitute for consulting with researchers or, at the least, reading the work they produce.

It sounds simple, but happens less often than it should.[49] Lawmakers and criminal justice officials typically call for "government accountability" and "evidence-based" policy. But that simply cannot happen without recourse to research.

One solution consists of institutionalizing research into decision-making. Another, simpler option is to forge greater ties between policy and the research community.[50] For organizations and companies that cannot afford to undertake research, there can be substantial benefit to be gained through research consultations. They might be able to identify approaches to improving performance or cost-effective steps that could be taken to collect relevant information for improving decision-making. In addition, they might work to forge mutually beneficial, "win-win" relationships with faculty at universities. Researchers gain access to research questions, data, and insights that they otherwise would not, and governments and organizations get answers to questions and researcher expertise that they otherwise could not afford.

---

[49] Mears (2010, 2017).   [50] Blomberg *et al.* (2016).

Obtain Information from Multiple Sources

Any one researcher or study may not well represent the universe of what is known about a given topic or issue. That is a certainty. Accordingly, listen to researchers, not any one researcher. Or, if consulting research, then read widely and look for reviews. Then scan for commonalities. If multiple reviews say that a particular criminal justice intervention can reduce recidivism, this finding can be better trusted than if the reviews disagree with one another.

Many sources exist for obtaining research. It should not be difficult, therefore, to collect information from diverse sources. However, what can be difficult is to filter out the good from the bad. For that reason, seek out non-partisan research organizations. "Left-leaning" (liberal) or "right-leaning" (conservative) organizations can undertake good, credible studies. Yet, more care is required to filter the potential biases that may affect their assessments and research. That does not mean that non-partisan organizations necessarily conduct better research. On average, though, you can trust more that you will receive unbiased (or less biased) information.

Seek Independent Research

Some organizations rely on their own research units. For example, many police departments, court systems, and departments of corrections have research divisions. Unfortunately, these divisions typically lack the resources and staffing to undertake more than descriptive analyses of organizational operations. Sometimes, though, they can evaluate these operations and some policies, programs, and practices. Their research can be useful and, indeed, essential to creating a ready supply of useful data and statistics for making decisions. Researchers in these divisions may understand far better than other researchers the intricate details of agency data and how to leverage them to gain insight.

Sometimes, though, those who work within an organization may be biased, whether intentionally or unintentionally. Where such a risk arises, it can be helpful to rely on independent research guidance from individuals or organizations with no "skin in the game." Such consultation does not have to mean a contract to conduct a study. It might simply mean a meeting or two to discuss an issue or to review an "in-house" study.

For the general public or anyone interested in criminal justice, the same advice holds true – consult multiple sources and prioritize studies or reviews conducted by independent researchers. Doing so can help to ensure that you obtain a more accurate picture of a given issue. The more you do so, the better your ability will be to discern good from bad research.

Create the Infrastructure Necessary to Provide the Research that You Need

Without the infrastructure – such as an independent division, staff, data collection capacity, and more – for research, lawmakers and agencies must rely on hunches. They make decisions based on gut instinct rather than science. There is, here, no free lunch. If we want better information, then we must invest in more and better research.[51]

This statement may seem to apply only to organizations, but it also applies to individuals. They of course will not have staff to do studies for them! But they can subscribe to science magazines and develop a bookshelf of research books, articles, and reports. Or they might regularly consult websites that discuss research and provide access to studies.

Check Whether a Study Used "Due Diligence"

As discussed above, researchers would do well to follow a "due diligence" checklist (see Table 11.2). Such a list can help them to conduct more rigorous studies. It also can help them to provide documentation that may be useful to other researchers seeking to replicate or build on their work. The same checklist can be useful to policymakers and practitioners in gaining insight into the strengths and limitations of research.

CONCLUSION

Criminological and criminal justice research should be the purview of everyone. However, research is like a weapon – it can be used carefully and to good effect or it can be used carelessly and cause harm. When done well, it advances our understanding of crime and justice and can credibly inform policy. When done badly, trees are destroyed in the process of publishing studies of little consequence. Worse, it can undermine efforts to promote safety and justice.

Good research requires a collective effort. Students – and ideally everyone – must be trained in it from a young age. Colleges and universities must have the resources to undertake cutting-edge studies. All organizations involved in combatting crime, helping victims, and improving criminal justice must have the ability to effectively request and use research. And lawmakers must place a premium on creating the infrastructure for evidence-based policy.

[51] Mears (2017).

We think that this collective effort is possible. But it will not happen of its own accord. Scholars, researchers, legislators, agency administrators, students, the public at large – all of us must improve our ability to conduct, evaluate, and use research. With a little appreciation of the science and art of research, we can create greater knowledge about crime and criminal justice. And just maybe we can create a safer and more just society.

References

Abbott, Andrew. 2004. *Methods of Discovery: Heuristics for the Social Sciences.* New York: Norton.

Abbott, Andrew. 1997. "Of Time and Space: The Contemporary Relevance of the Chicago School." *Social Forces* 75:1149–1182.

Acock, Alan A. 2013. *Discovering Structural Equation Modeling Using Stata.* College Station, TX: Stata Press.

Agnew, Robert. 2005. *Why Do Criminals Offend? A General Theory of Crime and Delinquency.* Los Angeles, CA: Roxbury.

Agnew, Robert. 1992. "Foundation for a General Strain Theory of Crime and Delinquency." *Criminology* 30:47–87.

Akers, Ronald L., Christine S. Sellers, and Wesley G. Jennings. 2016. *Criminological Theories: Introduction, Evaluation, and Application.* 7th edition. New York: Oxford.

Alexander, Michelle. 2012. *The New Jim Crow: Mass Incarceration in the Age of Colorblindedness.* New York: The New Press.

Allen, Francis A. 1954. "Pioneers in Criminology: IV – Raffaele Garofalo (1852–1934)." *Journal of Criminal Law, Criminology, and Police Science* 45:373–390.

Allison, Paul D. 2002. *Missing Data.* Thousand Oaks, CA: Sage.

Allison, Paul D. 2000. "Multiple Imputation for Missing Data: A Cautionary Tale." *Sociological Methods and Research* 28:301–309.

Allison, Paul D. 1999. *Multiple Regression: A Primer.* Thousand Oaks, CA: Sage.

Altschuler, Albert W. 2015. "A Nearly Perfect System for Convicting the Innocent." *Albany Law Review* 79:919–940.

Altschuler, Albert W. 1975. "The Defense Attorney's Role in Plea Bargaining." *Yale Law Journal* 84:1179–1314.

Anderson, Elijah. 1999. *Code of the Street: Decency, Violence, and the Moral Life of the Inner City.* New York: Norton.

Angrist, Joshua D. 2006. "Instrumental Variables Methods in Experimental Criminological Research: What, Why, and How?" *Journal of Experimental Criminology* 2:23–44.

Apel, Robert J., and Gary Sweeten. 2010. "Propensity Score Matching in Criminology and Criminal Justice," in Alex R. Piquero and David Weisburd (eds.), *The Handbook of Quantitative Criminology.* New York: Springer, pp. 543–562.

Applegate, Brandon K. 2016. "President's Message." *ACJS Today* 41:2–3.

Auty, Katherine M., Aiden Cope, and Alison Liebling. 2017. "A Systematic Review and Meta-Analysis of Yoga and Mindfulness Meditation in Prison: Effects on Psychological Well-Being and Behavioural Functioning." *International Journal of Offender Therapy and Comparative Criminology* 61:689–710.

Bachman, Ronet D. and Raymond Paternoster. 2017. *Statistics for Criminology and Criminal Justice*. 4th edition. Thousand Oaks, CA: Sage.

Bachman, Ronet D. and Russell K. Schutt. 2018. *Fundamentals of Research in Criminology and Criminal Justice*. 4th edition. Los Angeles, CA: Sage.

Bailey, Kenneth D. 1994. *Typologies and Taxonomies: An Introduction to Classification Techniques*. Thousand Oaks, CA: Sage.

Bardach, Eugene. 2012. *A Practical Guide for Policy Analysis: The Eightfold Path to More Effective Problem Solving*. 4th edition. Thousand Oaks, CA: Sage.

Bardach, Eugene. 2004. "Presidential Address – the Extrapolation Problem: How Can We Learn from the Experience of Others?" *Journal of Policy Analysis and Management* 23:205–220.

Barker, Vanessa. 2009. *The Politics of Imprisonment: How the Democratic Process Shapes the Way America Punishes Offenders*. New York: Oxford University Press.

Barlow, Hugh D. and Scott H. Decker (eds.). 2010. *Crime and Public Policy: Putting Theory to Work*. Philadelphia, PA: Temple University Press.

Barnes, J. C., John P. Wright, Brian B. Boutwell, Joseph A. Schwartz, Eric J. Connolly, Joseph L. Nedelec, and Kevin M. Beaver. 2014. "Demonstrating the Validity of Twin Research in Criminology." *Criminology* 52:588–626.

Barry, John M. 2005. *The Great Influenza: The Story of the Deadliest Pandemic in History*. New York: Penguin.

Bartol, Curt R. and Anne M. Bartol. 2017. *Criminal Behavior: A Psychological Approach*. 11th edition. New York: Pearson.

Basu, Onker N., Mark W. Dirsmith, and Parveen P. Gupta. 1999. "The Coupling of the Symbolic and the Technical in an Institutionalized Context: The Negotiated Order of the GAO's Audit Reporting Process." *American Sociological Review* 64:506–526.

Baumer, Eric P. 2013. "Reassessing and Redirecting Research on Race and Sentencing." *Justice Quarterly* 30:231–261.

Baumer, Eric P. and Janet L. Lauritsen. 2010. "Reporting Crime to the Police, 1973–2005: A Multivariate Analysis of Long-Term Trends in the National Crime Survey (NCS) and National Crime Victimization Survey (NCVS)." *Criminology* 48:131–185.

Beaver, Kevin M. 2016. *Biosocial Criminology: A Primer*. 3rd edition. Dubuque, IA: Kendall/Hunt.

Beaver, Kevin M., Matt DeLisi, Daniel P. Mears, and Eric A. Stewart. 2009. "Low Self-Control and Contact with the Criminal Justice System in a Nationally Representative Sample of Males." *Justice Quarterly* 26:695–715.

Beccaria, Cesare. 1986 [1764]. *An Essay on Crimes and Punishment*. Translated by David Young. Indianapolis, IN: Hackett Publishing.

Becker, Howard S. 1998. *Tricks of the Trade: How to Think about your Research while You're Doing It*. University of Chicago Press.

Becker, Howard S. 1991. *Outsiders: Studies in the Sociology of Deviance*. New York: Free Press.

Becker, Peter and Richard F. Wetzell (eds.). 2006. *Criminals and their Scientists: The History of Criminology in International Perspective*. New York: Cambridge University Press.

Beebee, Helen, Christopher Hitchcock, and Huw Price. 2017. *Making a Difference: Essays on the Philosophy of Causation*. New York: Oxford University Press.

Benforado, Adam. 2016. *Unfair: The New Science of Criminal Injustice*. New York: Penguin.

Berger, Bennett M. (ed.). 1990. *Authors of their own Lives: Intellectual Autobiographies by Twenty American Sociologists*. Berkeley, CA: University of California Press.

Berger, Joseph and Morris Zelditch, Jr. (eds.). 1993. *Theoretical Research Programs: Studies in the Growth of Theory*. Stanford University Press.

Berger, Peter L. and Thomas Luckmann. 1967. *The Social Construction of Reality: A Treatise in the Sociology of Knowledge*. Garden City, NY: Doubleday.

Berk, Richard A. 2012. *Criminal Justice Forecasts of Risk: A Machine Learning Approach*. New York: Springer.

Berk, Richard A. 2008. "Forecasting Methods in Crime and Justice." *Annual Review of Law and Social Science* 4:219–238.

Berk, Richard A. 1983. "An Introduction to Sample Selection Bias in Sociological Data." *American Sociological Review* 48:386–398.

Berk, Richard A. and Justin Bleich. 2013. "Statistical Procedures for Forecasting Criminal Behavior: A Comparative Assessment." *Criminology and Public Policy* 12:513–544.

Berk, Richard A. and Peter H. Rossi. 1997. *Just Punishment: Federal Guidelines and Public Views Compared*. New York: Aldine de Gruyter.

Berlin, Isaiah. 1953. *The Hedgehog and the Fox: An Essay on Tolstoy's View of History*. New York: Simon & Shuster.

Bernard, Thomas J. and Robin S. Engel. 2001. "Conceptualizing Criminal Justice Theory." *Justice Quarterly* 18:1–30.

Bernard, Thomas J., Eugene A. Paoline III, and Paul-Philippe Pare. 2005. "General Systems Theory and Criminal Justice." *Journal of Criminal Justice* 33:203–211.

Bibas, Stephanos. 2004. "Plea Bargaining outside the Shadow of Trial." *Harvard Law Review* 117:2463–2547.

Black, Donald. 2010. *The Behavior of Law*. Bingley, UK: Emerald Group Publishing.

Blalock, Hubert M., Jr. 1994. "Why Have We Failed to Systematize Reality's Complexities?" in Jerald Hage (ed.), *Formal Theory in Sociology*. Albany, NY: State University of New York Press, pp. 121–136.

Blalock, Hubert M., 1989. "Toward Cumulative Knowledge: Theoretical and Methodological Issues," in *Crossroads of Social Science: The ICPSR 25th Anniversary Volume*. New York: Agathon Press, pp. 15–37.

Blalock, Hubert M., 1967. *Toward a Theory of Minority Group Relations*. New York: Wiley.

Blalock, Hubert M., 1964. *Causal Inferences in Nonexperimental Research*. New York: Norton.

Blomberg, Thomas G., Julie M. Brancale, Kevin M. Beaver, and William D. Bales (eds.). 2016. *Advancing Criminology and Criminal Justice Policy.* New York: Routledge.

Blumberg, Abraham S. 1967. "The Practice of Law as Confidence Game: Organizational Cooptation of a Profession." *Law and Society Review* 1:15–40.

Blumstein, Alfred. 1997. "Interaction of Criminological Research and Public Policy." *Journal of Quantitative Criminology* 12:349–362.

Blumstein, Alfred and Kiminori Nakamura. 2009. "Redemption in the Presence of Widespread Criminal Background Checks." *Criminology* 47:327–359.

Booth, Wayne C., Gregory G. Colomb, and Joseph M. Williams. 2005. *The Craft of Research.* University of Chicago Press.

Bosworth, Mary and Carolyn Hoyle (eds.). 2011. *What Is Criminology?* New York: Oxford University Press.

Bottoms, Anthony E. 1999. "Interpersonal Violence and Social Order in Prisons," in Michael H. Tonry and Joan Petersilia (eds.), *Prisons.* University of Chicago Press, pp. 205–282.

Bradburn, Norman M., Seymour Sudman, and Brian Wansink. 2004. *The Definitive Guide to Questionnaire Design – for Market Research, Political Polls, and Social and Health Questionnaires.* 2nd edition. San Francisco, CA: Jossey-Bass.

Braga, Anthony A., Andrew V. Papachristos, and David M. Hureau. 2014. "The Effects of Hot Spots Policing on Crime: An Updated Systematic Review and Meta-Analysis." *Justice Quarterly* 31:633–663.

Braithwaite, John. 1989. *Crime, Shame, and Reintegration.* New York: Cambridge University Press.

Brayne, Sarah. 2017. "Big Data Surveillance: The Case of Policing." *American Sociological Review* 82:977–1008.

Breen, Richard. 2009. "Formal Theory in the Social Sciences," in Peter Hedström and Björn Wittrock (eds.), *Frontiers of Sociology.* Leiden: Brill, pp. 209–230.

Bridges, F. Stephen, Kimberly M. Tatum, and Julie C. Kunselman. 2008. "Domestic Violence Statutes and Rates of Intimate Partner and Family Homicide." *Criminal Justice Policy Review* 19:117–130.

Brown, Timothy A. 2015. *Confirmatory Factor Analysis for Applied Research.* New York: The Guilford Press.

Burnyeat, M. F. 1976. "Protagoras and Self-Refutation in Later Greek Philosophy." *The Philosophical Review* 85:44–69.

Burstein, Paul. 2014. *American Public Opinion, Advocacy, and Policy in Congress: What the Public Wants and What It Gets.* New York: Cambridge University Press.

Burt, Callie H. and Ronald L. Simons. 2014. "Pulling Back the Curtain on Heritability Studies: Biosocial Criminology in the Postgenomic Era." *Criminology* 52:223–262.

Bushway, Shawn and Robert Apel. 2010. "Instrumental Variables in Criminology and Criminal Justice," in Alex R. Piquero and David Weisburd (eds.), *Handbook of Quantitative Criminology.* New York: Springer, pp. 595–612.

Bushway, Shawn D., Allison D. Redlich, and Robert J. Norris. 2014. "An Explicit Test of Plea Bargaining in the 'Shadow of the Trial.'" *Criminology* 52:723–754.

Butts, Jeffrey A. and John Roman (eds.). 2004. *Juvenile Drug Courts and Teen Substance Abuse*. Washington DC: The Urban Institute.

Campbell, John L., Charles Quincy, Jordan Osserman, and Ove K. Pedersen. 2013. "Coding In-Depth Semistructured Interviews: Problems of Unitization and Intercoder Reliability and Agreement." *Sociological Methods and Research* 42:294–320.

Campbell, Michael C. 2014. "The Emergence of Penal Extremism in California: A Dynamic View of Institutional Structures and Political Processes." *Law and Society Review* 48:377–409.

Carlson, Christoffer and Jerzy Sarnecki. 2015. *An Introduction to Life-Course Criminology*. Thousand Oaks, CA: Sage.

Carpenter, James R., Michael G. Kenward, and Stijn Vansteelandt. 2006. "A Comparison of Multiple Imputation and Doubly Robust Estimation for Analyses with Missing Data." *Journal of the Royal Statistical Society* 169:571–584.

Carson, E. Ann. 2016. *Prisoners in 2015*. Washington DC: Bureau of Justice Statistics.

Caulkins, Jonathan P. and Peter Reuter. 2017. "Dealing More Effectively and Humanely with Illegal Drugs." *Crime and Justice* 46:95–158.

Cauvain, Stanley. 2015. *Technology of Breadmaking*. New York: Springer.

Chalfin, Aaron. 2014. "What Is the Contribution of Mexican Immigration to U.S. Crime Rates? Evidence from Rainfall Shocks in Mexico." *American Law and Economics Review* 16:220–268.

Chamberlain, John M. 2013. *Understanding Criminological Research: A Guide to Data Analysis*. Thousand Oaks, CA: Sage.

Chan, Janet and Lyria B. Moses. 2016. "Is Big Data Challenging Criminology?" *Theoretical Criminology* 20:21–39.

Charmaz, Kathy. 2014. *Constructing Grounded Theory*. 2nd edition. Thousand Oaks, CA: Sage.

Chawla, Dalmeet S. 2017. "Big Names in Statistics Want to Shake Up Much-Maligned P-Value." *Nature* 548:16–17.

Cicourel, Aaron V. 1976 [1968]. *The Social Organization of Juvenile Justice*. London: Heinemann Educational Books.

Clear, Todd R. 2001. "Has Academic Criminal Justice Come of Age? ACJS Presidential Address." *Justice Quarterly* 18:709–726.

Clear, Todd R. and Natasha A. Frost. 2013. *The Punishment Imperative: The Rise and Fall of the Grand Social Experiment in Mass Incarceration*. New York University Press.

Cochran, Joshua C. and Daniel P. Mears. 2017. "The Path of Least Desistance: Inmate Compliance and Recidivism." *Justice Quarterly* 34:431–458.

Cochran, Joshua C. and Daniel P. Mears. 2013. "Social Isolation and Inmate Behavior: A Conceptual Framework for Theorizing Prison Visitation and Guiding and Assessing Research." *Journal of Criminal Justice* 41:252–261.

Cohen, Lawrence E. and Kenneth C. Land. 1984. "Discrepancies between Crime Reports and Crime Surveys: Urban and Structural Determinants." *Criminology* 22:499–530.

Cole, Stephen. 1975. "The Growth of Scientific Knowledge: Theories of Deviance as a Case Study," in Lewis A. Coser (ed.), *The Idea of Social Structure: Papers in Honor of Robert K. Merton*. New York: Harcourt, pp. 175–220.

Contreras, Randol. 2013. *The Stickup Kids: Race, Drugs, Violence, and the American Dream*. Berkeley, CA: University of California Press.

Cooper, Harris M. 2017. *Research Synthesis and Meta-Analysis: A Step-by-Step Approach*. 5th edition. Thousand Oaks, CA: Sage.

Cooper, Jonathon and John L. Worrall. 2012. "Theorizing Criminal Justice Evaluation and Research." *Criminal Justice Review* 37:384–397.

Copes, Heith (ed.). 2012. *Advancing Qualitative Methods in Criminology and Criminal Justice*. New York: Routledge.

Copp, Jennifer E., Peggy C. Giordano, Wendy D. Manning, and Monica A. Longmore. 2016. "Couple-Level Economic/Career Concerns and Intimate Partner Violence in Young Adulthood." *Journal of Marriage and Family* 78:744–758.

Corbett, Ronald P., Jr. 2015. "The Burdens of Leniency: The Changing Face of Probation." *Minnesota Law Review* 99:1697–1733.

Corbin, Juliet and Anselm Strauss. 1990. "Grounded Theory Research: Procedures, Canons, and Evaluative Criteria." *Qualitative Sociology* 13:3–21.

Cowburn, Malcolm, Loraine Gelsthorpe, and Azrini Wahidin (eds.). 2017. *Research Ethics in Criminology: Dilemmas, Issues, and Solutions*. New York: Routledge.

Crank, John P. and Blythe M. Bowman. 2008. "What Is Good Criminal Justice Theory?" *Journal of Criminal Justice* 36:563–572.

Creswell, John W. and Vicki L. Plano Clark. 2011. *Designing and Conducting Mixed Methods Research*. Thousand Oaks, CA: Sage.

Cullen, Francis T. 2005. "The Twelve People Who Saved Rehabilitation: How the Science of Criminology Made a Difference." *Criminology* 43:1–42.

Cullen, Francis T., Bonnie S. Fisher, and Brandon K. Applegate. 2000. "Public Opinion about Punishment and Corrections." *Crime and Justice* 27:1–79.

Cullen, Francis T. and Karen E. Gilbert. 2013. *Reaffirming Rehabilitation*. 2nd edition. Waltham, MA: Anderson/Elsevier.

Cullen, Francis T., Cheryl L. Jonson, and Daniel P. Mears. 2017. "Reinventing Community Corrections." *Crime and Justice* 46:27–93.

Cullen, Francis T., Cheryl L. Jonson, Andrew J. Myer, and Freda Adler (eds.). 2011a. *The Origins of American Criminology*. New Brunswick, NJ: Transaction.

Cullen, Francis T., Cheryl L. Jonson, and Daniel S. Nagin. 2011b. "Prisons Do Not Reduce Recidivism: The High Cost of Ignoring Science." *Prison Journal* 91:48S-65S.

Cullen, Francis T. and Steven F. Messner. 2007. "The Making of Criminology Revisited: An Oral History of Merton's Anomie Paradigm." *Theoretical Criminology* 11:5–37.

Cullen, Francis T., Travis C. Pratt, and Jillian J. Turanovic. 2016. "It's Hopeless: Beyond Zero-Tolerance Supervision." *Criminology and Public Policy* 15:1–13.

Cullen, Francis T. and Brenda Vose. 2014. "How to Be a Successful Graduate Student." *Journal of Contemporary Criminal Justice* 30:362–377.

Cullen, Francis T. and Pamela Wilcox (eds.). 2012. *The Oxford Handbook of Criminological Theory*. New York: Oxford University Press.

Daigle, Leah E. and Lisa R. Muftic. 2016. *Victimology*. Thousand Oaks, CA: Sage.

Dantzker, Mark L., Ronald D. Hunter, and Susan T. Quinn. 2018. *Research Methods for Criminology and Criminal Justice*. 4th edition. Burlington, MA: Jones & Bartlett.

Danziger, Shai, Jonathan Levav, and Liora Avnaim-Pesso. 2011. "Extraneous Factors in Judicial Decisions." *PNAS* 108:6889–6892.

Darwin, Charles. 1859. *On the Origin of Species by Means of Natural Selection, or the Preservation of Favoured Races in the Struggle for Life*. London: John Murray.

Davies, Pamela, Peter Francis, and Victor Jupp (eds.). 2011. *Doing Criminological Research*. 2nd edition. Thousand Oaks, CA: Sage.

Davis, Robert C., Barbara E. Smith, and Bruce Taylor. 2003. "Increasing the Proportion of Domestic Violence Arrests that Are Prosecuted: A Natural Experiment in Milwaukee." *Criminology and Public Policy* 2:263–282.

Decker, Scott H. 2015. "From Theory to Policy and Back Again," in Alex R. Piquero (ed.), *The Handbook of Criminological Theory*. New York: Wiley, pp. 380–394.

Deigh, John and David Dolinko (eds.). 2011. *The Oxford Handbook of Philosophy of Criminal Law*. New York: Oxford University Press.

DeLisi, Matt and Michael G. Vaughn (eds.). 2015. *The Routledge International Handbook of Biosocial Criminology*. New York: Routledge.

Denver, Megan, Justin T. Pickett, and Shawn D. Bushway. 2017. "The Language of Stigmatization and the Mark of Violence: Experimental Evidence on the Social Construction and Use of Criminal Record Stigma." *Criminology* 55:664–690.

Devroye, Jennifer. 2010. "The Rise and Fall of the American Institute of Criminal Law and Criminology." *Journal of Criminal Law and Criminology* 100:7–32.

Dillman, Don A., Jolene D. Smyth, and Leah M. Christian. 2014. *Internet, Phone, Mail, and Mixed-Mode Surveys: The Tailored Design Method*. Hoboken, NJ: Wiley.

Dixon, Travis. 2008. "Crime News and Racialized Beliefs: Understanding the Relationship between Local News Viewing and Perceptions of African Americans and Crime." *Journal of Communication* 58:106–125.

Dooley, Brendan D. and Jason Rydberg. 2014. "Irreconcilable Differences? Examining Divergences in the Orientations of Criminology and Criminal Justice Scholarship, 1951–2008." *Journal of Criminal Justice Education* 25:84–105.

Dubin, Robert. 1978. *Theory Building*. 2nd edition. New York: Free Press.

Duffee, David E. 2015. "Why Is Criminal Justice Theory Important?" in Edward R. Maguire and David E. Duffee (eds.), *Criminal Justice Theory: Explaining the Nature and Behavior of Criminal Justice*. 2nd edition. New York: Routledge, pp. 5–26.

Dugan, Laura and Erica Chenoweth. 2012. "Moving beyond Deterrence: The Effectiveness of Raising the Expected Utility of Abstaining from Terrorism in Israel." *American Sociological Review* 77:597–624.

Duncan, Otis D. 1966. "Path Analysis: Sociological Examples." *American Journal of Sociology* 72:1–16.

Durkheim, Emile. 1933 [1893]. *The Division of Labor in Society*. New York: Free Press.

Durlauf, Steven N. and Daniel S. Nagin. 2011. "Imprisonment and Crime: Can Both Be Reduced?" *Criminology and Public Policy* 10:13–54.

Eck, John E. 2010. "Policy Is in the Details: Using External Validity to Help Policy Makers." *Criminology and Public Policy* 9:859–866.

Ekland-Olson, Sheldon and Jack P. Gibbs. 2018. *Science and Sociology: Predictive Power Is the Name of the Game*. New York: Routledge.

Elkhorne, J. L. 1967. "Edison: The Fabulous Drone." *73 Magazine* 46(3):52–54.

Ellenberg, Jordan. 2014. *How Not to Be Wrong: The Power of Mathematical Thinking*. New York: Penguin.

Elliott, Anthony (ed.). 1999. *Contemporary Social Theory*. Malden, MA: Blackwell.

Elliott, Deni and Judy E. Stern (eds.). 1997. *Research Ethics: A Reader*. Hanover, NH: University Press of New England.

Ellis, Havelock. 1913 [1890]. *The Criminal*. 4th edition. New York: Scribner and Welford.

Ellis, Lee. 2002. "Denominational Differences in Self-Reported Delinquency," in Thomas P. O'Connor and Nathaniel J. Pallone (eds.), *Religion, the Community, and the Rehabilitation of Criminal Offenders*. New York: Haworth Press, pp. 185–198.

Emerson, Robert M. 1969. *Judging Delinquents: Context and Process in Juvenile Court*. Chicago, IL: Aldine de Gruyter.

Engel, Robin S. and Michael R. Smith. 2009. "Perceptual Distortion and Reasonableness during Police Shootings: Law, Legitimacy, and Future Research." *Criminology and Public Policy* 8:141–151.

Entman, Robert M. and Andrew Rojecki. 2000. *The Black Image in the White Mind: Media and Race in America*. University of Chicago Press.

Fagan, Abigail and Andrea M. Lindsey. 2015. "Neighborhood-Based Prevention of Delinquency," in Marvin Krohn and Jodi Lane (eds.), *The Handbook of Juvenile Delinquency and Juvenile Justice*. New York: Wiley-Blackwell, pp. 387–404.

Fagin, Dan. 2013. *Toms River: A Story of Science and Salvation*. New York: Random House.

Farabee, David. 2005. *Rethinking Rehabilitation: Why Can't We Reform Our Criminals?* Washington DC: The AEI Press.

Farrington, David P. 2003a. "Developmental and Life-Course Criminology: Key Theoretical and Empirical Issues – the 2002 Sutherland Award Address." *Criminology* 41:221–225.

Farrington, David P. 2003b. "Methodological Quality Standards for Evaluation Research." *Annals of the American Academy of Political and Social Science* 587:49–68.

Farrington, David P. and Brandon C. Welsh (eds.). 2012. *The Oxford Handbook of Crime Prevention*. New York: Oxford University Press.

Farrington, David P. and Brandon C. Welsh 2005. "Randomized Experiments in Criminology: What Have We Learned in the Last Two Decades?" *Journal of Experimental Criminology* 1:9–38.

Feagin, Joe R., Anthony M. Orum, and Gideon Sjoberg (eds.). 1991. *A Case for the Case Study*. Chapel Hill, NC: University of North Carolina Press.

Feeley, Malcolm M. 1979. *The Process Is the Punishment: Handling Cases in a Lower Criminal Court*. New York: Russell Sage Foundation.

Feeley, Malcolm M. 1973. "Two Models of the Criminal Justice System: An Organizational Perspective." *Law & Society Review* 7:407–426.

Feld, Barry C. 2017. *The Evolution of the Juvenile Court: Race, Politics, and the Criminalizing of the Juvenile Court*. New York University Press.

Feld, Barry C. and Donna M. Bishop (eds.). 2012. *The Oxford Handbook of Juvenile Crime and Juvenile Justice*. New York: Oxford University Press.

Feldmeyer, Ben, Patricia Warren, Sonja E. Siennick, and Melisa Neptune. 2015. "Racial, Ethnic, and Immigrant Threat: Is There a New Criminal Threat on State Sentencing?" *Journal of Research in Crime and Delinquency* 52:62–92.

Felson, Marcus. 2017. "Criminology's First Paradigm," in Nick Tilley and Aiden Sidebottom (eds.), *Handbook of Crime Prevention and Community Safety*. 2nd edition. New York: Routledge, pp. 22–31.

Flanagan, Timothy J. and Dennis R. Longmire (eds.). 1996. *Americans View Crime and Justice: A National Public Opinion Survey*. Thousand Oaks, CA: Sage.

Forer, Lois G. 1994. *A Rage to Punish: The Unintended Consequences of Mandatory Sentencing*. New York: Norton.

Forst, Brian. 2004. *Errors of Justice: Nature, Sources, and Remedies*. New York: Cambridge University Press.

Freese, Lee. 1972. "Cumulative Sociological Knowledge." *American Sociological Review* 37:472–482.

Frost, Natasha and Carlos Monteiro. 2016. "Administrative Segregation in U.S. Prisons," in Marie Garcia (ed.), *Restrictive Housing in the U.S.: Issues, Challenges, and Future Directions*. Washington DC: National Institute of Justice, pp. 1–48.

Gaes, Gerald G., Scott D. Camp, Julianne B. Nelson, and William G. Saylor. 2004. *Measuring Prison Performance: Government Privatization and Accountability*. New York: AltaMira Press.

Garland, David. 2013. "The 2012 Sutherland Address: Penality and the Penal State." *Criminology* 51:475–517.

Garland, David. 2001. *The Culture of Control: Crime and Social Order in Contemporary Society*. University of Chicago Press.

Garofalo, Raffaele. 1885. *Criminologia: Studio sul Delitto, Sulle sue Cause e sui Mezzi di Repressione*. Turin, Italy: Fratelli Bocca.

Gartner, Rosemary, D. Wayne Osgood, and Eric Baumer. 2012. "Salami-Slicing, Peek-a-Boo, and LPUS: Addressing the Problem of Piecemeal Publication." *The Criminologist* 37:23–25.

Gastil, Raymond D. 1971. "Homicide and a Regional Culture of Violence." *American Sociological Review* 36:412–427.

Gawande, Atul. 2009. *The Checklist Manifesto: How to Get Things Right*. New York: Henry Holt.

Gawande, Atul. 2007. *Better: A Surgeon's Notes on Performance*. New York: Metropolitan Books.

Geertz, Clifford. 1973. *The Interpretation of Cultures*. New York: Basic Books.

Geis, Gilbert. 1996. "The Heavy Electrical Equipment Antitrust Cases: Price-Fixing Techniques and Rationalizations," in M. David Ermann and Richard J. Lundman (eds.), *Corporate and Governmental Deviance: Problems of Organizational Behavior in Contemporary Society*. New York: Oxford University Press, pp. 98–117.

General Accounting Office, US. 2003. *Justice Outcome Evaluations: Design and Implementation of Studies Require More NIJ Attention*. Washington DC: US General Accounting Office.

General Accounting Office, US. 1998. *Performance Measurement and Evaluation: Definitions and Relationships*. Washington DC: US General Accounting Office.

George, Alexander L. and Andrew Bennett. 2004. *Case Studies and Theory Development in the Social Sciences*. Cambridge, MA: MIT Press.

Gerstenfeld, Phyllis B., Diana R. Grant, and Chau-Pu Chiang. 2003. "Hate Online: A Content Analysis of Extremist Internet Sites." *Analyses of Social Issues and Public Policy* 3:29–44.

Gertz, Clifford. 2017. *The Interpretation of Cultures*. 3rd edition. New York: Hachette.

Gibbs, Jack P. 1997. "Seven Dimensions of the Predictive Power of Sociological Theories." *National Journal of Sociology* 11:1–28.

Gibbs, Jack P. 1989. *Control: Sociology's Central Notion*. Chicago, IL: University of Illinois Press.

Gibbs, Jack P. 1985. "The Methodology of Theory Construction in Criminology," in Robert F. Meier (ed.), *Theoretical Methods in Criminology*. Beverly Hills, CA: Sage, pp. 23–50.

Gibbs, Jack P. 1982. "Evidence of Causation." *Current Perspectives in Social Theory* 3:93–127.

Gibbs, Jack P. 1975. *Crime, Punishment and Deterrence*. New York: Elsevier.

Gibbs, Jack P. 1972. *Sociological Theory Construction*. Hinsdale, IL: Dryden Press.

Gibson, Chris L. and Marvin D. Krohn. 2013. *Handbook of Life-Course Criminology: Emerging Trends and Directions for Future Research*. New York: Springer.

Glueck, Sheldon and Eleanor Glueck. 1950. *Unraveling Juvenile Delinquency*. New York: The Commonwealth Fund.

Goffman, Alice. 2014. *On the Run: Fugitive Life in an American City*. University of Chicago Press.

Goffman, Erving. 1989. "On Fieldwork." *Journal of Contemporary Ethnography* 18:123–132.

Goffman, Erving. 1962. *Asylums*. Chicago, IL: Aldine.

Goode, Erich (ed.). 2008. *Out of Control: Assessing the General Theory of Crime*. Stanford University Press.

Gottfredson, Denise C., Stacy S. Najaka, and Brook Kearley. 2003. "Effectiveness of Drug Treatment Courts: Evidence from a Randomized Trial." *Criminology and Public Policy* 2:171–196.

Gottfredson, Michael R. and Travis Hirschi. 1990. *A General Theory of Crime*. Stanford University Press.

Gottschalk, Marie. 2013. "The Carceral State and the Politics of Punishment," in Jonathan Simon and Richard Sparks (eds.), *The Sage Handbook of Punishment and Society*. Thousand Oaks, CA: Sage, pp. 205–241.

Gottschalk, Marie. 2011. "The Past, Present, and Future of Mass Incarceration in the United States." *Criminology and Public Policy* 10:483–504.

Gottschalk, Marie. 2006. *The Prison and the Gallows: The Politics of Mass Incarceration in America*. New York: Cambridge University Press.

Gould, Mark. 1987. *Revolution in the Development of Capitalism*. Beverly Hills, CA: University of California Press.

Gould, Stephen J. 2003. *The Hedgehog, the Fox, and the Magister's Pox.* New York: Harmony Press.

Gould, Stephen J. 2002. *I Have Landed: The End of a Beginning in Natural History.* New York: Norton.

Gove, Walter R., Michael Hughes, and Michael Geerken. 1985. "Are Uniform Crime Reports a Valid Indicator of the Index Crimes? An Affirmative Answer with Minor Qualifications." *Criminology* 23:451–502.

Green, Donald P. and Daniel Winik. 2010. "Using Random Judge Assignments to Estimate the Effects of Incarceration and Probation on Recidivism among Drug Offenders." *Criminology* 48:357–387.

Griffin, Marie L. and John R. Hepburn. 2013. "Inmate Misconduct and the Institutional Capacity for Control." *Criminal Justice and Behavior* 40:270–388.

Groopman, Jerome. 2007. *How Doctors Think.* New York: Houghton Mifflin.

Groopman, Jerome and Pamela Hartzband. 2011. *Your Medical Mind: How to Decide What Is Right for You.* New York: Penguin Press.

Guo, Shenyang and Mark W. Fraser. 2010. *Propensity Score Analysis: Statistical Models and Applications.* Thousand Oaks, CA: Sage.

Hagan, John. 1989. "Why Is there so Little Criminal Justice Theory? Neglected Macro- and Micro-Level Links between Organization and Power." *Journal of Research in Crime and Delinquency* 26:116–135.

Hage, Jerald (ed.). 1994. *Formal Theory in Sociology.* Albany, NY: State University of New York Press.

Hagenaars, Jacques A. and Allan L. McCutcheon. 2002. *Applied Latent Class Analysis.* New York: Cambridge University Press.

Hammond, Phillip E. (ed.). 1964. *Sociologists at Work: The Craft of Social Research.* New York: Basic Books.

Haney, Craig, Curtis Banks, and Philip G. Zimbardo. 1973. "Interpersonal Dynamics in a Simulated Prison." *International Journal of Criminology and Penology* 1:69–97.

Harring, Sidney. 1983. *Policing in a Class Society: The Experience of American Cities, 1865–1915.* New Brunswick, NJ: Rutgers University Press.

Harris, Richard. 2017. *Rigor Mortis: How Sloppy Science Creates Worthless Cures, Crushes Hope, and Wastes Billions.* New York: Basic Books.

Hassin, Ran R., Kevin N. Ochsner, and Yaacov Trope (eds.). 2010. *Self-Control in Society, Mind, and Brain.* New York: Oxford University Press.

Hatry, Harry P. 2006. *Performance Measurement: Getting Results.* 2nd edition. Washington DC: The Urban Institute.

Hay, Carter and Ryan Meldrum. 2016. *Self-Control and Crime over the Life Course.* Los Angeles, CA: Sage.

He, Hua, Jun Hu, and Jiang He. 2016. "Overview of Propensity Score Methods," in Hua He, Pan Wu, and Ding-Geng (Din) Chen (eds.), *Statistical Causal Inferences and their Applications in Public Health Research.* New York: Springer, pp. 29–48.

Heilbroner, David. 1990. *Rough Justice: Days and Nights of a Young D.A.* New York: Pantheon.

Hemmens, Craig. 2015. "Which Is Bigger – Criminology or Criminal Justice?" *ACJS Today* 45:21–24.

Herman, Susan. 2010. *Parallel Justice for Victims of Crime*. Washington DC: National Center for Victims of Crime.

Higgins, Julian P. T. and Sally Green (eds.). 2011. *Cochrane Handbook for Systematic Reviews of Interventions*. London: The Cochrane Collaboration.

Hines, Denise A. 2009. "Domestic Violence," in Michael H. Tonry (ed.), *The Oxford Handbook of Crime and Public Policy*. New York: Oxford University Press, pp. 115–139.

Hirschi, Travis and Michael R. Gottfredson. 1993. "Rethinking the Juvenile Justice System." *Crime and Delinquency* 39:262–271.

Hirschi, Travis and Hanan C. Selvin. 1996. *Delinquency Research: An Appraisal of Analytic Methods*. Piscataway, NJ: Transaction.

Hoeve, Machteld, Judith S. Dubas, Veroni I. Eichelsheim, Peter H. van der Laan, Wilma Smeenk, and Jan R. M. Gerris. 2009. "The Relationship between Parenting and Delinquency: A Meta-Analysis." *Journal of Abnormal Child Psychology* 37:749–775.

Holtfreter, Kristy and Travis J. Meyers. 2015. "Challenges for Cybercrime Theory, Research, and Policy." *Norwich Review of International and Transnational Crime* 1:54–66.

Holtfreter, Kristy, Michael D. Reisig, and Travis C. Pratt. 2008. "Low Self-Control, Routine Activities, and Fraud Victimization." *Criminology* 46:189–220.

Homans, George. 1964. "Contemporary Theory in Sociology," in Robert E. L. Faris (ed.), *Handbook of Modern Sociology*. Chicago, IL: Rand McNally, pp. 951–77.

Hornblum, Allen M. 1999. *Acres of Skin: Human Experiments at Holmesburg Prison*. New York: Routledge.

Horney, Julie, Wayne D. Osgood, and Ineke H. Marshall. 1995. "Criminal Careers in the Short-Term: Intra-Individual Variability in Crime and its Relation to Local Life Circumstances." *American Sociological Review* 60:655–673.

Horton, Nicholas J. and Ken P. Kleinman. 2007. "Much Ado about Nothing: A Comparison of Missing Data Methods and Software to Fit Incomplete Data Regression Models." *The American Statistician* 61:79–90.

Huddleston, C. West, Douglas B. Marlowe, and Rachel Casebolt. 2008. *Painting the Current Picture: A National Report Card on Drug Courts and Other Problem-Solving Court Programs in the United States*. Alexandria, VA: National Drug Court Institute.

Huebner, Beth M. and Timothy S. Bynum (eds.). 2016. *The Handbook of Measurement Issues in Criminology and Criminal Justice*. New York: Wiley.

Humes, Edward. 1996. *No Matter How Loud I Shout: A Year in the Life of Juvenile Court*. New York: Simon & Schuster.

Inman, Thomas. 1860. *Foundation for a New Theory and Practice of Medicine*. London: John Churchill.

Ioannidis, John P. A. 2005a. "Contradicted and Initially Stronger Effects in Highly Cited Clinical Research." *Journal of the American Medical Association* 294:218–228.

Ioannidis, John P. A. 2005b. "Why Most Published Research Findings Are False." *PLoS Medicine* 2:0696–0701.

Israel, Mark and Ian Hay. 2006. *Research Ethics for Social Sciences*. Thousand Oaks, CA: Sage.

Iyengar, Radha. 2009. "Does the Certainty of Arrest Reduce Domestic Violence? Evidence from Mandatory and Recommended Arrest Laws." *Journal of Public Economics* 93:85–98.

Jaccard, James and Jacob Jacoby. 2010. *Theory Construction and Model-Building Skills: A Practical Guide for Social Scientists*. New York: Guildford Press.

Johnson, Brian D. 2010. "Multilevel Analysis in the Study of Crime and Justice," in Alex R. Piquero and David Weisburd (eds.), *Handbook of Quantitative Criminology*. New York: Springer, pp. 615–648.

Johnson, Brian D., Ryan D. King, and Cassia Spohn. 2016. "Sociolegal Approaches to the Study of Guilty Pleas and Prosecution." *Annual Review of Law and Social Science* 12:479–495.

Jolliffe, Darrick, David P. Farrington, Alex R. Piquero, John F. MacLeod, and Steve van de Weijer. 2017. "Prevalence of Life-Course-Persistent, Adolescence-Limited, and Late-Onset Offenders: A Systematic Review of Prospective Longitudinal Studies." *Aggression and Violent Behavior* 33:4–14.

Jones, David A. 1986. *History of Criminology: A Philosophical Perspective*. New York: Praeger.

Jones, Mark and Peter Johnstone. 2015. *History of Criminal Justice*. 5th edition. New York: Routledge.

Kahneman, Daniel. 2011. *Thinking, Fast and Slow*. New York: Farrar, Straus & Giroux.

Kee, James E. 2004. "Cost-Effectiveness and Cost–Benefit Analysis," in Joseph S. Wholey, Harry P. Hatry, and Kathryn E. Newcomer (eds.), *Handbook of Practical Program Evaluation*, 2nd edition. San Francisco, CA: Jossey-Bass, pp. 506–541.

Kellstedt, Paul M. and Guy D. Whitten. 2013. *The Fundamentals of Political Science Research*. 2nd edition. New York: Cambridge University Press.

Kelly, William R. 2016. *The Future of Crime and Punishment: Smart Policies for Reducing Crime and Saving Money*. Lanham, MD: Rowman & Littlefield.

Kelly, William R. 2015. *Criminal Justice at the Crossroads*. New York: Columbia University Press.

Kelly, William R., Robert Pittman, and William Streusand. 2017. *From Retribution to Public Safety: Disruptive Innovation in American Criminal Justice*. Lanham, MD: Rowman & Littlefield.

Khan, Shamus and Dana R. Fisher (eds.). 2013. *The Practice of Research: How Social Scientists Answer their Questions*. New York: Oxford University Press.

Kirk, David S. 2009. "A Natural Experiment on Residential Change and Recidivism: Lessons from Hurricane Katrina." *American Sociological Review* 74:484–505.

Kleck, Gary, Jongyeon Tark, and Jon J. Bellows. 2006. "What Methods Are Most Frequently Used in Research in Criminology and Criminal Justice?" *Journal of Criminal Justice* 34:147–152.

Kline, Rex B. 2016. *Principles and Practice of Structural Equation Modeling*. New York: The Guilford Press.

Knoke, David, George W. Bohrnstedt, and Alisa P. Mee. 2002. *Statistics for Social Data Analysis*. 4th edition. Belmont, CA: Wadsworth.

Kraska, Peter B. 2006. "Criminal Justice Theory: Toward Legitimacy and an Infrastructure." *Justice Quarterly* 23:167–185.

Kraska, Peter B. 2004. *Theorizing Criminal Justice*. Long Grove, IL: Waveland.

Kringen, Jonathan A., J. Pete Blair, and Meredith Emigh. 2018. "Pedagogical Issues in Criminal Justice: Often-Ignored Problems with Null Hypothesis Significance Testing." *ACJS Today* 43:13–22.

Krippendorff, Klaus. 2004. *Content Analysis: An Introduction to its Methodology*. Thousand Oaks, CA: Sage.

Krohn, Marvin D. and Chris L. Gibson (eds.). 2013. *Handbook of Life-Course Criminology: Emerging Trends and Directions for Future Research*. New York: Springer-Verlag.

Kubrin, Charis E., Marjorie S. Zatz, and Ramiro Martinez, Jr. (eds.). 2012. *Punishing Immigrants: Policy, Politics, and Injustice*. New York University Press.

Kuhn, Thomas S. 1962. *The Structure of Scientific Revolutions*. University of Chicago Press.

Kulig, Teresa C., Travis C. Pratt, and Francis T. Cullen. 2017. "Revisiting the Stanford Prison Experiment: A Case Study in Organized Skepticism." *Journal of Criminal Justice Education* 28:74–111.

Kupchik, Aaron. 2006. *Judging Juveniles: Prosecuting Adolescents in Adult and Juvenile Courts*. New York University Press.

Kurasaki, Karen S. 2000. "Intercoder Reliability for Validating Conclusions Drawn from Open-Ended Interview Data." *Field Methods* 12:179–194.

Kurlychek, Megan C., Shawn D. Bushway, and Robert Brame. 2012. "Long-Term Crime Desistance and Recidivism Patterns – Evidence from the Essex County Convicted Felon Study." *Criminology* 50:71–104.

Langton, Lynn, Marcus Berzofsky, Christopher Krebs, and Hope Smiley-McDonald. 2012. *Victimizations Not Reported to the Police, 2006–2010*. Washington DC: Bureau of Justice Statistics.

Lasley, James R. 1998. *Essentials of Criminal Justice and Criminology Research*. Upper Saddle River, NJ: Prentice Hall.

Lassiter, Daniel and Noah D. Goodman. 2015. "How Many Kinds of Reasoning? Inference, Probability, and Natural Language Semantics." *Cognition* 136:123–134.

Latessa, Edward J., Shelley J. Listwan, and Deborah Koetzle. 2014. *What Works (and Doesn't) in Reducing Recidivism*. Waltham, MA: Anderson Publishing.

Laub, John. 2012. "Translational Criminology." *Translational Criminology* 3:4–5.

Laub, John. 1983. *Criminology in the Making: An Oral History*. Boston, MA: Northeastern University Press.

Laub, John H. and Robert J. Sampson. 2003. *Shared Beginnings, Divergent Lives: Delinquent Boys to Age 70*. Boston, MA: Harvard University Press.

Lawrence, James R., Robert G. Demaree, and Gerrit Wolf. 1984. "Estimating Within-Group Interrater Reliability with and without Response Bias." *Journal of Applied Psychology* 69:85–98.

Lawrence, Sarah and Daniel P. Mears. 2004. *Benefit–Cost Analysis of Supermax Prisons: Critical Steps and Considerations.* Washington DC: The Urban Institute.

LeBel, Thomas P., Ros Burnett, Shadd Maruna, and Shawn Bushway. 2008. "The 'Chicken and Egg' of Subjective and Social Factors in Desistance from Crime." *European Journal of Criminology* 5:130–158.

Lewin, Kurt. 1952. *Field Theory in Social Science: Selected Theoretical Papers.* London: Tavistock.

Lieberman, Joel D. and Daniel A. Krauss. 2016. *Jury Psychology: Social Aspects of Trial Processes.* New York: Routledge.

Lieberson, Stanley. 1985. *Making It Count: The Improvement of Social Research and Theory.* Los Angeles, CA: University of California Press.

Liebling, Alison, Shadd Maruna, and Lesley McAra (eds.). 2017. *The Oxford Handbook of Criminology.* 6th edition. New York: Oxford University Press.

Lilly, J. Robert, Francis T. Cullen, and Richard A. Ball. 2015. *Criminological Theory: Context and Consequences.* 6th edition. Thousand Oaks, CA: Sage.

Linden, Ariel, S. Derya Uysal, Andrew Ryan, and John L. Adams. 2016. "Estimating Causal Effects for Multivalued Treatment Treatments: A Comparison of Approaches." *Statistics in Medicine* 35:534–552.

Lindsey, Andrea M., Daniel P. Mears, and Joshua C. Cochran. 2016. "The Privatization Debate: A Conceptual Framework for Improving (Public and Private) Corrections." *Journal of Contemporary Criminal Justice* 32:308–327.

Lipsey, Mark W. 2009. "The Primary Factors that Characterize Effective Interventions with Juvenile Offenders: A Meta-Analytic Review." *Victims and Offenders* 4:124–147.

Lipsey, Mark W. 1998. "Design Sensitivity: Statistical Power for Applied Experimental Research," in Leonard Bickman and Debra J. Rog (eds.), *Handbook of Applied Social Research Methods.* Thousand Oaks, CA: Sage, pp. 39–68.

Lipsey, Mark W., John L. Adams, Denise C. Gottfredson, John V. Pepper, and David Weisburd (eds.). 2005. *Improving Evaluation of Anticrime Programs.* Washington DC: The National Academies Press.

Lipsey, Mark W. and Francis T. Cullen. 2007. "The Effectiveness of Correctional Rehabilitation: A Review of Systematic Reviews." *Annual Review of Law and Social Science* 3:297–320.

Lipsey, Mark W. and David B. Wilson. 2001. *Practical Meta-Analysis.* Thousand Oaks, CA: Sage.

Liska, Allen E. 1992. *Social Threat and Social Control.* Albany, NY: State University of New York Press.

Liu, Hexuan and Guang Guo. 2016. "Opportunities and Challenges for the Social Sciences in the Era of Big Data: The Case of Genomic Data." *Social Science Research* 59:13–22.

Loehlin, John C. 1987. *Latent Variable Models: An Introduction to Factor, Path, and Structural Analysis.* Hillsdale, NJ: Erlbaum.

Lum, Cynthia and Daniel S. Nagin. 2017. "Reinventing American Policing." *Crime and Justice* 47:339–393.

Lynch, James P. and Lynn P. Addington (eds.). 2007. *Understanding Crime Statistics: Revisiting the Divergence of the NCVS and UCR*. New York: Cambridge University Press.

Lyons, Christopher J. 2006. "Stigma or Sympathy? Attributions of Fault to Hate Crime Victims and Offenders." *Social Psychology Quarterly* 69:39–59.

MacCannell, Dean. 1990. "Working in Other Fields," in Bennett M. Berger (ed.), *Authors of their own Lives: Intellectual Autobiographies by Twenty American Sociologists*. Berkeley, CA: University of California Press, pp. 165–189.

MacKenzie, Doris L. 2006. *What Works in Corrections: Reducing the Criminal Activities of Offenders and Delinquents*. New York: Cambridge University Press.

MacKenzie, Doris L. and David P. Farrington. 2015. "Preventing Future Offending of Delinquents and Offenders: What Have We Learned from Experiments and Meta-Analyses?" *Journal of Experimental Criminology* 11:565–595.

Macrina, Francis L. 2014. *Scientific Integrity: Text and Cases in Responsible Conduct of Research*. 4th edition. Herndon, VA: ASM Press.

Maguire, Edward R. and David E. Duffee (eds.). 2015. *Criminal Justice Theory: Explaining the Nature and Behavior of Criminal Justice*. 2nd edition. New York: Routledge.

Maguire, Edward R. and Charles M. Katz. 2002. "Community Policing, Loose Coupling, and Sensemaking in American Police Agencies." *Justice Quarterly* 19:503–536.

Maguire, Mike, Rod Morgan, and Robert Reiner (eds.). 2012. *The Oxford Handbook of Criminology*. New York: Oxford University Press.

Maier-Katkin, Daniel, Daniel P. Mears, and Thomas J. Bernard. 2009. "Towards a Criminology of Crimes against Humanity." *Theoretical Criminology* 13:227–255.

Malcolm, Norman. 1958. *Ludwig Wittgenstein: A Memoir*. New York: Oxford University Press.

Maltz, Michael D. 1984. *Recidivism*. Orlando, FL: Academic Press.

Mancini, Christina, James C. Barnes, and Daniel P. Mears. 2013. "It Varies from State to State: An Examination of Sex Crime Laws Nationally." *Criminal Justice Policy Review* 24:166–198.

Mancini, Christina and Daniel P. Mears. 2016. "Sex Offenders – America's New Witches? A Theoretical Analysis of the Emergence of Sex Crime Laws." *Deviant Behavior* 37:419–438.

Mancini, Christina and Daniel P. Mears. 2013. "The Effect of Agency Scandal on Public Views toward the Correctional System." *Criminal Justice Review* 38:5–28.

Mancini, Christina and Daniel P. Mears. 2010. "To Execute or Not to Execute? Examining Public Support for Capital Punishment of Sex Offenders." *Journal of Criminal Justice* 38:959–968.

Manning, Peter K. 2005. "The Study of Policing." *Police Quarterly* 8:23–43.

Manza, Jeff and Christopher Uggen. 2006. *Locked Out: Felon Disenfranchisement and American Democracy*. New York: Oxford University Press.

Marini, Margaret M. and Burton Singer. 1988. "Causality in the Social Sciences," in Clifford C. Clogg (ed.), *Sociological Methodology*. Washington DC: American Sociological Association, pp. 347–409.

Maruna, Shadd. 2011. "Reentry as a Rite of Passage." *Punishment and Society* 13:3–28.

Maruna, Shadd. 2001. *Making Good: How Ex-Convicts Reform and Rebuild their Lives.* Washington DC: American Psychological Association.

Maruna, Shadd and Russ Immarigeon. 2013. *After Crime and Punishment: Pathways to Offender Reintegration.* New York: Routledge.

Maxfield, Michael G. and Earl R. Babbie. 2015. *Research Methods for Criminal Justice and Criminology.* 7th edition. Stamford, CT: Cengage.

Maxwell, Christopher D., Joel H. Garner, and Jeffrey A. Fagan. 2002. "The Preventative Effects of Arrest on Intimate Partner Violence: Research, Policy and Theory." *Criminology and Public Policy* 2:51–80.

Maxwell, Christopher D., Joel H. Garner, and Jeffrey A. Fagan. 2001. *The Effects of Arrest on Intimate Partner Violence: New Evidence from the Spouse Assault Replication Program.* Washington DC: National Institute of Justice.

May, David C. and Peter B. Wood. 2010. *Ranking Correctional Punishments: Views from Offenders, Practitioners, and the Public.* Durham, NC: Carolina Academic Press.

McCleary, Richard, David McDowall, and Bradley Bartos. 2017. *Design and Analysis of Time Series Experiments.* New York: Oxford University Press.

McDavid, James C. and Laura R. L. Hawthorn. 2006. *Program Evaluation and Performance Measurement: An Introduction to Practice.* Thousand Oaks, CA: Sage.

McDowall, David. 2002. "Tests of Nonlinear Dynamics in U.S. Homicide Time Series, and their Implications." *Criminology* 40:711–736.

McGloin, Jean M. 2009. "Delinquency Balance: Revisiting Peer Influence." *Criminology* 47:439–477.

Meadows, Donella H. 2008. *Thinking in Systems: A Primer.* White River Junction, VT: Chelsea Green Publishing.

Mears, Daniel P. 2017. *Out-of-Control Criminal Justice: The Systems Improvement Solution for More Safety, Justice, Accountability, and Efficiency.* New York: Cambridge University Press.

Mears, Daniel P. 2016a. "Critical Research Gaps in Understanding the Effects of Prolonged Time in Restrictive Housing on Inmates and the Institutional Environment," in Marie Garcia (ed.), *Restrictive Housing in the U.S.: Issues, Challenges, and Future Directions.* Washington DC: National Institute of Justice, pp. 233–295.

Mears, Daniel P. 2016b. "Policy Evaluation and Assessment," in Thomas G. Blomberg, Julie M. Brancale, Kevin M. Beaver, and William D. Bales (eds.), *Advancing Criminology and Criminal Justice Policy.* New York: Routledge, pp. 26–39.

Mears, Daniel P. 2013. "Supermax Prisons: The Policy and the Evidence." *Criminology and Public Policy* 12:681–719.

Mears, Daniel P. 2012a. "The Front End of the Juvenile Court: Intake and Informal vs. Formal Processing," in Barry C. Feld and Donna M. Bishop (eds.), *The Oxford Handbook of Juvenile Crime and Juvenile Justice.* New York: Oxford University Press, pp. 573–605.

Mears, Daniel P. 2012b. "The Prison Experience." *Journal of Criminal Justice* 40:345–347.

Mears, Daniel P. 2010. *American Criminal Justice Policy: An Evaluation Approach to Increasing Accountability and Effectiveness.* New York: Cambridge University Press.

Mears, Daniel P. 2008a. "Accountability, Efficiency, and Effectiveness in Corrections: Shining a Light on the Black Box of Prison Systems." *Criminology and Public Policy* 7:143–152.

Mears, Daniel P. 2008b. "An Assessment of Supermax Prisons Using an Evaluation Research Framework." *Prison Journal* 88:43–68.

Mears, Daniel P. 2007. "Towards Rational and Evidence-Based Crime Policy." *Journal of Criminal Justice* 35:667–682.

Mears, Daniel P. 2006. *Evaluating the Effectiveness of Supermax Prisons*. Washington DC: The Urban Institute.

Mears, Daniel P. 2005. "A Critical Look at Supermax Prisons." *Corrections Compendium* 30: 45–49.

Mears, Daniel P. 2004. "Mental Health Needs and Services in the Criminal Justice System." *Houston Journal of Health Law and Policy* 4:255–284.

Mears, Daniel P. 2002. "The Ubiquity, Functions, and Contexts of Bullshitting." *Journal of Mundane Behavior* 3:233–256.

Mears, Daniel P. 2001a. "Critical Challenges in Addressing the Mental Health Needs of Juvenile Offenders." *Justice Policy Journal* 1:41–61.

Mears, Daniel P. 2001b. "The Immigration–Crime Nexus: Toward an Analytic Framework for Assessing and Guiding Theory, Research, and Policy." *Sociological Perspectives* 44:1–19.

Mears, Daniel P. 1998. "The Sociology of Sentencing: Reconceptualizing Decisionmaking Processes and Outcomes." *Law and Society Review* 32:667–724.

Mears, Daniel P. and Sarah Bacon. 2009. "Improving Criminal Justice through Better Decisionmaking: Lessons from the Medical System." *Journal of Criminal Justice* 37:142–154.

Mears, Daniel P. and James C. Barnes. 2010. "Toward a Systematic Foundation for Identifying Evidence-Based Criminal Justice Sanctions and their Relative Effectiveness." *Journal of Criminal Justice* 38:702–810.

Mears, Daniel P. and Avinash S. Bhati. 2006. "No Community Is an Island: The Effects of Resource Deprivation on Urban Violence in Spatially and Socially Proximate Communities." *Criminology* 44:509–548.

Mears, Daniel P. and Jennifer L. Castro. 2006. "Wardens' Views on the Wisdom of Supermax Prisons." *Crime and Delinquency* 52:398–431.

Mears, Daniel P. and Joshua C. Cochran. 2018. "Progressively Tougher Sanctioning and Recidivism: Assessing the Effects of Different Types of Sanctions." *Journal of Research in Crime and Delinquency* 55:194–241.

Mears, Daniel P. and Joshua C. Cochran. 2015. *Prisoner Reentry in the Era of Mass Incarceration*. Thousand Oaks, CA: Sage.

Mears, Daniel P. and Joshua C. Cochran. 2013. "What Is the Effect of IQ on Offending?" *Criminal Justice and Behavior* 40:1280–1300.

Mears, Daniel P., Joshua C. Cochran, William D. Bales, and Avinash S. Bhati. 2016a. "Recidivism and Time Served in Prison." *Journal of Criminal Law and Criminology* 106:83–124.

Mears, Daniel P., Joshua C. Cochran, and Kevin M. Beaver. 2013a. "Self-Control Theory and Nonlinear Effects on Offending." *Journal of Quantitative Criminology* 29:447–476.

Mears, Daniel P., Joshua C. Cochran, and Francis T. Cullen. 2015. "Incarceration Heterogeneity and its Implications for Assessing the Effectiveness of Imprisonment on Recidivism." *Criminal Justice Policy Review* 26:691–712.

Mears, Daniel P., Joshua C. Cochran, Sarah J. Greenman, Avinash S. Bhati, and Mark A. Greenwald. 2011. "Evidence on the Effectiveness of Juvenile Court Sanctions." *Journal of Criminal Justice* 39:509–520.

Mears, Daniel P., Joshua C. Cochran, and Andrea M. Lindsey. 2016b. "Offending and Racial and Ethnic Disparities in Criminal Justice: A Conceptual Framework for Guiding Theory and Research and Informing Policy." *Journal of Contemporary Criminal Justice* 32:78–103.

Mears, Daniel P., Joshua C. Cochran, and Sonja E. Siennick. 2013b. "Life-Course Perspectives and Prisoner Reentry," in Marvin D. Krohn and Chris L. Gibson (eds.), *Handbook of Life-Course Criminology: Emerging Trends and Directions for Future Research*. New York: Springer-Verlag, pp. 317–333.

Mears, Daniel P., Miltonette O. Craig, Eric A. Stewart, and Patricia Y. Warren. 2017a. "Thinking Fast, Not Slow: How Cognitive Biases May Contribute to Racial Disparities in the Use of Force in Police–Citizen Encounters." *Journal of Criminal Justice* 53:12–24.

Mears, Daniel P., Carter Hay, Marc Gertz, and Christina Mancini. 2007. "Public Opinion and the Foundation of the Juvenile Court." *Criminology* 45:223–258.

Mears, Daniel P., Joshua J. Kuch, Andrea M. Lindsey, Sonja E. Siennick, George B. Pesta, Mark A. Greenwald, and Thomas G. Blomberg. 2016c. "Juvenile Court and Contemporary Diversion: Helpful, Harmful, or Both?" *Criminology and Public Policy* 15:953–981.

Mears, Daniel P., Melissa Moon, and Angela J. Thielo. 2017b. "Columbine Revisited: Myths and Realities about the Bullying–School Shootings Connection." *Victims and Offenders* 12:939–955.

Mears, Daniel P., Matthew Ploeger, and Mark Warr. 1998. "Explaining the Gender Gap in Delinquency: Peer Influence and Moral Evaluations of Behavior." *Journal of Research in Crime and Delinquency* 35:251–266.

Mears, Daniel P. and Michael D. Reisig. 2006. "The Theory and Practice of Supermax Prisons." *Punishment and Society* 8:33–57.

Mears, Daniel P. and Sonja E. Siennick. 2016. "Young Adult Outcomes and the Life-Course Penalties of Parental Incarceration." *Journal of Research in Crime and Delinquency* 53:3–35.

Mears, Daniel P. and Mark C. Stafford. 2002. "Central Analytical Issues in the Generation of Cumulative Sociological Knowledge." *Sociological Focus* 35:5–24.

Mears, Daniel P., Eric A. Stewart, Sonja E. Siennick, and Ronald L. Simons. 2013c. "The Code of the Street and Inmate Violence: Investigating the Salience of Imported Belief Systems." *Criminology* 51:695–728.

Mears, Daniel P., Eric A. Stewart, Patricia Y. Warren, and Ronald L. Simons. 2017c. "Culture and Formal Social Control: The Effect of the Code of the Street on Police and Court Decisionmaking." *Justice Quarterly* 34:217–247.

Mears, Daniel P., Xia Wang, and William D. Bales. 2014. "Does a Rising Tide Lift All Boats? Labor Market Changes and their Effects on the Recidivism of Released Prisoners." *Justice Quarterly* 31:822–851.

Mears, Daniel P. and Jamie Watson. 2006. "Towards a Fair and Balanced Assessment of Supermax Prisons." *Justice Quarterly* 23:232–270.

Merton, Robert K. 1995. "The Thomas Theorem and the Matthew Effect." *Social Forces* 74:379–424.

Merton, Robert K. 1973. *The Sociology of Science: Theoretical and Empirical Investigations.* University of Chicago Press.

Merton, Robert K. 1968. *Social Theory and Social Structure.* New York: Free Press.

Merton, Robert K. 1938. "Social Structure and Anomie." *American Sociological Review* 22:635–639.

Messner, Steven F. 1983. "Regional and Racial Effects on the Urban Homicide Rate: The Subculture of Violence Revisited." *American Journal of Sociology* 88:997–1007.

Messner, Steven F., Marvin D. Krohn, and Allen E. Liska (eds.). 1989. *Theoretical Integration in the Study of Deviance and Crime.* Albany, NY: State University of New York Press.

Miles, Matthew B., A. Michael Huberman, and Johnny Saldaña. 2014. *Qualitative Data Analysis: A Methods Sourcebook.* 3rd edition. Thousand Oaks, CA: Sage.

Miller, Jody and Wilson R. Palacios (eds.). 2015. *Qualitative Research in Criminology.* New Brunswick, NJ: Transaction.

Miller, Walter B. 1973. "Ideology and Criminal Justice Policy: Some Current Issues." *Journal of Criminal Law and Criminology* 64:141–162.

Mills, C. Wright. 1959. *The Sociological Imagination.* New York: Oxford University Press.

Mitchell, Kimberly J., David Finkelhor, Lisa M. Jones, and Janis Wolak. 2012. "Prevalence and Characteristics of Youth Sexting: A National Study." *Pediatrics* 129:13–20.

Mitchell, Ojmarrh. 2005. "A Meta-Analysis of Race and Sentencing Research: Explaining the Inconsistencies." *Journal of Quantitative Criminology* 21:439–466.

Mitchell, Ojmarrh, Joshua C. Cochran, Daniel P. Mears, and William D. Bales. 2017. "Examining Prison Effects on Recidivism: A Regression Discontinuity Approach." *Justice Quarterly* 34:571–596.

Morgan, Stephen L. and Christopher Winship. 2015. *Counterfactuals and Causal Inference: Methods and Principles for Social Research.* Cambridge University Press.

Morris, Albert. 1975. "The American Society of Criminology: A History, 1941–1974." *Criminology* 13:123–167.

Morris, Norval. 2002. *Maconochie's Gentlemen: The Story of Norfolk Island and the Roots of Modern Prison Reform.* New York: Oxford University Press.

Mukherjee, Siddhartha. 2016. *The Gene: An Intimate History.* New York: Scribner.

Mukherjee, Siddhartha. 2010. *The Emperor of All Maladies: A Biography of Cancer.* New York: Scribner.

Mulvey, Edward P. and Carol A. Schubert. 2017. "Mentally Ill Individuals in Jails and Prisons." *Crime and Justice* 46:231–277.

Mumola, Christopher J. 2000. *Incarcerated Parents and their Children.* Washington DC: Bureau of Justice Statistics.

Nagin, Daniel S. 2013. "Deterrence: A Review of the Evidence by a Criminologist for Economists." *Annual Review of Economics* 5:83–105.

Nagin, Daniel S. 2005. *Group-Based Modeling of Development*. Cambridge, MA: Harvard University Press.

Nagin, Daniel S. 2001. "Measuring the Economic Benefits of Developmental Prevention Programs." *Crime and Justice* 28:347–384.

Nagin, Daniel S., Francis T. Cullen, and Cheryl L. Jonson. 2009. "Imprisonment and Reoffending." *Crime and Justice* 38:115–200.

Nagin, Daniel S. and John V. Pepper (eds.). 2012. *Deterrence and the Death Penalty*. Washington DC: National Academies Press.

National Institute of Justice. 2006. *Drug Courts: The Second Decade*. Washington DC: National Institute of Justice.

Okasha, Samir. 2002. *Philosophy of Science: A Very Short Introduction*. New York: Oxford University Press.

Oliver, William M. 2014. *The History of the Academy of Criminal Justice Sciences (ACJS): Celebrating 50 Years, 1963–2013*. Greenbelt, MD: Academy of Criminal Justice Sciences.

Oreskes, Naomi and Erik M. Conway. 2010. *Merchants of Doubt: How a Handful of Scientists Obscured the Truth on Issues from Tobacco Smoke to Global Warming*. New York: Bloomsbury Press.

Osgood, Wayne D. 2010. "Statistical Models of Life Events and Criminal Behavior," in Alex R. Piquero and David Weisburd (eds.), *Handbook of Quantitative Criminology*. New York: Springer, pp. 375–396.

Osgood, D. Wayne, Barbara J. McMorris, and Maria T. Potenza. 2002. "Analyzing Multiple-Item Measures of Crime and Deviance I: Item Response Theory Scaling." *Journal of Quantitative Criminology* 18:267–296.

Parker, Karen F. 2008. *Unequal Crime Decline: Theorizing Race, Urban Inequality, and Criminal Violence*. New York University Press.

Parsons, Talcott. 1977. *Social Systems and the Evolution of Action Theory*. New York: Free Press.

Parsons, Talcott. 1968 [1937]. *The Structure of Social Action*. New York: Free Press.

Parsons, Talcott, Edward Shils, Kaspar Naegele, and Jesse R. Pitts (eds.). 1961. *Theories of Society*. Glencoe, IL: Free Press.

Paternoster, Raymond. 2010. "How Much Do We Really Know about Criminal Deterrence?" *Journal of Criminal Law and Criminology* 100:765–824.

Paternoster, Raymond, Ronet Bachman, Erin Kerrison, Daniel O'Connell, and Lionel Smith. 2016. "Desistance from Crime and Identity: An Empirical Test with Survival Time." *Criminal Justice and Behavior* 43:1204–1224.

Paternoster, Raymond, Robert Brame, and Sarah Bacon. 2007. *The Death Penalty: America's Experience with Capital Punishment*. New York: Oxford University Press.

Patton, Michael Q. 2015. *Qualitative Research and Evaluation Methods: Integrating Theory and Practice*. 4th edition. Thousand Oaks, CA: Sage.

Peffley, Mark and Jon Hurwitz. 2010. *Justice in America: The Separate Realities of Blacks and Whites*. New York: Cambridge University Press.

Petersilia, Joan. 2011. "Community Corrections: Probation, Parole, and Prisoner Reentry," in James Q. Wilson and Joan Petersilia (eds.), *Crime and Public Policy*. New York: Oxford University Press, pp. 499–531.

Petersilia, Joan. 2003. *When Prisoners Come Home: Parole and Prisoner Reentry*. New York: Oxford University Press.

Petersilia, Joan. 1991. "Policy Relevance and the Future of Criminology." *Criminology* 29:1–16.

Petersilia, Joan and Kevin R. Reitz (eds.). 2012. *The Oxford Handbook of Sentencing and Corrections*. New York: Oxford University Press.

Pickett, Justin T. 2017. "Methodological Myths and the Role of Appeals in Criminal Justice Journals: The Case of Response Rates." *ACJS Today* 42:61–69.

Pickett, Justin T., Christina Mancini, and Daniel P. Mears. 2013. "Vulnerable Victims, Monstrous Offenders, and Unmanageable Risk: Explaining Public Opinion on the Social Control of Sex Crime." *Criminology* 51:729–759.

Pickett, Justin T., Christina Mancini, Daniel P. Mears, and Marc Gertz. 2015. "Public (Mis)Understanding of Crime Policy: The Effects of Criminal Justice Experience and Media Reliance." *Criminal Justice Policy Review* 26:500–522.

Piehl, Anne M. and Shawn D. Bushway. 2007. "Measuring and Explaining Charge Bargaining." *Journal of Quantitative Criminology* 23:105–125.

Piehl, Anne M. and Stefan F. LoBuglio. 2005. "Does Supervision Matter?" in Jeremy Travis and Christy Visher (eds.), *Prisoner Reentry and Public Safety in America*. New York: Cambridge University Press, pp. 105–138.

Pifferi, Michele. 2016. *Reinventing Punishment: A Comparative History of Criminology and Penology in the 19th and 20th Century*. New York: Oxford University Press.

Piquero, Alex R. and David Weisburd. 2010. *Handbook of Quantitative Criminology*. New York: Springer.

Pollack, Harold A. 2017. "Dealing More Effectively with Problematic Substance Use and Crime." *Crime and Justice* 46:159–200.

Popper, Karl. 2002. *The Logic of Scientific Discovery*. New York: Routledge.

Pratt, Travis C. (ed.). 2012. *Advancing Quantitative Methods in Criminology and Criminal Justice*. New York: Taylor & Francis.

Pratt, Travis C., Jillian J. Turanovic, and Francis T. Cullen. 2016. "Revisiting the Criminological Consequences of Exposure to Fetal Testosterone: A Meta-Analysis of the 2D:4D Digit Ratio." *Criminology* 54:587–620.

President's Commission on Law Enforcement and Administration of Justice. 1967. *The Challenge of Crime in a Free Society*. Washington DC: US Government Printing Office.

Pridemore, William A. and Tony H. Grubesic. 2013. "Alcohol Outlets and Community Levels of Interpersonal Violence: Spatial Density, Outlet Type, and Seriousness of Assault." *Journal of Research in Crime and Delinquency* 50:132–159.

Rafter, Nicole. 2011. "Origins of Criminology," in Mary Bosworth and Carolyn Hoyle (eds.), *What Is Criminology?* New York: Oxford University Press, pp. 143–156.

Rafter, Nicole. (ed.). 2009. *The Origins of Criminology: A Reader*. New York: Routledge.

RAND. 1996. *Guidelines for Preparing Briefings*. Santa Monica, CA: RAND.

Raphael, Steven and Rudolf Winter-Ebmer. 2001. "Identifying the Effect of Unemployment on Crime." *Journal of Law and Economics* 44:259–283.

Ratcliffe, Jerry, Travis Taniguchi, Elizabeth R. Groff, and Jennifer D. Wood. 2011. "The Philadelphia Foot Patrol Experiment: A Randomized Controlled Trial of Police Patrol Effectiveness in Violent Crime Hotspots." *Criminology* 49:795–831.

Reaves, Brian A. 2013. *Felony Defendants in Large Urban Counties, 2009 – Statistical Tables*. Washington DC: Bureau of Justice Statistics.

Reichertz, Jo. 2014. "Induction, Deduction, Abduction," in Uwe Flick (ed.), *The Sage Handbook of Qualitative Data Analysis*. Thousand Oaks, CA: Sage, pp. 123–135.

Reisig, Michael D. 2010. "Community and Problem-Oriented Policing." *Crime and Justice* 39:1–53.

Reisig, Michael D. and Robert J. Kane (eds.). 2014. *The Oxford Handbook of Police and Policing*. New York: Oxford University Press.

Reynolds, Paul D. 2006. *A Primer in Theory Construction*. New York: Routledge.

Ridgeway, Greg. 2013. "Linking Prediction and Prevention." *Criminology and Public Policy* 12:545–550.

Ridgeway, Greg and John M. MacDonald. 2014. "A Method for Internal Benchmarking of Criminal Justice System Performance." *Crime and Delinquency* 60:145–162.

Ripley, Amanda. 2016. "At Least 22 States Make It a Crime to Disturb School in Ways that Teenagers Are Wired to Do. Why Did This Happen? How America Outlawed Adolescence." *The Atlantic Monthly*, November, pp. 86–96.

Riveland, Chase. 1999. *Supermax Prisons: Overview and General Considerations*. Washington DC: National Institute of Corrections.

Roberts, Julian V. 2008. "Punishing Persistence: Explaining the Enduring Appeal of the Recidivist Sentencing Premium." *British Journal of Criminology* 48:468–481.

Roberts, Julian V. and Mike Hough. 2005. *Understanding Public Attitudes to Criminal Justice*. Maidenhead, UK: Open University Press.

Roberts, Julian V. and Loretta Stalans. 2000. *Public Opinion, Crime, and Criminal Justice*. Boulder, CO: Westview.

Rocque, Michael. 2017. *Desistance from Crime: New Advances in Theory and Research*. New York: Macmillan.

Rodriguez, Nancy. 2010. "The Cumulative Effect of Race and Ethnicity in Juvenile Court Outcomes and Why Preadjudication Detention Matters." *Journal of Research in Crime and Delinquency* 47:391–413.

Rojek, Jeff, Geoffrey P. Alpert, and Hayden P. Smith. 2012. "Examining Officer and Citizen Use-of-Force Incidents." *Crime and Delinquency* 58:301–327.

Roman, John and Christine DeStefano. 2004. "Drug Court Effects and the Quality of Existing Evidence," in Jeffrey A. Butts and John Roman (eds.), *Juvenile Drug Courts and Teen Substance Abuse*. Washington DC: The Urban Institute, pp. 107–135.

Roman, John, Terry Dunworth, and Kevin Marsh. 2010. *Cost–Benefit Analysis and Crime Control*. Washington DC: The Urban Institute.

Rossi, Peter H. 1980. "The Presidential Address: The Challenge and Opportunities of Applied Social Research." *American Sociological Review* 45:889–904.

Rossi, Peter H., Mark W. Lipsey, and Howard E. Freeman. 2004. *Evaluation: A Systematic Approach*. 7th edition. Thousand Oaks, CA: Sage.

Rossman, Shelli B., John K. Roman, Janine M. Zweig, Michael Rempel, and Christine H. Lindquist (eds.). 2011. *The Multi-Site Adult Drug Court Evaluation: The Impact of Drug Courts*. Washington DC: The Urban Institute.

Rubin, Ashley T. 2012. "The Unintended Consequences of Penal Reform: A Case Study of Penal Transportation in Eighteenth-Century London." *Law and Society Review* 46:815–851.

Sampson, Robert J. 2013. "The Place of Context: A Theory and Strategy for Criminology's Hard Problems." *Criminology* 51:1–32.

Sampson, Robert J. 2012. *Great American City: Chicago and the Enduring Neighborhood Effect*. University of Chicago Press.

Sampson, Robert J. and John H. Laub. 1993. *Crime in the Making: Pathways and Turning Points through Life*. Boston, MA: Harvard University Press.

Sampson, Robert. J., Stephen. W. Raudenbush, and Felton Earls. 1997. "Neighborhoods and Violent Crime: A Multilevel Study of Collective Efficacy." *Science* 277:918–924.

Sampson, Robert J., Christopher Winship, and Carly Knight. 2013. "Translating Causal Claims: Principles and Strategies for Policy-Relevant Criminology." *Criminology and Public Policy* 12:587–616.

Sanders, Lisa. 2009. *Every Patient Tells a Story: Medical Mysteries and the Art of Diagnosis*. New York: Broadway Books.

Scarborough, Kathryn E. and Pamela A. Collins. 2002. *Women in Public and Private Law Enforcement*. Woburn, MA: Butterworth Heinemann.

Scarre, Geoffrey. 2003. "Corporal Punishment." *Ethical Theory and Moral Practice* 6:295–316.

Schaefer, Lacey, Francis T. Cullen, and John E. Eck. 2016. *Environmental Corrections: A New Paradigm for Supervising Offenders in the Community*. Thousand Oaks, CA: Sage.

Seife, Charles. 2000. *Zero: The Biography of a Dangerous Idea*. New York: Penguin.

Shaw, Clifford and Henry McKay. 1969. *Juvenile Delinquency and Urban Areas*. University of Chicago Press.

Sherman, Lawrence W. 2004. "Research and Policing: The Infrastructure and Political Economy of Federal Funding." *Annals of the American Academy of Political and Social Science* 593:156–178.

Sherman, Lawrence W. 2003a. "Misleading Evidence and Evidence-Led Policy: Making Social Science More Experimental." *Annals of the American Academy of Political and Social Science* 589:6–19.

Sherman, Lawrence W. 2003b. "Reason for Emotion: Reinventing Justice with Theories, Innovations, and Research – the American Society of Criminology 2002 Presidential Address." *Criminology* 41:1–38.

Sherman, Lawrence W. 1993. "Defiance, Deterrence and Irrelevance: A Theory of the Criminal Sanction." *Journal of Research in Crime and Delinquency* 30:445–473.

Sherman, Lawrence W. and Richard A. Berk. 1984. "The Specific Deterrent Effects of Arrest for Domestic Assault." *American Sociological Review* 49:261–271.

Siennick, Sonja E., Daniel P. Mears, and William D. Bales. 2013. "Here and Gone: Anticipation and Separation Effects of Prison Visits on Inmate Infractions." *Journal of Research in Crime and Delinquency* 50:417–444.

Silver, Nate. 2012. *The Signal and the Noise: Why So Many Predictions Fail – But Some Don't*. New York: Penguin.

Simon, Dan. 2012. *In Doubt: The Psychology of the Criminal Justice Process*. Cambridge, MA: Harvard University Press.

Singer, Simon I. 1996. *Recriminalizing Delinquency: Violent Juvenile Crime and Juvenile Justice Reform*. New York: Cambridge University Press.

Skolnick, Jerome. 1966. *Justice without Trial: Law Enforcement in Democratic Society*. New York: Wiley.

Smith, Sven, Chris Ferguson, and Kevin Beaver. 2018. "A Longitudinal Analysis of Shooter Games and their Relationship with Conduct Disorder and Self-Reported Delinquency." *International Journal of Law and Psychiatry* 58:48–53.

Snipes, Jeffrey B. and Edward R. Maguire. 2015. "Foundations of Criminal Justice Theory," in Edward R. Maguire and David E. Duffee (eds.), *Criminal Justice Theory: Explaining the Nature and Behavior of Criminal Justice*. 2nd edition. New York: Routledge, pp. 27–54.

Sokol, Daniel K. 2013. "'First Do No Harm' Revisited." *British Medical Journal* 347:1–2.

Sorensen, Jon, Clete Snell, and John J. Rodriguez. 2006. "An Assessment of Criminal Justice and Criminology Journal Prestige." *Journal of Criminal Justice Education* 17:297–322.

Sparks, Richard, Anthony E. Bottoms, and Will Hay. 1996. *Prisons and the Problem of Order*. Oxford University Press.

Spohn, Cassia. 2018. "Reflections on the Exercise of Prosecutorial Discretion 50 Years after Publication of *The Challenge of Crime in a Free Society*." *Criminology and Public Policy* 17:321–340.

Spohn, Cassia. 2013. "Racial Disparities in Prosecution, Sentencing, and Punishment," in Sandra M. Bucerius and Michael Tonry (eds.), *The Oxford Handbook of Ethnicity, Crime, and Immigration*. New York: Oxford University Press, pp. 166–193.

Stafford, Mark C., Louis N. Gray, Ben A. Menke, and David A. Ward. 1986. "Modeling the Deterrent Effects of Punishment." *Social Psychology Quarterly* 49:338–347.

Stafford, Mark C. and Daniel P. Mears. 2015. "Causation, Theory, and Policy in the Social Sciences," in Robert A. Scott and Stephen M. Kosslyn (eds.), *Emerging Trends in the Behavioral and Social Sciences: An Interdisciplinary, Searchable, and Linkable Resource*. Hoboken, NJ: Wiley, pp. 1–14.

Staley, Kent W. 2014. *An Introduction to the Philosophy of Science*. New York: Cambridge University Press.

Starr, June and Jane F. Collier (eds.). 1989. *History and Power in the Study of Law*. Ithaca, NY: Cornell University Press.

Steffensmeier, Darrell J. 1986. *The Fence: In the Shadow of Two Worlds*. New York: Rowman & Littlefield.

Steiner, Benjamin and John Wooldredge. 2014. "Comparing Self-Report to Official Measures of Inmate Misconduct." *Justice Quarterly* 31:1074–1101.

Steinmetz, Kevin F., Brian P. Schaefer, Rolando V. del Carmen, and Craig Hemmens. 2014. "Assessing the Boundaries between Criminal Justice and Criminology." *Criminal Justice Review* 39:357–376.

Stewart, David W. and Prem N. Shamdasani. 2015. *Focus Groups: Theory and Practice*. Thousand Oaks, CA: Sage.

Stewart, Eric A. and Ronald L. Simons. 2010. "Race, Code of the Street, and Violent Delinquency: A Multilevel Investigation of Neighborhood Street Culture and Individual Norms of Violence." *Criminology* 48:569–605.

Stults, Brian J. and Eric P. Baumer. 2007. "Racial Threat and Police Force Size: Evaluating the Empirical Validity of the Minority Threat Perspective." *American Journal of Sociology* 113:507–546.

Sullivan, Christopher J. 2013. "Computer Simulation Experiments and the Development of Criminological Theory," in Brandon C. Welsh, Anthony A. Braga, and Gerben J. N. Bruinsma (eds.), *Experimental Criminology: Prospects for Advancing Science and Public Policy*. New York: Cambridge University Press, pp. 65–89.

Surette, Ray. 2015. *Media, Crime, and Criminal Justice: Images, Realities, and Policies*. 5th edition. Stamford, CT: Cengage.

Sutherland, Edwin H. 1934. *Principles of Criminology*. Philadelphia, PA: Lippincott.

Swanson, Richard A. and Thomas J. Chermack. 2013. *Theory Building in Applied Disciplines*. San Francisco, CA: Berrett-Koehler.

Swedberg, Richard. 2014. *The Art of Social Theory*. Princeton University Press.

Sweeten, Gary. 2012. "Scaling Criminal Offending." *Journal of Quantitative Criminology* 28:533–557.

Sykes, Gresham M. 1958. *The Society of Captives*. Princeton University Press.

Takhteyev, Yuri, Anatoliy Gruzd, and Barry Wellman. 2012. "Geography of Twitter Networks." *Social Networks* 34:73–81.

Tanner-Smith, Emily E., Mark W. Lipsey, and David B. Wilson. 2016. "Juvenile Drug Court Effects on Recidivism and Drug Use: A Systematic Review and Meta-Analysis." *Journal of Experimental Criminology* 12:477–513.

Taxman, Faye S. (ed.). 2017. *Handbook on Risk and Need Assessment: Theory and Practice*. New York: Routledge.

Taylor, Rae. 2009. "Slain and Slandered: A Content Analysis of the Portrayal of Femicide in Crime News." *Homicide Studies* 13:21–49.

Theall, Katherine P., Zoe H. Brett, Elizabeth A. Shirtcliff, Erin C. Dunn, and Stacy S. Drury. 2013. "Neighborhood Disorder and Telomeres: Connecting Children's Exposure to Community Level Stress and Cellular Response." *Social Science & Medicine* 85:50–58.

Thomas, W. I. and Dorothy S. Thomas. 1928. *The Child in America: Behavior Problems and Programs*. New York: Knopf.

Tita, George E. and Steven M. Radil. 2010a. "Theorizing Space and Place for Spatial Analysis in Criminology." *Journal of Quantitative Criminology* 26:467–479.

Tita, George E. and Steven M. Radil. 2010b. "Spatial Regression Models in Criminology: Modeling Social Processes in the Spatial Weights Matrix," in Alex R. Piquero and David Weisburd (eds.), *Handbook of Quantitative Criminology*. New York: Springer, pp. 101–121.

Thistlewaite, Amy B. and John D. Wooldredge (eds.). 2014. *Forty Studies that Changed Criminal Justice: Explorations into the History of Criminal Justice Research*. 2nd edition. Upper Saddle River, NJ: Pearson.

Tonry, Michael H. 2014. "Why Crime Rates Are Falling throughout the Western World." *Crime and Justice* 43:1–63.

Tonry, Michael H. (ed.). 2011. *The Oxford Handbook of Crime and Criminal Justice*. New York: Oxford University Press.

Tonry, Michael H. (ed.). 2009. *The Oxford Handbook of Crime and Public Policy*. New York: Oxford University Press.

Travis, Jeremy, Bruce Western, and Steven Redburn (eds.). 2014. *The Growth of Incarceration in the United States*. Washington DC: The National Academies Press.

Turanovic, Jillian J. and Travis C. Pratt. 2014. "'Can't Stop, Won't Stop': Self-Control, Risky Lifestyles, and Repeat Victimization." *Journal of Quantitative Criminology* 30:29–56.

Turanovic, Jillian J. and Nancy Rodriguez. 2017. "Mental Health Service Needs in the Prison Boom: The Case of Children of Incarcerated Mothers." *Criminal Justice Policy Review* 28:415–436.

Turco, Catherine and Ezra Zuckerman. 2017. "Verstehen Sociology: Comment on Watts." *American Journal of Sociology* 122:1272–1791.

Turow, Scott. 1977. *One L: The Turbulent True Story of a First Year at Harvard Law School*. New York: Farrar, Straus, & Giroux.

Tyler, Tom R. 2006. *Why People Obey the Law*. Princeton University Press.

Tyson, Neil deGrasse. 2016. "In Science, When Human Behavior Enters the Equation, Things Go Nonlinear. That's Why Physics Is Easy and Sociology Is Hard." [Tweet]. Available online at https://twitter.com/neiltyson/status/695759776752496640?lang=en.

Tyson, Neil deGrasse. 2014. *The Pluto Files: The Rise and Fall of America's Favorite Planet*. New York: Norton.

Uggen, Christopher and Suzy McElrath. 2014. "Parental Incarceration: What We Know and Where We Need to Go." *Journal of Criminal Law and Criminology* 104:597–604.

Ulmer, Jeffery T. 2012. "Recent Developments and New Directions in Sentencing Research." *Justice Quarterly* 29:1–40.

Ulmer, Jeffery T. and Julia Laskorunsky. 2016. "Sentencing Disparities," in Thomas G. Blomberg, Julie M. Brancale, Kevin M. Beaver, and William D. Bales (eds.), *Advancing Criminology and Criminal Justice Policy*. New York: Routledge, pp. 170–186.

Unnever, James D. 2014. "Race, Crime, and Public Opinion," in Sandra M. Bucerius and Michael H. Tonry (eds.), *The Oxford Handbook of Ethnicity, Crime, and Immigration*. New York: Oxford University Press, pp. 70–106.

Useem, Bert and Anne M. Piehl. 2008. *Prison State: The Challenge of Mass Incarceration*. New York: Cambridge University Press.

van der Werff, Steven J. A., Bernet M. Elzinga, Annika S. Smit, and Nic J. A. van der Wee. 2017. "Structural Brain Correlates of Resilience to Stress in Dutch Police Officers." *Psychoneuroendocrinology* 85:172–178.

Van Ness, Daniel W. and Karen H. Strong. 2015. *Restoring Justice: An Introduction to Restorative Justice*. 5th edition. New York: Routledge.

Villettaz, Patrice, Gwladys Gilliéron, and Martin Killias. 2014. *The Effects on Re-Offending of Custodial versus Non-Custodial Sanctions: An Updated Systematic Review of the State of Knowledge*. Stockholm: Swedish National Council for Crime Prevention.

Vito, Gennaro F. and George E. Higgins. 2015. *Practical Program Evaluation for Criminal Justice*. New York: Elsevier.

Vohs, Kathleen D. and Roy F. Baumeister (eds.). 2016. *Handbook of Self-Regulation: Research, Theory, and Applications*. 3rd edition. New York: Guilford.

von Hirsch, Andrew and Andrew Ashworth (eds.). 1992. *Principled Sentencing*. Boston, MA: Northeastern University Press.

Walker, Samuel. 1998. *Popular Justice: A History of American Criminal Justice*. New York: Oxford University Press.

Walker, Samuel and Charles M. Katz. 2017. *The Police in America*. 9th edition. New York: McGraw-Hill.

Wallander, Lisa. 2009. "25 Years of Factorial Surveys in Sociology: A Review." *Social Science Research* 38:505–520.

Wang, Xia and Daniel P. Mears. 2015. "Sentencing and State-Level Racial and Ethnic Contexts." *Law and Society Review* 49:883–915.

Wang, Xia and Daniel P. Mears. 2010a. "A Multilevel Test of Minority Threat Effects on Sentencing." *Journal of Quantitative Criminology* 26:191–215.

Wang, Xia and Daniel P. Mears. 2010b. "Examining the Direct and Interactive Effects of Changes in Racial and Ethnic Threat on Sentencing Decisions." *Journal of Research in Crime and Delinquency* 47:522–557.

Wang, Xia, Daniel P. Mears, Cassia C. Spohn, and Lisa Dario. 2013. "Assessing the Differential Effects of Race and Ethnicity on Sentencing Outcomes under Different Sentencing Systems." *Crime and Delinquency* 59:87–114.

Warren, Patricia Y., Donald Tomaskovic-Devey, William R. Smith, Matthew Zingraff, and Marcinda Mason. 2006. "Driving While Black: Bias Processes and Racial Disparity in Stops." *Criminology* 44:709–736.

Warren, Robert. 2016. "One Thing I Learned by Editing Sociology of Education." *Sociology of Education Newsletter* 19:3–5.

Watts, Duncan J. 2017. "Response to Turco and Zuckerman's 'Verstehen for Sociology.'" *American Journal of Sociology* 122:1292–1299.

Watts, Duncan J. 2014. "Common Sense and Sociological Explanations." *American Journal of Sociology* 120:313–351.

Weber, Max. 1978. *Economy and Society: An Outline of Interpretive Sociology*. Vol. 1. Translated by Guenther Roth and Claus Wittich. Los Angeles, CA: University of California Press.

Weber, Max. 1949. *On the Methodology of the Social Sciences*, translated and edited by Edward A. Shils and Henry A. Finch. Glencoe, IL: Free Press.

Weber, Max. 1946. "Science as a Vocation," in H. H. Gerth and C. Wright Mills (eds. and trans.), *From Max Weber: Essays in Sociology*. New York: Oxford University Press, pp. 129–156.

Weinberg, Steven. 2015. *To Explain the World: The Discovery of Modern Science.* New York: Harper.

Weiner, Tim. 2012. *Enemies: A History of the FBI.* New York: Random House.

Weisburd, David, David P. Farrington, and Charlotte Gill. 2017. "What Works in Crime Prevention and Rehabilitation: An Assessment of Systematic Reviews." *Criminology and Public Policy* 16:415–449.

Weiss, Carol H., Erin Murphy-Graham, Anthony Petrosino, and Allison G. Gandhi. 2008. "The Fairy Godmother – and Her Warts: Making the Dream of Evidence-Based Policy Come True." *American Journal of Evaluation* 29:29–47.

Welsh, Brandon C., Anthony A. Braga, and Gerben J. N. Bruinsma (eds.). 2013. *Experimental Criminology: Prospects for Advancing Science and Public Policy.* New York: Cambridge University Press.

Welsh, Brandon C. and David P. Farrington. 2000. "Monetary Costs and Benefits of Crime Prevention Programs." *Crime and Justice* 27:305–361.

Welsh, Brandon C., Gregory M. Zimmerman, and Steven N. Zane. 2018. "The Centrality of Theory in Modern Day Crime Prevention: Developments, Challenges, and Opportunities." *Justice Quarterly* 35:139–161.

Wener, Richard E. 2012. *The Environmental Psychology of Prisons and Jails: Creating Humane Spaces in Secure Settings.* New York: Cambridge University Press.

Williams, Franklin P., III and Marilyn D. McShane. 2014. *Criminological Theory.* 6th edition. New York: Pearson.

Williams, Matthew L. and Pete Burnap. 2016. "Cyberhate on Social Media in the Aftermath of Woolwich: A Case Study in Computational Criminology and Big Data." *British Journal of Criminology* 56:211–238.

Wilson, David B., Ojmarrh Mitchell, and Doris L. MacKenzie. 2006. "A Systematic Review of Drug Court Effects on Recidivism." *Journal of Experimental Criminology* 2:459–487.

Wincup, Emma. 2017. *Criminological Research: Understanding Qualitative Methods.* 2nd edition. Thousand Oaks, CA: Sage.

Winship, Christopher and Stephen L. Morgan. 1999. "The Estimation of Causal Effects from Observational Data." *Annual Review of Sociology* 25:659–707.

Wolfgang, Marvin E. 1963. "Criminology and the Criminologist." *Journal of Criminal Law, Criminology, and Police Science* 54:155–162.

Wolfgang, Marvin E. 1961. "Pioneers in Criminology: Cesare Lombroso (1825–1909)." *Journal of Criminal Law and Criminology* 52:361–391.

Wolfgang, Marvin E. and Franco Ferracuti. 1967. *The Subculture of Violence.* London: Tavistock.

Wooldredge, John, James Frank, Natalie Goulette, and Lawrence Travis III. 2015. "Is the Impact of Cumulative Disadvantage on Sentencing Greater for Black Defendants?" *Criminology and Public Policy* 14:187–223.

Wooldredge, John and Paula Smith (eds.). 2016. *The Oxford Handbook of Prisons and Imprisonment.* New York: Oxford University Press.

Wright, John P. and Kevin M. Beaver. 2014. "Teaching Criminological Taboo." *ACJS Today* 39:1–13.

Wright, Ronald F. 2017. "Reinventing American Prosecution Systems." *Crime and Justice* 47:395–439.

Wright, Ronald F. and Marc L. Miller. 2002. "The Screening/Bargaining Trade-off." *Stanford Law Review* 55:29–118.

Yaffee, Robert A. 2000. *Introduction to Time Series Analysis and Forecasting.* New York: Academic Press.

Yau, Nathan. 2011. *Visualize This: The FlowingData Guide to Design, Visualization, and Statistics.* Indianapolis, IN: Wiley.

Yoffe, Emily. 2017. "Innocence *Is* Relevant." *The Atlantic Monthly* 320:66–74.

Završnik, Aleš (ed.). 2017. *Big Data, Crime and Social Control.* New York: Routledge.

Zimbardo, Philip G., Curtis Banks, Craig Haney, and David Jaffe. 1973. A Pirandellian Prison: The Mind Is a Formidable Jailer." *New York Times Magazine* 8:38–60.

Index